T0244149

CODE NAME PURITAN

Code Name Puritan

NORMAN HOLMES PEARSON AT THE
NEXUS OF POETRY, ESPIONAGE,
AND AMERICAN POWER

Greg Barnhisel

The University of Chicago Press

Chicago and London

The University of Chicago Press, Chicago 60637
The University of Chicago Press, Ltd., London
© 2024 by The University of Chicago
Published 2024
Printed in the United States of America

33 32 31 30 29 28 27 26 25 24   1 2 3 4 5

ISBN-13: 978-0-226-64720-3 (cloth)
ISBN-13: 978-0-226-64734-0 (e-book)
DOI: https://doi.org/10.7208/chicago/9780226647340.001.0001

Library of Congress Cataloging-in-Publication Data

Names: Barnhisel, Greg, 1969- author.
Title: Code name Puritan : Norman Holmes Pearson at the nexus
  of poetry, espionage, and American power / Greg Barnhisel.
Description: Chicago : The University of Chicago Press, 2024.
  | Includes bibliographical references and index.
Identifiers: LCCN 2024005599 | ISBN 9780226647203 (cloth) |
  ISBN 9780226647340 (ebook)
Subjects: LCSH: Pearson, Norman Holmes, 1909-1975. | Yale
  University—Faculty—Biography. | Yale University. American
  Studies Program. | United States. Office of Strategic
  Services. | Literary historians—United States—Biography. |
  American poetry—Study and teaching—United States—History—
  20th century. | Intelligence service—United States—History—
  20th century.
Classification: LCC PS29.P43 B37 2024 | DDC 810.9—dc23/
  eng/20240311
LC record available at https://lccn.loc.gov/2024005599

♾ This paper meets the requirements of ANSI/NISO Z39.48-1992
(Permanence of Paper).

CONTENTS

INTRODUCTION

Norman Holmes Pearson's influence in twentieth-century American cultural life was profound, although it has remained stubbornly invisible. Pearson midwifed an academic field, helped build its dominant program, and then nudged the infant discipline to serve US interests in the Cold War. He used his position at Yale, and his extensive connections with writers, to shape the public's understanding of literary modernism, above all the work of women authors such as H.D. and Gertrude Stein. And he was a spy. In World War II, Pearson created and headed "X-2"—the Office of Strategic Services (OSS) counterespionage program that, working with British MI6, rolled up the entire Nazi spy network in Allied territory—and then applied his experience to the formation of the Central Intelligence Agency.

It's not really news that a privileged, well-connected, *Mayflower*-descended white man from New England could live a fascinating life at the upper echelons of American culture in the mid-twentieth century. So why is Pearson's story any different from those of dozens of his better-known peers like McGeorge Bundy or Kingman Brewster or Averell Harriman? Pearson is unique because of how he brought together the two rarefied worlds in which he moved (academe and national security), how this produced a new relationship between the government and universities and foundations and the publishing industry, and how it changed our understanding of modern American literature.

Nor was he, like those men, at the very top of the pyramid. Instead, he was one of those who did the largely behind-the-scenes work to keep that system running. At a time when elite institutions enjoyed Americans' trust more than during any period before or since, Pearson's carefully cultivated social skills and extensive personal networks let him enter into and move frictionlessly among them, serving them even as they benefited him. Pearson helped knit these institutions together, reinforcing what he and others of his class assumed was their benevolent hegemony. He was, deeply and fundamentally, an Organization Man in a time of organization men, and in this perhaps even the emblematic figure of the truncated American Century. And privileged as he certainly was, Pearson did all of this while coping with a significant and visible disability that not only limited him physically, but marked him as defective in the eyes of his peers.

He hides in plain sight, and springs up everywhere once you know to look for him. He cameos in dozens of Yale memoirs as the genial, eloquent, bent-over little professor whom everyone knew was a spy. William F. Buckley Jr.—who clashed with Pearson while an undergraduate—fictionalized him in his 2000 novel *Spytime*. Alec Baldwin plays a Pearson stand-in in the 2006 Hollywood film *The Good Shepherd*. Histories of the OSS inevitably mention him, but generally only in passing, as X-2 kept its secrets long after many of the other branches had spilled theirs. Fans of modern poetry likely know that he was important to H.D.'s career, but he also passes through the biographies (and even sometimes the work) of dozens of other poets and novelists. Like some dapper, mustachioed Zelig, he is there on just about every midcentury literary prize committee, cultural board of directors, or award banquet dais.

But because he operated interpersonally and institutionally, traces of his impact were evanescent, even to those who knew him. When I asked his colleague Alan Trachtenberg if I could interview him about Pearson, Trachtenberg bluntly asked, "Why would you want to write about *him*?" He wrote no enduring scholarly studies, and Yale named no room in its libraries for him. His name isn't on the front of so many of the books that he helped bring into the world; instead, it is inside, in small print, after "Edited by" or "Introduction by" or "Dedicated to."

The only monument to him is, appropriately enough, an institutional one: the American Studies Association's Carl Bode–Norman Holmes Pearson Prize, which "recognizes the outstanding achievement of an individual who has dedicated a lifetime of work to the mission and values of American studies."[1]

At its most simple, his is the story of a young man who developed skills that would precisely suit him for his times, and because of this ended up shaping that era in a small but significant way. Accordingly, the first five chapters of this biography closely follow the events of Pearson's life until the Second World War. Struck at a young age by a serious injury that became a permanent disability and a sometimes life-threatening chronic infection — "most of my life so far has been spent in getting well," he said when he was twenty-two — Pearson compensated for not being a physically "normal" child by becoming, in many ways, a little grown-up. As a preadolescent he learned how to impress older people with his maturity and intelligence, and how to cultivate them into something between mentors and friends. "He is not tiresome nor does he overrate himself," the poet Marianne Moore remarked upon meeting him for the first time. Often finding himself "in heady society for an ephebe," Norm came to understand the value of being the person that someone else wanted him to be. He also learned that for someone facing personal obstacles, institutions provided safety and support and security, and that joining those institutions could imbue him with social and cultural capital.[2]

He also, from an early age, immersed himself in books and words and letters. He didn't just read books but collected them as well, reveling in the materiality of the written word. And through this, he learned that just like institutions, language and collecting could bring him security, respect, and recognition. Norm became a master of words, but even more than that a master of conventional discourses: the academic paper, the after-dinner speech, the thank-you letter, the book review, the polemic, the proposal, the solicitation for a donation. And a mastery of discourses, he quickly learned, solidified one's place within an institution.

At first, the institutions Norm inhabited were small and local. But even as a boy, he used language to enter into and get attention from larger communities and institutions. Language and writing won him an award at Phillips Academy Andover, and then at sports-crazy Yale they helped him be active on campus when athletics weren't a possibility. As a graduate student he gained entry to institutions with broader reach, higher visibility, more status, and more influential members. He also started to assemble a remarkable network of prominent figures in the literary and academic worlds, becoming a collector of people as well as of books. And increasingly, he wanted to use his talents on behalf of his nation, to show readers that American literature was just as worthy as English, that the United States had a civilization to be proud of.

His service in World War II beginning at the age of thirty-three was a kind of hinge in his life, marking the end of his extended apprenticeship; and thus chapters 6 and 7, covering his war years and just after, serve the same purpose in this biography. Even among the erudite crowd in the Office of Strategic Services, Pearson stood out, and for the first time he started to build, not just inhabit, an institution. Pearson was one of four men selected to create X-2, the OSS's counterespionage branch, and ran all the OSS's counterintelligence programs in the last years of the war, making him one of the Allies' leading intelligence officials. His extraordinary achievements earned him the Medal of Freedom in 1945, among other distinctions. After the war, he was offered several top intelligence positions, and although ultimately he chose to return to his academic career, he was instrumental in designing the CIA's counterintelligence branch and moved comfortably in the Yankee insider intelligence milieu fictionalized in such novels as Don DeLillo's *Libra* and Norman Mailer's *Harlot's Ghost*. Pearson's service in the war also forced him to think more deeply about what the United States, newly victorious and unprecedentedly powerful, really stood for, what values and beliefs made it unique, and how those values and beliefs should guide it as it led the Western alliance against communism.

The book takes a structural shift in its last five chapters, which I hope will not be too jarring for the reader. Because the day-to-day, or even year-to-year, professional life of an academic tends not to be all that varied or eventful, these chapters depart from the chronological structure of the first seven, and instead each explores a sphere of postwar American culture in which Pearson operated. Chapters 8, 9, and 10 cover his relationships with, and work on behalf of, modernist writers such as Ezra Pound, William Carlos Williams, Marianne Moore, Wallace Stevens, W. H. Auden, John Gould Fletcher, and above all H.D. and Bryher. It might seem incongruous that a tweedy Yale professor, Hawthorne expert, and neo-Puritan would be so central in convincing stuffy Yale or the Poetry Foundation or the State Department to embrace experimental modernist literature, which is so at odds with the ethos of those institutions. Modernist poetry is mystical instead of logical, often antireligious, frequently antidemocratic and skeptical of liberal individualism, and implacably opposed to middle-class values. H.D. was a notorious sexual bohemian, and Ezra Pound a Fascist sympathizer and indicted traitor. Certainly, on one level Pearson saw an opportunity to be part of an important and prestigious network. But it wasn't just a status play. Pearson had truly loved modernist poetry since he was a teenager. He was in awe of H.D.'s clipped, gnomic poems, which seem to have been excavated from a Mediterranean archeological dig. He also loved Pound's work and saw in the modernism that they and others created the Puritan desire for renewal, for spiritual cleansing, for an intensely personal relationship with the divine.

It's good to have friends in influential places. Pearson brought these writers to Yale to read and receive honoraria, and he included them in the anthologies he edited. He helped broker deals that brought many of their papers to Yale, where they became available for scholars to use (and to write about, giving them and their associated authors even more exposure). As a member of award and grant committees, Pearson pushed them to give these poets money and recognition. He taught their work in his classes and trained graduate students who then became professors who taught the modernists' work to their students. And for H.D., he did *all* these things, as well as editing her new works, preparing them for American publication, lining up reviewers for them, and acting as her literary agent and then her executor after her death. In the end, the real product of his work for these writers was the mundane but essential assembly of an infrastructure for the scholarship that built both individual literary reputations and an alternative American modernist canon: one centered not on the gloomy Christianity of the then-inescapable (and not particularly American) T. S. Eliot, but rather on Williams's regional rootedness, Pound's autodidactic European-Chinese-American understanding of history, and H.D.'s Freudian hermeticism and Greek-Egyptian mystic visions. Invisibly, unglamorously, Pearson rewrote the story of American modernism.

Chapter 11 turns to Pearson's role in serving the American Cold War cultural consensus. After the war, major US institutions entered into an unprecedented collaboration to define, strengthen, and defend what they saw as the American "way of life," which was rooted in liberal individualism, pragmatism, suspicion of rigid ideologies, democratic self-governance, and capitalism. Unsurprisingly, those major institutions saw themselves not just as advocates for but as the very expression of these American values. The citizens of a democracy had built them to pursue and defend their interests, and the people that rose to prominence in them did so because of their expertise, training, and merit. That they were populated almost entirely by one tiny and homogenous slice of the population was, to them, evidence not of their insularity but of the special responsibility this small sliver of Americans had to the nation.

In the academy, the new field of "American studies" helped give this postwar consensus scholarly backing. Pearson was one of the first students trained in (and later one of the first professors of) American studies, and throughout the 1940s and 1950s he helped foster the new field and assemble its institutions. Then, starting in the 1960s, he frequently traveled abroad to teach American studies at institutions that had been established, often with US government and foundation assistance, to promote understanding of and sympathy with America abroad. He became a gracious ambassador for the United States in places like Australia, New Zealand, South Korea, and Japan, and he brought scholars and students from those nations to the United States to study. This was certainly "people-to-people diplomacy," as the Eisenhower administration called it; but through it, Pearson didn't just introduce these foreign students and scholars to America and to a singular American, but also to the institutions that asserted themselves as the cornerstones of America's resilient democratic society. For over twenty years the field of American studies and the US cultural-diplomatic establishment were in a symbiotic relationship, each one strengthening the other. Pearson, as much as any other figure, orchestrated this collaboration.

This cultural-diplomatic work came from Pearson's conviction that the United States should be an example for the rest of the world, a belief rooted in Pearson's lifelong reconsideration of the Puritans. A descendant of the earliest English settlers of New England, Pearson was ever conscious of his ancestry, thinking and joking frequently about his "Puritanism." For Pearson, Puritanism wasn't the unforgiving faith that led to banishments and witch trials, or the insistence that anything pleasurable in life was sinful. Instead, he saw in its intricate and unforgiving theology not callousness and rigidity but rather an intense drive for self-criticism and self-improvement, for the renewal of a corrupted world. In this, he was thinking very much against the grain. In fact, in 1936 the prominent Spanish American philosopher George Santayana published his "memoir in the form of a novel," *The Last Puritan*. In this book, Puritanism represents an uncompromising, moralistic "passion for reality," a "merciless pleasure in the hard facts," and a refusal to pursue worldly or aesthetic experience in favor of keeping oneself pure for "what was best."[3] In *The Last Puritan*, Santayana portrays Puritanism as both admirable and tragic. It's unclear if Pearson read this book, although he certainly would have known of it, as it appeared just as he was immersing himself in his graduate study of the Puritans. What is certain is that he would have deeply disagreed with Santayana's condemnation of the Puritan strain in American culture, and would have found his depiction of Puritanism partial and simplistic.

Ten years later, as the Cold War dawned, the Puritans improbably thrust themselves again onto center stage. In a 1630 sermon aboard the *Arabella*, which was bringing the first Puritans to the Massachusetts Bay Colony, John Winthrop had told the settlers that they would be founding a "city on a hill," a community that would be an example of godliness to the nations. Long considered simply an example of religious fanaticism, Winthrop's "Model of Christian Charity" speech started to sound like a prefiguration of Henry Luce's argument in "The American Century" that the United States had to lead the postwar world and spread the benefits of its culture. If America's obligation was to be an example to the nations and a light unto the world, it had begun with the Puritans—and Pearson, an ambassador for American civilization, had made himself into the very model of a modern Puritan, at least in his understanding of the term.[4]

Pearson's deep-grained Puritanism suited him well for his habitat, and the last chapter of this book explores his symbiotic relationship with Yale University from the end of the war until his death in 1975. For forty-four years, he was a creature of Yale, a school founded in 1700 by Puritan ministers. Yale formed him intellectually and personally and socially; it was the matrix in which he moved, the institution that provided him with a foundation for everything else he did and gave him access to those elite networks. In the 1950s and 1960s he was one of its most beloved professors, in the words of one student a "black-browed, black-mustached man with [a] grotesquely hunched back, whom many of his pupils had pitied at the beginning of the term but who had gradually and completely forgotten his deformity and had grown to marvel at the brilliance of his delivery and the sincerity of his teachings."[5] Yale's centrality in American elite culture did not diminish over Pearson's life, but just as that culture became unrecognizable to itself between the 1920s and the 1970s, Yale did as well. Over the course of Norm's time there, the university evolved into something quite close to what it is today: an international-caliber research institution, immensely wealthy, intensely meritocratic, and increasingly diverse while still disproportionately serving the most privileged children of the northeastern establishment. Pearson didn't just witness those changes but played a part in many of them.

Yale connections also pulled Pearson into the spy business. In X-2, Norm supervised classmates and friends and brought his own students into the service. After the war, Norm recruited promising Yale men into the Central Intelligence Agency, itself dominated by Yalies in its early years. Pulling the camera back, we would see similarly pervasive networks of Yale (or Harvard, or Princeton) men at the top levels of all the institutions that drove and oversaw the postwar cultural consensus. Pearson first benefited from this expansive Yale network, then after the war became a crucial node in it.

But being plugged in didn't help Norm's status among the faculty, where the most valuable capital is scholarly renown. Pearson did not make a lasting mark as a scholar or critic, and his work is rarely read today. The project he intended as his great contribution to American literary studies, a complete edition of Nathaniel Hawthorne's correspondence, remained incomplete at his death. As he watched generations of eminent scholars pass through Yale's English department, he grew more marginal, more of an afterthought among his high-powered colleagues. Was this merely the result of spending so much time helping others accomplish their goals, as one of his friends concluded? Or was this intentional, a conscious opting out of the chase for academic prestige because he found another type of status more personally fulfilling?

Just as he was present at its genesis, Pearson was also there when Americans' broad-based faith in a Cold War order led by these institutions and his class crumbled. That is where the book, and his life, come to a close. The Vietnam War, racial and gender and economic injustice, environmental degradation, and young people's refusal to be trained to fuel the military-industrial-corporate complex eroded the postwar consensus in the late 1960s. American society and its institutions had to change. Pearson watched, quietly, as Yale College began to admit a more economically and ethnically diverse group of students in the mid-1960s, and then in 1969, women. Even the larger institutions in which he circulated, such as the Department of State, began to question whether they should be peopled by such a limited segment of the population. In response Pearson evolved, changing his teaching, his scholarship, even the language in which he described the American character. Only weeks before he passed away in 1975, this paragon of New England WASPdom argued to audiences in Japan and South Korea that America's belated and halting moves toward diversity proved that its democracy was still vital and vibrant.

Because Pearson lived so much of his life out in public, and in writing, in some ways his biography is easy to write. His inveterate, even compulsive collecting is a godsend for the biographer, for his archive at the Beinecke Library holds seemingly every piece of paper that passed through his hands. And letters from him are in the archives of many of the thousands of people he corresponded with, making for a great deal of research travel but even more documentation of his daily life. There is so much evidence of *what he was doing*: in letters and speeches and radio appearances and meeting minutes and pocket calendars and the like. But he remains difficult to get to know. A highly social man who had few close friends, Pearson kept his deepest thoughts and feelings mostly to himself and channeled his energies into work and networking. Introspective he was not. Part of this came from his inherent New England reticence and stoicism, and three years in the spy services certainly solidified this inclination. But there were a few people—most of them women—to whom he would open up, who can help us understand why he was so driven to do so much for others even though it might have prevented him from achieving the scholarly prestige that he also craved.

Through this biography, I hope to offer an explanation of how an unprepossessing former spy became one of the master operators of postwar American culture, expertly navigating and even manipulating the world of this new "power elite." I seek to answer why a man with such endless energy, such keen intellectual and emotional intelligence, such relentless ambition and wide-ranging talent, had such a huge impact on postwar American culture but was never able to complete the single project that he considered his life's work. I also investigate the psychological roots of Pearson's compulsion to collect and network, his love for modernist poetry, his championing of women artists even though he spent his life in institutions that were almost entirely male, and his beliefs about the American character and America's Puritan legacy. But Pearson's biography is, I hope to show, not just about one man, for his life and work also provide the opportunity to explore larger questions about postwar America: about the role of experimental art in American culture; about the collaboration of artistic and educational and national-security institutions; and about the creation, inner workings, and ultimate demise of the Cold War consensus, and the birth of a new America in the 1970s.

+ 1 +

BORN A PURITAN

You have a very promising son who has the spirit
of America imbedded in his heart.
MARY GUYTON TO CHESTER PEARSON

Norman Holmes Pearson was born a Puritan in 1909. Not literally, of course. But the New England physical and social environment in which he was raised, and the values that his close-knit family held, retained powerful traces of the English settlers from three centuries past, and this ghostly Puritanism would shape his personality and his understanding of himself and of America. He even had Puritanism in his blood, thanks to his descent from several old and distinguished New England families. His father's side were Pearsons, prominent citizens of Rowley, one of the earliest Massachusetts Bay Colony settlements. The Reverend Ezekiel Rogers, Puritan minister in the Yorkshire village of Rowley, had emigrated to America with twenty families from his congregation in 1638. (Stephen Daye, a fellow passenger on that voyage, brought along his printing press, which two years later produced the first book printed in North America.) North of Cape Ann, between Newbury and Ipswich, Rogers and his twenty families founded the town that they named after their Yorkshire home. This area, the north shore of Essex County, was in sociologist E. Digby Baltzell's words "the nursery of the strictest Puritanism," as well as of many of Boston's First Families, including the Cabots, Lowells, and Peabodys.[1]

Yorkshire was England's textile-manufacturing center, and Rogers's settlers brought those skills with them. In the first history of the colony, Edward Johnson wrote that, "having been clothiers in England," the people of Rowley were among "the first that set upon making Cloth in this Western World." Supplied with cotton from Barbados, as well as hemp and flax, "Rowley . . . exceeded all other towns" in providing the Massachusetts Bay Colony with textiles, Governor John Winthrop wrote in his journal entry of June 12, 1643.[2]

John Pearson wasn't among Rogers's party of original settlers of Rowley. Instead, he came over in 1643, bringing with him his wife, Dorcas. He was made a freeman—that is, he paid off the indenture that had funded his passage to America—in 1647, by which time he had already built and begun operating a "fulling-mill," which took raw cloth, soaked it in a foul-smelling ammoniac solution (often including stale horse urine), and beat it to thicken and strengthen it. For fifty years, it was the only fulling-mill in eastern Massachusetts, and Pearson provided fabric for hundreds of families. The entrepreneurial Pearson soon added to his assets both the town gristmill and its sawmill, making him one of the most prominent men in Rowley. His fellow citizens recognized this by choosing him for selectman, assessor, and for nine sessions their deputy at the Great and General Court in Boston. John Pearson embodied the New England Puritan combination of businessman and civic leader, which became a Pearson hallmark.

Puritans such as Rogers and Winthrop sought to build an ideal godly society that would cleanse the Church of England and be an example to the world. The Puritans and the New England landscape, in this view, had been divinely bequeathed to each other, and even centuries later the descendants of these settlers held to that idea. "The land was ours before we were the land's," Robert Frost asserted at President John F. Kennedy's 1961 inauguration in his poem "The Gift Outright." The Wampanoag, Massachuset, and Pennacook peoples disagreed, though, and the Pearson family took part in the conflicts with the native peoples and, later, the British government that shaped American self-imagining. In all his writing and speaking about early America, Norman never expressed any doubt that the English settlers had been right to claim and settle Massachusetts.

Proud of his heritage, Pearson was quite familiar with his geneal-ogy. John and Dorcas Pearson had thirteen children in all, three of whom died in infancy, and one of whom, Joseph, was killed at nine-teen when Wampanoags ambushed his "Flower of Essex" infantry unit in King Philip's War in 1675. Their tenth child, Benjamin (born 1658), was to be Norman's great-great-great-great grandfather. Benjamin's son David (1701–73), like his forebears a miller by trade, moved Nor-man's line out of Rowley—but just to Newbury, the neighboring town to the north. David and Jane Noyes Pearson's seventh child, Noyes Pearson (1741–1805), fought in the Revolutionary War in the Second Infantry Company, under the command of Lieutenant Colonel Joshua Gerrish, and returned the family to Rowley. Noyes's son David (1765–1824) married Lydia Welch of Plaistow, New Hampshire, and defin-itively displaced Norman's line from Essex County when he settled in Canaan, New Hampshire. David's son Moses (1808–99) and wife, Eliza Cowles, then moved the family even farther away, into Orleans County, Vermont, just below the Canadian border. Moses was an im-portant member of the community and a deacon in the Congregational church. Samuel Howe Pearson (born 1842), Moses's son, grew up to be a prominent farmer in Coventry and even served in the Vermont state legislature. Samuel and his first wife, Sarah Gray Pearson, had four children: Henry (born 1871), James (1874), Emma (1879), and Chester Page Pearson, Norman's father, who was born in 1873.[3]

Chester took after his father and grandfather in combining civil ser-vice with a head for business, and he moved south to Worcester, Mas-sachusetts, to attend Becker's Business College. After a short time as a railroad and telegraph clerk there, Chester took a job at the Goodnow Brothers dry-goods store in East Jaffrey, New Hampshire. In 1899, he married Fanny Kittredge, who had grown up in Nelson, New Hamp-shire, attended Fitchburg Teachers College in Massachusetts, and was teaching school in East Jaffrey when she met Chester. After their wed-ding, the two moved across the border to Gardner, Massachusetts, to open a store in partnership with the Goodnows. Chester's brothers James and Henry also entered the business at the same time, both opening Goodnow stores in the vicinity.[4]

Like the Pearsons, Fanny Holmes Kittredge's family also dated back to the Massachusetts Bay Colony. Fanny claimed direct matrilineal descent from Elder William Brewster, the Pilgrim leader who came to Massachusetts on the *Mayflower*, and was also a member of the prominent Holmes family, but saw herself primarily as a Kittredge. In the mid-seventeenth century, John Kittredge was a ship's captain from Lowestoft, on the coast of East Anglia. Captain Kittredge, "being of a surgical turn of mind" and apparently an autodidactic bent, used "medical receipts" on board his vessel to teach himself medicine. "He began experimenting by breaking animals' limbs," a family chronicler recorded, "then setting them, and seeing how fast he could get them to heal." When a shipmate broke his leg, Captain Kittredge saw his opportunity. Unfortunately, the laws against practicing medicine without a diploma were quite inflexible, and so Captain Kittredge fled to Billerica, northwest of Boston, in 1660. His descendants would remain in that general region for the next several generations before settling in southern New Hampshire, where Fanny was born in 1873.[5] Fanny's older brother Alfred Beard Kittredge (1861–1911) had taken his Yale degree to the Dakota Territory to work in journalism and politics and eventually was appointed as a US senator from South Dakota in 1901, upon the death of James Kyle, serving until 1909. As he died when Norm was only two years old, Uncle Alfred was never a great personal influence on him, but he did frequently note to people that he had an uncle who was a senator. Alfred left $62,000 in stock and Sioux Falls real estate—almost $2 million in 2024 dollars—to Fanny and Chester, which would help the Pearsons and their store through the Depression.

Chester and Fanny both maintained close relationships with their extended families, but the Kittredges were particularly important presences in the family's life. When their first child was born in 1903, he was named after Fanny's brother: Alfred Kittredge Pearson. Norman came next, in April 1909, then Eleanor in 1912. Although her sons each carried a name of one of her prominent New England clans, Fanny opposed using lineage for social status and refused to even consider joining the Daughters of the American Revolution or the Mayflower

Society. The Puritan tenets of modesty and self-effacement were as strong in her as those of hard work, achievement, and public service were in Chester.

The Pearsons and Kittredges were not "Puritans" in any real sense, but neither was anyone else in 1900. The Puritan strain of Anglicanism that the seventeenth-century settlers brought, and the Calvinist theology underpinning it, were essentially dead by the twentieth century. But many of the ideas, practices, and approaches to social organization and individual life persisted, in a mutated and attenuated form, among New Englanders, and they continued to color the region's political, educational, and cultural institutions even after immigrants from other parts of the world brought their own practices beginning in the mid-nineteenth century. These are the people we call "Yankees," and the striving Pearsons and Kittredges were part of that group just as much as the elevated Lowells and Cabots of Boston's Beacon Hill or the humble Frosts of rural New Hampshire. Yankee culture and values cut across class and geography, and across religion to some degree—they were Congregationalists, Episcopalians, Methodists, Presbyterians, Baptists, and eventually Unitarians—but not ethnicity. These were the original WASPs.

"Puritan" today evokes a stereotypical prude or moral scold, and shame about sex and the body is certainly part of the Puritan legacy. But this impetus derives as much from a more general valuing of modesty and reticence, of not glorying in the things of this world—pleasure, physicality, even one's own possessions and accomplishments—because they are fleeting illusions at best, and the traps of Satan at worst. Puritans prized education, as it helped one better understand the ways and demands of God. (Harvard, like Yale, was founded by and for Puritans.) Work was crucial in Puritan life, so long as it was performed not to amass individual wealth or to strive for fame or earthly glory. Puritans, sociologist Baltzell writes, "sought to replace the personal pride of birth and status with the professional's or craftsman's pride of doing one's best in one's particular calling."[6] As instantiated in the New England town meeting and the congregationalist church, self-governance was essential. However, as human beings were fundamentally and irreducibly sinful, Puritans also demanded obedience to authority: parental, pastoral, educational, governmental. Puritan society, and the Massachusetts that evolved from it, combined a lively small-scale democracy with "deference and hierarchy." Norman's life-long faith in American democracy and American institutions came in part from this facet of the Puritan worldview.

The Pearsons were not devout, but the Congregational Church of Gardner was a regular part of their lives. The children attended Sunday school, and Norm was a devoted reader of the church's national youth magazine, the *Wellspring*. The church's spiritual lessons influenced Norm less than its reinforcement of the values Fanny and Chester sought to instill in their children: modesty, hard work, public service, education, sociability, humility. In truth, everything in small-town Massachusetts did, from the schools to church magazines to the dozens of civic organizations and social clubs to which Fanny and Chester belonged.

Moreover, for many, Puritan-inflected life in Massachusetts had become conflated with the nation itself. Settlement and expansion, the special divine mission of the Puritans, the intertwinement of theology with government, the dispossession of the native population, the productive development and use of the land and its natural resources, the idealizing of the small farmer or craftsman: even as the Puritans themselves became disfavored, their legacy in New England became the essence of America in the public mind. In the nineteenth century, Boston, along with Philadelphia, was the center of the US publishing industry, and New England home to the nation's preeminent schools and colleges. New England writers like Longfellow and Hawthorne, educated at New England schools like Bowdoin, published poems and stories of New England such as "Paul Revere's Ride" or *The Scarlet Letter* with Boston magazines like the *Atlantic Monthly* or Boston publishers like Ticknor and Field. Roger Williams and Anne Hutchinson, and later Emerson and Thoreau and Fuller, provided models of principled dissent from authority and conformity, which would be crucial in building a pluralist society. The powerful cultural influence of New

England then encouraged schools and readers all over the country to see these stories as *the* essential American stories.

As a result, New England Yankees like the Pearsons took for granted that they were the most American of Americans, both embodying and tasked with carrying forth the mission of the nation. This view, of course, ignored the diversity even of the earliest British immigrants. Royalist Cavaliers settled Virginia and the Carolinas and established an aristocratic social structure in the South. Freethinking Quakers founded Philadelphia and made Pennsylvania the most liberal of the colonies. English Catholics settled Maryland to escape persecution under the Stuarts, and the Scots Irish populated the Appalachian frontier. Other ethnic groups—Dutch in New York, Spanish in Florida, French in upper New England, Huguenots in coastal cities, Germans in Pennsylvania and New York, Africans all through the colonies, and of course the hundreds of Native nations—all left their indelible marks on American character and identity long before the Revolution. Norm grew up to be a broad-minded, cosmopolitan, curious person, but in his scholarly career of thinking and writing and teaching about what made America America, his perspective would rarely stray far from New England and its English-descended settlers.

Pearson's birthplace of Gardner was for much of the nineteenth and twentieth centuries a center of furniture manufacturing and home of the Heywood-Wakefield furniture factory, accounting for its self-bestowed nickname "Chair City." Heywood-Wakefield opened in 1826 and by the 1920s employed hundreds in the city, and over five thousand in factories and warehouses across the country. Several other well-known chair manufacturers also operated in Gardner, including S. K. Pierce and Son, Royal Furniture, Greenwood Carlton, and Arlington Chair, but like Heywood-Wakefield they all closed up shop in the last decades of the twentieth century. Not coincidentally for a factory town, Gardner also claims to be the birthplace of the first punch-clock time recorder (the Simplex, in 1894).

With the furniture industry starting to boom in 1909, the year Norm was born, Gardner had a population of about fourteen thousand. When

Chester had opened his store in 1899 on Vernon and Parker Streets, it offered only men's clothing, but he added a women's department in 1903, and by 1915 the store had taken over the stock and buildings of several other downtown retailers. It eventually occupied three contiguous buildings on Main Street. The 1924 *History of Worcester County, Massachusetts* notes admiringly that Goodnow Pearson's started with one clerk, "but under [Chester Pearson's] efficient and progressive management has developed into one of the largest and most important department stores of any city of similar size in the State of Massachusetts. The concern here now employs as many as 112 clerks."[7]

The store made Chester and his family prosperous, and he built a seven-bedroom house in a prominent location at 88 Elm Street. When Gardner became a city in 1923, Chester was elected its first mayor, and today a major boulevard is named for him.[8] He was also a joiner, like most leading small-city businessmen, and it's difficult not to hear faint echoes of Sinclair Lewis's George Babbitt in Pearson's fraternal-organization lineup:

> Hope Lodge, Free and Accepted Masons of Gardner; Gardner Chapter, Royal Arch Masons; Ivanhoe Commandery, No. 146, Knights Templar; Massachusetts Consistory, Ancient and Accepted Scottish Rite of Boston[;] . . . Aleppo Temple, Ancient Arabic Order Nobles of the Mystic Shrine of Boston[;] . . . Gardner Lodge, No. 1426, Benevolent and Protective Order of Elks; William Ellison Lodge, International Order of Odd Fellows[;] . . . Ridgely Club[;] . . . Gardner Boat Club[;] . . . Gardner Luncheon Club, Worcester Country Club[;] . . . Oak Hill Country Club of Fitchburg; [and] chairman of the Home Service Committee of the Gardner Red Cross.[9]

Chester's example showed Norm the value of joining and belonging.

The family had a warm and loving home life, although taciturn and reserved Chester spent much of his time working, so the more outgoing Fanny handled most of the parenting responsibilities (assisted, eventually, by a cook). The Pearson children saw their aunts, uncles, and cousins frequently, as most lived no farther than Boston, and busi-ness ties kept Chester and his brothers in close contact.

When he was no more than eight years old, Norm experienced a devastating event that would fundamentally alter the course of his life. While visiting a playmate, Norm fell off of a barn roof, breaking bones in his lower back as well as the left side of his pelvis and his left femur. A compound fracture ripped through the skin of his hip. Gardner's hospital wasn't equipped to handle the complexity of his injury, so he was transferred to the hospital in Fitchburg. Even still, his leg was set poorly and healed crookedly, resulting in a malformed left femur and pelvis wing and "severe structural rotary curve" in the hip.[10] He devel-oped a scoliotic curvature of the back. Even worse, in the hospital, he was exposed to tuberculosis bacteria, which colonized the surface of the pelvis and the bursa. He lost weight and had breathing troubles. In this pre-antibiotic era, little could be done to combat this infection when it flared up, as it often did, both in the hip and to a lesser degree in the lungs. He was in real danger of dying on many occasions, and fre-quently on crutches or even in a wheelchair. Then the infection would relent for periods of time, and his mobility would return. All through his youth his ill health was a consistent concern, and he often had to spend extended periods in the hospital.

Rest helped; warm weather did too. Doctors would also sometimes use mercury injections and "phototherapy" (exposure to UV light) to treat tuberculosis infections in the bones, and Norm underwent both treatments regularly. In December 1920 he started receiving more aggressive interventions from the pioneering Boston orthopedic sur-geon William R. MacAusland, whose surgeries also included excruciat-ingly painful "curettages," literal scrapings-away of the top layer of the pelvic surface in an effort to eliminate the bacteria.[11]

The family were well aware that Norm could die from his infec-tion, and so Chester and Fanny decided early on that Alfred would take Chester's position as the head of Goodnow Pearson's. Nominally a desk job, running the store was physically demanding, requiring twelve-hour days and few or no vacations. Chester felt that a Pearson had to be on the premises or at least in town whenever the store was open. Alfred was never given much choice in the matter and at times later in life resented the wide latitude, and considerable subventions, the family provided Norm, when Alfred himself yearned for the cosmopolitan, academic, art-filled life that his younger brother led.

In the 1920s, the store and the family's fortunes were carried upward by Gardner's roaring economy. Chester and Fanny were able to provide their children with some of the cultural and educational—and thus social—advantages that Chester's side of the family had lacked, such as trips to Europe, extended summer vacations on Cape Cod, and frequent excursions to Boston theaters. Chester and Fanny, though, realized that Alfred would need more than Chester's Becker's Business College degree to advance Goodnow Pearson's and his own prospects, so in 1918, when he was fifteen, they sent Alfred to the prestigious Philips Academy in nearby Andover, to prepare him eventually to attend college at Yale.

Philips Academy (known colloquially as "Andover") was, along with New Hampshire's Philips Exeter Academy, the epitome of the elite New England boarding school as well as one of its oldest examples, having been founded in 1778. As the eastern ruling class grew in the 1800s, it created a set of restricted cultural institutions that served to reinforce and pass on the group's power and traditions: law firms, social and civic clubs, country clubs. (Edith Wharton's novels, which Pearson taught and adored, chronicle the efforts of this class to build and then police the borders of their society.) Better public education meant that a broader variety of students had access to Harvard, Yale, Princeton, Brown, Williams, Bowdoin, and other colleges, so the network of English-inspired prep schools intended to funnel its young men into, and confirm its dominance of, those colleges proliferated. St. Paul's, Hotchkiss, Choate, and Groton were all founded between 1856 and 1891, and they joined Andover, Exeter, Milton, and Deerfield as austere and demanding academies inculcating the beliefs and practices of the New England WASP into young men. Andover led, customarily, to Yale, and its nineteenth-century alumni included Samuel Morse,

Frederick Law Olmstead, Josiah Quincy, Henry Stimson, and Norm's distant relative Oliver Wendell Holmes Sr.

Most of the students, though, didn't grow up to be notables like these. They were wealthy and privileged young men from wealthy and privileged northeastern families, and a school like Andover was just part of that group's shared life experience. Although the Pearsons' distant ancestor Eliphalet had been Andover's first preceptor from 1778 to 1786, the Pearsons weren't among that elite, and Alfred keenly felt the difference between himself and his classmates. Writing to Norm in 1921, he remarked that "I'm probably the only fellow in school who hasn't been to New York many times, but I haven't a chance of going until I get enough money to go on my own hook."[12] Nevertheless, Chester and Fanny reasoned, entering into the networks of Andover and Yale would be invaluable. Eleanor could not access these all-male schools, but her parents saw to it that she, too, was put on an upward trajectory passing through Vassar, one of the "Seven Sisters" women's colleges that also served this class.

In early December 1921, with Alfred in his first year at Yale, Fanny pulled the two younger children out of school and moved them to Florida for the winter, in the hopes that the warm weather would ameliorate twelve-year-old Norm's stubborn TB. Norm found the journey thrilling and the sights exotic. He and his sister explored St. Augustine, saw unfamiliar wildlife, and were delighted by a young boy selling fresh pecans on the train. Coming from Gardner—whose ethnic diversity at the time consisted of a small colony of Finns, about ten Jewish families, and fifteen African Americans—Norm was struck by seeing a "mob of negroes" at the train station.[13] After a few days in the Jacksonville area, the family checked into the Hollenbeck Hotel in St. Petersburg, where Alfred joined them, leaving Chester alone in Gardner to handle the store. "We had a strange Christmas for us," Norm noted; "80 degrees in the shade and we ate corn on the cob and strawberries."

What started out strange soon became unremarkable, as they settled into a rental cottage in Pass-a-Grille Beach, near St. Petersburg, which was rebuilding after a devastating hurricane and fire the previous

October. In Norm's journal for the winter of 1922, almost every day is the same: "sunned on the beach. Did my schoolwork." He collected shells and rocks and patiently waited for shipments of the *Gardner News* every week or so. The Gunnisons, friends from Gardner, lived in St. Petersburg, and weekly services at the Congregational church (which also hosted meetings of the New England Tourists Club) also provided a touch of home. Once or twice a week Fanny would take the kids into town for dinner and the movies—silent films such as *Little Lord Fauntleroy, Is Matrimony a Failure?*, and *The Three Muske-teers* with Douglas Fairbanks. Children are introduced to the ideas and assumptions of the larger culture through public entertainments, and the racial and political codes of the South made an impression on this observant Yankee boy. At a screening of D. W. Griffith's racist epic *Birth of a Nation*, he marveled at how the audience erupted in cheers at the appearance of the Confederate flag. But like most white Americans of the time, Norm himself used racist language and uncritically accepted racist ideas. One night in St. Petersburg the family saw a medicine show "where a man was selling things to negroes. There was a darky playing a banjo and there was a cowboy. Mr. Gunnison said that the cowboy costume was very catching to the negroes."

The children loved their time at the beach, and Fanny was a skilled and effective homeschooler, but even the daily sun exposure failed to clear up Norm's infection, so in early May, the family returned to Gardner. But Norm, Eleanor, and Fanny had developed an especially close relationship that would last the rest of their lives, and Norm would remain far closer to his sister and mother than to his father and brother. This may, as well, have made him more comfortable around women, especially accomplished women, than many other men of his generation were.

Back in Gardner, Norm tried to lead a normal, active life. He took part in school sports and attended summer camps in Maine. Also every summer, the family vacationed at the Snow Inn on southern Cape Cod's Harwich Port, where the regular crowd included several young people who would become lifelong friends and fellow academics. But many of his pastimes were those that a bedridden boy had to develop.

Norm was an avid reader and in early adolescence relished the popular boys' sports and adventure books by American writers like Joseph Altsheler and John R. Tunis. Certainly he read Nathaniel Hawthorne, as Fanny had a passion for his novels and stories. Even better, though, were British authors G. A. Henty, R. M. Ballantyne, and Ralph Henry Barbour, as well as the *Boy's Own Paper* magazine, which he treasured. Norm even subscribed to the *Sea Breeze*, the newsletter of the Boston Seaman's Friend Society, because of its true-life stories about mariners. With friends, he convened a book club in the garage apartment at his house, where they would talk about, and reenact, the exploits of Henty's and Ballantyne's heroes, Barbour's athletes, or the *Sea Breeze*'s sailors. He didn't just read, either, but also collected. On family trips to Boston, he always requested to be taken to Ashburton Place, where many of the city's new and antiquarian bookstores were located, often accompanied by his older cousin Edward "Kit" Kittredge, a Boston lawyer, who shared his bibliomania.

He had also begun to write, and his writing reflected his love for books and literature. His sixteen-line iambic-pentameter poem "Reverie," published in the Gardner High School magazine in Norm's senior year, is mostly about sitting on the "seashore" (Harwich Port, presumably) and "think[ing] / Of sailing days now ended and long past," and especially of pirates and privateers, the subjects of his reading. But the poem ends with a surprisingly dark quatrain in which Norm switches to iambic tetrameter and, perhaps, begins engaging with serious modern literature:

> There is a fascination to the sea
> Which only sailing ships can bring,
> And somehow now that they have gone
> It seems an empty, worthless thing.

While far from brilliant, it shows a facility with meter and conventional poetic voice, and definitely some talent. By design or coincidence, it also carries an echo of the greatest New England poet of the day, Robert Frost, whose melancholy 1916 sonnet "The Oven Bird" concludes with similar tone and wording. (Norm certainly knew Frost's work at the time.)

Like many teenagers, he was attracted to the morbid and depressing. A much earlier poem, from when he was thirteen, exhibits this tendency, but more interesting is its form: it is in free verse, with short lines inspired by the imagist verse of poets like William Carlos Williams, H.D., and Amy Lowell whom he had just started to read:

> It was fall
> The birds have flown
> to their winter's home
> the lovers deserting
> the benches of the park
> A man
> Out of work with no home
> balances on the end of the
> bridge
> A splash
> then silence

If that poem's sentiments are conventional, for the most part Norm's tastes in and critical appreciation for literature were far more advanced than those of a typical teenage boy. During his senior year, the *Wellspring* held a national "Book Letter Contest," in which *Saturday Review of Literature* editor May Lamberton Becker asked her readers to suggest titles for a list she called "I Take for Granted You Read These Books before You Were Sixteen." Prizes—books Becker selected for them— would go to three winners from across the nation who wrote the best letters or submitted the best lists.[14] Norm recommended the novels of Horatio Alger, even though his letter made it clear that he was reading much more challenging material and already viewed literature with the distance and analytical approach of a critic. "There is an appeal in his work," he wrote, "not because there is any doubt as to the end, for whoever heard of an Alger story whose bootblack did not become a baronet or whose farmer-boy did not pay off the mortgage? But rather because they are genuine and because everyone loves success."[15] In April 1927, the *Wellspring* congratulated Norm on submitting the finest list among thousands. The prize book, a color-plate edition of Dickens's *A Tale of Two Cities*, struck Becker as a bit juvenile for him, so she offered, instead, a Harcourt anthology of modern biographies and *Split Records: Tales of the Cinder Track* by American Olympic sprinter Jackson Scholz.

Whichever one he selected, it found its place in his growing collection. In a class essay titled "Book-Collecting," he elaborated on the pleasures of owning association copies (books owned by famous people), guessing which first editions would eventually become valuable, and finding overlooked treasures in the back shelves of bookshops. "There is nothing, I believe, which would give me greater pleasure than to have a piece of a Gutenberg Bible in my hand and to think that I could actually touch the first book printed," he wrote. (He would soon be able to do so—the Yale Libraries obtained their Gutenberg Bible the year he wrote this essay, and he often had the chance to handle it.) Another paper, "A Man's Library," cautioned that books should not be bought for their covers alone, unless one is a connoisseur of bindings, and "promiscuous pure having of sets should be avoided" ("sets" were the expensive multivolume collections middle-class families used to display their refinement). "A few books well chosen are better than many picked up without care," he concluded. "The library should express the individuality of the owner."

Unsurprisingly, his other hobbies also centered around reading and writing. His stamp collection motivated him to write, and thus receive, even more letters: to classmates, family friends, pen pals, even national radio hosts. A faithful listener to the *George W. Ludlow, Friend to Boys* program, Norm wrote several letters about his stamp collection that Ludlow read on the air.[16] He was already collecting historical documents and letters, as well. When he was only twelve, he ordered a set of "War-Record-Prints" from a shop in Harwich Port.[17] Collecting— initially stamps and documents, and then letters, art, and always books—would be one of his great loves and enduring obsessions, and he even wrote about his passion for auctions and estate sales in the Gardner High School magazine.

His condition, though, often kept him out of school, sometimes for weeks in an ankle-to-armpit cast. In 1921, Alfred wrote to suggest that Norm look at the bright side: "You're pretty lucky to get to stay in bed all day. It will be a good chance to fix up your stamp collection!" But this confinement would have been terribly difficult. As an adult, in a letter to his little niece Joan when she was sick in bed, Norm described one strategy he had developed for handling the monotony of convalescence and hospital care:

> In a hospital bed one is anywhere one wants to be. I remember how I used to raise my knees under the sheets. Suddenly, rising up from the valleys of white creases was a Monadnock of a mountain! Two knees up, and there was a Rocky Mountain range! Groups of people climbed up the sides of the slopes in springtime. Like a flash of lightning, someone came skiing down one side. A band of soldiers crossed the mountains by a secret pass to surprise the enemy. A score of pioneers in covered wagons searched about the base until they found the pass that would let them through to where they could build new homes. Every now and then I had to wiggle a toe to remember where I really was.[18]

Books, always, formed the way he understood and viewed the world.

> The Alps for Heidi, or the Concord fields for the Five Little Peppers, or a bull-ring for Ferdinand. [Imagination] can make a hospital bed whatever you want to make it. All you need to do is to think back over the books you have read at home or with grandma, or your geography lessons, or your history texts. Think how lonely the seven dwarfs must be now that Snow White has left them, and without even asking them to visit her, or thanking them for all they did for her. How rude! Set them a-sail with Columbus—and when their boat comes scudding around the corner of the sheets they'll be singing a new "Heigh Ho!" for you!

Norm missed out on some of the social opportunities and activities of young adolescence but spent a great deal of time playing cards and going out with friends, and he took girls to school dances and local functions. For his eighteenth birthday, his friends took him to see the 1926 film version of *The Scarlet Letter*, starring Lillian Gish as Hester Prynne, perhaps further fueling his interest in Hawthorne. And once he learned to drive, he was rarely home and roamed from Worcester to Winchendon to Fitchburg and even as far as Boston. Cars and driving, in fact, soon became one of Norm's greatest pleasures. Because of his injury and illness, he was very skinny, stooped over, and walked strangely. His clothes fit oddly, too. But in a car none of this mattered. Like so many other young people in the 1920s, Norm realized that an automobile gave him freedom, creating a protected space free from parental supervision. But unlike most, for Norm the car also concealed his handicap: behind the wheel, he was just like everyone else.

He was popular and active, a cutup who liked to show off his intelligence, as demonstrated by lackluster "conduct" marks on his report cards. And he was already an inveterate joiner and leader. As a senior, he was vice president of the chemistry club, president of the debating club, manager for the swim team, business manager for the school play, and editor in chief of the *Argus*, the school magazine. (He was merely a member of the science, dramatic, senior dance, junior decorating, and nominating clubs that year.) His editorials in the *Argus* took stands on the burning issues of whether high school students should have after-school jobs (no), the importance of making good memories to cherish later (considerable), and the desirability of presenting varsity athletes with frameable certificates as well as large cloth letters (great).

While he was never the top student, ranking fifteenth in a class of 118, his schoolwork showed both an instinctive knack for academic writing and an interest in early American history and thought. Although he was neither valedictorian nor salutatorian, his selection to give the "Ivy Oration" at commencement attests to his reputation as the school's leading wordsmith. Rather pedestrian in itself, the speech demonstrates his precocious mastery of conventional discourses and also expresses his enduring faith in small-d democracy as the cornerstone of the American character. "We are coming to the end of a great adventure and are entering upon another equally as great," he opened.

The control of our government lies not in the hands of a few but in the hands of the masses. We are the people who go to make up those masses and if we wish our country to mean the most to us, we must use judiciously that power which is granted us. . . . Above all these are the true purposes of our schooling: the logical development of the mind so that we may more easily be able to master the difficult things which we are about to face, and the molding of the individual into good citizenship.[19]

Even if Norm's speech wasn't memorable, the class of 1927's graduation was quite so, as the relatively unknown Duke Ellington and His Orchestra played the after-party. In his diary, Norm simply called it "A Wow!"

In August, Norm embarked on an extensive driving trip in the Pearson Chrysler through eastern Canada with friends Curtis White and Allen Keyworth. The teenagers drove to Maine, where they boarded a ferry to Yarmouth, Nova Scotia. From there, they continued north, through undeveloped New Brunswick. Passenger cars had been common for only twenty years, and so infrastructure such as frequent service stations, traffic controls, even reliable and hardy tires just didn't exist. The roads were small and poorly maintained, and the boys were traveling through largely unpopulated areas. Norm described this portion of the trip to his father as "the muddiest and slipperiest [roads] I have ever seen" through "thick forest" for long stretches at a time, with "perhaps five houses" along the way, "50 miles between places to eat," and "only one filling station." "Every once in a while we saw hunters' cabins, it is about the best moose section there is," he added.[20] It was a genuine adventure—three eighteen-year-olds on a road trip through the wild.

Norm's health had withstood his taxing senior year well enough that his parents felt it an acceptable risk to send him to board at Philips Academy for a postgraduate year, which they hoped would guarantee admission to Yale. It was only fifty-one miles from Gardner to Andover, but it took Norm to a different and much more challenging world. Andover's academic and behavioral standards were more strin-

FIGURE 1 Norm and his roommate, Allen Keyworth, in their dorm room at Andover, 1929 (Norman Holmes Pearson Papers, Yale Collection of American Literature, Beinecke Rare Book and Manuscript Library).

gent than Gardner High's. Soon after he entered the school, Chester received a disappointed letter reporting that Norm was being put on disciplinary probation for smoking. (Norm would be a heavy smoker his entire life.) In February 1928, he was put on academic probation. He struggled with languages, with C's in French and Latin, and pulled A's only in English and geometry.[21] His difficulties weren't just academic. In December, Dr. MacAusland informed him that he would need a major surgery the upcoming summer, "which of course means no Yale," he wrote dejectedly in his journal. "C'est la vie."

Still, he was continuing to develop his taste for modern American poetry, and to cultivate his critical voice and a sense of American literary history. In one essay, he denigrated the New England poets of the nineteenth century, who "copied the sugared sentimentality of English poetry. . . . Literature was chiefly confined to New England and New England was disintegrating in a literary sense" because "Puritanic influences were starting to tell on its works." (Norm's pedestrian opinion of the Puritans would soon change.) But "the opening of the West [awakened] the American people to something vibrant and tingling which took them out of the rut into which they were rapidly settling.

Whitman was the first exponent of this new type of poetry." Praising contemporary poetry and free verse in particular, he calls out Frost, Edgar Lee Masters, Edwin Arlington Robinson, Vachel Lindsay, Louis Untermeyer, Carl Sandburg, Amy Lowell, and—in his first recorded mention of the woman who would play such an outsized role in his life—Hilda Doolittle. And his interest in women writers is also prefigured here: "when the country can boast of such lyrists as Edna Millay, Sara Teasdale, Louise Guiney, and Emily Dickinson," he concludes, "it need have no fear that there are some left who can write good poetry and still have it rhyme." The essay merited only a B: "too short, of course, for adequate treatment. Result: unsound generalizations."[22]

At Andover, Norm roomed with his Gardner pal Allen Keyworth and also struck up a close friendship with the athletic senior Franz "Ingie" Ingelfinger. Befitting a one-year student, Norm's yearbook entry has very little to it, but does indicate that Norm was a member of "Philo"—the Philomathean Society, Andover's century-old debate club. In the yearbook photo of that year's student orators, Pearson stands on the far edge of the back row, an outsider much like his brother had been.[23]

But as always, writing and language provided Norm with a way into the club. He took third place and won $10 in Andover's annual "Means Prize" oratory competition for his speech titled "The Problem of Assimilation."[24] Although most of his writing was utterly conventional, uncannily mimicking the rhythm and diction and sentiments of the authority figures he so carefully studied, this essay marks the first well-thought-out statement of ideas that were actually his, and that might even be controversial. This is not to say it's a remarkably original or independent piece of writing; it's not. But "The Problem of Assimilation" prefigures much of Norm's later thinking on the character of America.

The essay is essentially a liberal argument for the value of immigration and diversity, an endorsement of the "melting-pot" vision of America, and a refutation of the xenophobic "Americanism" ideas that had arisen in the 1920s. With one-third of America's population of 120 million being foreign-born or second-generation immigrants,

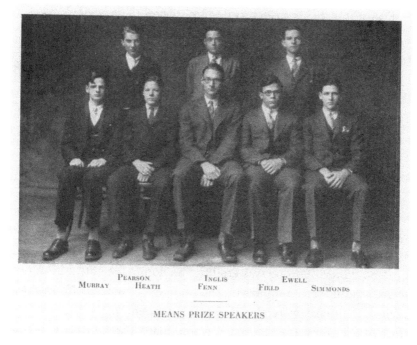

MURRAY   PEARSON   INGLIS   EWELL
          HEATH   FENN   FIELD   SIMMONDS

MEANS PRIZE SPEAKERS

FIGURE 2   The Means Prize speakers, 1928–29, Phillips Academy, Norm at top left, from *Pot-Pourri*, 1929 (Phillips Academy Archives).

Norm opens, assimilation of these immigrants into the American cultural body is imperative. But a forcible program of "compulsion" would bring only "social chaos and economic ruin." Rather, "it is a slow development, ending not with the fathers but carrying on even to their children." Moreover, immigrants must be not just allowed but actively encouraged to retain their own traditions, which are "too often cast aside in a mad rush for uniformity." Indeed, "it is a spirit of toleration which we must develop, an effort to work understandingly with [the immigrant], to see that his ignorance is not taken advantage of, and to help him adjust to his new surroundings and conditions."

The essay gets more pointed when Pearson turns to nativism:

One of the curses under which our country labors is the so-called "race nightmare." Any person whose name has the tang of peasant

Europe is placed in a category decidedly below those whose families have lived in America for some time. He may be accepted economically, but never socially. . . . We frown upon intermarriage with the alien lest it hasten the dissolution of what we call "the pure American race." There is no belief more absurd than that which shows the United States at any time a country of a truly pure race. It has always been a haven for different nationalities, and the result of inevitable intermarriage and consequent fusion has been what we call "our old stock."

In context, these claims were contentious, for immigration was an explosive issue in 1928. The immigration restriction acts of 1921 and 1924, spurred by public sentiment that mass immigration from southern and eastern Europe was eroding the dominance of "pure Americans," had put strict quotas on the numbers of entrants from those regions. (Chinese were already barred from entry, and immigration from regions outside of Europe was minimal.) The Ku Klux Klan and other nativist groups were at the height of their influence in local and state governments. Norm's liberal sentiments wouldn't have been out of the mainstream, but they responded directly to a powerful xenophobic movement of the day.

Norm's speech also would have landed with particular resonance at Andover, whose student body was almost entirely composed of white Protestant boys of Anglo-Saxon heritage. (Ingie, a first-generation immigrant born in Dresden, was a rare exception.) The nonwhite population of Massachusetts was just over 1 percent, but 53 percent of the white population were either foreign-born or children of foreign-born parents.[25] So these Andover boys and their families likely *did* feel troubled that something fundamental was changing in the makeup of New England and—by extension—in America. Although his own WASP lineage was pure, Pearson did not feel that this made him a truer American than any other. But his openness to what would be called today "diversity" had its limits. Norm understands "immigrants" as being exclusively European and is blind to the prohibition on Chinese immigration, much less the exclusion of African Americans from the "melting pot."

Perhaps because he received only third place—in Gardner, he always could assume that he was the best writer in any room—Norm wasn't particularly proud of the essay. "Please don't think it necessary to tell the *News* about it," he instructed Fanny. "I absolutely mean this. You or anyone else."[26] But his declamation somehow reached and impressed the Massachusetts Department of Education. Mary Guyton, the state supervisor of adult alien education, wrote Chester that "you have a very promising son who has the spirit of America imbedded in his heart. Youths of today who have this spirit of Americanism are going to make our Democracy stronger and better."[27]

It was a heartening way to end his Andover stint. More good news came when the dreaded hip surgery was temporarily stayed, and Yale sent official notice of his admission. Norm returned to Gardner for the early part of the summer, then in July took a three-week Thomas Cook Mediterranean cruise with Fanny and Eleanor. Departing from Naples, the ship made stops in Athens, Istanbul, Beirut, Haifa, Alexandria, and Nice, ending in Le Havre, where the Pearsons embarked on their voyage home. Thomas Cook and Son specialized in cultural tours, and this one offered an onboard orchestra and lectures on history, art, and anthropology by the popular radio commentators Charles C. Batchelder and Hans von Kaltenborn. It was just Norm's kind of trip, combining culture, opportunities to socialize and make connections with fellow passengers, and of course the pleasure of "collecting" cities and experiences.

The Norman Holmes Pearson who would matriculate at Yale in October 1928 was in many ways a typical example of the Yankee upper bourgeoisie. He shared their cultural outlook, their politics, their sense that they were the most American of Americans. He was what the Puritan heritage had produced, a true believer in the institutions who also understood that institutions must evolve with the times in order to accommodate the rapid cultural and demographic changes of modernity. The adult Norm who was emerging was very much like his adult models: civic leaders and socializers and networkers and *doers*. But he was also precociously intelligent, witty, with a sly and sometimes sideways sense of humor. Most important, he had an iron determination, born from his days hovering near death, to make the most of his time, and enjoy himself in doing so. Optimistic, entrepreneurial, gregarious, diligent, and always highly self-aware, he was just the kind of striver that Yale saw as its ideal raw material and its signature product.

+ 2 +

BRIGHT COLLEGE YEARS

When Norm arrived in New Haven, Connecticut, in the fall of 1928, he had come to the place where he would spend virtually the rest of his life. The old Puritan city, one of the first English settlements in America, was still dominated by its WASP population in the 1920s, but over the past decades immigration had brought significant Jewish, Portuguese, and especially Italian inhabitants to New Haven to work in the city's thriving industries, particularly firearms and garments. Like the rest of New England, New Haven's character and power structure remained WASPy, but it was visibly changing.

Norm had also come to the institution that would mold him intellectually, socially, personally, and professionally. For most people today, and in fact even a hundred years ago, the so-called Big Three schools (Harvard, Yale, and Princeton) can all seem essentially the same — insular northeastern universities whose alumni precipitate to positions of power. But they always had distinct characters and played different roles in training the American elite. By the early 1900s, a set of widely read books conveyed to people who would never attend them the distinctions among these schools. Harvard, the oldest, was considered the most intellectual and most connected with the old Puritan establishment, so it was appropriate that the best-known literary depiction of Harvard was 1907's *The Education of Henry Adams*, the autobiography of a member of one of Boston's First Families. Princeton, the youngest, was the most socially oriented, an identity both reflected in and popularized by F. Scott Fitzgerald's early novels and stories so beloved by the flapper generation.

Yale, then, was for the ambitious, the ones seeking to become leaders, those who valued success above all, as portrayed in Owen Johnson's 1912 novel *Stover at Yale* (which Fitzgerald himself called the "textbook" for his generation). For Fitzgerald, Yale was "November, crisp and energetic" in comparison to Princeton's "lazy spring day."[1] It was less academically demanding than Harvard, drawing people for whom "college was an attractive social experience, to be paid for by a certain intellectual minimum," in the words of Yale historian George Pierson.[2] Yale's ethos was "the importance of being 'well-rounded'—of not focusing excessively on academics, but instead achieving success in the extracurricular world," as historian Daniel Horowitz writes.[3] "The 'Yale System' harnessed individual ambition and effort into team efforts for the greater good and honor of one's academic class and the college," educational historian John Thelin explains. "It provided the critical formula whereby American individualism could be reconciled with cooperation."[4]

Yale also liked to distinguish itself—at least in its own self-imagining—as a more diverse, democratic, meritocratic, and representatively American institution than its Puritan sister Harvard. Yale, closer to boisterous New York City while still geographically in New England, saw itself as leavening its Puritan fiber with the looser, more commercial, and less Anglo-Saxon population of New York, Pennsylvania, and "the West" (Ohio and points beyond). "We were not impressed by the Great Names of plutocracy—by Vanderbilts, Astors, Rockefellers," the editor and critic Henry Seidel Canby (class of 1899) preened, for the "qualified democracy" of Yale ranked men only on their accomplishments and personal qualities.[5] Unlike at Harvard and Princeton, where the final clubs and eating clubs based their admission largely on one's lineage, at Yale "even boys of relatively modest social origin could dream of membership in Bones" if they could combine "extraordinary accomplishment . . . with personal charisma."[6] Approximately 25 to 30 percent of Yale students at the time, most of them products of public schools, received scholarships or financial aid.

But Yale's own officials acknowledged that the school was really for one group. "The sons of the wealthy parents are the best material we get here at Yale," Dean Frederick Jones frankly noted in 1914. "This may sound undemocratic . . . but it's true."[7] The affluent, prep school–educated men dominated social life, athletics, and important student organizations like the newspaper, the glee club, the senior societies, and the fraternities. And in the 1920s, its growing preference for "legacies" was making the school even more inbred. (Yale, in fact, was the first of the Big Three schools to formally favor alumni children in admission.)[8] In 1924, 13 percent of incoming freshmen had family members who had attended Yale; by the late 1930s, this number was over 50 percent. With a brother and uncle who were alumni, Pearson was among these. Also, by the 1920s up to a third of the student body at the Big Three colleges came from schools such as Andover, and 60 percent of Social Register families in Boston and New York sent their boys to Harvard, Yale, or Princeton. They had always been schools serving the WASP elite, but now they were schools *primarily* for the WASP elite.

An important part of Yale's allure to students beyond the Northeast, though, was how popular culture depicted the vitality and vibrancy of its undergraduate life. Popular novels like *Stover*, dime-novel characters like Frank Merriwell (a standout Yale athlete who solved mysteries between games and classes), and songs like "Bright College Years" or Yale alumnus Cole Porter's "Bingo Eli Yale" made life at Yale seem irresistibly fun, a place where studying was of secondary importance to clubs and sports and parties. Moreover, at this time Yale's athletes and teams were often successful on national and international stages; the eights rowing team, featuring the future Dr. Benjamin Spock, won the 1924 Olympic gold medal for the United States, and the football team had shared the national championship in 1927. By the time Norm matriculated, Yale had become the model for American college life. In the 1920s, "Yale was America's college," Thelin claims.[9]

Although Yale's character and self-imagining remained much the same as they had been for decades, Pearson's undergraduate years marked a period of dramatic change. Most significant was the creation of the residential college system, the feature of the university most visible today in the colleges' gated quadrangles. They were added to solve a couple of problems: overcrowding, and the perceived attenuation of "school spirit," one's attachment not only to Yale itself but to one's graduating class. Picking out the big men in each class, and guessing who would be invited to join a prestigious sophomore society, started as soon as the freshmen matriculated. Being admitted to a sophomore society, in turn, would then lead to being "tapped" for one of the three most elite senior societies: Wolf's Head, Scroll and Key, or best of all, Skull and Bones.

But as Yale College's enrollment burgeoned—going from 3,820 in 1921 to 5,914 in 1931—faculty, alumni, and President James Angell grew concerned that with so many students in each class they were just not sufficiently connected to their peers, that "the old closeness of the class and the college were being lost," in the words of a Yale historian.[10] So in 1930, philanthropist Edward Harkness gave $15.7 million to create a system of residential colleges, "intermediate between a dormitory and the true English college," for students who had completed their freshman year.[11] Although Norm just missed the opportunity to be a member of one of the residential colleges, he witnessed the massive physical transformations to the campus as seven new colleges, the monumental Sterling Memorial Library, and other landmarks were erected.

Yale wasn't just physically changed in these years. It was starting to modernize its campus life and program of study. Compulsory chapel for undergraduates was eliminated in 1927, and in the early 1920s, a small group of students and alumni had agitated for a loosening of the required curriculum and a tightening of academic expectations. Admissions standards would have to be strengthened, as well. Angell, not himself a Yale graduate, "was anxious to make the stimulation of the intellect the prime goal of Yale."[12] In effect, Angell sought to emphasize the educational component of Yale over its role as an incubator and distributor of social capital among a small group of privileged young men.

Angell's focus on learning and producing knowledge certainly affected Pearson, who entered the school with the modest intention merely to go into the family business, but left resolved to become a scholar. For many alumni, though, this struck at the very heart of Yale's identity. For them, Yale's purpose was to identify the nation's future leaders and mold its elites, and academic achievement was only one—and certainly not the most important—marker of this group. Breeding, social status, and family reputation absolutely mattered; athletic achievement was also important; but leadership potential, "clubbability," team spirit, and other intangibles were paramount. Because of these criteria, the sophomore and senior societies often took men whose academic performance wasn't particularly stellar, a tradition threatened by Angell's reforms. "Yale will soon reach the sorry state when her sons will be mere brain specimens," the *Yale Daily News* fretted in 1926, and will "no longer be a heterogeneous group of average citizens."[13]

The increasing dominance at Yale of Social Register–listed, prep school–trained boys intensified the resistance to Angell's changes. Emphasizing academics would open Yale up to a more diverse group of students: graduates of public high schools, young men from outside the Northeast, less affluent students, and even members of ethnic and religious minority groups, Catholics and Jews in particular. (An unwritten policy entirely excluded African Americans from consideration for admission to Yale College.) These were strivers and climbers who had internalized the idea that in America, hard work and achievement could get you anywhere you wanted to go. In the view of many students and alumni, these interlopers didn't understand that true status wasn't something you could obtain; status was something one was born with, and Yale's purpose was to distill out the best among those who already possessed that status.

If Yale's students were largely responsible for creating and sustaining that ethos, even many faculty and administration (a significant percentage of whom were alumni) had little respect for students who put their studies first. Nor were they coy about how class and ethnic prejudice colored their distaste. In his memoir of his college years, Henry Seidel Canby, who taught literature at Yale for two decades, sneered at the "greasy grind . . . [who] seldom changed his collar. He had a sneaking cleverness. . . . Education for him was a coin, useless unless you could buy something with it." Somehow, Canby distinguishes this ugly anti-Semitic stereotype from another purported "undesirable" group, the children of immigrants who were trickling in to Yale: "Polish Jews with anemic faces on which were set dirty spectacles, soft-eyed Italians too alien to mix with an Anglo-Saxon community, seam-faced Armenian boys, and now and then a Chinese. These, except the last, were all in college to learn how to live in America. Their mien was apologetic; you could see them watching with envious curiosity the courteous indifference of the superior race."[14] When the Jewish component of incoming classes began to rise in the years just before Pearson arrived, Angell took a number of measures to halt the increase. In 1924, for instance, the administration restricted transfer privileges for public-school students from the New Haven, Bridgeport, and Hartford school districts; not coincidentally, 75 percent of Yale's few Jewish students had came from those three systems.[15] These restrictions were a response not just to the fear that Harvard and Yale were losing their "character," but to the larger anti-immigrant, nativist backlash that Norm had decried in his Means Prize declamation.

Like Alfred, Norm fell between the scholarship boys and the prep school aristocracy, and he knew that he would never be among the chosen. What people would have noticed about him first was his disability: he was rail thin and stooped over because of the curvature of his spine and the fact that his left leg was two inches shorter than the right. Concerned about his brother, Alfred wrote both the dean of Yale College and the freshman dean the month before Norm arrived in New Haven to request that he be given a first-floor room "to save him unnecessary exertion" for "he has been laid up for a total of three of the last five years with an infected hip [which] has left him with a leg he cannot bend."[16] ("His spirit and health," Alfred was quick to add, are "excellent, and by taking proper precautions, there is no question but that he will be able to carry on well at Yale.")

As it had at Gardner High and Andover, his condition prevented him for going out for any sports. Norm was on crutches or even in a wheelchair for long stretches of his college career. While he didn't report any ugly incidents in letters home, in this era before the Americans with Disabilities Act, discrimination and bias against the disabled were common, and Norm certainly had to endure ugly comments from classmates about his "deficiency." Moreover, in an age and place saturated with anti-Semitism, Norm's disability tracked closely with the physical shortcomings commonly associated with Jews: a weak physique, stooped posture, and gait that indicated poor health.

Although he tried not to let it, the stubborn infection still very much hindered him, physically and psychologically. He was always reminded of what he couldn't do, and he had to take the realities of a chronic condition into consideration—his letters home requesting money often asked for medical supplies such as crutch tips as well. The effect his condition had on his family also weighed on him. By the time Norm started at Yale, Alfred was back in Gardner and had embarked, somewhat begrudgingly, on the career and life that his family had "chartered" (in the words of his niece Elizabeth) for him.[17] After graduating in 1925, Alfred had moved to New York City to enroll in Macy's training program for careers in the retail trade. He adored the New York life unavailable to him in Gardner. But inevitably, the family called him back, and Alfred dutifully returned to Goodnow Pearson's. His first daughter, Joan, would be born in 1929, followed by Barbara in 1932 and Ann in 1934. Although Alfred rarely complained, Norm was aware of his regrets and even resentments.

But the injury had never interfered with Norm's instinct, honed over his homebound youth, to connect with others and create networks, and to show team spirit and leadership. Ingie, Norm's roommate for their entire undergraduate careers, had lettered in track and football at Andover and joined the Yale freshman football squad and crew. Their first home was in Fayerweather Hall, which was torn down in 1933 to make way for Berkeley College. In their sophomore year, they then moved into a quad with two other young men who had become Pearson's other closest friends: Steve Van Cortlandt Morris and Eugene O'Neill Jr., son of the playwright. The four remained together for the next two years as well, with rooms near each other first in Dickinson

Hall and finally in the Harkness Memorial Quadrangle for their senior year.

Gene had come into Yale with the glittering prep school résumé that Norman lacked, with scholarship awards at Horace Mann and numerous poems in the school's literary magazine. He was a brilliant undergraduate as well, winning a number of prizes as well as election to Phi Beta Kappa and selection as Ivy Laureate of the class of 1932. Most important of all, he was tapped for Skull and Bones. His impressive achievements in classical studies, in fact, partly inspired his father to write *Mourning Becomes Electra* in 1930.[18] That the son would influence the father is somewhat ironic. Eugene O'Neill and Gene's mother, Kathleen Jenkins, barely saw each other after they married in a secret ceremony in 1909; the playwright was out of the country when his son was born; Gene Jr. did not even meet his father until he was eleven years old; and father and son rarely saw each other.[19]

The fourth member of Norm's group of friends was Stephanus (Steve) Van Cortlandt Morris, a descendant of several distinguished old New York families, including the Schermerhorns and the Morris clan. His grandfather was the Gilded Age society figure Augustus Newbold Morris, and his mother Helen Schermerhorn Kingsland was granddaughter of New York City mayor Ambrose Kingsland. Like Ingie, Morris was an athlete, playing tennis on club and varsity teams.

On campus Norm socialized avidly and took part in literary clubs, although he would not be selected for the exclusive Elizabethan Club, Yale's leading literary society. Yale was a national football power, playing almost all its games at the giant Yale Bowl, and Norm and his friends attended many Bulldog games to watch Ingie, who started for the varsity team as a senior. He also, as a freshman, joined the staff of the *News Pictorial*, the weekly supplement to the *Yale Daily News*, and became its vice chairman as a senior. While the *Yale Daily News* was one of the most prestigious and high-profile organizations on campus, its staff members often selected for senior societies, the *Pictorial* was a step down in status.

More than with most Yale boys of the day, though, much of Norm's social and extracurricular life took place away from campus. Chester had bought a Ford Model T for Norm, and he frequently drove back and forth to Gardner to see his parents, to Poughkeepsie to see Eleanor, and to both ends of Massachusetts to visit friends. He, Ingie, Steve, and Gene drove frequently to New York to see plays, generally staying at the Morris house. The modern drama and music that he experienced in New York City shaped his artistic tastes far more than did the hidebound curriculum at Yale. In 1930, for instance, he saw Marc Connelly's play *The Green Pastures*, which featured the first all-Black cast in a Broadway show. Pearson found it "quite unusual and alternately funny and inexpressibly touching."[20] A recital by the African American tenor Roland Hayes, and Lillian Gish in *Uncle Vanya*, also made an impression on him.

Not all his trips were cultural. Because there was no women's college in New Haven—or at least not one that drew girls of the right social class—Yale men often had girlfriends or steady dates out of town. At Harwich Port in the summer of 1927, Norm had met Mary Elizabeth Thomson of Schenectady, New York, and the two immediately began a flirtatious and at times intense relationship, conducted through the mail and through his visits to her, that lasted for several years. Norm grew more and more attached to Mary Lib over the course of 1929 and 1930, while she increasingly played the coquette. For months, she wrote him almost every day, addressing him as "dear" and "love," even as she blithely talked about her fiancé Don. His letters to her grew emotional and even, only partly jokingly, toyed with the idea of marriage. The correspondence got even more heated in the summer of 1930, and in one letter, she responded to his (again, only partly tongue-in-cheek) plan for them to live off his Goodnow Pearson's dividends by both shutting him down and giving him hope: "Glad you know I'm not in love with you," she wrote, "or you could never understand these remarks of mine—never the less we would have fun if only I'd change my mind and you really meant the things you seem to think."[21] Ingie saw through her game, though, and warned Norm that she was stringing him along. She realized he had sussed her out: "Tell Ingie I don't like him particularly either now that he is interfering with our perfectly nice correspondence," she told Norm in the summer of 1930.

Weeks later, she told Norm that her engagement had been announced in the Schenectady papers.[22]

Mary Lib was Norm's first big crush. In part because of his insecurity about his appearance, he was hungry for the validation she gave him, and vulnerable to falling in love with her. It didn't help that even after she was engaged and married, she continued to flirt. "Your letters are so intelligent and interesting," she wrote him not long after her engagement announcement was published, "that they fascinate me always—though sometimes they are only sheets of paper completely and nonsensically covered with 'all my love'—at least they are unique—they seem to be a part of you—perhaps I'm only gullible and fooling myself—and I want that part dreadfully because it is annoying to know you and like you and then have you miles away all of the time."[23]

Even as the drama with Mary Lib put Norm in an emotionally inflamed state, his medical condition worsened things. His infection flared up in early 1930 and had started eating away at the ball of his left femur and the acetabulum of the pelvis. With his left leg largely immobilized, he was barely able to walk during the spring term and often relied on a wheelchair. In June, he returned to Dr. MacAusland, who concluded that the treatment he had received up to this point wasn't doing the job and the hip joint had stiffened up almost entirely. Norman's left leg jutted out at an angle of fifteen to twenty degrees (although he had learned to balance on the ball of his foot) and he was having regular attacks resulting in discharge from the hip. The infected areas had to be fully scraped out and a bone graft performed on the eroded bone surfaces.[24] The time had come for the radical intervention that had been postponed in 1928. This surgery would permanently fuse the ball of his left femur to the pelvis, making him unable to bend at the hip on the left side. He would be able to walk, by swinging his left side over laterally rather than lifting the knee, but it would prevent him from sitting on sofas or armchairs for the rest of his life unless he could hang his left leg off of the seat, or (as in a car) recline so far back that he was barely bent at the hip.

Norm knew from experience that this surgery would require serious

FIGURE 3 Ingie, Eleanor, and Norm, eating sandwiches on the banks of the Hudson about 1930 (Photo courtesy of Elizabeth Rice-Smith).

convalescence. He had told Mary Lib, who offered to visit him, that "you could not see me so soon after the 'fixings.'"[25] In fact, much of his recovery over the summer of 1930 would have to happen alone, with occasional visits from Ingie. His father and brother needed to be at the store, and his mother and Eleanor were traveling in Europe. (Norm had accompanied Chester on their own three-week European trip the previous year: a tour of England, France, and Germany for the Berlin convention of the International Advertising Association, a conclave of back-slapping Babbitts in the teetering Weimar Republic.) He had the surgery in late June and remained at Brooks Hospital in Brookline until mid-September, when he returned to Yale for his junior year.

Slipping back into the life of a college student, Pearson continued to stay engaged with art, literature, and music through trips to New York. In January 1932, he saw the famous retrospective for Diego Rivera, "the Mexican who is causing so much excitement right now," at the two-year-old Museum of Modern Art, for which Rivera famously created eight "portable murals."[26] In February, he saw Ethel Barrymore in *School for Scandal* on Broadway, and a few weeks later, he and Steve returned for *Parsifal* at the Met. Accompanied by Eleanor's friend Anais von Kaltenborn (daughter of the radio commentator they had met on their

1928 cruise), the two went to Adolph Lewisohn's Fifth Avenue mansion to view his famous modern art collection. The Lewisohns were in Florida, so Norm and his friends "had the run of the house."[27]

Norm's road-tripping was curtailed, though, in May, when his car was totaled. In May 1932, just before he graduated, for a little pocket money he charged a group of freshmen $10 to borrow his Model T to drive up to Miss Hall's School in Pittsfield, Massachusetts, for a dance. ("One boy across the hall has lived for a year on the money he gets from" renting his car, Norm explained to his parents.) But near Torrington, the boys ran the car off the road in the foggy night. The Ford rolled, caught fire, and was a total wreck. Norm didn't want to report it to the police as renting a car without a license was illegal in Connecticut, and lending a car to freshmen against Yale's rules. The $250 that the boys promised him in compensation wasn't enough for a new car, and he had no way of ensuring they'd even pay up. He wrote a chagrined letter to Chester, who knew everything already, as the state police had contacted him as soon as they found the burned, melted vehicle. He and Fanny were forgiving—at least of Norm. "You and the rest of us are sorry that you did the combination of friendly and profitable transaction which you did; however, you did it with your eyes open, and probably I would have done the same thing," his father told him. "Don't," he admonished, "be kindhearted with these boys—they shouldn't get the idea that they can duck *full* responsibility."[28]

His return to school after his hospitalization did bring one major change of course to young Norm's life. He had entered Yale intending to major in economics, in preparation for a career at Goodnow Pearson's. Trying to interest himself in business, he closely followed the volatile stock market in the fall of 1929 from the bulletin board of a downtown New Haven brokerage.[29] For his first two and a half years, he was a good but not outstanding student. At the time, Yale used a 400-point scale for grading, and in his first semester he pulled a 295 average—equivalent to a 79 percent. His grades hovered right around the 80 percent mark, with difficulties in French, geology, and psychology, until the second semester of his junior year, when his average jumped to an 87 percent and, by his senior year, to an 89 percent.

English, though, was a different matter. He started loading up on English classes in his sophomore year, even though he was still pursuing an economics major, and in his junior year took twelve hours in the subject, pulling outstanding grades. Then, Professor Stanley T. Williams's Studies in American Literature (English 52), which Norm took in the spring of 1931, energized him like nothing he had ever done. As Pearson reminisced years later, it wasn't even the class that did this, but just a tossed-off aside in one of Williams's lectures: "nobody really knows very much about Hawthorne as an undergraduate at Bowdoin." He took that as a challenge, and the resulting term paper, "Hawthorne's College Years," earned Norm the highest grade he received in any Yale class, a 360 (92 percent).[30] It also caught Williams's attention so much that he hired Norm to help him compile a list of the books that Hawthorne would have read while he was in college.

Today, a college student like Norm who falls in love with Nathaniel Hawthorne (or Herman Melville or Emily Dickinson) can easily imagine a career teaching and writing about that author. But that wasn't the case in 1928. When Williams kindled Norm's interest in the idea of becoming a teacher of American literature, in effect he was recruiting his student into what had very recently been an insurgent faction in the profession, a faction of which Williams was a ringleader.

In fact, literature itself, apart from the Greek and Latin classics, had only recently been considered worthy of inclusion in a curriculum. The influential 1828 "Yale Report," which expressed the dominant "philosophy of education in the liberal arts" well into the twentieth century, insisted that only the classics could instill the "mental discipline" that a college education was intended to deliver.[31] The modern languages, on the other hand, were "frivolous subjects."[32] When English literary works did appear in the curriculum of schools and colleges, it was for instruction in rhetoric and oratory. Unsurprisingly, Yale held to the standard demanded by its eponymous report even longer than other schools, and in 1895 a Yale-educated scholar remembered that he never heard "the name of a single English author or the title of a single English classic" in a Yale classroom. But by the time Pearson arrived, this had finally changed. Undergraduates still had to take at least a yearlong course in the classics, but they also needed to complete a year of study in "English, Art, or Music." That English was grouped with art and music shows that these were meant as courses in aesthetic expression. Matthew Arnold's influential Victorian view that great literary works should be studied because they embodied "the best that has been thought and said," and thus instilled appreciation for high cultural achievement, also helped make literature a part of the education of privileged young men. Unlike their predecessors of a couple of decades before, therefore, Yale men of Pearson's vintage would have been expected to learn something about literature written in their own language and could even "major" (itself a relatively new innovation) in English.

But they wouldn't read much — or perhaps any — American literature at Yale, or in their earlier schooling. Generations of high schoolers struggling through *The Scarlet Letter* might be surprised to know that before about 1940, their counterparts didn't have to read Hawthorne, or many other American writers. "In this country," Howard Mumford Jones of the University of Michigan wrote in 1936, "education in English literature is education in British literature."[33] Well into the twentieth century, most literary scholars and critics in England and the United States took it for granted that American literature was just a low-quality, vulgarized imitation of English models. Sydney Smith's infamous 1820 dismissal of American culture and American literature stung native writers for decades and was reiterated, in strikingly similar terms, throughout the rest of the century. "During the thirty or forty years of [Americans'] independence, they have done absolutely nothing for the Sciences, for the Arts, for Literature. . . . In the four quarters of the globe, who reads an American book? or goes to an American play? or looks at an American picture or statue?"[34] And to some degree Smith was right. Well into the twentieth century, even Americans preferred English literature to homegrown writing. Certainly, some of the writers who have come to be considered major American authors were popular in their home country — Hawthorne, Longfellow, Emerson, and of course Harriet Beecher Stowe — but more notable is that Walt

Whitman was widely considered a vulgar curiosity, Emily Dickinson was barely known, and Herman Melville had been largely forgotten.

So even when literature started to enter the American higher education curriculum, American literature was widely treated as a sideshow to the real story, and not until the 1920s did Harvard or Yale regularly offer an American literature class for undergraduates. This marginalization characterized scholarship as much as the curriculum. Scholars who wanted to produce research on American literature commonly had "feelings of inferiority," in the words of early critic Jay Hubbell, and for an early twentieth-century professor to specialize in American literature was "close to professional suicide."[35] In fact, many American literature teachers were critics and writers rather than PhD-credentialed scholars. At Yale, Canby, Phelps, and Henry Augustin Beers—only Phelps with a PhD—taught the subject until Williams took on the task in 1925.[36]

The changing nature of college professors' jobs also impeded the acceptance of American literature. In the nineteenth century, faculty rarely had advanced degrees and often taught in a wide range of subjects in a standard curriculum: mathematics, basic science, theology, Greek and Latin, rhetoric. But a new, German-influenced research-university model had come to the United States at the end of the 1800s and spread quickly to elite colleges like Yale. At such schools, professors were no longer expected to be gentlemen generalists, spiritual and intellectual guides. Instead, they were PhD-prepared researchers, and publishing scholarship, not just teaching and tutelage, became a central part of their jobs.

Scholarly research in literature at this time generally took the form of "philology." Philology's main concern was what English literature could show about the evolution of the English language, and so professors were trained in Anglo-Saxon, Old German, Old Icelandic, and other dead languages that had contributed to modern English. And to this approach, American literature just wasn't that useful, as it was even further removed from those sources than Chaucer, Spenser, and Shakespeare. One might imagine that the American language, on the other hand, was worth studying as a linguistic phenomenon, but the dominant view was that any unique characteristics of the American language were nothing but bastardizations and corruptions of the real English tongue.

So the philological scholars said that American literature wasn't interesting, and the men of letters said it wasn't any good. But for Williams and others in this first generation of American literature professors, something even more urgent was at stake: "to demonstrate the existence of an American civilization," as literary historian David Shumway put it.[37] Williams had begun his career as a specialist in eighteenth-century English drama, but the early 1920s shifted his interests to American literature, and he wrote a widely read two-volume biography of Washington Irving. Williams was one of the most active agitators in the profession for the status of American literature. He had helped to found the American Literature Group within the Modern Language Association in 1921 and the scholarly journal *American Literature* in 1929. As American literary studies spread to more and more universities over the course of the 1920s and 1930s, and its journals and scholarly meetings grew, Williams became one of the field's leading figures.

The feisty self-justification typical of American literary study at the time comes across in Williams's lecture notes for English 52, the class Norm took at the end of his junior year. Williams swipes away the prejudice that American literature was second-rate, countering that there are professors of American literature in France and Holland, that Poe letters now sell for $500, and that two hundred undergraduates are in this particular Yale class. "I cannot help thinking that something has happened since the sneer of Sydney Smith. . . . We are no longer afraid to study scientifically Emerson, Hawthorne, Poe, or Whitman. We have come to realize that it may be as well to study first-rate Americans as fourth-rate Englishmen." He refutes the commonplace idea that American literature is merely an inconsequential outcropping of the Anglo-Saxon tradition, and he emphasizes Frederick Jackson Turner's well-known "frontier thesis" about American culture: only the frontier could create "a Daniel Boone, an Abraham Lincoln, a Jackson"—and even Hawthorne and Emerson.[38] And he concludes by saying that the modern movement, embodied by Willa Cather and Sinclair Lewis, isn't a clean break from this American tradition, but rather a further development of Puritan ideas and themes traceable back to Cotton Mather.[39] In his own teaching and scholarly work, Pearson would reiterate and refine these arguments of his mentor.

Pearson also appreciated that Williams was one of the few Yale English professors to include in his class modern authors such as Cather, Robert Frost, Carl Sandburg, and Vachel Lindsay. Norman's interest in modern writing had turned into a passion in his freshman year, when he bought Mark Van Doren's groundbreaking *Anthology of World Poetry*. In Van Doren's collection, Pearson's Yale colleague Robin Winks points out, Pearson "encountered the world's range of poetic expression — translations from the Chinese, Sanskrit, Hebrew, Greek, Russian. . . . Emerson, Longfellow, Poe, Whitman were there of course, but so were poets that had not been taught, even at Andover: Ezra Pound and H.D."[40] Pearson had imbibed Longfellow and Emerson as part of his New England cultural heritage, and the more daring (and less Yankee) Whitman and Poe were also part of that education. But to meet as well the very experimental Pound and Hilda Doolittle, both of whom would figure prominently in Pearson's adult life: it's almost as if Van Doren's anthology materialized so as to prefigure Pearson's eventual career.

Energized by his first American literature class, Pearson enrolled in Williams and Ralph Gabriel's American Thought and Civilization (History 37) the next fall. Offered for the very first time that year, History 37 was a daring class at conservative Yale, crossing academic departments at a time when disciplinary boundaries were jealously policed. Norm, unsurprisingly, was the star student in the class. American Thought and Civilization is today widely credited as the first American studies course at any university. The syllabus certainly didn't suggest that the course would be groundbreaking, but what made Williams and Gabriel's first American studies class distinctive and original, and what came to define American studies as a field, were its premises: that there was such a thing as an American civilization, a characteristic "culture" or way of life separate from that of Great Britain; that one could use history and literature to define and explore that unique culture; and that doing so was a worthwhile endeavor and could help young Americans better understand, and ultimately serve, their nation.

Norm earned a solid A in History 37 and excelled in almost all his classes his senior year, with the telling exception of economics. He also relished his work as Williams's research assistant and how learning about Hawthorne's life got him thinking about his own family's Puritan roots and history. In the spring he won a $125 prize for his scholarly work—a prize, he warned his mother, that was intended "only for people going on to more work." Later that term, his now ninety-page essay on Hawthorne's college years won the $500 Henry Strong Prize in the English department, a sum greater than that year's tuition.[41] In an obscure New England Sunday school magazine Pearson had also unearthed "The Good Man's Miracle," a long-lost 1843 Hawthorne story. Williams encouraged Pearson to send the story, along with his own accompanying observations, to the New England Quarterly, which published the article and story in 1933, making it Pearson's first scholarly publication.[42]

Williams and his classes also "struck the spark" that set him on his career path, Norm reminisced later, showing him that a life in retail was no longer his only plausible future.[43] Although he joked that he was born a "natural ladies' ready-to-wear, stylish stout, and young misses' man," a career at Goodnow Pearson's had always been more a default than an aspiration.[44] Ironically, one of the original reasons for his family's plan for Norm to work under Alfred at the store—his disability and the tenuousness of his health—also gave him cause to think of alternatives. His hospital stay the previous fall, and the shattering of the illusion that he and Mary Lib would marry and move to Gardner, made him crave some time and distance to think over what he would do with his life. The Depression, as well, made going into the retail trade in 1932 a grim prospect.

Although they were certainly disappointed that Norm would not be returning to Gardner, it was probably a relief to his family that Norm opted out of working at the store. The life of a teacher was certainly less taxing than that of a store owner and was unlikely to damage his health. Norm's choice likely wasn't a surprise, either, as the previous summer he had already floated the idea of delaying his entry into the family business. He wasn't ready, he had told them, and felt that his illness had cheated him of his youth a bit. So he had proposed to spend a year doing what middle-class Americans have often done when they are done with school: wander around Europe. As he explained to his mother,

> I want to go abroad for a year—not studying but going places and staying there until I became tired of them. If I got sick of it I should come home. . . . Most of my life so far has been spent in getting well. Before I settle down and go to work and am unable to get away for long, I want one year of just being well and enjoying being normal. Life is short and if I don't take it now I never shall. Then I will settle down and make you both proud of me in a business way—but I want to forget the past for a little while first.[45]

He asked his father for $3,000 to fund at least a year of travel. His parents agreed (and Alfred, likely, stewed a bit).

Norm was the aimless exception in his group of friends, who all started training for their careers immediately after graduation. Ingie would begin his studies at Harvard Medical School in the fall, and Steve had secured a place in the diplomatic service. In June 1931, Gene had shocked everyone by secretly marrying a woman named Betty Green, telling none of his friends or even his mother or father about his plans. Norm found out only when Gene, ever the classicist, telegrammed him the news in Latin. Betty and Gene found an apartment off campus for his senior year and prepared to move to Germany, where he had won a yearlong fellowship to study at the University of Freiburg.[46]

Norm's new career aspirations gave some shape to his nebulous overseas plans, and he began to consider studying at an English university. And as German was the most helpful language for philology, which even an American literature scholar would have to master, Norm also intended to pick up that tongue. Ineligible for a Rhodes Scholarship because he was not an athlete, Norm decided to apply for a "lesser" scholarship Yale offered to Oxford's Magdalen College, where he would earn a second bachelor's degree in two years. He sought out Dr. John Fulton, a professor in Yale's medical school who had studied at Magdalen, for his advice and a recommendation. In April, he wrote his mother that he had received "a radiogram sent to the Dr. at the Medical School saying that they would take me at Magdalen College, Oxford. He certainly must have had a good deal of prestige, and I had a lucky break to meet him. . . . At any rate I'm in and my academic career started."[47] Norm was headed to Europe: this time, on his own.

He immediately began preparing for his time abroad. That summer, Ingie and his family were going to visit relatives in Germany, so Norm planned to join them on the voyage over. Dr. MacAusland cleared him to travel. Theodore Sizer of the Yale Art Gallery provided him with letters of introduction to the heads of various European art museums and galleries, including Bernard Berenson at Villa I Tatti in Florence. Stanley Williams requested his continued assistance, this time on a massive project to collect and publish Hawthorne's entire correspondence, which he had undertaken with Randall Stewart of Vanderbilt University. And as Oxford's term didn't begin until early October, Norm arranged to stay in Munich for ten weeks to study German. But he was disappointed to learn, when registering to "read" (major in) English literature, that the course of study laid out for him was even more fusty and backward looking than Yale's, with a hefty dose of Anglo-Saxon required. If he was going to equip himself with the training expected of a serious scholar in 1932, American literature would have to wait.

+ 3 +

THE CREAM OF AMERICAN
INTELLECTUALITY

In late June, Norm sailed from Boston to Europe on the Hamburg-American Line with the Ingelfingers. This wasn't his first time in Europe, but it was his first time there alone, and his letters to his mother indelibly record his impressions. Poor weather during the crossing forced everyone to stay indoors, which Norm complained has "complicated the problem of association with the German Jews who make up the greater part of the boat," showing the persistence of his class prejudices. Passing by the Aran Islands off the west coast of Ireland, Norm noted that "the houses were all thatched and looked as though they kept the pig in the parlor, a thing which I seem to associate with the country." After Ireland, the ship docked at Cherbourg, Southampton, and Boulogne before its final port of call, Hamburg.

Upon disembarkation, Norm received a nasty surprise when customs officials told him that he owed a duty of forty-five pfennigs apiece on the six hundred cigarettes he had brought. With Ingie's help, though, he distracted them and managed to avoid paying. In Hamburg, Norm and the Ingelfingers met Gene O'Neill, who accompanied them on visits to family and old friends in Stuttgart and Dresden. After about a week Norm and Gene traveled on their own south to Munich, via Austria. Norm had arranged to lodge with Frau Elisabet Lessing at 2 Maria Josepha Strasse through the end of September for ten marks a night.[1] He also arranged for Frau Elisabet Mayer to tutor him in German several times a week.

In the summer of 1932, the nation was on the cusp of becoming Nazi Germany. In April, Adolf Hitler had lost the presidential election to Paul von Hindenburg, but in the July parliamentary elections the Nazis became the largest party in the Reichstag (while still lacking an outright majority). Over the summer of 1932, both before and after the July 31 election, Hitler had traveled throughout Germany, giving speeches and appearing at Nazi Party rallies. The Third Reich would soon be born. Pearson's mid-July arrival in Munich came at the height of campaigning for the parliamentary elections, and he noted the growing influence of the Nazi Party in German life. In Dresden, for instance, Norm spoke to a Fräulein Fricke, "who . . . is all for Hitler as the savior who can make things a little easier for everyone." Remarking on Germany's increasing affluence, especially compared to the poverty he had seen on his summer 1929 Berlin trip with Chester and the admen, he told his mother that "I don't believe anyone need worry about Germany being prosperous or that they are not paying for the war."[2] It was no surprise, then, that this intellectually curious and culturally adventurous young man, accompanied by O'Neill, made a point of attending the insurgent party's rally in Munich on September 7.

Notwithstanding the generally blithe attitude toward daily manifestations of Nazism expressed in his letters home during this period, Pearson sensed that this was a significant event, and the description he recorded in his journal and in a letter to Fanny is careful and detailed:

Last night I saw Hitler speak. It was at the Circuskrone Building, a circular structure in the Marsfeld. There must have been three or four thousand there, and many more in other cafes in the city, listening by loudspeaker. . . . On the walls hung banners with the Nazi swastica [sic], and signs "Workers, against a Jewish Marxism and for a German Socialism." A line of Nazis formed on either side of the center aisle. The band played with loud trumpet calls, and heavy beats of traps and kettledrum. In walked several Nazi officials, then Hitler. Everyone stood, raised their arm in the salute, screamed cheers. Behind Hitler came a giant Roman standard with an eagle surmounting the circle which enclosed the swastika. Behind it were the banners of the party arranged like flags for the legions. . . . Overhead was a gigantic cloth, Nazi-red with a swastika and beneath—"Freedom and Bread." In the center of the stand was a small table draped with the party insignia. Everywhere was this red. It seemed to inflame, to make the hall seem revolutionary, vital.[3]

In his account of the Circus Krone rally, Pearson pointedly avoids expressing how *he* responded. He is a pure observer interested only in the self-presentation of the Nazis and their leader, and the connection between the speaker and the audience.

A man spoke, then another, then Hitler stood. There were flowers for him, as if he were a prima donna, there were enormous cheers, again the salute. He stood there, heels together, arms folded, unsmiling. This was a serious meeting. He was come to talk of the politics of the moment. He began to speak in a low voice. People quieted as he wanted them to. He spoke quietly, unemotionally, confidentially. This was a man who was talking heart to heart with the party. They could trust this man; he relied so much in their judgment. Never moving, never smiling, only occasionally lifting his palms outward in a confidential gesture. Then his mouth began to curl. He used scorn, wit against the government. The people screamed with delight. They felt easier now. Now they felt both intimacy and ease.[4]

Pearson's letters home were always filled with detail—shows seen and the actors who starred in them, menus at restaurants, friends visited and itineraries of driving trips—but rarely does he *report* quite like this. Later, when he began to meet famous writers, he would record his encounters with them in similar short sketches, but this is the first such vignette he produces. Something he would write about Hawthorne just a few years later here seems to apply to himself: "he was alert for detail to be jotted down in journals [and told a friend], 'Think nothing too trifling to write down, so be it in the smallest degree characteristic. You will be surprised to find on reperusing your journal what an importance and graphic power these little particulars assume.'"[5] But this journal entry also seems sickeningly blind. Norm makes no mention of the hatred and bigotry that charged these rallies, the contempt for democracy and equality and the rule of law, the fetishization of strength and power. Like many other Americans in those Depression years, he was wondering whether some sort of strongman rule was not in fact the answer for the times—if not for the United States, then for the nations of Europe.

Norm left Munich for Oxford at the beginning of October in time for Michaelmas term, the first of the university's three eight-week teaching periods. During Norm's college years Yale had been a massive construction site, transforming itself into a New World Oxford. Now, for the first time, he was seeing the real thing: Oxford's self-contained colleges with their ancient buildings, courtyards, and vaulted dining halls. Magdalen is perhaps the loveliest of these, sitting on the Cherwell River and with its own deer park. And it was ancient. The college had been founded in 1458, and its "new building," where fellows lived, dated from 1733.

Norm was one of only three Americans at Magdalen that year. The others were upperclassmen like himself, one a Rhodes Scholar from Harvard's medical school and the other from West Point. The Harvard student, William Sweet, became Norm's roommate (they shared Oscar Wilde's old quarters) and one of his closest friends for the rest of his life. Also at Oxford, but not at Magdalen, was William Weedon, a childhood friend from Cape Cod summer vacations. The Americans quickly had to deal with the culture shock of Magdalen's rituals: dinner, gowned, with the president and dons precisely at 7:15 p.m., preceded by a recitation of "Benedictus, Benedictus"; innumerable political and sporting and artistic clubs that seemed to spontaneously generate "at the spur of the moment"; and being incessantly nickel-and-dimed for "battels," Oxford's name for expenses. "They exact more money out of one . . . than you would think possible," Norm grumbled. He was charmed by the enthusiasm of the "freshies" but, as an upperclassman, felt obliged to maintain "a haughty aloofness in accordance with all instructions."

Class distinctions, in fact, were still explicit at this college, where he was officially classified as a "commoner."

Norm also quickly noticed that Oxford's expectations were higher than Yale's "gentleman's C" standards, and students could not fade into the anonymity of a large lecture hall. In Oxford's tutorial system, each student is assigned a tutor, and the two meet individually or in small groups once or twice a week for intense discussions about course material. Students are required, as well, to turn in weekly essays. To Norm's chagrin, he learned that because he had signed up to read English, dreaded Anglo-Saxon and Middle English would be *the* central part of his Oxford education. He found most of it "pretty bad stuff," seeing "very little value in it for my American literature," and as a result struggled. "My first assignment in Anglo-Saxon left me completely stumped," he reported glumly. Mr. Lewis, his tutor, "won't think that the cream of American intellectuality has landed in his midst."[6]

"Mr. Lewis" was, in fact, Clive Staples Lewis, later and much better known as C. S. Lewis, author of the Chronicles of Narnia series as well as many works of Christian apologetics. Not yet a published author in 1932, Lewis had been a fellow and tutor at Magdalen for almost ten years by that point and took his teaching seriously. Students reported to Lewis's thick door in the New Building and had to wait until Magdalen's bell tower struck the hour before they could knock. Admitted to Lewis's study, the student would then (in the words of Lewis's close friend George Sayer) "defend and enlarge upon the opinions and statements he had made in his essay. . . . Afterward [Lewis] would make wide-ranging criticisms, some of them semantic or philological, for he always hated the inexact use of words."[7] Lewis was a literary conservative with a strong "anti-American bias" and hated the modernist poetry that appealed to Norm, so it was probably best that the two of them mostly discussed Old English and the Elizabethan and Restoration writers. (He also complained repeatedly that Norm didn't "write like an Englishman.")[8] Lewis was Norm's most important academic influence during his Oxford years, but because of their conservatism and disdain for Americans and American literature, Lewis and Oxford in general did little to shape Norm's intellectual trajectory.

The real impact of Norm's time at Oxford would be social and professional. Norm threw himself into university life, attending the Oxford-Cambridge "rugger" match (which he found not as interesting as football), Oxford Union debates, plays, and speakers' and musical events. That fall, he hosted a Thanksgiving dinner in his room for fifteen friends complete with a pumpkin pie from Selfridge's in London, and he enjoyed a visit from Steve Morris. He even met a member of the royal family: Magdalen alumnus Edward, Prince of Wales (later Edward VIII before abdicating in 1936), who came to officially open the college's library. "He seemed nice, and easy to talk to," Norm reported to his mother. But "we were all told not to get drunk until after he left, and since he had such a good time he stayed until about a quarter to eleven and made everyone quite impatient."[9] Edward's well-known pro-German sentiments, as well, must have been intriguing to Norm, who was working through his own.

In the turbulent 1930s, radical politics were roiling everywhere, even in Britain's elite universities. While some, like the Prince of Wales, admired or were at least intrigued by the new fascist governments in Germany and Italy, others were pushing for socialism or even communism in Britain. (The so-called Cambridge ring of future Soviet spies Kim Philby, Don Maclean, and Guy Burgess were all studying at Trinity College while Norm was at Magdalen.) On November 17, Pearson attended the Oxford Union debate on whether Britain should adopt a "socialist government," with the Tory MP Alfred Duff-Cooper speaking against, and Labour Party head George Lansbury speaking for. (The affirmative carried the day.) The United States, of course, had its own momentous 1932 election, which brought Franklin Roosevelt and his New Deal to the presidency. Pearson had received an absentee ballot, but not soon enough to return it in time. "I'm not sure who I would have voted for," he told his mother, "but I suspect Roosevelt. . . . At any rate I wasn't forced to decide, so my republican record is clean." The Republican Fanny was less sanguine about the results. "We all must be very brave and trust that things will turn out all right," Norm reassured her. "It's a relief to know that Roosevelt isn't a Catholic, at any rate, and the Pope won't be in power."[10] (Like the aristocrats at Yale, provincial

New England bourgeoisie like the Pearsons feared the growing influence of urban Catholics as embodied in politicians like 1928 Democratic presidential nominee Al Smith, who to their relief lost the 1932 nomination to Roosevelt.)

Germany's political and cultural transformation had progressed even further when Pearson returned to Munich after Michaelmas term for several weeks with the Lessings, to catch up on his Anglo-Saxon and improve his German. Pearson noted seeing a Christmas tree with swastikas as ornaments, and watching a child choose a swastika rather than a Mickey Mouse pin as a trinket. Mostly, though, Pearson was a tourist. He visited all the Christmas markets, took driving tours into the mountains, and attended plays or concerts every night. On December 12 he and Frau Lessing saw Gerhard Hauptmann's play *Die Ratten* at a Hauptmann festival, sitting only a few feet from Hauptmann himself, and directly behind Thomas Mann's wife and mother. (He was disappointed that Mann was not there.) Lacking in self-consciousness but certainly not in confidence, he was even taking dance lessons, unconcerned with the awkwardness of his lame left leg.[11] He saw friends as well. The O'Neills came down from Freiburg and spent a week with him. In January Norm visited Steve Morris in Paris and in a week managed to squeeze in attendance at two École Libre des Sciences Politiques lectures, two shows at the Opéra Comique, dancing, and shopping for paintings. One night, he took a date to the Casino de Paris to see Josephine Baker dance before ending the evening at Chez Bricktop, the legendary bar run by the African American expatriate Ada "Bricktop" Smith.

Back in Oxford for Hilary term, he settled in quickly to his routine: attending lectures and artistic performances, meeting with Lewis, and studying Anglo-Saxon (which he admitted he was coming to tolerate, just as he had accustomed himself to "nux vomica or cod-liver oil" when he was a child). He was quite impressed by W. B. Yeats's June 1933 reading and by Paul Robeson in *All God's Chillun Got Wings* in the West End, but an Oxford production of William Congreve's 1700 comedy *The Way of the World* spurred him to reflect to his mother that "we often delude ourselves into thinking something is great art, only because it is old art."[12] On the side, he continued to help Williams and Stewart with their Hawthorne project, tracking down letters and either transcribing them or even purchasing them outright. ("I think I can promise you a pretty damned thorough covering of the English field," he boasted to Williams.)[13] Norm was in almost constant motion, creating networks of friends and acquaintances and contacts as well as tending to those he had already assembled, such as with several Gardner families he entertained when they came to Oxford as part of their English holidays. The social skills he had developed as a teenager had become almost a compulsion, and he was now working on his "host pose, which should stand me in good stead in life."[14]

Money, of course, was always an issue, as he spent freely on travel, entertainment, art, rare books, and restaurants and catering. Because of the unusual proportions of his body, he also had his suits and shoes custom made. His parents send him checks and drafts, but those often took up to four weeks to cash, and because of the Depression the dollar had been devalued to two-thirds of its previous rate. And Oxford's incessant battels always brought a new surprise—at the end of his first term, Norm had to explain to Fanny that the "argent" fee was for rental and insurance on the silver he used for entertaining.

He wasn't going to let a lack of money stand in the way of taking full advantage of his European time, though, and after cashing in some stock, Norm set off with Morris on a spring 1933 driving trip through France (Paris, Limoges, Toulouse, Carcassonne) and Spain (Barcelona, Zaragosa, Madrid, and Toledo). Steve's car was a convertible, and Norm could "hardly think of a lovelier time to drive in a car through the country." He even saw a bullfight in Madrid: "I thought I should not enjoy the fight and leave early," he reported, "but as they went on I got more and more enthusiastic, until at the end I was almost a fan."[15] The two parted ways in Madrid, and Norm returned to London swollen with the ecstasy of being young and hungry for experience. "I don't think it would be exaggerating to say that I've never enjoyed a year as much as I have this," he told his mother. Trinity term passed rapidly as he wrapped up his classes, continued his socializing, and prepared to spend the summer in Germany. "It hardly seems I have been here a moment since Spain," he wrote his mother on June 1, "but I am already having to plan on leaving for Berlin."

He arrived on June 11 at the Institut für Ausländer, where he was to take German-language courses. Hitler had been named chancellor in January, and after the Reichstag fire a month later the Nazis began to suspend democracy and civil liberties. "Things are looking very troubled now in Germany," Norm wrote his mother just after the fire, and he worried whether "there should still be considerable unrest when I return there."[16] But he found less tumult than he expected, and instead a country revolutionized by the rapid Nazi takeover. Like his description of the Circus Krone rally the previous summer, Norm's reports on the changes in Germany are remarkably sanguine and even-handed, even obtuse. In Berlin, an American family he knew, the Howlands, had set him up with a room with their neighbors, a Jewish family whose father "was a director for UFA pictures, but who has lost his job as a result of the anti-Semitic movement."[17] When that Jewish family fled, Norm just moved across the garden to the Howlands', struck more by how convenient this was for him than by the cruelty that gave him the opportunity. The 1933 film S.A.-Mann Brand, which apotheosized a Nazi martyr, was "rather crudely obvious, but they made no attempt to conceal its purpose, and as propaganda it was not so bad. It was all a part of the program of educating the people in the doctrine now in power."[18] And he was disappointed when the Nazi choir didn't show up at Berlin's famous Kroll Biergarten when he went there specifically to hear them. "Many of their songs are extremely good, particularly the famous 'Horst Wessel Lied.' I have heard a good many of them," he added, "because I go quite often to eat at the Nazi official restaurant, which has good food and is reasonably inexpensive."[19] He even attended an "interesting talk by a member of the Nazis on the place of art and literature in the new German state, and how the Party intends to control them."

At first Norm had a lot of time on his hands in Berlin, as his classes were only for two hours a day, four days a week. But after a few weeks he transferred into a more intensive teacher-training program and as a result spent almost all day every day at the institute, even auditing a seminar in American literature. He completed his programs in mid-August, leaving with a certificate attesting that he had enough German to study in a German university. On the seventeenth Norm left on a driving trip with his friend Roger Black, stopping in Dresden and Sukohrad on the way to Prague, where the young men drove their Morris Oxford right up to the castle gates on Hradčany, unaware that it was still a secure government facility. Predictably, the soldiers guarding the castle pounced, brusquely informing Norm and Roger that the castle was accessible only to diplomats. A sticker on the car's windshield, though, drew the guards' attention: the British royal coat of arms over the initials "H.R.R." and a set of instructions in English below. Thinking quickly and with, he later reminisced, "the spirit of Satan," Norm told them (in German) that this sticker indicated that they were diplomats on an official mission from His Majesty's government, and that the guards were causing a grave international incident. Immediately, the guards parted, lined up on each side of the car, and saluted the young men as they drove through the gate. (In fact, "H.R.R." stood for Henley Royal Regatta, in which Black had rowed as part of the Oxford eights the previous year, and the instructions simply said "please admit this competitor's car.")[20]

From Prague the two then went via Karlsbad, Marienbad, and Nurnberg to Munich, where Norm planned to stay until his Oxford term began in October. With no room at the Lessings', he stayed in a hotel for a few days while he looked for longer-term lodgings, and he saw shows every night at the Munich Festival, including the *Götterdämmerung* and Agnes Straub in *Hedda Gabler*.[21] This year, though, he had decided that he wanted a quieter place outside of the city so he could concentrate on the difficult Old English readings he needed to complete before Magdalen's term began again. He found a peat-heated, ground-floor flat in a village called Oberallmanshausen. "The countryside is unbelievably beautiful," he reported to Fanny. The bucolic setting didn't make the work any easier, though. "Anglo-Saxon and Middle English are uncongenial enough to me to mean that my head droops every few minutes, and my mind wanders," he confessed to his mother.[22] To Stanley Williams, he was more blunt about the archaic languages: "God how I hate them!"[23]

Although he mostly studied, he did make it in to the city a few times a week to see the Lessings and Mayers. He was saddened to learn that the Mayers were also selling their belongings in preparation to leave Germany. Although Elisabet was from a prominent Protestant family, her psychiatrist husband, Wilhelm, was Jewish, and a set of national laws passed in April 1933 had limited "Jewish activity" in medicine. Later that year, Munich prohibited Jewish doctors from treating non-Jewish patients. Dr. Mayer was hopeful that the Nazis would not retain power for long, but Elisabet foresaw what was to come and realized that the family had to emigrate. Seeming to us today disturbingly callous, Norm noted to his mother that he bought two etchings from her and "in that way I helped her and also myself, paying only about ten dollars apiece for them, which is a price incredibly below their value."[24] The Mayers' collection—"all of it modern," Norm pointed out—is notable, because in addition to being a freelance language tutor, Elisabet was, as Pearson himself would become, one of those figures whose lives and work brought together many of the artists and writers of the twentieth century. Forty-eight when Pearson met her, she had already established herself as a translator, art collector, and member of artistic circles in Germany. Her work as a language tutor, as well, put her in contact with English and American students active in arts and literature.

Norm's sanguinity or obliviousness here at the sinister prefigurations of Nazi horror is telling both of the perspective of his class—New England Republicans found the Nazis of 1933 vulgar and distasteful but didn't necessarily condemn their anti-Semitism or authoritarianism—and of the larger blindness of many Europeans and Americans to what the dawn of Nazi rule portended. While he had never exactly admitted to an attraction to fascism or Nazism, it is clear that he had seen some of its appeal since the Circus Krone rally: its determination, its sense of being the voice of a people, its aesthetics. And even Norm's friends were open to fascism at this point: in April 1935 Steve told Norm that being stationed at the Rome embassy was making him "more an admirer of Mussolini while my distaste for Herr Hitler increases."[25]

Norm returned to Oxford in late September, regretting that he hadn't gotten enough work done over the summer and immediately throwing himself back into his social whirl. Curious "to compare English fascism with the German brand," in November he attended a rally led by Oswald Mosley, the head of the British Union of Fascists Party. He was "surprised to find the audience reasonably pleased with him. . . . There might be a chance for that form of government here someday." And he surmised that "they think that with Italy, Germany, and America already headed in that direction they might as well hop on the bandwagon." (It's unclear here whether he is referring to a sense that Roosevelt's interventions in the economy were similar to fascist corporatism, or to the rise of American demagogues like Father Charles Coughlin.) Mostly, he reported on their "blackshirt" uniform: "a little silly . . . a variation of a high-necked Russian shirt with buttons down the side, and the shirt drawn in at the waist. It gives pretty much the effect of an adagio dancer . . . but I suppose variations of shirts and colors become fewer." Again displaying his obtuseness, he was "astonished to hear what sounded very much like the beginning of an anti-Semitic feeling, at least as far as Mosley was concerned. It sounded as though he were saying as much as he dared, and sounding out the crowd."[26] Although Norm at times expressed the disdain for Jews that was endemic in his milieu, fascism's vicious anti-Semitism did not appeal to him at all.

After Thanksgiving he returned again to Germany and spent the Christmas holidays in Vienna, this time accompanied by Bill Sweet. Now even he was sensing that things were getting darker. He had come to know several German Jewish exiles in England and linked them to people like the Mayers whom he genuinely loved. And on his December train trip to Munich, he encountered a Belgian soldier who "told us about the preparations Belgium was making for the war with Germany. They certainly fear one." "I haven't written you much about the German situation," he told his mother, "because it is too complicated, somewhat unwise when one is in Germany and too far back when one is in England."[27]

Norm spent his final two terms at Magdalen much as he had the previous ones: seeing shows, entertaining, dining out, traveling, and spending time with American friends and one of his few close English friends, Herbert Lewisohn. Over the spring break he took a driving tour of Lincolnshire and Yorkshire. He also had to prepare for a supernatural visitor, he realized, when his next-door neighbor encountered Oscar Wilde's ghost. "Since I have Wilde's old bedroom," he told his mother, "I have been expecting a visit myself. He has seen him on two occasions, the second time the ghost was writing at the center table, the place where he wrote a poem which won him the Oxford prize for poetry."[28] His mother and sister came over to visit him, and Norm was particularly happy that Eleanor could attend the white-tie Commemoration Ball, one of Oxford's biggest galas, which Magdalen hosted that year.

That winter, Norm had started to make plans in earnest for what came next. Although he occasionally joked to his mother about returning to Gardner, he had largely settled on enrolling in graduate school. In this he was like many of his classmates. The Depression had "broken the spell of Wall Street and big business" that had enthralled Yalies and brought "a more serious tone" to Norm's generation, many of whom were staying in school because of the lack of jobs.[29] Through his family's business Norm had seen firsthand the precariousness of life in the retail business. A university increasingly seemed like a safe and, if not exciting, potentially satisfying place to spend one's life.

But Stanley Williams's advice wasn't promising. He informed Norm that universities weren't entirely shielded from the Depression and that some of Yale's "best men" had failed to find jobs after earning their PhDs. Funding for graduate study was shrinking as Yale was facing operating deficits for the first time in decades.[30] In addition, he frankly told Norm that "those who are chosen are invariably persons who have exceptional records and are not handicapped in any way. . . . Health might be a factor, and I want you to keep that in mind." Discrimination against the disabled was a reality.

Williams was also coldly realistic about employment prospects. Slogging through years of Anglo-Saxon and Middle English at Oxford had convinced Norm that he did not want to follow the traditional course of study for a PhD in English. He wanted to study and write about American literature, and especially about how that literature arose from the history and thought of the nation. He wanted to do the kind of work that he had done under Gabriel and Williams back at Yale, in a field that was just starting to be known as American studies. But there just weren't any *jobs* there, Williams told him. Yale's tiny History, Arts, and Letters (HAL) graduate program had only five students, "hand-picked, exceedingly able men." "Departments like these do not exist in great numbers throughout the country," Williams warned. (Harvard's and Penn's American Civilization graduate programs wouldn't come into being until 1937.) "They will exist, but this is a hazard which . . . you should keep in mind."[31]

Norm applied anyway and was accepted to HAL in the spring of 1934. But now money became an obstacle. After relying on them for financial support during his two years in Europe, Norm didn't want to ask his family to underwrite his graduate education just as Goodnow Pearson's was struggling. And in April, Williams told him that he had not received one of the very few fellowships. This hit him hard. At Oxford he had worked so diligently, in so many areas he found distasteful, to prepare himself for this profession. Because of his work with Williams and Gabriel, he was already better prepared than many advanced graduate students and had even published a scholarly article. Now, he would have to either give up the dream, or defer it. He reached out, in measured tones, to his parents, asking their advice: should he work for a few years to save up for school, or would they be willing to lend—*lend*, he emphasized—him the money?

In the end, though, they didn't need to make this decision. In July, Williams wrote him to offer a "readership," a teaching-assistant position that would pay almost as much as the fellowship. And the work it required—meeting with the two hundred students in Williams's American literature class, attending the lectures, and grading their essays and exams—would be ideal if also grueling professional training. He may not have been among the elect, but as a good Puritan he knew that the ways of God, and Yale, are mysterious, and that our lot on earth is to earn our bread by the sweat of our brows.

+ 4 +

BIG SHOTS

Norm returned home in September to start his graduate work, now with an Oxford BA to match his Yale one. Magdalen, with its endless Anglo-Saxon drudgery, had been difficult, but its tutorial system and eight-week terms afforded one a great deal of free time. Graduate school was different: it was professional training, an apprenticeship. Specifically, this meant taking two classes a term, with all the attendant essay writing and note transcribing, while also serving as Williams's reader, which paid him $700 a year.

This was more work than it sounded. Williams's class enrolled two hundred students, and Norm's responsibility was to be the "middleman . . . between him and his pupils, correct their daily papers and their essays and tests." As any teacher knows, marking up papers is time-consuming drudgery, particularly if one wants to do a thorough job, and a pile of two hundred papers that must be returned in forty-eight hours is a bleak prospect. Norm was also a meticulous and diligent student, who every evening typed up all the notes he took in longhand during classes. "I certainly have never known what it is to be busy before I started graduate work here," he reported.[1]

Norm was also moving into adulthood in other ways. He was now living in his own apartment, on Cottage Street in the East Rock neighborhood. "Having my own establishment is perfect," he told Fanny, "and I am infinitely happier than I would be in a dormitory."[2] Gene O'Neill had also returned to New Haven to pursue his own PhD, and he and Betty lived nearby. Norm avoided cooking for himself, paying ten cents a day to eat breakfast with the O'Neills, and taking the rest of his meals in the dining halls. Later, fellow Gardner High graduate Calvin Tenney moved in with him and, after his marriage broke up, O'Neill as well, who slept on a custom-made mattress Norm obtained for him from Goodnow Pearson's.

Norm had loved being overseas, but it was good to be back in a familiar place, close to his friends and family. With Gardner just a few hours' drive from New Haven, Norm also saw his parents and Alfred frequently. As a part owner of the store, he also attended quarterly directors' meetings when he could but never regretted his choice to go into academia. Norm also frequently visited Eleanor, who was living the life of a young career woman in New York City, lodging at the brand-new Barbizon women's hotel on the Upper East Side. She worked first as a Macy's window dresser, then for the Broadway press agent Lodewick Vroom, and, finally, for the designer Dorothy Draper's "Learn to Live" correspondence course.

Norm's studies were far more appealing than they had been at Magdalen, and he excelled, taking honors even in the required history class. With his "not being a historian the professors were always surprised at my knowing anything at all," he self-deprecatingly told Fanny.[3] But even as Norm was immersing himself in his conventional training, he was drawn ever more to daring modernist literature—particularly poetry—that in his view captured the reality of twentieth-century life. Gertrude Stein catalyzed this inchoate interest into a genuine passion. On her six-month tour of the United States in 1934 and 1935, Stein gave a private lecture at the Choate School in nearby Wallingford as a guest of the poet-translator and teacher Dudley Fitts, who "smuggled" Norm in. (Conservative Yale had refused to host her, which Norm deemed "very stupid.") In a detached journal entry much like the one he wrote about the 1932 Hitler rally, Norm described the sight of the "ugly" Alice Toklas, Stein's partner, sitting on the side of the stage, "never smil[ing] in approval or show[ing] any signs that she was responding to what Stein was saying." Stein's lecture, Norm recorded, argued that the primary literary problem of the twentieth century was how to depict motion in a way that counteracts how "events occur and are made accessible to us with too great rapidity, so they lose their significance." "I found her very fascinating," he told his mother, but it's not clear what he found fascinating.[4] He would come to admire Stein and her work, but he never saw her as one of the most accomplished writers of the day. Instead, for him she was a kind of necessary transitional figure, someone who "had done the great pioneering work of freeing writers from the nineteenth century and giving them a tool for expression of the twentieth century. . . . This work of transition had resulted in a kind of awkward ugliness at times [but] at the same time possessed a beauty through its activity and virility."[5] She made possible the breakthroughs of the writers he admired most.

But most of Norm's time was spent studying, grading, and reading. Unusually for a brand-new grad student, though, he was also starting to publish his work. Williams's Hawthorne-project partner Randall Stewart, a contributor to Scribner's planned twenty-volume *Dictionary of American Biography*, let Norm know that the dictionary could provide an opportunity for him. By January 1935, Norm had signed a contract to deliver, by September, a capsule biography of the minor nineteenth-century writer and editor Robert William Wright.[6] In addition to the professional boost the publication provided, the small fee was welcome, for as his second year in school began Norm's stipend was cut from $700 to $450 because of smaller-than-expected enrollments, and he had to pick up extra work as a research assistant for Ralph Gabriel.

Just as he was adjusting himself to straitened circumstances at home, Norm's attention was urgently drawn abroad. Since returning from Oxford, Norm had stayed in touch with the Mayers, and had come to consider himself a close friend. The warm letters between Norm, Elisabet, and Wilhelm were mostly quotidian until they got significantly darker in September 1935, in the shadow of the Nuremberg Laws. While Elisabet was an Aryan under those racial-classification codes, Wilhelm and their children were not and thus fell under new national and local restrictions. The anti-Semitism and violence swirling in German society were never far from their lives. "I tell you today in a great hurry," Elisabet wrote Norm on October 28, "that life in Germ. becomes intolerable and we must leave. . . . Excuse me that

I am just exploding with an important question,—do you know anybody who would be so kind as to give his name for an affidavit for my husband that he may enter the U.Sts.?"[7]

But the 1920s anti-immigration laws meant that only about twenty-five thousand German nationals were allowed in the United States annually, out of hundreds of thousands of applicants. Potential emigrants had to prove that they were not "likely to become a public charge," but Germany forbade Jewish emigrants to take their money out of the country. Norm turned first to his father, not only a business owner but the mayor of Gardner, and explained that if he was forced to remain in Germany, the Mayers' teenage son, Christopher, "will grow up to be a man who cannot work for anyone outside his own race; who cannot go to college; who cannot even ask an Aryan girl to go to a dance with him."[8] Moved by his son's concern for his friends overseas, Chester agreed to provide the affidavit, even though this would legally oblige him to financially support the family if the Mayers could not find employment.

Although the Pearsons were confident that Wilhelm would eventually find a job as a psychiatrist, Norm had to concoct for him a kind of factotum position in the interim. In his own affidavit submitted to the US consul in Stuttgart, Norm attested that upon arrival in the United States Dr. Mayer would serve "as my medical companion and my secretary," assisting with his clerical needs related to the Hawthorne and Oxford projects and providing "such medical attention as is necessary to my condition, suffering as I have from tuberculosis of the hip for the past twenty years." For this, Norm would pay Dr. Mayer $20 a week.[9]

To save Dr. Mayer's dignity, Norm also tried to arrange for him to do some (unpaid) work in the Yale Medical School neurology lab run by Dr. Fulton, who had provided his recommendation to Magdalen. Fulton was welcoming, but his response to Norm's request also starkly illustrates other practical impediments to Jewish emigration:

I hope you have taken adequate precautions to protect yourself from the extraordinarily embarrassing situation which have [sic] arisen in connection with other people of this sort who have come to this country without funds. . . . In the past few years we have had a dozen or more come to our attention, and thus far we have accepted only one, because the request has generally been to give them facilities with a promise ultimately of permanent tenure and salary. In representing the interests of the University I feel that this is a commitment which we cannot make no matter how strong the humanitarian appeal may be in individual cases and however great the potential contribution of the man in question.[10]

It's hard to find fault with what Fulton says here. Yet this response, multiplied tens or hundreds of thousands of times, contributed to untold death and misery and is an important part of the story of America's grave failure to respond as the Holocaust began to take shape. It is only because Chester had, in fact, agreed to provide just such a guarantee that the Mayers were eventually allowed to enter the country.

The urgency of the Mayers' situation increased in February. Beata, their daughter who was attending school in Italy, told Norm that Wilhelm's and Elisabet's passports had been confiscated, as "has happened to nearly all non-Aryans, especially in Bavaria and south Germany."[11] Only if they provided evidence of plans for permanent emigration would they be returned. With these plans made, thanks to Chester, the Mayers' passports were restored to them, and they were granted US entry visas in the spring of 1936. In July, Dr. Mayer sailed to America on the RMS *Berengaria*. Elisabet and the rest of his family joined him in December. Dr. Mayer never did have to serve as Norm's "medical companion and secretary." He worked briefly at Yale University Hospital before obtaining a position as a psychiatrist at the Howard State Hospital in Cranston, Rhode Island, and then in mid-1937 at a hospital on Long Island.

Notwithstanding his failure to obtain a fellowship for his protégé, Williams was already treating Norm as something between a student and a colleague, inviting him to faculty dinners and talent spotting him for work on various projects. He also continued to employ Norm on the Hawthorne letters and was trying to carve out a corner of this undertaking that Norm could claim as his own and perhaps use as an eventual dissertation project. In this, Norm started to work especially closely with Stewart, and during the summer following his first year of grad school, the two traveled to Concord and Boston to transcribe several letters, and Norm went on his own to Pittsfield, Massachusetts, in the fall of 1935 to secure another one.

Collecting and editing the letters was only one part of Stewart's Hawthorne work. In 1932, he had published an edition of Hawthorne's *American Notebooks* and at this time was completing his edition of the English notebooks. Stewart and Williams proposed that Norm edit the French and Italian notebooks for publication as a scholarly edition, a project that could also be his dissertation. Such "scholarly editions" were typical of the work that early twentieth-century American literature scholars were taking on: making available complete, authoritative texts of the work of the authors who were only then coming to be considered important. Such collected editions of English authors had been common at least since the famed 1623 "First Folio" amassed most of Shakespeare's plays in one place for the first time, but in the Victorian era, sets of major authors became obligatory accoutrements for any middle-class parlor or library. Such collected editions—and the editorial choices that go into producing them—"forg[e] authorial legacies, produc[e] regional and national propaganda, and generally work . . . as a determinant for what and how we consider American literature," in the words of scholar Amanda Gailey.[12] Until the early twentieth century, American authors rarely enjoyed this kind of prestige publication, because American literature just wasn't considered worthy of it; but now the new generation of American literature scholars were editing these complete-works projects in part to stake a claim for these authors' importance as a subject of research and scholarship, not just pleasure reading.

Nathaniel Hawthorne was particularly ripe for this kind of newly authoritative treatment. His novels and stories were widely published and circulated, but he'd produced other important writing that wasn't generally available to readers. Throughout his life, Hawthorne kept extensive journals containing worked-out story ideas and drafts, detailed sketches and observations, and philosophical meditations. These notebooks (which scholars and biographers came to refer to by the locations Hawthorne was living when he produced them) are invaluable for understanding his life, thought, and creative process. Hawthorne's widow, Sophia, had published excerpts from his American notebooks in 1866, but they were bowdlerized and hardly representative of Hawthorne's actual ideas. Stewart's faithful 1932 edition, then, was a sensation in American literary studies, deepening readers' and scholars' understanding of Hawthorne's early artistic and intellectual development, as well as filling in countless gaps in his life story. Starting in 1857, Hawthorne and his family traveled in France and Italy for three years. The notebooks from these years illuminate the great swerve Hawthorne took between his masterworks *The Scarlet Letter* (1850) and *The House of the Seven Gables* (1851) and his next and final novel, *The Marble Faun* (1860), which was deeply influenced by his time in Rome.

The prospect of editing the French and Italian notebooks was irresistible to Norm. The Morgan Library in New York held five of the seven notebooks, the Huntington Library in Pasadena held one other, and the last was in the hands of a private collector. In October 1935, Norm asked the Morgan's permission to edit a volume of the notebooks, and to his surprise the librarian agreed. "An unbelievably lucky thing," he told his mother, for "at least half of the professors of American literature . . . would give anything for the chance." But as he was learning, connections and reputation were as important in scholarship as in any other field. "My connection with the edition of the letters helped a great deal, and it was really put through by Randall Stewart. . . . Everyone had expected that he would do them himself; but it was quite a gesture of friendship on his part to turn them over to me."[13]

Norm came to rely on Stewart in what was coming to look more like a collaboration than a teacher-and-student project. In December 1935, he accompanied Stewart to his first Modern Language Association conference. For decades, aspiring English professors' "first MLA" symbolically marked their formal debut into this ritual-bound and status-obsessed community. The MLA was also, to put it crudely, both a meat market and a debutante ball: the convention was where schools interviewed candidates for faculty positions, and where senior professors paraded their protégés.

Debuting under the wing of an eminent senior scholar such as Stewart gives the ephebe advantages both concrete (a speaking slot, invitations to cocktail parties) and more intangible (buzz that this person is "one to watch"). But Norm wasn't, yet, feeling the pressure of the job market, and the self-confidence he had developed fooled people into thinking that he wasn't just a second-year student. "I made no references to the fact that I would eventually be job-hunting," he told his mother. "Everyone seemed to take it for granted . . . that I was a member of the faculty; and there will be time enough to disillusion them later."[14]

Attending the conference, in fact, was only an incidental reason for the trip. The last of the Italian notebooks resided near Cincinnati, in the possession of William T. H. Howe, president of the American Book Company, who took advantage of the rare opportunity of having almost all the leading experts in American literature visit his city by hosting a lavish luncheon. "Since he is one of the largest publishers in the field," Norm told his mother afterward, "it was a really good contact to make."[15] Playing hooky from the conference, Stewart and Pearson crossed the Ohio River to Howe's Kentucky estate, Freelands, where they "got the lay of the land" of his library. Howe's treasures—at the time the greatest collection of American literary materials in private hands—also included such priceless gems as a copy of "The Raven" that Edgar Allan Poe had inscribed to Elizabeth Barrett Browning and the copy of *Walden* that Thoreau gave to Emerson. The house itself wasn't particularly opulent or extravagant, but its furnishings were, as Norm told Fanny: "The chair by the fireplace was Conrad's, the book case in the corner was Dickens's, another belonged to Thackeray. The silverware is all by Paul Revere, and a rare book dealer who was over here Sunday assured me that there was $200,000 worth of books in the top of one secretary alone in this room, and well over $2,000,000 worth in the house itself."[16]

They would return for several weeks of transcription work the next summer, which gave Norm the opportunity for his first road trip into the American interior to experience the American landscape beyond New England. He gloried in the drive through the Great Smokies and was particularly pleased to see how the Victorian-era utopian community of Rugby, Tennessee, had been transformed into a village for Tennessee Valley Authority electrification workers, noting with local pride that "the government had put Heywood chairs into their drugstores."[17] He deplored the "squalor" of the coal-country hollows of West Virginia and remarked on how the Cumberland region was "spoiled" by "shacks of coal miners, and poverty."[18]

The work on the Hawthorne project was enormously satisfying to Norm, who by this time was already a seasoned researcher, expert with rare books and manuscripts. Unfortunately, all the time spent chasing down and transcribing Hawthorne manuscripts was time he couldn't spend studying, marking up papers, or working for Gabriel. And another alluring distraction soon presented itself. In late 1935, Williams asked Norm to serve as an editorial assistant on a new anthology of American literature, covering its beginnings to the present day, to be published by Oxford University Press. Williams gave the project academic heft, but the project's coeditor, William Rose Benét, was really the top-line name. Although a poet like his brother Stephen Vincent, William Rose was best known as one of the founding editors of the *Saturday Review of Literature*, the leading voice of middlebrow literary taste. Williams had no desire to do the scut work an anthology requires and offered Norm the opportunity to help select texts and excerpts to be included, and write headnotes for some of the selections. This would certainly slow down his progress in school even more, but a graduate student with major ambitions couldn't turn an offer like this down. Norm reasoned that his current position as Williams's teaching assistant had him reading excerpts from American writers anyway, and the Oxford job provided $300.[19] He jumped at it.

Like scholarly editions and sets, anthologies help shape the category of literature. The anthology as we understand it now came about in the later eighteenth century and really began to proliferate with the expansion of education and general literacy in the later nineteenth century. Francis Palgrave's *Golden Treasury of English Songs and Lyrics* appeared first in 1861 and then, with heavy revisions by Tennyson, again a few decades later. The *Golden Treasury*, as much as anything else, established a "canon" of English poetry that could be taught in schools. Working on an Oxford anthology, thus, would give Norm a role in shaping this new field of "American literature."

We might think of an anthology as simply a record, a transparent and self-evident collection of texts that a culture has collectively decided are great or important, the literary version of a sports hall of fame. But like a hall of fame, the point of an anthology is not just to enshrine the best, but for the best to embody the unspoken assumptions of the judges (the editor, in the case of an anthology) about what makes something "best," and in the case of the anthology, how readers should approach and understand those texts. An anthology "functions in the academy to create a tradition, as well as to define and preserve it," as Henry Louis Gates, himself an influential anthology editor, said.[20] Leah Price adds that anthologies "determine not simply who gets published or what gets read, but who reads, and how."[21] And the criteria for inclusion change. The eighteenth century esteemed classical refinement, wit, and erudition; the Romantic era flipped this on its head and prized raw emotion and nature; the Victorians loved florid craft; the mid-twentieth-century moderns wanted everything stripped down and oblique; the late twentieth and early twenty-first century demand diversity and representation and engagement with social and political issues. Even to call something "literature" is a value judgment, and values change.

In addition to broader evolutions in public taste, literature anthologies are also shaped by material factors such as the structure of the publishing industry and the educational system. Like current anthologies, pre-twentieth-century anthologies were aimed primarily at students, but the publishers didn't differentiate between college students and high school students. The point was appreciation of the nation's literary heritage. But as universities, in the early twentieth century, started to teach stand-alone American literature courses, professors started looking for anthologies that reflected that approach. "By 1925," Joseph

Csicsila writes, "scholars were compiling collections specifically for year-long college courses, interspersing historical background with the poetry and prose together in the now-familiar, same-volume format."[22]

Oxford already had a hit anthology in circulation, the portable *Oxford Book of English Verse*, its answer to the *Golden Treasury*. The 1890 first edition, edited by Arthur Quiller-Couch, sold half a million copies. But the publisher was looking to broaden its anthology offerings and expand into the vast American educational market. Oxford University Press had had an American office only since 1896, and until the 1930s its US business consisted almost entirely of selling Bibles and titles that it had previously published in Great Britain. But the Depression forced it to seek new revenue streams. One possibility, an executive insisted in 1930, was to develop "a series of advanced educational books written by Americans and produced in America." For an editor, Oxford would need a credentialed scholar who also taught in the classroom, someone familiar with American secondary and higher education, in both the elite northeastern schools and the more far-flung colleges, and it hired Howard Lowry, a recent Yale PhD, who became the general editor and education manager for Oxford's New York office.[23] For this first product, Lowry envisioned an American version of its English anthologies, a collection that would supplant the two most popular such books at the time, Norman Foerster's 1925 *American Poetry and Prose* and Fred Pattee's 1919 *Century Readings in American Literature*. As with the English collections, there would be two volumes, and Lowry selected Benét to choose the poetry and Williams to handle the prose. Pearson was also hired to write the bulk of the headnotes for a $350 fee.[24]

Soon, he received a promotion as well. Early in 1936, Williams sailed for Europe, where he would spend much of the year in Liverpool working on the Hawthorne letters. It was impractical for him to continue on the Oxford project, so Norm moved up from assistant to de facto coeditor, even though Williams's name stayed on the project, and began accompanying Benét to editorial meetings in New York. This change bolstered his confidence and allowed him to put into practice the schmoozing and networking chops he'd been assiduously cultivating. Almost immediately he reached out to Lowry, opening with effusive praise: he had wanted to speak with Lowry after his MLA talk the previous December, but "there seemed as much of a chance of a talk with you after your paper . . . as of meeting the President on a New Year's reception."[25] But he quickly moved from obsequiousness to business, proposing one of the more innovative features of the volume: that each (living) contributor provide a kind of "opening statement" about the intent, or technique, or background of his or her works that were included. Such a statement would put the spotlight on the work itself, not on how it illustrated a school or historical tendency, which was the case with most previous American literature anthologies. It also gave Pearson the assignment to contact—and potentially meet—almost all of America's most important living writers.

To make it more practical and affordable to use in a yearlong survey class, Pearson suggested that the anthology be published as one volume, its two chronological parts corresponding not to genre but "to the two semesters of the academic year."[26] (This would also make it easy to publish a more "deluxe" two-volume edition.) Conscious that Lowry likely did feel that an anthology of American literature didn't merit the same bulk as one of English letters, Norm cleverly made pragmatic, market-based arguments: "a year's course requires the same amount of material whether it be in a more or less important subject," and teachers and readers should be afforded "a certain leeway of choice." He closed by reminding Lowry of his own Oxford bona fides: "if you see [C. S.] Lewis, my former tutor at Magdalen, remember me to him."[27] Here, this twenty-six-year-old is already exhibiting the professional and rhetorical deftness that would characterize his entire career: a principled, without being strident, defense of the value of American writing in comparison with English literature; a drive to avoid inflammatory disputes and instead ground arguments on practical matters; an instinct to shape his own self-presentation in the way that his interlocutor would find most appealing and trustworthy. Working on the anthology plunged Norm into an entirely new world, one in which he immediately found himself comfortable. But the importance of his promotion on the anthology went beyond just moving to another level of professional responsibility. For many years an observer of the contemporary literary scene, he would now be a participant in it.

Norm and Benét established a cordial collaboration, with Norm appropriately deferential in their regular meetings. He was beginning, as well, to meet other major players, including Benét's *Saturday Review* coeditor Henry Seidel Canby, the powerful embodiment of the middlebrow literary establishment. Canby, Benét, and Pearson lunched together in the fall of 1936, just three Yale men talking over which contemporary writers would be in the canon and who wouldn't. (Norm wisely observed that Canby's "recommendation in case I needed it would be a very useful thing.")[28]

Lowry was happy to allow the editors to produce an anthology of the size they thought appropriate, but his real practical concerns regarded timing. The anthology had been under contract since 1934, but by the end of 1936 there was still no end in sight, largely because Benét, Williams, and Pearson couldn't agree on which authors to include. Benét seemed to want essentially every poet he had ever read or admired, ballooning the project far beyond what would be feasible and affordable even for a two-volume edition. He was approaching it, Williams and Pearson worried, like a critic, not like a teacher, and didn't really understand the target market for the book.[29] Pearson let Benét know that the numerous college-level teachers to whom he'd shown their working table of contents had been unanimous: "there were far, far too many modern poets." "We must be ruthlessly restrictive if we want to sell the book," Norm warned Benét, and Williams backed him up: "If we do not," he insisted, "create a book to compete with Foerster, and to reach the audience which Foerster reaches, we had better not have any anthology at all—at least one which is allegedly designed for college classes."[30]

The press was getting impatient. "It would be nothing short of a tragedy if the book is not ready for sale next summer," Lowry told Pearson in December, because there has been "the most remarkable advance interest in the book." "I'm afraid," he added, "that the reputation of the Press would be seriously jeopardized" if the book's release were postponed anytime beyond the fall of 1937. "You are giving the Oxford University Press as bad a case of jitters as it has had in some time." Oxford's "jitters" came from the fact that it had invested significantly more in this project than in any of its other anthologies: rather than the customary budget of $3,000 plus a negligible sum for copyright fees (because most of the works in an English literature anthology were in the public domain), Pearson and Benét ultimately spent $15,000 of Oxford's money to produce their collection.[31] Norm and Williams promised him a third of the manuscript by the start of the year even though it meant Norm "dropping his graduate tasks" for a time to focus on bringing the poetry side under control.[32] With Lowry's endorsement, Pearson culled Benét's initial list of ninety modern poets to thirty-two "important and teachable" figures "representative . . . of the direction and accomplishment of poetry in our time," with a particular emphasis on the "technically radical."[33]

By distilling the modern poetry section to its most daring practitioners, Norm put experimental writing at the center of American literature rather than presenting it as simply one of many strains of contemporary poetry. The texts chosen reflected Norm's own thinking and experience: one of the Gertrude Stein selections, for instance, was the very lecture she delivered on her 1934–35 tour. Tilting his anthology so much toward the contemporary and the experimental was also a rejoinder to the conservatives in American academic circles who believed that "modern literature ends with such poets as Robinson and Frost."[34] Lowry, who saw something of himself in the young, energetic editor trying to promote recent writing, knew that Pearson would "throw the weight of choice in favor of twentieth-century American literature" and bet that this would not just distinguish the Oxford collection from its competitors, but potentially make it "significant."[35]

Norm's selections also subtly—invisibly, in fact, to all but the most sophisticated readers—shifted the story of earlier American literature. Far more of Washington Irving's short stories were included in the *Oxford Anthology* than had appeared in any of its competitors, and the headnote claimed that these tales "mark the beginnings of the development of the short story in America," signaling not just Norm's (and

NORMAN HOLMES PEARSON is becoming well known to scholars and the general public as an authority on American literature. He edited *The Complete Novels and Selected Tales of Nathaniel Hawthorne,* and is now engaged in editing the Complete Letters of Hawthorne, in collaboration with Randall Stewart, Stanley T. Williams, and Manning Hawthorne.

Mr. Pearson has received degrees from Yale and Oxford, and has studied at the University of Berlin, in Munich, and in Vienna. During the summer of 1938 he was visiting Associate Professor of English at the University of Colorado.

Lotte Jacobi

FIGURE 4 Publicity flyer for the *Oxford Anthology of American Literature* (Horace Gregory Papers, Special Collections Research Center, Syracuse University Libraries).

Williams's) greater esteem for Irving but a reorientation of idea of the American short story. Irving's tales had much more in common with Hawthorne's than with the local-color humorists like Twain and Harte, suggesting that the form was essentially Yankee and Knickerbocker rather than frontier, and psychological rather than plot driven.[36] The anthology also reflects the Melville revival that Williams himself was helping to drive, with eighteen selections from the writer, far more than in any previous collection. Most notably, Benét and Pearson completely reframed the importance of Henry James with half a dozen selections, two of which were novel excerpts — not from his early, more popular works such as *Washington Square* or *The American,* but rather from his difficult late masterpieces *The Wings of the Dove* and *The Golden Bowl,* novels that had deeply influenced the stream-of-consciousness technique and psychological analysis practiced by modernists like Virginia Woolf and James Joyce. The main current of American literary history, Pearson and Benét's anthology quietly argued, led to the modernists.

The conflict between the academic (Pearson and Williams) and the critic (Benét) also gave Pearson the chance to fulfill the role that Price ascribes to anthology editors: being both "the voice of authority and a challenge to prevailing modes of authorship."[37] Previous anthologies—Foerster's, as well as earlier ones, and parallel critical projects like Parrington's *Main Currents in American Thought* or Van Wyck Brooks's books on American literature—were too historical, in Pearson's view. They presented the sweep of American literature as an illustration of the changing ways Americans thought about their new country and identity, as "social matters or social history." This approach, Pearson feared, implicitly conceded that American literature was substandard. Instead, teachers and critics of literature should primarily concern themselves with the "artistic consciousness" and "literary value"; "a course in literature ought to be primarily a study of the art of literature, and not a survey of the social or intellectual life of the nation." And American literature, Pearson was convinced, could now stand up to this scrutiny and judgment, because "the gradual emancipation of American literature from provincialism of expression by American authors as well as from self-conscious patronizing by American critics has brought about a time when there is no need for apology or subterfuge in its teaching."[38] It was time, Pearson insisted, to drop what he called this "defensive enthusiasm." "Such estimates," he contended, "leave unanswered the old problem of *literary values*." We mustn't hesitate to present and evaluate American literature through a purely literary, aesthetic sense. On the contrary, Pearson was convinced, America was experiencing its "greatest period" of literature yet—"never before have our writers of prose been leading influences for the writers of other nations," he told Bryher at this time.[39]

Norm's profile on the anthology increased when Lowry asked Williams to fully withdraw from the project in the summer of 1937. Williams had been simultaneously working on another multivolume anthology with Gabriel and Harry Warfel: *The American Mind, Selections from the Literature of the United States*, which was eventually published by Howe's American Book Company. Realizing that the two titles were in direct competition, Lowry asked Williams to step down. It was now just Benét and Pearson's baby, and the publicity brochure Oxford issued in 1937 (with a portrait of Norm by Elisabet Mayer's expatriate photographer friend Lotte Jacobi) made that clear. "Pearson," the brochure claimed, "is becoming well known to scholars and the general public as an authority on American literature." Although more aspirational than completely accurate, this claim wasn't too distant from the truth. Certainly among the very small community of literary editors and American literature professors, Norm was announcing his presence, and doing so quite strategically.

With the possible exceptions of his injury and his marriage, nothing affected the course of Norm's personal and professional life as much as editing the anthology. Strictly in terms of his career, it allowed him to develop practical skills including dealing with writers and publishers and agents, figuring out how to shape a book for a nonacademic audience, and working with celebrity literary editors. The anthology forced Norm to think about not just what contemporary writing merited inclusion in such a collection, but how to present it for use in actual college classes. Furthermore, through it he learned to write for an audience of students, teachers outside research universities, and the general public.

Norm had long instinctively used his natural talents and carefully developed his social and communications skills to attain a leading position in the institutions he inhabited. Now, through working on the anthology, Norm not only entered into another, even more exclusive and prestigious institution (Oxford University Press) but used his position in that institution to assemble two overlapping networks that he would deploy, in the postwar period, to alter the course of contemporary American literature and the public's understanding of modernism.

Probably the more important of these two new networks consisted of the writers he met. The endless letters he sent to writers, asking their permission to reprint their work, became dozens of relationships. Some—with Ezra Pound, William Carlos Williams, Wallace Stevens, Thomas Wolfe, Thornton Wilder, Marianne Moore, Gertrude Stein, Archibald MacLeish, and many others—became the connections that allowed him a truly singular perspective on twentieth-century American writing. "I have known so many figures from this period with somewhat unusual intimacy (when one considers my age)," Pearson said later, that "I know a good deal without having been actually involved in it."[40] Others, as with Horace Gregory and John Gould Fletcher and H.D. and particularly Bryher, became some of the closest friendships of his life.

One of the most colorful and omnipresent figures in twentieth-century avant-garde English art and literature, Bryher, born Annie Winifred Ellerman, was a prolific writer, but her primary role in the avant-garde scene was as a patroness and impresario. She came from an enormously wealthy family—her father owned one of the world's largest shipping companies and was believed to be Britain's richest man when he died in 1933—and used her money and connections to promote writers, painters, architects, filmmakers, photographers, and psychoanalysts whose work she found stimulating and important. She relished being the woman who makes things happen. At the time Norm met her, Bryher (who today might call herself "transgender" or "genderqueer" or "nonbinary") had been H.D.'s partner for almost twenty years. She conducted her romantic and sexual relationships exclusively with women, but when she met Norm in January 1937 she was also on her second marriage, to the gay English photographer and filmmaker Kenneth Macpherson. Her first had been to the gay American writer Robert McAlmon.

Bryher's marriages were arrangements of convenience by which she could satisfy her parents' insistence that she *appear* to be living a "normal" life, and she was willing to acquiesce because it kept the family funds flowing to her and the artists she supported. McAlmon, for example, used her money not only to write his own books, but to found the Paris-based private press Contact Editions, which published early works by William Carlos Williams, Ford Madox Ford, and H.D., as well as Ernest Hemingway's first book. She financed the construction of Hermann Henselmann's Bauhaus architectural masterpiece Villa Kenwin (named for *Ken*neth Macpherson and *Win*ifred Ellerman) on Lake Geneva in Switzerland, and the production of many films, including the groundbreaking 1930 interracial love triangle movie *Borderline*, starring Paul Robeson. She also provided innumerable small grants and gifts to artists and writers, many of which have been lost to history. Drawn to psychoanalysis partly as a way to understand her own gender identity, she arranged for H.D. to undergo analysis with Sigmund Freud himself in 1934.

Eventually, Bryher would become one of Norm's models for how to use connections to benefit writers and artists. At first, though, she tutored him in contemporary European literature. After the two first met, Norm reported to his mother, "she took me to task for not knowing some of the younger French writers better, and . . . sent over some ten or fifteen novels from France, plus a subscription to the *Nouvelle Revue Française* [and a] package of English books and a two years subscription to her own magazine [*Life and Letters*]."[41] "She keeps sending me . . . great packages of books," he added the next month.[42] This continued until the war made such regular shipments impossible.

In part because of his work on the anthology, Norm was also assembling a network of those people, most of them men, whose work brought writers to the public: New York literary editors and publishers and agents including Benét, Canby, Alfred A. Knopf, James Laughlin, Kurt and Helen Wolff, Harold Ober, and others. One of these, Saxe Commins of Random House, which was aggressively expanding following its daring 1934 publication of Joyce's *Ulysses*, provided Pearson with another early break into publishing. Early in 1937, Commins had contacted Pearson (through Gene O'Neill) about possibly including an edition of Nathaniel Hawthorne's complete novels in the publisher's new Modern Library Giants series of thousand-plus-page books. Within a few weeks, Norm had submitted a full proposal for all of Hawthorne's published novels as well as three "pretty bad" works that the author had left incomplete. But a better idea, Norm suggested, would be to omit those and instead include most of Hawthorne's stories, making for an approximately thirteen-hundred-page book.[43] A contract was signed and executed a month later, specifying a $200 fee for Norm's editorial and introductory work. "A pleasant payment for a comparatively few pages," he told Fanny, and the work "will help towards making my name better known, and be a good link with Hawthorne."[44] As always, he delivered his work on time and in polished form. Commins wrote to tell him "how impressed I am by the skill and feeling you have gotten into this best-of-all forewords. I'm damn proud of you. Not a syllable will be changed by me."[45] The book came out a month later and is still in print.

Pearson's introduction is a compact, confident, and assured piece of writing, proof of his ability to speak to audiences beyond the professoriate, and Eugene O'Neill (senior), Fletcher, and the poet Lola Ridge all wrote to compliment him on it. The essay is justifiably preoccupied with the impact of New England Puritanism on American literature and culture, saying of Hawthorne that "there was no truer child of the religious mood and cultural heritage of New England." In fact, Norm reads Hawthorne as inescapably American, even when the writer felt compelled to draw on Europe in order to pursue his art. Hawthorne "complained in his preface to *The Marble Faun* that America lacked the antique detail necessary to a writer like himself," but Pearson sees Hawthorne at his weakest when he was most immersed in that "antique detail." Instead, "its very absence in the American scene led him to substitute for concrete background the highly developed mental metaphor," as in the "Clifford's chamber" section of *The House of the Seven Gables*.[46] Norm approached the "curious kind of writing" in this essay quite deliberately, trying to "seduce the subway and rooming house reader into believing that the long turned sentence is not entirely an archaism"—in other words, to use his own sentences to accustom these casual or untrained readers to Hawthorne's long sentences. "I wanted the reader to come on a cadenced sentence first of all in the introduction."[47]

Norm had offered this explanation to yet another of the new friends whom he wanted to impress with his sophistication: Horace Gregory. Barely remembered today, Horace Gregory and his wife, Marya Zaturenska, were prominent literary figures of the midcentury. Born in Milwaukee in 1898, Gregory had moved to New York City after college to work as an advertising copywriter but also contributed to cultural magazines ranging from the *New Republic* to the Communist-aligned *New Masses*, for which he eventually became poetry editor. He also started writing poetry, and his first book, the acclaimed *Chelsea Rooming House*, appeared in 1930. Marya's own collection *Cold Morning Sky* would win a 1938 Pulitzer Prize in poetry. The two were friendly with many poets of their own generation as well as of the previous, such as Yeats and T. S. Eliot.

Gregory taught at Sarah Lawrence College with Norm's friend Helen Neill McMaster, who introduced the two, and after their first meeting in June 1937 they saw each other often. Norm greatly admired Gregory's work, calling him "so full of such technical knowledge and ability . . . that he has the necessary equipment for a great American poet."[48] (Pearson concluded the *Oxford Anthology* with Gregory's work, in fact, giving him more pages than Sherwood Anderson, Marianne Moore, Wallace Stevens, William Faulkner, Ernest Hemingway, or Gertrude Stein!) Gregory quickly became a mentor to Pearson, encouraging his critical sense and advising him on selections for the anthology. "Gregory was the one man I had met . . . whom I would travel distances in order to study under," he wrote in his journal.[49]

The Gregorys were embroiled in the fiery literary politics of the day, and their involvement drew Norm in. In the mid-1930s, the American literary scene was consumed with the question of how political art and literature should be. While a group of traditionalists, and many of the avant-garde modernists, held that art should only serve aesthetic aims, the loudest voices called for art and literature to lead the way in catalyzing social change. And the change they were calling for was a radical shift to the left. The Depression showed that capitalism had failed, the Soviet Union and international communism were seemingly making remarkable advances, and fascism was threatening freedom everywhere. In these circles the real debate wasn't between left and right; it was between left and lefter. Communists, with no real political power in the United States but highly influential among writers, followed the Soviet Union's lead and sought to produce strictly and transparently political art in works like Mike Gold's 1930 novel *Jews without Money* or Clifford Odets's 1934 one-act play *Waiting for Lefty*.

Many artists and writers, even on the left, rejected this directiveness, this insistence on so-called tendentious work, and a split emerged between Stalinists and Trotskyites. "Stalinoids," as their detractors called them, submitted to the party's guidance on what and how they wrote, and the party proscribed experimental modernism. Art and literature, the party insisted, had to be easily understandable to the masses, and to focus on the class conflict and other realities that a Marxist lens on the world brought into view. The psychology of the individual, a primary concern of both modernist and nineteenth-century art and literature, was less important than the forces of history. But Trotsky-ites argued in publications like *Partisan Review* that art didn't need to be simplistic and two-dimensional, that experimentation and psycho-logical exploration weren't marks of bourgeois decadence but could be revolutionary in a deeper way.

Gregory was not a Trotskyite, but superficially he could be seen as aligned with them. While he served as the poetry editor for the *New Masses*, he often refused to toe its line. This conflict boiled over in 1937, when Granville Hicks—an influential Communist literary critic, as well as former editor of the magazine—reviewed Gregory's collec-tion of younger poets called *New Letters* and found its contributors too "pessimistic" about the possibility of a Communist revolution in the United States. "Communism is good news," Hicks proclaimed. "Once understood, once believed in, it holds out hope to all but capitalism's pampered few."[50] (Despite their differences, both Gregory and Hicks took for granted that writers should advance leftist causes.)

Pearson's response to the debate, in letters to Gregory, shows him starting to develop the literary and political outlook that would vary little over the remaining decades of his life. It was based, first of all, on pragmatism and a rejection of any overarching ideologies. Commu-nism, he granted, offered "hope" and "faith," which might have been a sufficient "moral pick-me-up for the lost generation" (the generation of Hicks and Gregory), but his own generation "isn't lost. Mine didn't, doesn't, know which way to turn, but that's not being lost. We know where we are!" And unlike the "lost generation" and previous gener-ations of Americans, Pearson saw his generation as inescapably and fundamentally American, a grounding that couldn't be overcome with an "inoculation" of a foreign philosophy like Communism. "We know that Mather, Edwards, Franklin, and Jefferson are behind us. We feel that they and Emerson and others are still to be reckoned with. . . . Our hope doesn't come in setting up a false stage or waving a magician's wand and muttering abracadabra over the countryside. Our hope is based on facing complexity and resolving if possible a solution."

Pearson positioned himself in the midpoint of the spectrum between tendentious or "committed" art and "art for art's sake" or aesthetic formalism, the late nineteenth-century philosophy that art cannot and should not do social or political work or be judged by its social or political impact. The 1930s writers' advocacy of committed art, in fact, derived in part from their rejection of the modernists' embrace of aesthetic formalism. But for Pearson, this was all incidental. "Many young writers today turn their eyes leftward," he told Gregory.

> Yet in any true test of their ability as writers it is coincidental only. There are many impulses that lead to literature. Whether the result is literature or not does not depend on whether [what] we as individuals or a group favor exists in this particular work; and even more fully it does not depend on whether the expression of that impulse be one of happy hope. . . . Most leftish criticism today . . . will stifle the literary expression of our own age by trying to push everything into one channel. We recognize that art for art's sake is not the only aim in writing. God knows we needed the vitality which is coming with the reaction! God also knows that if art is done for art's sake it can still be art! . . . What writers have got to do is to stop going around self-consciously saying to the world, "See how happy I am!" Their business is to think and feel and write. And our business as editors and critics is to choose the best that's written.[51]

He had said similar things just a few months earlier in his introduction to Hawthorne. "Criticism is relearning a respect for the didactic in art," he neutrally asserted. "Literature may serve as well as merely satisfy. At least it may do one or the other, and yet be art." But literature can never be reduced to its social message, its "moral tag," which is merely the "jewel toward which the design of a circlet is traced; it is the truth toward which the story points."[52] This preference for the aesthetic over the political is clear in the table of contents for the Oxford anthology as well, which includes none of the so-called proletarian writers of the time: no Odets, no Gold, no Upton Sinclair or Jack London or Kenneth Fearing. Instead, the most contemporary writers are safely middlebrow (Stephen Vincent Benét, MacLeish), politically conservative (Eliot, John Crowe Ransom, Allen Tate), or apolitical (Léonie Adams, Thomas Wolfe). When soliciting their critical statements about their work, he even asked at least one of the writers for "a little more emphasis on the art of literature and a little less on literature as a social document."[53]

This taste of being part of the literary scene made Norm realize that he was not interested in being just a scholar with a conventional academic career. But he still was going to need a job. His editing and publishing work would not tempt a university search committee, and his dissertation had stalled because of his outside commitments. Luckily, prompted by Pearson's friend Dixon Wecter, the chairman of the University of Colorado's English department approached Norm in November 1937 about teaching in Boulder's prestigious summer session the following year. Wecter, a Texan and Rhodes Scholar, had studied American cultural history at Yale with Norm and wanted a kindred spirit working with him: both men took a proto–American studies approach to their work, trying to understand how history influenced literature and vice versa. (Wecter in fact credited Pearson in the acknowledgments to his first book.)[54]

"This is really an unbelievable stroke of luck," Norm reported to his mother, as "the summer school is one of the three or four best in the country, and as Randall Stewart told me when he heard: 'Only the big shots get in.'"[55] Wecter, like Stewart, Benét, Gabriel, and Williams, was helping Norm amass capital in what one might call "the economy of prestige," and Norm knew it. Connections, Norm was learning, were the most important asset one could have. Connections gave one entry into prestigious institutions, from Yale to Random House to the Modern Language Association; connections also led to other connections, as Williams led to Benét who led to the authors he met through the anthology. Norm had exquisite social skills that made older people comfortable around him, and the ideal combination of defer-

ence, respect, intelligence, affability, and ambition to earn their affection and loyalty.

Wecter also provided Pearson with an introduction to at least one
important person outside of the academic world: Thomas Wolfe, the
North Carolina writer whose 1929 autobiographical novel *Look Homeward, Angel* had made him a literary celebrity, a sort of Marcel Proust of
Asheville. Pearson was among his fans. "I have thought for some time
that he is really a brilliant writer," he told his mother, and after their
first in-person meeting he remarked that "I like him enormously."[56]
Pearson had wanted to include scenes from *Angel* in the anthology,
but by 1936 Wolfe felt he had left that stage of his writing, and his life,
behind: "I was a young man when I wrote 'Look Homeward, Angel,'"
he told Norm. "I am approaching middle age now. I think I know more
about life, more about living, more about people now than I did then."
He proposed that Benét and Pearson include, instead, a long section—
twenty-three chapters!—from his 1935 sequel *Of Time and the River*,
and in the end Pearson did include about half of that.[57]

At that time, Wolfe was living in Brooklyn, having made himself
unwelcome in Asheville. Only about nine years Norm's senior, Wolfe
recounted to his new friend his feelings of alienation from the dod-
dering or irrelevant old writers at his first American Academy of Arts
and Letters meeting in January, which was "very sad. I went away and
drank, and wished someone like yourself had been with me that I could
talk to."[58] Pearson visited Wolfe in New York several times over 1937
and 1938, by which time Wolfe had moved into that notorious writers'
haunt, the Chelsea Hotel on Twenty-Third Street in Manhattan. A few
months later they got together to celebrate Wolfe submitting a million-
word manuscript for the novel he was calling *The October Fair*. "He's
in good form, and is working on his next novel," Norm reported to his
mother.[59] Wolfe invited Norm to join him on a planned western road
trip in June 1938, which would begin in Portland and then trace an
enormous circle through Oregon, California, Nevada, Arizona, Utah,
Colorado, Wyoming, Montana, and Idaho, and finally to Seattle.[60] This
worked out nicely for Pearson, who was scheduled to start work in
Boulder in early July, and loved nothing more than a driving vacation—

Wolfe could just drop him off halfway through. However, when Oxford let Norm know in no uncertain terms that it needed the full anthology manuscript as soon as possible, he realized a three-week meander was no longer possible.

He never saw Wolfe again, who developed pneumonia and miliary tuberculosis at the end of his trip and died on September 15, 1938. "I've lost other great friends, but none who seemed so much a symbol of life in himself," Norm told Benét.[61] To Wecter, Pearson expanded on the sentiment: "no other man in American literature or in any other literature as far as I know was able to accomplish just what Tom did accomplish. His attempt to synthesize through the sensibilities of a single man the entire physical impressions of a continent is, not might be, a great achievement."[62]

His Colorado trip had been preceded by another loss. Ever since Mary Lib Thomson had broken his heart in 1930, Norm had not had any significant romantic relationships, although he dated frequently. But in 1937, he hired as his secretary for the Oxford project Virginia Lee Donaldson, the eighteen-year-old daughter of Yale University Press editor Norman Donaldson. Virginia Lee—or Midge, as she preferred to be called—was an aspiring actress, with delicate features and a milkmaid braid. Norm, ten years her elder, was soon smitten. By December, he was writing love poems to her, many of which depict a work environment that no modern HR department would tolerate:

MOTHER'S TASK A DIFFICULT ONE

Sure, Norman's the boss, which
Is treacherous;
For like any employer,
He's lecherous.

But poor Midget must work.
Can you blame her,
If she fears an attempt
To inflame her?

No mother is there as
A chaperone,
To prevent falls from grace in
A room alone.

From fright at it all,
We're delirious.
What might happen, God knows!
God's mysterious.[63]

Steeped in poetic history, with very little actual romantic experience, in this poem and several others Norm draws on the venerable form of the wooing poem—the poet/speaker's entreaty to a hesitant but interested woman to dispense with propriety and give in to love and, presumably, sex. Other poems, though, were more earnest, and uncharacteristically old-fashioned, almost Victorian in their sentiments.

In May, as he prepared to leave for Colorado, Norm proposed marriage, recording the moment in an ominous poem:

WHEN ASKED

Midge was silent, but her smile tinkled
With the sound of tiny silver bells sway-
ing slowly above a white frosted cake.

But Norm was, it seems, fooling himself. Midge declined Norm's marriage proposal just before he left for Colorado, leaving him bereft and heartsick.

+ 5 +

HEADY SOCIETY

Deprived now of his love and his road trip, Norm flew to Denver on June 25, 1938, on what he told Bryher was "only the second time I had crossed the Hudson." (This was an exaggeration, but his experience of the United States beyond the Eastern Seaboard was indeed minimal.) He tried to mirror Bryher's own love of travel and dramatic prose style in describing the trip to her: "to see America spread out below me was a rare privilege. From the plane I looked down on the erosion with a terrified awe at the destructive power of nature. It was like a great corpse with its nervous system laid bare and a thin pall of green laid over it, but concealing nothing. I shuddered to think what had happened to the good earth beneath."[1] To his mother, he extolled the creature comforts of the flights. "I have never seen so much done to make passengers comfortable," he told Fanny. "Food all day if one wanted it, attractively served on little trays with sunken holes to hold the dishes. Gum, candy, and cigarettes passed out all the time; plenty of magazines to read; and at every landing we were handed the latest edition of the local paper."[2] The next day, the Wecters shuttled him to Boulder, where he spent a week working on the seventy-five remaining introductions for the anthology and preparing for his classes. Elizabeth Mayer (who, like her husband, Wilhelm, and son, Christoph, had Americanized their names) and his Oxford friend Doreen Lewisohn, who had come there for a holiday, mothered him by unpacking his trunks and buying housewares for his temporary lodgings.

Colorado's summer session was not only prestigious; it was popular.

FIGURE 5 Norm with Dixon Wecter, Boulder, 1938 (Alfred A. Knopf Literary File Photography Collection, Harry Ransom Center, University of Texas at Austin).

Prefiguring his teaching career at Yale, Norm's classes were all overenrolled. "Having to pretend to be an experienced teacher hasn't let me dare not to act as though I knew what to do in each circumstance," he told his mother. "Probably that is an advantage." The students were hungry for contemporary writing, and Norm, then finishing up the most modern anthology of American literature yet, was able to bring personal insights into his lectures on writers like Pound, Williams, H.D., and Gregory.

In August, Fanny came to visit. Norm had implored her to persuade Chester to come along, but he did not yet feel that Alfred was ready to have full responsibility over the still-struggling store. "I've never had but one trip with him since I can remember," Norm lamented.[3] Over one of his last weekends in the West, Norm and Fanny, accompanied by the Gregorys (who had come out from Milwaukee), drove through Yellowstone National Park and on to Santa Fe and Taos, where they saw John Gould Fletcher and his wife, Charlie May, and tried unsuccessfully to look up D. H. Lawrence's wife, Frieda.

Between teaching, grading, entertaining guests, and writing introductions for the anthology, Norm was brutally overworked. As the Oxford deadline loomed, Gregory sympathetically stepped up to help him complete the last sixty-five headnotes in a frantic week of eighteen-hour days.[4] He posted the completed anthology just as he left Colorado. From there, he went to Chicago, to copy Hawthorne manuscripts held at the University of Chicago Library. "No one had used the material before," he told Fanny, "and there was not even a caretaker for the collection, so I was given a key and had complete freedom."[5]

But it wasn't just Hawthorne work that drew him to Chicago. He also examined the University of Chicago's archive of the papers of Harriet Monroe, the editor of *Poetry* magazine in the period before World War I when it was a leading outlet for avant-garde literature (Pound famously claimed he "discovered" Eliot when he urged the younger man to submit "The Love Song of J. Alfred Prufrock" to *Poetry* in 1914).[6] Norm left convinced that any experimental tendencies in that magazine emerged in spite of Monroe's nearly "reactionary" instincts and only because of collaborators such as Pound. He had begun to help Yale's library amass a collection of the so-called "little magazines" like *Poetry* that had published the first generation of modernist artists. "What I want to do, and am trying to do, is to get every damned little mag from 1890 to date" for Yale, he told William Carlos Williams when the poet sent him some from his own collection.[7] "The literary accounts of our times are going to be written from the little mags, and there ought to be one place where people can go knowing that they can find the whole batch. Yale is enthusiastic about" this collection, he added—or "at least the library is, and the English department is succumbing to an oblique attack on the part of modern writing." Norm here tips his hand about what he was starting to do and would continue to do throughout his career: conduct a rear-guard action, not through the academic departments but through secondary institutions like the library, to inject contemporary literature into Yale's stodgy curriculum and staid campus artistic scene.

To help him save money, his old Magdalen friend Bill Sweet, then completing his residency at the University of Chicago Hospital, arranged for Norm to lodge in the hospital dormitory. It was a fortunate choice, for while there his hip injury flared up. Initially, he attributed it to rheumatism brought about by damp weather, but it quickly worsened, and he "suddenly went lame," as he told a friend.[8] Sweet referred him to Dr. C. Howard Hatcher, one of the leading orthopedic surgeons in the country, who discovered that the bone graft Dr. MacAusland had performed in 1930 had undergone significant deterioration, and the tuberculosis bacteria were active again. Hatcher proposed another operation to "refix" the hip and, at the same time, reposition the femur within the pelvis so as to effectively lengthen Norm's left leg. The surgery would be a complicated one.

The operation would be performed in Chicago, and as a result Norman would be under the care of someone besides Dr. MacAusland for the first time in over a decade. From Boston, Ingie reassured him that Dr. Hatcher and his supervisor Dr. Dallas Phemister were well known and well respected. Chicago's Rockefeller-funded staff was among the best in the world, and as it was "somewhat of a charity hospital" it could adjust the fees to Norm's meager income. Norm made the arrangements and returned to New Haven on September 25, finding that the Great New England Hurricane of 1938 had left his apartment "without lights or telephone, and surrounded by the corpses of great trees blown down by the storm."[9] He settled his affairs for the fall and prepared for an extended absence. Having gathered the materials he would need to work on his dissertation and edit the proofs for the anthology, two weeks later Norm returned to Chicago.

Back in Chicago, even though he was preparing for a major surgery and extensive recovery, Norm quickly turned to what was always his first priority: tending to his friendships and connections, and making sure he would be able to work as much as possible. He took the Northwestern University American literature professor Leon Howard and his wife, Henrietta, out to dinner before checking in with Sweet. And the networks he had been laboring to establish reached out to him, as well. Hearing that Norm would be undergoing a major surgery and extended recovery, new friends such as Gregory, Bryher, H.D., and Fitts sent their best wishes. "You are one of the finest guys in the world,"

Benét wrote sympathetically, "and of course, for that very reason, one of the fellows who has to have a close acquaintance with pain." Norm also hired a secretary to help him keep up with his correspondence.

At the hospital on Sunday, October 10, Norm immediately underwent a lumbar puncture and full physical workup. He underwent surgery on October 14, and that afternoon Sweet reported to Fanny and Chester that it was a complete success—a surprise to both of them, for to save his mother anxiety Norm had avoided telling her when the operation was going to take place.[10] Dr. Hatcher had grafted large sections of bone from farther down the left femur and tibia on top of the original graft. He also curetted away the diseased tissue that showed indications of exposure to tuberculosis and was able to reposition the left femur by three degrees so that Norman's posture would improve. The operation effectively lengthened his leg by over an inch, leaving him less lopsided. Nonetheless, as Norm told Fitts, "the new position of my leg swung south by south-southeast is very impressive. I shall roll along with a merry sailor's roll."[11]

After two postoperative days in a narcotic haze, his initial recovery went very well. He was encased in a bilateral plaster spica—a body cast covering his entire left leg, down to the knee of his right leg, and reaching up to his chest—for four weeks. He described being "turned like a cartwheel from flat on my face to flat on my back."[12] The bright side was that this cast was lighter than the one in which Dr. MacAusland had imprisoned him eight years before. Norm was touched at Sweet's constant attention to him despite his own full schedule: "that certainly is friendship! Any I've shown for anyone pales besides what he's shown for me."[13] For his part, Sweet reported to Fanny that "he is behaving in a model fashion . . . complains of nothing, and is very hesitant in calling on the orderlies and nurses."[14] "I shouldn't be surprised if he found himself able to dictate again in a few more days," he added.

October 24 provided another lift to the patient's spirits, for he received his author's copies of *The Oxford Anthology of American Literature*, barely six weeks after he had turned in the final copy for the headnotes. Later that week, Lowry wrote to say that, looking at the book "in its glory on the table in the Library for the crowding multitudes to buy," he was "really terribly pleased by it."[15] Norm was enormously proud, even though he self-deprecatingly told Bryher that "there are all kinds of silly mistakes in it" that he would have to correct in future editions. He sent complimentary copies not just to the contributors but to many of his new literary friends who didn't appear in the volume, and of course to his family, prompting an impressed Alfred to tell him that "you are made professionally if you never reached for a pen again." Important people in important places were indeed talking about him: in December, Yale's William Lyon Phelps featured the anthology in a Brooklyn lecture called "Important Books Worth Reading." As all editors learn, though, publication day isn't the end of their work. Norm immediately had to deal with follow-up requests from Oxford, which wanted to publish a deluxe two-volume edition, and would he please produce a preface for the second volume? And divide the bibliography into two sections? And submit a full list of corrections for that edition within the next few weeks? And clear up some ambiguous copyright clearances? And explain why Ezra Pound's literary agent was so incensed at her permissions check?

The initial forecast for a three-week hospital stay had been optimistic; he would spend more than that just in his body cast. But by early November, Norm was put in a "more manageable" cast and began several hours of daily physical therapy. By the middle of the month, he stopped paying for private twenty-four-hour nursing care and resumed feeding himself and, soon, working. Over October and November 1938 he produced a truly staggering number of letters, most dictated to his part-time secretary. "The whole period in the hospital has been very useful to me, and I already feel all sorts of new energy and vitality to go back to my work," he told Bryher.[16] In fact, this interval helped him solidify and strengthen many of the friendships that he had started to cultivate with anthology contributors, for there was little to do *besides* write letters. He'd reached the gossiping stage with many of them, metaphorically rolling his eyes to Fletcher, for instance, at the news that middlebrow author Pearl S. Buck had received the Nobel Prize in Literature.[17] Notwithstanding their mutual formality of address, "Mr. Pearson," "Mrs. Macpherson" (Bryher), and "Mrs. Aldington" (H.D.) were developing a particularly warm relationship, and when she didn't hear from Norm directly, Bryher often asked their mutual friend Gregory for updates on his condition.[18]

The past few months had also brought the Gregorys and Norm especially close. "It would be impossible," he told them in a Christmas letter, "to express how much I owe to you both for [my] maturation. . . . I can only helplessly gesture with my hands to indicate its enormity and my gratitude and my friendship and my love."[19] Horace and Marya returned his affection, and their son, Patrick, later said that Norm was in his "earliest memories" as a "close personal friend" of both of his parents whom they held in "deep regard."[20] The Gregorys were struggling to raise Patrick and his sister on paltry incomes and whatever fees or royalties they could earn from their writing, and both had health problems. Seeing this, Norm started to give them money. He lived frugally, and in addition to the dividends he received from his stake in Goodnow Pearson's, he now was making money from his writing. In September, he signed over to Horace his $200 advance from Oxford to help fund an operation for their daughter, Joanna, assuring him that it was "a very slight part of your rightful share in" the anthology. Two months later, he asked Marya's permission to privately print her poem "Summer to Lapland," which the Atlantic had rejected, as his Christmas card, but "only on condition that you would allow me to pay you for its use the precise sum you would have received." His new experience in the publishing industry also prompted him to give them professional advice, such as that Marya should publish her next collection with Harcourt, with its "prestige and sales" and the "best list of poets," rather than the larger Macmillan.[21]

Gregory had connected him with Morton Dauwen Zabel, a Loyola University professor who had just stepped down as the editor in chief at Poetry magazine, and Zabel came to visit frequently. And while Norm disdained Poetry's aesthetic conservatism, its apoliticality and enduring prestige aligned well with his tendency to associate with well-established institutions rather than insurgent new ones. Other local

American literature scholars stopped in to visit: the Howards, Lowry, Percy Boynton of the University of Chicago, Frederick Mulhauser of Northwestern. Even Carl Sandburg dropped by.

But his release from the hospital kept receding. On October 30, he expected to be in Chicago for only "two or three weeks longer," but on November 20, he ruefully told his mother that although Dr. Hatcher cleared him to return to Gardner briefly for Thanksgiving, his rapid rehabilitation indicated that it would be best if he stayed close to his physical therapists.[22] "I shall unquestionably be here well into December, and possibly over Christmas," he told Gregory a week later. The lengthening of his left leg promised to improve his walking, but in the near term it meant much time spent "unlearn[ing] old habits," and learning "to walk more nearly correctly for the first time."[23] This retraining meant he was not even allowed to use crutches until after the New Year, but typically, he threw himself into the work. "I have been making good progress," he told his father on January 2. "For the last two or three days I have been walking in the ramp for a little while without my cast."[24] Sweet was amazed at Norm's good spirits, telling Fanny that "I marvel at his ability to adapt himself to such inconveniences."[25] Norm even reported putting on weight, a welcome development as he had weighed only 113 pounds at admission.

Once he was more mobile, he began to visit the "crippled children's ward" and befriended a number of the patients there. As the children's section was a charity ward, he told his mother, "the children have far more presents than they would have at home. . . . Children have been known not to open all of theirs, because they knew their brothers and sisters would be having none."[26] (Norm gave the staff $5 for candy for all the children and bought stamps and a model airplane for his juvenile companions in the physical therapy room.)

By January, he was able to leave the hospital to work for short periods of time in the University of Chicago and Northwestern University libraries, and even for evening excursions (such as to a performance of *The Swing Mikado*), but the endless hospital routine and uncertainty of when he would be able to leave were getting to him. Marya reached out in January, concerned at reports that Norm appeared depressed.[27]

His release had had to be delayed again because although the bones were healing well, the underlying infection persisted, and the sinus in his hip stubbornly refused to dry up. So in early February he underwent another surgery. "The surgeon burns, snips, and curettes as if he were eating a cantaloupe—to little avail," Norm complained to William Carlos Williams.[28] Recovery from this required another eight weeks of bed rest, during which he fell uncharacteristically silent, causing many of his friends to worry. In April Gregory let him know that "lack of word of you is causing a small ripple of worry among your New York friends." Bryher also checked in with the Gregorys in June as to whether they'd heard from him—"I fear that he may not have gone on so well as was thought," she fretted.[29]

But rather than suffering from depression, Norm had finally embraced the solitude and isolation of convalescence, rather than trying to perform normality and live up to the Puritan ideal of constant productivity. In December, he had told Bryher that "the whole period in the hospital has been very useful to me" because it had reenergized him for his work.[30] But after the second operation, he didn't see the point in keeping that up any longer. "There really isn't any excuse," Norm finally wrote in early April, "for not having written to anyone, and certainly no cause for anyone's having worried. . . . Some people would explain my recent life as a crawling back into the womb. . . . Yet the atmosphere was peaceful, and I found the situation surprisingly pleasant. Now that I'm told to shake myself and get back into life I find it difficult to shake off the lethargy."[31] He remained at the hospital throughout the spring (celebrating his thirtieth birthday by treating the children to "a huge chocolate cake and ice-cream") and was finally allowed to leave in late May.[32]

Norm had come to see these extended hospitalizations that he had endured since his boyhood as punctuating or even delineating stages of his life. As he wrote the Gregorys that Christmas, this one marked "the termination of a delayed adolescence. I have kept thinking of myself as a bright young boy, far too long. I have put off, delayed the events. I still must clean up, but I know that I am cleaning up. Hospitalization doesn't change one; it simply gives one the chance to catch up with one's self and what has happened."[33] But these periods of medical confinement also catalyzed his lifelong drive to use his privileges, his advantages and assets, for others' benefit. Writing Bryher in 1961, he looked back:

> When I was seven years old, when I was fourteen, when I was twenty-one, and when I was twenty-eight I knew in the hospitals that I might easily die on the operating tables. I knew it from the eyes of the people about me, I knew it sometimes from what they said to each other or to me. And I was definitely told that each time I became sick in the future it would be more difficult to recover. Life became very precious to me, and increasingly I became aware of how difficult it was for others. I wanted to make life happier for those others, but on their terms rather than my own, so that by their becoming free I could be all the freer.[34]

After leaving the hospital, Norm returned to Gardner for about six weeks of further recuperation before a progress check in Chicago in June. Released, he bounced back to New Haven, where he spent the balance of the summer seeing friends and attending to publicity tasks for the anthology. Because the primary audience for this book wasn't consumers but rather professors who would adopt it for their courses, this involved traveling to colleges and cajoling colleagues. Norm (and Oxford) especially craved the coup of an adoption at Harvard, where he had established professional friendships with Perry Miller and F. O. Matthiessen, who taught the American literature class. Unfortunately, both seemed satisfied with Foerster's book. A number of schools, though, adopted the anthology in 1940 and 1941, including Penn State and other major state universities. (By 1947 it was being used at Berkeley, NYU, UCLA, Minnesota, Wisconsin, Indiana, Washington, Georgia, Utah, Stanford, Cornell, Caltech, MIT, San Francisco State, and many other large schools.)

While *The Oxford Anthology of American Literature* had been conceived largely as an educational product aimed at professors, Oxford also marketed it as a "trade" book intended for noneducational consumers. Because of that it was widely and positively reviewed in newspapers and magazines. To the *New York Times*, it was the "liveliest and most useful anthology of American literature that has come this way in a long time." The *San Diego Sun* called it "necessary to every home," and the *Chicago Tribune* praised it as being "fine" and "comprehensive." The *New Masses* disapproved of the book's primarily "esthetic" principle of selection but applauded how its inclusion of leftist selections such as one from John Reed's *Ten Days That Shook the World* showed that "social relevance and creative art are far from being incompatible." And even though Norm had significantly reduced the number of modern writers from Benét's original proposal, the anthology was still by far the most modern-heavy one on the market, and many of the reviews lauded Benét's and Pearson's emphasis on modern writers. The *Rocky Mountain News*, for example, praised the "young critical genius" Pearson for deciding "not to treat contemporary American writers as sketchy offshoots of the Mathers and Longfellows, but to stick out [his] own neck by ranking Ernest Hemingway . . . with Thomas Paine and other fellows who can be called the classic American writers." This emphasis on the moderns, the *Dallas News* adjudged, "fills a very definite void."[35]

His convalescence over, the anthology in circulation, and his first teaching job successfully executed, Norm resolved to complete his degree. He declined a number of offers from publishers for projects such as histories of American literature or surveys of the American novel and spent the next two academic years fully immersed in graduate school for the first time.[36] And unusually for an advanced-stage graduate student, he was broadening, not narrowing, his interests. In the fall of 1939 he audited an undergraduate philosophy class, an American history class, and Theory of Cultural Analysis, taught by the eminent Polish anthropologist Bronislaw Malinowski. (Malinowski's ideas so excited him that he typed out the anthropologist's "synoptic tables of culture" and sent them to his new friend Daniel Aaron, who was in the process of earning the first PhD in Harvard's new American Civilization department.)[37] He then attended the 1939 MLA conference in

New Orleans. "It would be pretty difficult to estimate concrete results from a trip like this," he wrote to Fanny, "but it certainly is useful to meet the men in one's field."[38]

Norm's Hawthorne edition had given him some visibility in the profession, but an old boys' network controlled the allocation of prestige jobs in academia. In 1958, two researchers found that nepotism—"the bestowal of patronage by reason of relationship rather than merit"— was the most powerful factor influencing hiring in academia, and this had been all the more true for Norm in 1939, with many fewer jobs available.[39] Within the small but growing world of American literature professors, Stanley Williams and Randall Stewart were boldface names, and both talked Norm up. His web now also included Wecter, F. O. Matthiessen, Northwestern's Leon Howard, and many others. But Norm had even better-known people advocating for him, including Benét, Canby, Gregory, Fitts, Zabel, and others who straddled the academic and literary worlds. Because of this, some job offers had already started to trickle in even before Colorado had provided him his first professional audition. The University of Illinois, for instance, had approached him in the spring of 1938 and noted that "you were very highly recommended to us by Mr. Canby and Mr. Benét."[40] Just weeks after he left Boulder, the University of Colorado also offered him a permanent job.

The offers really started coming in after the anthology appeared in 1939. Tulane, Scripps, Stanford, Vassar, Sarah Lawrence, even two departments at Yale (English and history) tried to lure him onto their faculties. A back-channel missive from Robert Hutchins, celebrity president of the University of Chicago, tempted Norm with teaching "the best things to be taught to the best students they can be taught to. Let me know when you are ready."[41] But he always demurred. Both he and Williams reasoned that he should finish his degree first. He was right—"my stock is higher than it ever was before" because of his willingness to wait, he noted in 1938.[42] This rising stock led to invitations for speaking engagements at Harvard, Wesleyan, and other New England schools over the next two years.

Almost as important to Norm's professional development as Williams's guidance was his model as a navigator of the world of academia. Williams showed him that the academy was no different from any other sector of American society: in it, power resided in and flowed from its institutions, and from the connections one made within them. Williams had helped create the professional institutions that legitimated American literary study, but he also spoke to a larger public through his anthology projects. Norm would soon surpass him in status and influence by working through his own institutions and using his own networks, but from Williams he learned that he needed to be more than just a scholar and a teacher.

The talks, job offers, and editing opportunities weren't the only indications that Norm was getting noticed. He contributed a critical article on so-called survey courses in American literature to the teaching-focused journal *College English*, criticizing the "confused" way most instructors approached those increasingly common classes—not knowing enough about the Puritans and colonial period, professors rushed to get to the nineteenth century, where they were on safer ground with Emerson and Hawthorne and Whitman. Such an article would seem to have required years of experience and a familiarity with many different kinds of colleges, but the piece is assured and confident, evidence both of Pearson's broad network of contacts and of his ability to convincingly impersonate the voice of a much older and more experienced professional.[43]

Such professionals were noticing him. Early in 1940, through Williams's intercession he was asked to lecture at the second annual English Institute. Rutgers University's Rudolf Kirk, its creator, envisioned the institute as a kind of supercharged, superstar MLA conference, where the highest-profile scholars would talk not about specific research projects but about the "ways, means, and ends of scholarship in English literature." Norm would be "much the youngest person" at the English Institute, he told his mother, but "there is no person my age in the academic world of American literature who would be recognized as my peer."[44] Still, at the conference Pearson still felt himself "in heady society for an ephebe," he later reminisced.[45] In addition to Gregory, poets W. H. Auden and Allen Tate spoke there, as well as Randall Stewart and several of the literary scholars who would come to dominate the 1940s and 1950s with their New Critical approach to literature: René Wellek, Cleanth Brooks, and Princeton's Willard Thorp. For this meeting, Kirk explained, the organizing committee wanted "speakers who were definitely experimental in ideas and techniques and who were themselves so immersed in their work that they were more interested in processes than in results of a final nature."[46] It's hard to imagine that Norm's work could have been considered "experimental"—he was, after all, doing very traditional scholarly editing—but his paper wasn't even on Hawthorne. Rather, he spoke about Polonius, the tragicomic character from *Hamlet*.

Or, at least that was what his title promised. Instead, Pearson's talk was a kind of philosophical state-of-the-discipline report on literary study, influenced not just by his practical experience as an anthology editor but by an unlikely person to bring up in a meeting of literature scholars in 1940: Malinowski. Pearson opened by arguing that two of the most widespread ways of approaching and interpreting American literary works—as illuminating their authors' lives, and as mere documents of the mind of the time and place in which they were created—were showing themselves to be insufficient. "Biography has done us an ill turn," he asserted. "We have got to the point where we study *Moby Dick* to understand Melville, rather than Melville to understand *Moby Dick*." Similarly, the sociohistorical approach of American studies pioneers like Vern Parrington, "which would examine all works of art as though they were significant solely as documents of social and intellectual history," fails: "a critic and historian of literature ought not to confuse his role with that of a sociologist simply because his materials may also serve the sociologist."[47]

Rather, the proper domain for the literary historian is form—those features that make a verbal text "literature." Here, Pearson begins to sound like the formalist critics who insisted that a literary critic should pay attention only to those things actually present in the text itself, such as images, symbols, motifs, characters, sounds. But Pearson swerves, moving not into sociology but into anthropology. "A formalized examination of literature is not unlike that of a formalized examination of cultures," he argued, and thus literary historians needed to look to the work of scholars such as Malinowski, for whom culture itself is a "vast instrumental reality—the body of implements and commodities, charters of social organization, ideas and customs, beliefs and values—all of which allow man to satisfy his biological requirements through cooperation and within an environment refashioned and adjusted." And the study of literature, he continued, "may without torture to the fancy be said to comprehend a 'vast instrumental reality,'" encompassing "the aspects of a culture [and] the forms and types in which the writing takes shape." Pearson's mention of "biological requirements" comes directly from Malinowski, who held that culture was, in its essence, a response to an individual organism's biological needs—food, shelter, health, reproduction, and so on—and that anthropologists needed to start with those needs in analyzing any aspects of a culture.[48]

He doesn't, however, then opine on how Hawthorne's preoccupations stemmed from the climate and geography of coastal New England. Instead, his somewhat verbose and abstract explanation leads to a relatively simple and utterly pragmatic principle: in studying literature, we need to balance our attention between the conditions affecting the work's creation (e.g., when it was written, the author's advanced age or provincial upbringing), the things being written about (marriage, the Crimean War, a summer's day), and the way things are written (as a novel, in Whitmanesque catalogs, as a villanelle). This seems intuitive, but in the 1930s it was fiercely contested and politicized, often pitting Marxists against formalists. In the end, Pearson proclaimed, "the critic," or those concerned with form, "and the literary historian," or those concerned with conditions and content, "emerge, therefore, as the same person." And Norm asserted that he would be that person for the next stage of literary studies.

This audacious rhetorical gesture was Pearson's public nod that the profession had identified him as its promising young star. In New York, he was asked to dinners every night by the field's eminences, and the institute selected his essay for its annual collection of the meeting's best papers. Kirk himself then chose Norm to run the Literary Criticism section of the institute the following year.

The English Institute also showed him how he could take advantage of networking not just for his own benefit, but for others'. He relished being the person who could connect other people, who could plug young scholars and writers into the opportunities that would help their careers. "I think that I got a job for this winter for a young protégé of mine who has just married and is jobless," he told his mother soon after returning from the institute. "If this alone works out it will have been worth the trip."[49] Among others he helped as he finished up at Yale was Eric Bentley, an English émigré who had earned his PhD at Yale and was trying to find a paying job but at the time teaching at the experimental Black Mountain College for only room and board. Pearson connected him with Wecter, by then at UCLA, who found Bentley employment there in 1941.[50] (Bentley would go on to be an influential theater critic.)

But the more attention Norm received as the top prospect of the academy, the less he relished that future. He didn't want to spend his career writing dry, incremental scholarship on Hawthorne and teaching undergraduates. The world of modern and contemporary literature beckoned to him. He wanted to attend gala New York awards ceremonies; he wanted eminent writers to call themselves his friend. And he also wanted his own *collecting*—of books, magazines, artworks, people—to be part of his career. But in 1940, there really wasn't a model for this kind of career in the academy. One could be a well-known public critic and editor who sometimes taught in the university (like Canby), or one could be a well-respected scholar whose name sometimes appeared on more public-aimed products like a literary anthology (like Williams). Norm, though, wanted both, and neither.

Williams was aware of this, and respected it, even if it implicitly slighted his own accomplishments. In 1938, Williams perceptively laid out "two pictures" of Norm's dual ambitions—as scholar and as public literary intellectual—that ended up being uncannily prescient. "In one," he told Norm, "you are the free-lance critic, with all of his virtues and none of his defects, an authority on American literature, a critic of distinction, liberal and sound. . . . You are free in spirit for all the adventures which delight you."[51] But Williams was a creature of the academy, aware of both its virtues and its insularity, and wanted Norm to bring his talents there to help improve it—to be exactly the kind of critic-historian that Pearson had called for in his English Institute talk: "without any danger of the faults that stiffen many of us, you are in a large university, using these same powers not merely for the dung-hill scholarship but for better critical writing than comes from our English departments. Here is where your gifts are needed!"

Because of how he crossed between academia and the larger world of letters, Pearson had also become a kind of node for students with literary aspirations. When undergraduate roommates Reed Whittemore and James Angleton approached Gregory in 1939 soliciting a submission to their ambitious new magazine *Furioso*, Gregory redirected them to Norm. Norm was glad to help, especially after he learned from Zaturenska that Angleton and Whittemore had money to match their ambition.[52] *Furioso* would be aggressively avant-garde, much in the model of James Laughlin's annual *New Directions in Prose and Poetry*, which also began appearing at this time. Angleton was brilliant and obsessed with poetry, but this passion got in the way of his actual schoolwork, and he had come close to flunking out. Despite the young man's desultory academic performance, Norm wrote Angleton a recommendation letter for Harvard Law School, describing him as a "young man of great, and on occasion, not always practical enthusiasms . . . one of the few undergraduates who has made their mark on Yale."[53] This equivocal letter would not mark the end of their association.

Pearson was also nudging Yale itself to accept modern literature. In 1940, along with librarians Donald Gallup and Bernard Knollenberg, he assembled the Sterling Library's 1941 exhibition of its Gertrude Stein collection, selected from the extensive materials that Stein had been donating and loaning to the university for a number of years. (Gallup and Pearson had both worked on Stanley Williams's Hawthorne projects, sparking a lifelong friendship spent collecting books and manuscripts.)[54] Stein, of course, had been a key figure in Norm's intellectual and aesthetic development, and he wanted a broader public to appreciate her accomplishments. "Miss Stein deserves serious as well as loving attention," he wrote in 1941. "An academic exhibition on the part of Yale can help call her to the attention of a wider audience than she has had before."[55] But the importance of the Stein exhibit concerned more than just Stein: the exhibit was further evidence to Norm of how one could shape public opinion, and thus literary history, not just as a writer or a critic. Libraries were powerful. Objects—manuscripts, rare editions, photographs, a writer's possessions—were powerful. A collection, exhibited to the public, could make an argument just as much as an article or a monograph did.

Stein was already a celebrity, and a saint to the avant-garde, but this exhibition was pivotal in making representatives of the middlebrow literary establishment take her seriously. Thornton Wilder delivered the opening address to a "spellbound," "overflowing" crowd, and Gallup wrote later that "the interest aroused by the arrival at the Library of the first part of the Stein bequest was so great that even before it was completely sorted some of the more important items were placed on exhibition in the four cases in the main corridor. Here they attracted so much attention, particularly from the undergraduates, that the display was gradually increased and eventually filled sixteen cases." ("Dear Jesus," Pearson remarked sarcastically to William Carlos Williams, "only think of smug Yale proudly exhibiting Gertrude Stein on its Alumni Day!")[56] Columbia University then borrowed Yale's materials to mount its own equally popular show. "It has been one of the most successful exhibitions in every respect that we have had since I have been here," Knollenberg told Pearson, "and a large part of the credit is due and given to you."[57] Norm proposed a similar exhibition of the little magazines he had been collecting for Yale, and with the Yale and Columbia libraries he was also developing a plan to record albums of readings by the best modern poets.[58] The profession saw in him a Hawthorne expert in the making, but Norm had a story he wanted to tell about modern literature, and he was learning how to use institutions and side channels to tell it, and to get exposure for himself in the process.

The retail book trade was another such institution. Through his book collecting, he had come to know Frances Steloff, owner of New York's Gotham Book Mart, at the time America's best-known avant-garde bookstore, and Pearson used his friendship with Steloff to further expand his network. At a Gotham Book Mart party, Norm even met the notorious literary eccentric and cadger Joe Gould, a *New Republic* book reviewer who told everyone he met that he was completing the longest book ever written, *An Oral History of Our Times*. As attentive to a good opportunity as Pearson, Gould unsuccessfully tried to use this acquaintance to secure a paid lecture at Yale.[59]

In 1939, Steloff asked Norm for a quote about Williams for the store's twentieth-anniversary catalog, *We Moderns*. His purple blurb shows him chafing at the conventions of dusty academic writing.

William Carlos Williams is the Wordsworth of Rutherford, NJ, a Wordsworth—thank God—without the bleat. London? Paris? Rapallo? This little poet stayed home! . . . His prose is as experimental, as imaginative, as first-rate as his poetry. There are no literary snoods or form-flarers for either. I don't see how anyone can hope to understand modern writing without knowing Williams' work. I don't see how, knowing it, he can feel anything except adoration for one of America's finest writers.[60]

Steloff invited him to put together the introduction for the "Forerunners" section of the catalog, listing books by the writers who had been the inspirations for the great modernists such as Joyce and Stein and Williams. Norm put in an emphatic plug for including Bryher among the "Moderns." "Half of the list have broken her bread, her bank account, or her spirit," he told Steloff, and "she has done things that can be read—that ought to be read. In every sense of the term she is a modern. Please! Please!"[61] Steloff declined.

Pearson had also become a member of the artistic salon that Elizabeth Mayer had gathered around her in Long Island, which included a number of German writers and artists such as Lotte Jacobi and the painter Josef Scharl who, like the Mayers, had fled the Nazis. (Norm had provided a "moral affidavit" when Scharl applied for legal residency in the United States in 1940.)[62] The English pianist and composer Benjamin Britten and his partner, the tenor Peter Pears, were frequent visitors to Mayer's house after they came to America in 1939, and Pearson befriended them. Also through the Mayers, Norm met the expatriate German publishers Helen and Kurt Wolff, who would become key connections for him after the war. (In 1943, he even identified himself as the "editorial director" for their just-founded Pantheon Books, although it's unclear whether he ever did anything editorial for them in that period; if the position wasn't entirely speculative, it was certainly informal.)[63]

Through Mayer, Pearson also knew W. H. Auden, who had dedicated his 1940 poem "New Year Letter" to her. Pearson wrote Auden a recommendation letter for his application for a Guggenheim Fellowship, for a joint project with Britten, in 1941, attesting to the widespread perception that Pearson was plugged in to prestigious cultural institutions, and could influence those institutions. The letter, though, is as much about Pearson's feelings about America as it is about Auden and barely touches on Auden's actual proposal. Pearson praised the poet for having resolved to become an American citizen even before the war began, which "seems to me a conclusion not very different than that made by my Puritan ancestors in the early seventeenth century who left before the Puritan Revolution and did not return after its success."[64] (Auden won the fellowship but declined it.)

Pearson had also grown increasingly friendly with the young poet Muriel Rukeyser, a leftist whose *Theory of Flight* had won the Yale Younger Poets Prize in 1935. Norm had initially met her at a party at the Gregorys' house in January 1938 and admired her verse; she returned his enthusiasm by sending him a copy of her latest collection, *U.S. 1*, which featured the poetic sequence now considered her masterpiece, "The Book of the Dead."[65] Rukeyser considered herself a "radical," but like Gregory maintained her distance from the Stalinist / *New Masses* side of the furious literary disputes of the 1930s. She asked Norm to review F. O. Matthiessen's new book *American Renaissance* for *Decision*, a short-lived antifascist cultural magazine where she was an associate editor.[66] It wasn't the *New Republic* or the *Saturday Review*, but any chance to review Matthiessen's book was an opportunity. The brilliant "Matty," as he was known, was not much older than Pearson, but already one of the most respected scholars of American literature, widely recognized as someone who would take the field in a new direction. Much like Pearson, his interests were divided between the moderns and the writers of the period that he indelibly dubbed the "American Renaissance": Melville, Emerson, Thoreau, Whitman, and Hawthorne. His writing and scholarship, moving effortlessly between formal literary analysis and cultural history, were touchstones of early American studies. The two even shared an editor: Howard Lowry had handled *American Renaissance* for Oxford. In fact, while working on *American Renaissance*, Matthiessen had written to commend Norm on his Hawthorne volume, learn more about the Hawthorne letters and notebooks projects, and invite him to Cambridge. "I have been hearing of you and your work for years from Harvard and Yale friends like Gene O'Neill," he wrote.[67] Norm returned the invitation, but the two never met in person.

Running as it did just as the United States was about to enter the war, and only a few months after Norm's dissertation was accepted and he moved from being student to being faculty, Pearson's review of this landmark book marks a transition in his understanding of the purpose of his own academic field, and of the nature of great literature. Beginning by reiterating his English Institute argument—the importance of evaluating a work of literature's "fusion of form and content" rather than how it responds to "trends of the time, as directly social critics" do—he then moved to an interpretation of Matthiessen's work that seems almost mystical.[68] The main figures in *American Renaissance*, Pearson argues, realized that meaning in words "had more than just a level of sense, that the arrangements of words in patterns of sound and rhythm enabled them to create feelings and tones that could not be included in a logical or scientific statement." This idea—that a literary work cannot be paraphrased or boiled down to just "sense" or an argument or a statement, and that its "meaning" also included feelings and rhythms—was dogma among the formalist critics who were coming to dominate the field of literary studies.

But this isn't a formalist statement any more than his English Institute talk was. Words charged with such power become "symbols"; then the symbols are put into order by the artist, creating a "myth." "Myth," Pearson claimed, "is the common denominator of full reality, and removes the restrictions of nominalism. It destroys the distance to the past by making the words of the past represent things of the present. It particularizes the general, and generalizes the particular." ("Nominalist" here means that abstractions are merely names humans give to things that have no actual existence in the real world, and is opposed to "realism," or the belief, held by Plato and many others, that such abstractions actually exist outside of the mind. Pearson here is likely using terms he picked up from auditing an undergraduate philosophy course.)

This approach, Pearson continued, made these writers of the American Renaissance Neoplatonists: that is, they believed that there were universal truths that persisted across history, and that symbols, not pure logic, could convey those truths. This put the writers of the American Renaissance in conversation with the great modernist writers of sixty years later, such as "Mann, Yeats, Eliot, Joyce and Kafka," who are all seeking for "a common recognition of the value of myth, of the literary means by which one may give the precise description of reality." And for Pearson, "until the organic and objectively interdependent quality of existence is recognized it will remain, like our words, coreless."

So what were these writers writing about by using these myths and symbols? For Matthiessen, but even more for Pearson, it was democracy. "When they were writing with words they were dealing directly with things, and were in the highest sense the best realists. The thing dealt with in common was . . . democracy." Democracy, though, doesn't simply mean elections. For Emerson and Whitman, it meant "a land of enlarged individuals." For Thoreau, it was the idea that "man might pursue life without encumbrances." But Melville and Hawthorne, with their greater moral and tragic vision, "emerge from Matthiessen's study as the greatest figures of the American Renaissance, by virtue of their fuller comprehension of reality. All of the men reached for the center; these two approached the core."

Like his English Institute talk, Norman's review was a self-conscious attempt to thrust himself into a conversation among the leaders of the field through proposing a new direction for the field itself, one influenced equally by anthropology's and modernist literature's understanding of the power of myth. This preoccupation with myth would only grow stronger as he became a more confident and knowledgeable critic of contemporary poetry, and it was one of the reasons he, almost alone among critics, would come to argue that H.D. was perhaps the greatest of the American modernist poets. But this was also of course a performative gesture, meant to claim what Norm saw as his rightful place in the field.

Privately, Norm was no more deferential. In a letter to Matthiessen, he charged that he underplayed Emerson's Neoplatonism, and he disputed that Melville was "devoted to the possibilities of democracy." He had long felt that it was an error to read Melville as some kind of Whitmanian tribune of democratic man. Norm also audaciously criticized the "confusing" structure of Matthiessen's book: "Genius must organize or it dies," he advised, and he added that "shaping isn't cheating intellectually. Shaping is order, and order is understanding." (Matthiessen's Harvard colleague Perry Miller, another giant of the field, "has this difficulty more severely," Norm added.)[69] That's some real chutzpah here from a young man who hadn't yet written a book, and never would.

But this review, and his other writing of the time, was also an effort to articulate what was at stake in understanding American identity, what it meant to be an American, and how an academic field could transmit those values at a time when they were threatened by domestic political movements and possibly a foreign war. The key term here for Norm is "democracy." American democracy promised each citizen the right of self-determination and was grounded on the intrinsic importance of the individual. Whatever callow appeal Hitler and Nazi populism had ever held for him had long since disappeared. He was revolted on a personal level by Nazi anti-Semitism, after seeing how it had affected the Mayers, and its collectivism repelled him as much as Communism did. Although many would see him as the product of great privilege, Pearson viewed himself as ordinary and middle class. He also felt, from growing up with the children of immigrant factory workers, that he had an understanding of the American working classes, and that American-style democracy, individualism, and capitalism were the best hopes for these people to pursue "life without encumbrances." But where Communism and Nazism and even Puritanism were highly theorized and explicit about their philosophical underpinnings, American democracy wasn't. Scholars of American literature and culture — people who would pursue what would become known as "American studies" — needed to do that work, to explain to Americans what their civilization meant in order to prepare them to defend it.

For all his closeness with Fanny, among all the details of parties and plays seen and people visited in Norm's correspondence with his mother, there is rarely a mention of his romantic life. He often mentions taking dates to plays and games but rarely names them. But in spring 1940, a new person entered Norman's orbit, and his correspondence. "Tonight I'll have a little relaxation by going to hear a Haydn opera with the O'Neills and a friend of theirs," he told his mother on May 17. A week later, she gets a name: "The Haydn opera on Friday night with the O'Neills and Mrs. Tracy was very fine."[70]

"Mrs. Tracy" was Susan Silliman Bennett Tracy, a New Haven Junior League friend of Gene's second wife, Elizabeth Green. Five years older than Norman, Mrs. Tracy was also a divorcée with two daughters — Susan and Elizabeth, who were ten and six at the time. Like Norman, Susan Silliman Bennett Tracy descended from distinguished old families on both sides, but hers were closely linked with both Yale and New Haven. Her great-grandfather Oliver Fisher Winchester had served as lieutenant governor of Connecticut from 1866 to 1867 but is best known for founding the famed firearms company that bears his name. The Winchesters became one of the richest families in New England, and after Oliver died, his wife, Jane, devoted her efforts to philanthropy, including funding the construction of Winchester Hall on the Yale campus.[71]

Oliver Winchester's third child, Hannah Jane, married Thomas G. Bennett, an 1870 Yale graduate who joined the Winchester company.

With his scientific education and business talent, Bennett helped the company thrive and was central in the development and marketing of the famed Winchester Model 1873 rifle, the "Gun That Won the West." He quickly rose through the ranks and became president of the company in 1890, guiding its rapid growth.[72] "Although not as famous by name as his father-in-law," the Winchester company itself says, "it is T. G. Bennett who was responsible, in large part, for creating the firearms empire of Winchester and for making the name 'Winchester' a household word."[73] T. G. Bennett was Susan's grandfather.

Susan's father Winchester ("Win") Bennett, Thomas's second child, had taken over the presidency from 1915 to 1919. And while one might think that a war would be a great time to run a gun company, this wasn't the case. Massive contracts with the British military obliged Winchester to expand dramatically but also sell its arms below cost, and so the company unsuccessfully tried to expand into consumer products to make up the difference. The slogan "As Good as the Gun" apparently didn't sell many lunchboxes, irons, lawnmowers, or roller skates, and the pressure of presiding over a failing company drove Win Bennett into a physical and emotional breakdown and a stay in a sanatorium after the war.[74]

Susan, the oldest of Win and Susan's five children, was born in 1904 and grew up among the several Winchester and Bennett households in New Haven, which had itself become "inexorably entwined" with the Winchester Repeating Arms Company, its biggest employer by the time of the war. Her mother, Susan Silliman Bennett, was a pillar of New Haven society and avidly pursued gardening, a pastime that she passed on to her daughter Susan. The younger Susan grew up in her parents' nine-bedroom house in East Rock, one of the most desirable parts of the city. But the real center of the extended Winchester family was the "Big House," a mansion and compound overlooking Long Island Sound on Johnson's Point, near Branford, fifteen miles away. Susan attended Miss Day's School in New Haven and Smith College, graduating from the latter in 1926. By the time Norman met her, Susan was, like her mother, already well known in New Haven society, and active in the Junior League, the Colonial Dames Society, and the Lawn Club.

And although she couldn't attend Yale, of course, on her mother's side she came from a long line of Yale faculty who were instrumental in developing academic scientific research in America. Her maternal grandfather Arthur Williams Wright was the first recipient of a PhD in the United States.[75] At Yale, Wright had studied with the chemist Benjamin Silliman Jr., often considered the father of the American petroleum industry—but for our purposes, notable as Susan's great-grandfather. Both Silliman Jr. (1816–85) and his father, Benjamin Silliman Sr. (1779–1864), attended Yale and taught geology and chemistry there. (Silliman Sr. founded the *American Journal of Science*, the longest continually published scientific journal in the United States.) All three were members of the National Academy of Sciences, and hallowed names at Yale: when the residential colleges were created in the early 1930s, one of them was named for the senior Silliman. Through the Silliman line, as well, Susan was related to Jonathan Trumbull, the Revolutionary War hero and eponym of another Yale residential college.

Susan came from genuine wealth and privilege, while Norman didn't. His immediate family was certainly well-off, and by 1940 Goodnow Pearson's was starting to recover from the Depression, but the difference between being a leading family of little Gardner and being one of the industrial dynasties of New England was vast. And Norman himself, partly by choice, didn't enjoy all the comforts that the store afforded Chester, Fanny, Alfred, and Eleanor, living very much like a graduate student (albeit one who collected rare books and manuscripts). Some family investment income and dividends from the store, along with proceeds from his writing, supplemented his meager stipend, but until the later 1940s this amounted to relatively little, two or three hundred dollars a year. He often relied on family gifts and grants to cover unexpected expenses. But despite her family wealth, Susan herself didn't have a great deal of money. Her parents gave her some, but after she got married, her husband, Tom Tracy, had refused to work, and thus they ran through most of her funds. After divorcing Tracy in 1935, Susan took a job at the Yale Child Study Center, working under the eminent child psychologist Dr. Arnold Gesell.

Norm and Susan saw each other frequently over the spring and early summer of 1940 until, in late June, Norman left for a scheduled checkup with Dr. Hatcher in Chicago. In Chicago, the news from Dr. Hatcher was good; the main graft was growing "regularly and well."[76] For years, Norm had been undergoing phototherapy for his infection, using ultraviolet light to stimulate the body's immune response (and giving Norm a healthy glow, he often said), and Hatcher recommended continuing with that therapy.[77] He tacked some personal and professional tasks onto the trip as well. He "talk[ed] over various problems of American literature" with University of Chicago faculty; Horace Gregory had asked him to check in on his father in Milwaukee; Oxford University Press wanted him to promote the anthology at the University of Michigan, and Norm looked in on the progress of Michigan's planned American Studies program; and at the invitation of professor and poet Paul Engle, Norm stopped in at the recently founded Iowa Writers' Workshop.

He returned to New Haven in August, giving him only a few weeks to prepare for the English Institute, but his attention was distracted: Norm was experiencing the glow of his first serious adult relationship. Susan, too, was smitten and told her daughters that after four dates she knew that the two would marry.[78] By October Norm was spending much of his free time with "Mrs. Tracy," as he still called her in letters to his mother, and was also growing close to Lizzie and young Susan. Norman and Susan took the girls on walks in the "pheasant lot," a Winchester-owned tract in the woods near New Haven, to admire the asters, gentian, goldenrod, and wild apples. "He always used to keep chocolate in his pockets," his stepdaughter Susan remembered of those walks, "and from the time we got out of the car and started to walk we'd be tugging at his pants and asking for the chocolate, and at some point he gave it to us." He even let them help him fill in his ballot in the November elections, the selections "all Republican."[79] And although he maintained his own apartment on Cottage Street, he was also spending most of his evenings with Susan, though he never stayed the night at their house until after the two were married. When he was in New York for the institute, she wrote him sometimes twice a day, even though they spoke on the phone every night. "You can't imag-

FIGURE 6 Norm, Susan, and the girls, 1941 (Norman Holmes Pearson Papers, Yale Collection of American Literature, Beinecke Rare Book and Manuscript Library).

ine how I miss having you here in the morning," she wrote. "I feel so lost!"[80]

"Mrs. Tracy" finally became "Susan" at Thanksgiving, when Norman brought her home to Gardner to meet the family and announce their engagement. (Little Susan and Lizzie spent the holiday with their father.) Susan easily won Fanny and Chester's approval. And even if they were ambivalent about him marrying a divorced mother of two, they certainly approved of the jump in social status it meant for Norm to become part of the Winchester clan.[81] Later, Norm also joked about the match between these two children of multiple illustrious New England lineages: "I felt that since [my] family had come from such a long line of Massachusetts people, I had to break out and marry someone from the West . . . a New Havener."[82]

With the couple now publicly affianced, society opened to Norm. At a Lawn Club badminton tournament Norman found himself the "prize exhibit. It seemed to me that half of New Haven must have come up and asked if I was their new cousin; and if I could ever keep straight the names of all my relations-in-law I'd be a genius." Susan and Norman started going to her parents' for lunch every Sunday, and he was "extremely pleased" that they were starting to see him as a member of the family. In January, they brought the girls to Gardner to meet his family, leading Lizzie to conclude that Gardner English was different from her native dialect.[83]

Momentous news came in late January: Norman was offered, and this time accepted, a job in Yale's English department. It was a more attractive offer than the one tendered in 1939. While it was a one-year job, it would almost certainly roll into a second year, and then into an assistant professorship, which meant that he would enter the tenure track and potentially indefinite employment. His salary was $2,500—the maximum for an instructor. He would have to complete and defend his dissertation before starting, but that project was almost complete (and in June 1941 was formally accepted by the department). "I hope nothing will seem to have quite the same pressure in the future," he told Fanny about the mad rush to finish his dissertation and plan a wedding.[84]

That problem sorted, the rest of his life slipped into place. He and Susan would live in her house; they would not have to deal with the hassle of moving to some other college town or finding schools for the girls. There would be family around to support them. Norman and Susan thus decided to get married as soon as possible—February 21, in just three weeks! This allowed for only a small ceremony, held at Susan's parents' house and officiated, appropriately enough for Yankees like the Bennetts and Sillimans and Pearsons and Kittredges, by a "distinguished old Congregationalist minister."[85]

Norm was ecstatic about his new married life, glowing about it in letters to friends and reporting to the Andover alumni newsletter that "I have become a confirmed Calvinist now that I know I am one of God's elect."[86] To William Carlos Williams, he was even more effusive: "I already feel very much the family man, very cock-'o-the-walk, very kitten with tongue in a bowl of cream. Not only am I getting a very swell gal, but two sweet little girls, of six and nine, thrown in for God's good measure. It's one of those times when you walk into an open door and find yourself quite unexpectedly at home. God, it's good!"[87] There was friction, though, from Tom Tracy and his father, John, a professor in Yale's civil-engineering department. Tom at first was amenable to Susan's burgeoning romance and Norman's presence in the girls' lives. A sense of this comes through in Norman's description of Thanksgiving 1940. "The day with their father," he wrote, "was a little of a strain on them, and our good-night kisses established a family feeling again. But their father was very good to them about me, told them that he was glad for their sake, and that they would need a father in their home. For which I am grateful."[88] But things soon turned more contentious over which name the girls would use. Little Susan had mused to a teacher about whether Norman would make them change their names from Tracy to Pearson. He wouldn't, he assured her; but their mother would not keep her own name, of course. When it dawned on Susan that she wouldn't have the same last name as her mother, she started to reconsider and reported to Norman that she'd allow her close friends to call her Susan *Pearson*, which Norm had hoped for. "They'll come around," Norman told his mother, "particularly if we have another child, and that's the best way."[89]

But the Tracys were not coming around. The week before the wedding, Tom protested the idea of changing his daughters' last name and threatened a lawsuit. Norm calmly but firmly responded that the girls had independently chosen to adopt the Pearson name. "Shall I tell them," he asked, "that you object to this situation? It will be a terrific blow to them, and rob them of the sense of security to which they have been growing accustomed, and to which in all eagerness they have been looking forward." A lawsuit, Norman warned, would "torture their spirits and split their personalities. It would make them hunted instead of loved." He concluded by explaining that the name change would be "by use" only—that there would be no *legal* change of their name.[90]

A polite but firm telegraph the next day—Norman and Susan's wedding eve—reiterated Tracy's objection. Nor did the wedding put an end to this dispute. Two weeks later, John Tracy sent an aggressive letter of his own, copied to Susan's parents, accusing Susan of trying to "conceal" her marriage to Tom and claiming that this name change "takes something precious from" his son. "The argument that the change of name will contribute to the unity of the Pearson family seems to me to be naive and a bit of wishful thinking," he snorted, and then added, cattily, that there was "widespread criticism" of the couple's behavior among New Haven society.[91] Susan stayed quiet throughout this dispute but certainly burned with resentment and anger at the Tracys' imperiousness. Her marriage with Tom had been miserable. He was such a sponger that, as a condition of the divorce, he insisted that she reimburse his half-ownership of a house and car that she had entirely paid for herself and then registered in both of their names.[92] Ultimately, Norman and Susan agreed to wait until the fall, and the new school year, to start using "Pearson" with the girls' names.

Tom Tracy's estrangement from his daughters only grew over the years, and he grew ever more spiteful toward Norm. But this push for adoption, the sense that he was trying to supplant their real father, initially turned the girls against Norm. "Liz and I got more and more resistant," Sue Addiss said later, "and during our teen years we gave him a rough time. . . . We just treated him horribly." The episode hurt Norm, too, and roused an emotion that he rarely displayed: anger. Norm vented to Bryher, calling Tom "an unbelievable swine and a sworn enemy of mine, who will stop at nothing to disaffect these girls from me. It is not so much that he cares for them, as that he hates me for Susan's affection. She divorced him and he sees me in that succeeding where he so miserably failed."[93]

Norm was going through one of the most eventful times of his personal and professional life, but of course the nation and the world were also in turmoil in 1940–41, as the Nazi war machine overran Europe, and the United States struggled to decide how or whether to support its friends in France and Great Britain. For years, Norm had held a strong pro-Allied position at odds with many of his peers at Yale, a stronghold of isolationist opinion. Yale was the site of the founding of the America First Committee, the largest and most influential isolationist political group, and many prominent Yalies (including future university president Kingman Brewster) were among its early members. New England Republicans, especially elites, tended to oppose involvement in the European war.[94]

It was a long journey from what Norm had felt in Europe back in 1932 and 1933, watching with interest, and some degree of attraction, as Germany became fascist. Many of the English aristocrats he encountered at Magdalen had been sympathetic to the Nazis and to the British Union of Fascists. But by the mid-1930s he wanted Britain to be even more aggressive in countering Hitler. "I have become very strongly anti-Chamberlain [and] I cannot understand how Britain is willing to endure this kind of suicide," he wrote in November 1938.[95] By the late 1930s, he was thoroughly antifascist. "The fall of Barcelona is a grievous thing," he lamented to Gregory in 1939. "Have we begun an era of rendering unto Mussolini that which was Caesar's?"[96] When war came that September, he wanted the United States to get involved on the Allied side—immediately. His friendship with the Mayers and role in helping them escape Germany had also forced him to acknowledge the reality of that nation's institutional anti-Semitism (and begin to leave behind his own). By 1938 there was no ambivalence in his feelings: the Nazis were simply evil, and even American figures like radio commentator Charles Coughlin, who echoed Nazi-style anti-Semitism, were "poisonous."[97]

The time he had spent trying to understand the American character and the nature of democracy had also erased his brief attraction to fascism. In a diary entry dated September 3, 1939, Norm had reflected on the start of the war, weighing the two sides and remarking on the experience of being bombarded by the news from the radio and "newsboys outside my apartment all day: hi-yi—read all about it—war declared—read all about it—extra, extra." He has come to a new understanding of what is at stake, he writes. This will be a confrontation between passion and reluctance, spectacle and introspection, emotion and restraint.

On Friday [September 1, the day Hitler invaded Poland] I heard a transcript of Hitler's speech before the Reichstag. Perhaps if I had been already in agreement with him I would have thought it the words of the Son of God. As it was it was shouted, cursed, and raged by a mad Lucifer. The wildest moments of the speech I once heard at the Circuskrone in Munich were multiplied to every breathing space, every sentence, every paragraph. But Chamberlain's speech from Downing Street . . . was simply uttered, in a dignified manner . . . full of honest emotion which gave me a cold grip about the heart that I have only rarely felt. King George's speech . . . too was a dignified appeal, simply given, directly stated. . . . I prefer to lend my support to the side whose tradition leads it to enter war with dignity and reluctance.[98]

Interestingly, in neither reflection does Pearson mention much of the *substance* of Hitler's rhetoric. Instead, the very thing that enticed Pearson in 1932 repels him in 1939: the emotional rawness of Hitler's delivery, which in the end strikes Pearson as a mad demagogic performance, lacking in the sincerity and honesty and "dignity" of Chamberlain's and King George's own speeches. Looking back seven years, he felt that he had matured through his studies, and come into his birthright as the very avatar of these values, self-consciously carrying his Puritan inheritance.

Bryher also stoked Norm's pro-British and anti-Nazi feelings. From her home at Kenwin in Switzerland, she had been using her money, connections, and mobility to help refugees — especially artists, writers, and members of the psychoanalytic profession — escape the "mass cruelty" in Germany, Austria, Czechoslovakia, and elsewhere, which was getting worse. "Nothing that happened in Berlin in 1933 touches what has happened in Vienna [after the Anschluss]," she told Norm in May 1938.[99] In November 1939, H.D. returned to London while Bryher chose to stay. But as the threat of a German invasion of Switzerland, and of her own capture and torture for acting as a British agent, grew through 1940, she obtained French, Spanish, and Portuguese transit visas and fled for London. She arrived on September 28, 1940, just in time to endure the worst of the Blitz, and described the harrowing experience in a number of letters:

We sleep downstairs on mattresses, while . . . the house rocks like the *Normandie* in a gale. . . . Shells whistling, guns thundering, one thinks nothing can survive the night and crawls up from the basement to listen to the early news and our dear BBC says, "last night's attacks were on a somewhat smaller scale than usual."

We have to cook supper by the light of one candle. We have to eat it early so as not to swallow it hastily with gunfire overhead as that, oddly enough, is enough to make one sick if one combines it with food.

Most people here . . . are annoyed, or angry, or bored, but they are certainly confident and sure of themselves. . . . The more the small houses are knocked about, the more eager the people are to fight back, nobody has weakened yet that I've heard.

"I loathe this war," she wrote him in January 1941. "I knew it was coming and nobody would listen to me."[100] But she wasn't going to let the war get in the way of literature: all through the conflict, she and H.D. wrote frantically, and she and Robert Herring kept publishing their literary magazine *Life and Letters*, even though it had to relocate when the offices were bombed.

Once the war began, Pearson wanted to join up, telling Fletcher in May 1940 that "I should throw aside this academic life of mine, and become the man of action that the scholar and the poet were once supposed to be." He decried how the literary left, under the influence of the Communist Party (and Stalin's pact with Hitler), now opposed US entry into the war: "The boys in the League of American Writers who used to cry for intervention in Spain, who used to prate of writers as legislators of the universe now sanction such statements as 'Remember, poetry by its very nature is opposed to war.' . . . Surely there must be some things in the world worth fighting for! Some referent by which we can decide our action! Or is the aesthetic of evil a sufficient solace for the presence of evil?"[101]

Even before Pearl Harbor, Yale's sense of national obligation had started to erode the isolationist sentiment on campus, and in 1940 President Charles Seymour wrote that "we must all of us, students and professors, recognize that whatever demands the necessities of national defense lay upon us, they are paramount." Yale had already begun mobilizing in support of Great Britain, hosting the families of Oxford faculty members who fled the country. The Yale medical and nursing schools began collaborating with military medical units, and over a hundred faculty members were called into service. Students lost their draft deferments in July 1941, leaving many "gaunt, unshaven, and hollow-eyed" with worry, in the words of the *Yale Alumni Magazine*.[102]

Norm, though, was relieved, even celebratory, when on December 7 what he had long considered "inevitable" finally came. "The War is on," he wrote Elizabeth Mayer, "and I am glad because things will be lined up if not straightened out. War is here; and Christmas too. A Merry Christmas to you all, and a Successful War Year."[103] Because of its thriving small-arms industry, after the declarations of war against Japan and Germany on December 8 and 11, New Haven was immediately on alert, with blackouts every night. Few Yale men immediately enlisted, but Norm knew that "many will not come back after Christmas." And only days after the declaration of war, one faculty member had already been drafted.[104]

Because of a rule stating that no faculty member who goes off to war could be replaced, and the university's transition to a wartime twelve-month calendar of classes, Norm foresaw major changes in his working conditions but assumed that his job would be safe. Just a few days later, though, his outlook was much less sanguine, as Yale announced that it planned to lay off everyone below the rank of assistant professor. "I shall keep this job if I can [but] if I'm out here," he told his mother,

> then I will . . . get into one form or other of the service. By pulling wires I think I can arrange to get a desk job somewhere, or sign up for some medical unit. . . . The whole thing will simply be an unpleasant interruption of my career and married life, but certainly no worse for me or for Susan than for thousands of other families in the country. It

will be worth it if we can only win the war; and if we don't, or the war drags on too long, there won't be any private universities anyhow.[105]

As it turned out, though, Norm wasn't laid off and instead took over responsibilities for faculty members who had gone into the service. "I've never had my days so full," he told Rukeyser. "A class to teach, thirty boys to prepare on all of English literature for their comprehensives, and a bunch to advise for their military service, and the Jonathan Edwards library to buy for, etc., etc."[106] Yale, also, became a different place. Its undergraduate population plummeted to only 565 by the middle of the war, the university rented out seven of the ten residential colleges to the military, and the Army Air Force instituted a training camp on campus. It became, in many ways, a military installation.

With fewer students to teach, the academic departments needed something to do. Pearson, the junior man in English, was assigned to see what other departments across the country were doing to "be of some use in the war effort." This was partly an exercise in self-preservation. If they could not explain how they were "capable of rendering services" to the nation in wartime, these departments would be forced by their administrations to "release the younger members of the English departments who are for one reason or another not taken by the draft": in other words, men like Norm would lose their jobs.[107] But even if his job was in jeopardy, his profile was rising in Yale's rump wartime community. He made his first formal public appearance as a faculty member in February and was also made a fellow of one of the residential colleges, Jonathan Edwards. The anthology had also sold enough of its initial five-thousand-copy run that, by mid-1941, Oxford had ordered a second printing.[108] Even though he would have preferred to be serving his country, professionally things were going quite well for him.

This wasn't true, though, in his personal life. Tom Tracy continued to make trouble, and the girls began resisting their father's role in their lives. Dr. Hatcher had summoned Norm to Chicago for a checkup in June and after examination performed a minor surgery, though Norm was back home in July. There were also problems in Gardner. In April,

Eleanor lost her newborn baby and was battling depression. After a suicide attempt in October she was hospitalized. Norm immediately called on Dr. Mayer, who brought Eleanor to Amityville for evaluation and, eventually, residential treatment in the Long Island Home. This caused him to reflect on the nature of friendship and service, and, perhaps, on the ripple effects of his networking and his drive to do favors for others. "How fortunate we are to be able to call on the Mayers at this time," Norm observed to his mother, "and how the wheel of fortune turns."[109]

+ 6 +

THE PURITAN GOES TO WAR

Only days after Pearl Harbor, Norm was itching to get into the war, to "help get the boil over with so that peace might be established," as he explained to Fanny. He was classified 3-A (family hardship) in the draft, and because of his disability even volunteering for the armed services was likely out, but he hoped that he would be able to find a way to contribute something "of very real importance."[1] And in 1942, Pearson finally had his chance, through the intercession of Donald Downes, a graduate school friend since 1934.[2] Like Norm impatient to get involved in the fight, Downes had, in contravention of a number of American laws, joined British intelligence in 1939 and was quickly posted to Istanbul. From there, he went everywhere and, in the summer of 1941, regaled Norm with stories of his escapades in Beirut, Greece, Damascus, the Balkans, Iraq, Egypt, Java, and South Africa.[3] (Downes was back in New Haven partly on assignment, in fact: his handler in British Security Coordination had asked him to sniff out potential German agents on the America First Committee.)[4]

When President Roosevelt created the Coordinator of Information (COI) foreign intelligence agency in the summer of 1941, Downes immediately reached out to its director, General William Donovan, to express his interest in joining but ultimately remained with the British until after Pearl Harbor. Hyperactive and indiscreet, gay and overweight, Downes presented some liabilities as a field intelligence officer, especially to the buttoned-down types who built the COI and then transformed it into the Office for Strategic Services (OSS). But Downes was also immensely energetic, brave, and creative, and a top-notch talent scout, especially for unlikely types like himself. Downes understood that Pearson—who appeared to most like a frail and crippled professor—would bring genuine assets to an intelligence agency.

For almost a year, Norm did piecework for Downes, such as investigating a suspected German spy in New Haven and recruiting a Portuguese-speaking faculty member.[5] In the summer of 1942, Downes and Wallace Notestein, a distinguished history professor, concocted a plan by which Yale would send a professor to Switzerland ostensibly to "collect materials for the library's War Collection," but who would spy for the OSS among the aristocrats and book dealers of Geneva and Zurich. The library would be told that an anonymous donor was financing acquisitions, but in reality this person would be paid by OSS. Norm seemed perfect for the job. "I hope you will give Notey the opportunity to tell you in what connection we discussed your possibly going far afield on a war job," Downes prodded Pearson from Mexico in August. "I would prefer not to put it in type."[6]

"Notey," as it turned out, ultimately decided that another Yale man would be better suited, as his German was superior. But Downes and Notey continued to try and find a place for Norm. While on vacation in Quebec in October 1942, Pearson received an urgent phone call at his hotel, ordering him to report to Washington for an interview with the OSS. "I ought to warn you not to be too surprised if FBI men or otherwise turn up in Gardner to investigate me," he told his mother after the interview. After eight weeks with no offer, though, he reasoned that OSS had found someone "better qualified." But just a few weeks later, he received a cryptic letter from David Seiferheld in the OSS's Secret Intelligence branch. "Our friend Donald Downes has mentioned you in connection with some work that is now being undertaken down here. . . . You would be eminently qualified," Seiferheld wrote. (Norm's background check recommended him "most highly as to loyalty, ability, and personal character.") Soon he was asking for a leave of absence from Yale. "I have been offered a position with the office of Strategic Services," he explained to Fanny, "and I am accepting it as the only kind of draft to which I can respond. The work I shall do will be of a confidential nature, but will not . . . take me out of the country."[7]

At first this was true. Just before Christmas, he reported to Washington, DC, where he became an "Assistant Editor" in the censor unit, part of the OSS's Research and Analysis branch. This unit didn't actually censor anything but rather read materials that censors of other Allied nations had flagged, particularly correspondence between Europe and South America, and noted anything potentially important on an index card. These cards, in turn, joined a growing "card index" whose awe-inspiring comprehensiveness soon became "the talk of Washington" and certainly appealed to the collector in Norm.[8] It was interesting work, aligning with Norm's training as a scholarly researcher and his talent for drawing unexpected connections between seemingly random details. "I enjoy my work a great deal, find it possibly useful in the war effort, and at any rate more satisfactory than teaching *Romeo and Juliet* to freshmen," he told Fanny. But this work did definitively convince him that a career as a civil servant, with its petty "jealousies" and "needling" and "wasted effort," held no appeal.[9]

Some of that "needling" came from Wilmarth "Lefty" Lewis, the fussy and haughty chief of the Central Intelligence Division (CID), who like Pearson came to OSS from academia. One of many aristocrats loosely attached to Yale, Lewis saw as his life's work collecting, editing, and publishing Horace Walpole's complete correspondence. And he did so: by 1942 several volumes had already appeared from Yale University Press. Pearson knew Lewis and was aware of the parallels between their scholarly projects, and how Lewis's wealth and connections had brought his so much further along. The two had directly clashed in 1942 when Pearson had, perhaps unadvisedly, stuck his neck out on an issue of faculty politics of importance to Lewis.[10] Personal animus then charged the bureaucratic rivalry between the men's respective branches of OSS, and Pearson "soon found that he could not get along with Lefty Lewis, and perhaps did not want to."[11]

Office politics were aggravating, and he was sad to be separated from Susan and the girls so soon after their wedding, but Washington was in other ways a pleasant reunion. He roomed with Steve Morris in his Georgetown townhouse and soon discovered that his childhood buddy Bill Weedon was also working in intelligence in Washington. At the time of Pearl Harbor the OSS had six hundred employees working in a cluster of buildings just northwest of the Lincoln Memorial.[12] A year later, when Pearson joined, its ranks had more than tripled, and it had become a large and lively community. No doubt Norm encountered many others whom he knew from his networking, as OSS was well stocked with academics, and its analytical offices especially were "something of a branch of the Harvard and Yale humanities divisions," as Michael Holzman has noted.[13]

Research and Analysis in particular—wryly dubbed the OSS's "Chairborne Division"—"came to shelter a community of scholars without precedent in modern intellectual history," according to OSS historian Barry Katz, who put these scholars in three broad strains: midcareer established scholars, "broadly conservative in political outlook but motivated by a fierce detestation of fascist regimes" and an eagerness to contribute to the war effort; graduate students and younger scholars like Pearson, "who would redirect the course of postwar scholarship in a dozen disciplines"; and what he calls "the community of the uprooted," exiles and refugees who wanted to bring down the Nazi regime. As was the academy at the time, these scholars were overwhelmingly male. But women played important roles in R&A, as in the OSS more broadly, in the form of "a women's army corps of typists, secretaries, and filing clerks whom Donovan patronizingly called 'the invisible apron strings of an organization which touched every theater of war.'" (Not all OSS women were relegated to clerical roles; the future television chef Julia Child worked in Asia and with the Emergency Sea Rescue Equipment Section, where she helped develop shark repellent.)[14]

Within two months, OSS's talent spotters had taken notice of this skinny, lopsided man who arrived forty-five minutes early to work every day (owing less to dedication than the schedule of his carpool), and who exhibited an exceptionally sharp intelligence, instinctive collegiality, language skills, and comfort with British aristocrats. "He combined penetrating insight with an abundance of social grace," as Tim Naftali aptly put it.[15] He might, though, have overplayed his own worldliness. In a biographical statement, Pearson noted that "when I was at Oxford, I was there not as a Rhodes scholar but on my own resources. I made many friends in England, political and social, with whom I have continued to maintain relationships. . . . In Germany I lived not only in Berlin and Munich but I had my country place at Starnberger and I lived also in Vienna. I am reasonably familiar with Germany, Austria, Czechoslovakia, France, and Spain. During the summer of 1927 I was in North Africa, Greece, Turkey, Egypt, and the Near East."[16]

While this statement is mostly, technically, true, Pearson's experience in "North Africa, Greece, Turkey, Egypt, and the Near East" was in ports of call on a pleasure cruise with his parents, and his French and Spanish sojourns were on his 1933 driving tour with Steve Morris. But a good spy can fake it. His English connections "should keep him contented in the country," the OSS personnel evaluator remarked, and his *Mitteleuropean* experience and facility with German were "all to the good." "His training seems good for the work and his background should contribute," the evaluator concluded.[17]

By late February 1943, Donovan had informed Pearson that he would be sent overseas on an unspecified mission for a new branch of the OSS. This pleased him enormously. He would be returning to England, making an active contribution to the war effort, and escaping Washington's petty politics. Donovan wrote the draft board on March 1 requesting that Pearson be permitted to leave the country "on a confidential mission for [my] organization." Pearson and his team took the OSS field training course outside Washington in early March, and he showed himself to be unexpectedly adroit at small arms and hand-to-hand combat—the instructor commented that Pearson had an "unusually strong grip."[18]

"How long I'll be away I don't know," Norm informed his mother. "I may get back occasionally for liaison, but otherwise I suppose it will be for the duration." Susan was "a wonderful sport about it," although she, like Fanny, certainly must have feared for Norm, given his health problems and, of course, the war. "The job is not spectacular," he added, "but should be even more interesting than what I have been doing. . . . There's no danger; people come and go all the time. And I am in a way proud to be able to help, and proud too to be thought worth sending over."[19] He wouldn't be lonely there, either. Susan's sister Molly and her husband, Humphry Trevelyan, a Cambridge professor, lived in London, where Humphry was with the Foreign Office; Bill Sweet had been transferred to a hospital near Oxford; and H.D. and Bryher were in London. Auden told him to look up his father if he ever found himself in Birmingham.[20] Although most of his salary ($5,000, double what he was earning at Yale) would go to Susan, he would also enjoy $2,600 a year in living expenses, and an entertainment account. The team even had its own cook.

Donovan had tapped his lawyer friend James Murphy to head this new group, and Murphy departed for England to find quarters in March, soon followed by several others, including Captain John McDonough, a Rhodes Scholar and former University of Chicago quarterback. Bureaucratic snags delayed the departure of civilians Dana Durand and Pearson, but on April 9, they left for England on a "thrilling" series of hops through Bermuda, the Azores, Lisbon, and Foynes and Shannon in Ireland, before finally to Bristol, where they arrived four days later, on Pearson's thirty-fourth birthday.[21] His long training and apprenticeship finished, Pearson would now see what he could do with the skills he had been so diligently developing his whole life, even though he never would have expected that he would use them in quite this way.

After landing in Bristol, Pearson and Durand—soon joined by Murphy, McDonough, Hubert Will, and Robert Blum (another Yale faculty member)—were escorted to the headquarters of Section V, British military intelligence (MI6)'s counterespionage division, at St. Albans, near London, where they learned the real purpose of their unit. The OSS's team been created specifically to handle the information produced by the British ULTRA program, which collected, processed, and guarded so-called signals intelligence—radio and telegraph messages. ULTRA's most precious intelligence came from intercepts of messages generated by the Germans' fiendishly elusive Enigma coding machine, whose codes the British had broken in 1940 through the heroic efforts of Alan Turing and his team of cryptanalysts at the Bletchley Park compound. The British were determined to conceal that the Enigma codes had been compromised, in order to ensure the Germans continued using the system. As a result, the ULTRA program was extraordinarily tightfisted about who could have access to the intelligence gleaned from Enigma decodes.

Even after Pearl Harbor, MI6 had refused American intelligence services access to ULTRA material. But Donovan had learned that the Brits had some sort of intelligence goldmine and in 1942 sent his special assistant George Bowden to Bletchley Park to suss it out. After much negotiation, in December 1942 the British agreed to share this information but only with a small and exclusive team, and thus Donovan offered to create a special division within OSS specifically to handle this intelligence and carefully parcel it out. This division would be the sole link between the British and American counterespionage services and would receive not only the precious ULTRA decrypts but also access to, and the right to copy, British intelligence's own legendary card catalogs—hundreds of thousands of names of spies and subversives and suspects.[22] To establish this collaboration, Murphy had to agree to adopt British security practices for this new branch, even segregating its communications from those of other OSS branches. This arrangement had advantages for the British, as well, who knew that the Americans had the resources and determination to build the largest intelligence agency in the Western world, and (as Naftali explains) "participation in its formative period would align British intelligence with its counterpart."[23] Because it had access to the most secret and consequential intelligence in the European theater, X-2 would become "an elite within an elite," whose officers would hold veto power even over the undertakings of the Secret Intelligence and Secret Operations branches of OSS.[24]

The branch received its moniker when Pearson suggested that "X-2" would stand out in the alphabet soup of government agencies, and rhyme with British counterparts such as "X-B" (the Secret Intelligence

Service's [SIS] counterintelligence team) or the "XX Committee," the high-level Committee of Twenty that oversaw counterespionage, intelligence gathering, and disinformation. (Later, both the British and the Americans would get much mileage from how both X-2 and XX could also mean "double-crossing.") But even beyond its name, X-2's character was shaped by Pearson as much as by Murphy or Donovan. His keen intelligence and facility with textual interpretation became crucial qualifications for X-2 agents, who needed to analyze ambiguous information, and so the branch sought out highly educated humanities professors and students trained in that kind of work. But Pearson's "soft" skills also marked the agency from its conception. The British intelligence services were the province of the upper classes, and its agents could be aloof, insular, and snobbish. In order for the British to trust them, these Americans had to be accepted not just professionally but socially. Pearson was already deft at cultivating and winning over people who assumed themselves superior to him, and he knew the folkways and predilections of the English upper crust, while never seeming to presume to be *of* them: he did not try to hide his middle-class, colonial identity and always affected a self-deprecating deference. Still, he employed some subtle tricks for establishing his own status. As he held no military rank, he insisted on being called "Professor" rather than "Doctor," for he knew that at Oxbridge "Professor" referred to a high-ranking senior faculty member, while "Doctor" was rarely used and subtly denigrated.[25]

Over the spring and summer of 1943, Pearson and the rest of the team lodged in two farmer's cottages in the tiny village of Ayot St. Lawrence, about thirty miles southeast of Bletchley and an equal distance north of central London. There, they intensely studied counterintelligence practice and mapped out the structure for X-2. By early June, Murphy's departure for North Africa to take part in Operation TORCH made Pearson the de facto chief of the unit, for he was already the primary liaison with MI6's counterespionage chief Felix Cowgill. Country life could be idyllic. They ate better than Londoners because local markets and their own gardens provided them with fresh vegetables like

FIGURE 7   Norm, Dana Durand, and John McDonough trying on gas masks, Ayot St. Lawrence, 1943 (Norman Holmes Pearson Papers, Yale Collection of American Literature, Beinecke Rare Book and Manuscript Library).

cauliflower, asparagus, tomatoes, and brussels sprouts, which Durand used to prepare dinners. For his part, Norm used the garden's endless rhubarb to make breakfasts and tarts. "The other boys are sick of it," he told his mother after several weeks, "but I can still take it." In the air, they listened to the RAF's Flying Fortress bombers bound for Germany, and on the wireless they listened to William "Lord Haw-Haw" Joyce, an Englishman who conducted pro-Nazi propaganda broadcasts. They played a weekly cricket match — Norm attempted to keep score — and drank warm pints at the Brockett Arms pub. Learning that George Bernard Shaw lived in the village, Pearson lightheartedly staked his house out until he finally witnessed the great gray eminence emerge into his garden. On weekends, Norm would travel down to bombed-out, blacked-out London to see the Trevelyans and the theater productions that the English stubbornly insisted on staging in the devastated city, including John Gielgud in Congreve's *Love for Love* and operas like *Rigoletto* and *The Marriage of Figaro*. If there hadn't been a war going on, it would have been an enviable vacation. "After the jealousies of Washington, and all the wasted effort that went on there," he wrote Fanny, "this seems like a complete paradise."[26]

Nor did his literary networking cease. He had just missed the defiant April 14, 1943, Reading of Famous Poets in London—a benefit for the Free French organized by Edith Sitwell and featuring H.D., T. S. Eliot, the Sitwells, and many others—but rushed down to see H.D. and Bryher within his first month in England. His close rapport with Bryher immediately resumed. "I feel immediately at ease. . . . One had the feeling of our having been separated only a few weeks at best, and that one picked up the conversation where it had been dropped before," he wrote her afterward. To Hilda, he simply said that "you and Bryher must be my suns." Bryher shared his sentiments, gushing after his first visit that "it was hard to believe that you were really here. . . . It was hard to calm down for the rest of the day."[27] His arrival in England transformed his relationship with the women. Perdita Aldington, H.D.'s biological daughter (and Bryher's adoptive daughter), remembered how the previous "formal businesslike" relationship between Pearson and her mother changed immediately into "a new rapport—instantaneous, total and mutual. He became a confidant and mentor."[28] He also eased some of the tension roiling between H.D. and Bryher, who were living together for the first time and felt "trapped and frustrated" at being "thrown together, day and night, in close quarters," Perdita recalled. Pearson energized the women for their work, "gave them focus. They had someone to write for, rather than an anonymous unresponsive public."[29] (Perdita didn't live at Lowndes Square, but she worked with Pearson: while still in Washington a year before, he had pulled OSS strings to get her a job at Bletchley, and once he set up shop in London he had her transferred to his department, where she could be closer to her two mothers.)

Pearson soon added to his circle of friends and contacts. On that May 1943 visit, Bryher introduced him to her *Life and Letters* coeditor Herring and other members of their London literary circle such as Norman Douglas, Faith Compton Mackenzie, and the Sitwells. In Bletchley, he had also befriended the cryptographer Oliver Strachey—

brother of *Eminent Victorians* author Lytton Strachey—and they discovered that they had a common friend in Benjamin Britten. Pearson often went to Britten's flat to listen to Britten and Strachey play. At a Reform Club lunch, E. M. Forster begged Pearson's opinion of his still-unpublished gay novel *Maurice*.[30] Pearson didn't only socialize with queer writers and artists: he also met T. S. Eliot at his club, but the stuffy Eliot and the puckish Pearson didn't particularly hit it off. The collecting continued, as well. Pearson obtained from Bryher a complete run of *Close-Up*, the film magazine she had edited with Macpherson in the late 1920s and early 1930s, for the Yale library, and Bryher brought him to the famed antiquarian bookstore Maggs, a "dangerous" place for her because she always left with armloads of "late Elizabethan quartos" and early editions of Renaissance playwrights Beaumont and Fletcher. (Most of these books would eventually make their way to Pearson's own collection and, finally, to Yale.)

The bucolic interval soon ended, though, and the real work began. X-2's official date of birth was June 15, 1943, when General Order 13 established the new branch's responsibilities:

1. To collect from every authorized source appropriate intelligence data concerning espionage and subversive activities of the enemy
2. To analyze and process such intelligence
3. To institute such measures as may be necessary to protect the operational security of OSS
4. To cooperate with the counterintelligence agencies of the United States and our Allies
5. To prepare secret lists of subversive personalities.[31]

In short, X-2 would be charged with helping to ferret out German spies in Allied territory in Europe, using both American intelligence and whatever intelligence the British were willing to share. Admittedly, in mid-1943, this didn't amount to much territory: the Nazi empire controlled the entire continent, with the exception of neutral Sweden, Switzerland, Spain, and Portugal, and the only Allied nation still standing was Britain. But this would soon change, and Pearson—the primary liaison between OSS, the ULTRA team at Bletchley Park, and MI6 Section V—thus found himself a key player in the American war effort in the European theater of operations. (Because of the bitter rivalry between Donovan and J. Edgar Hoover of the FBI, OSS was not allowed to operate in the Americas, and General Douglas MacArthur refused to allow OSS into the Pacific theater until 1944.)

Fearing that ULTRA information would be lost or intercepted traveling between OSS's headquarters in Washington and England, the British insisted that X-2's operational offices remain in the UK.[32] On July 18, then, the team moved to London, where Pearson, Durand, McDonough, and Blum were allocated cramped offices at 7 Ryder Street, a "shabby, grotesque, Victorian layer-cake" pile with a roof badly damaged from German bombing, near St. James's Square.[33] X-2's offices were on the top floor "because it was closest to the air raids," the staff joked. Although the team remained small, throughout the fall it gradually grew to several dozen officers, mostly professors or lawyers. "Of the two," Pearson quipped later, "I preferred the lawyers because they had been trained to make up their minds, while the professors preferred to meditate."[34]

With other X-2 men, Pearson shared a house and flat in Belgravia and hired a neighborhood woman, Alice Hitchcock, as a housekeeper and cook—"a good soul, unmarried, about fifty-five, and full of attention and devotion," he told Fanny.[35] (Alice appears to have been in a "Boston marriage," and as she became comfortable with Pearson she shared details about her life with her partner, Queenie.) Pearson would take his dinners either at the officers' mess or at one of the many gentlemen's clubs in Mayfair. "I rather like the high-ceilinged solemnity of these meeting-houses," he told his mother, "the dark library windows where the clubmen sit looking out at hoi polloi passing on the sidewalks; the voices never above a whisper; the dining rooms where one cannot smoke until after seven-thirty in the evening." This access to upper-class London life thrilled the Anglophile in Pearson, and he not only soaked up the experience but put it to use in his dealing with his MI6 counterparts.

While the small team continued to assemble the infrastructure for

X-2, establish satellite stations outside of Britain, and prepare for expansion, Pearson received a summons to join one of the most secret bodies in the UK. The Twenty Committee consisted of high-level officials from British military intelligence, MI5 (the domestic security service), Home Forces, and others. Beginning in 1941, by using ULTRA decrypts as well as human sources, the Twenty Committee and its agents had succeeded in identifying every German spy operating in British territory. In what came to be called the "Double-Cross System," instead of merely imprisoning or executing these spies the British flipped them, converting them into double agents. These double agents, then, could be used to feed disinformation to the Germans, as well as to supplement the information from the ULTRA decrypts. Over the course of the war, the British turned 120 Nazi spies into double agents, accounting for the vast majority of all agents that the Abwehr, the German military intelligence organization, had sent into Great Britain. (The remainder were executed or jailed.) By 1943, "we actively ran and controlled the German espionage system" in the United Kingdom, John Masterman, the Twenty Committee's head, boasted afterward.[36] Pearson himself noted, pithily, that "one is not frightened of an 'enemy's' or 'friend's' intelligence service so long as it is gelded."[37] In addition to double-crossing, the Twenty Committee had developed successful deception campaigns such as Operation MINCEMEAT, which misled the Germans about the plans for the invasion of Sicily through fake documents planted on an English corpse washed up in Spain. By the time Pearson joined the committee it was producing disinformation to persuade the Germans that the planned OVERLORD invasion of Normandy would take place near Calais and be spearheaded by an entirely fictional "First US Army Group" headed by General George Patton.

Pearson's first major task was developing "Special Counter-Intelligence Units" (SCIUs) to engage in counterintelligence work against German agents encountered in retaken territory in France after OVERLORD. But in December 1943, Murphy dispatched Pearson and his secretary Susan Tully to Madrid to establish an X-2 field station there. Spain was officially neutral, although Franco's friendly government allowed Abwehr agents to operate more or less openly.

Because of this, Allied spies were drawn to the Spanish capital and to Lisbon as well, both of which quickly became bustling marketplaces of secrets. "It was not possible to learn in Berlin what was happening in London," Masterman wrote later, "but it might well be possible to hear, or guess, or deduce in neutral Portugal what was happening in both."[38] In Spain from December 28, 1943, to January 19, 1944, Pearson observed the double-cross system in action: British agents had flipped a number of German agents in Madrid and were running them from the UK territory of Gibraltar or from secret locations in Spain or Portugal. Although it was mostly an observation trip, there were some thrills. Upon checking into the Ritz, he noted with alarm that an SS man with a machine gun was stationed outside the room opposite his. Lodging there was Walter Schellenberg, the head of the Sicherheitdienst (SD), the German counterintelligence agency, and the Spanish hotelier had placed them in facing rooms apparently as a practical joke. Pearson relished telling his stepdaughters this story. "We said to Pop," his stepdaughter remembered,

> "Why didn't you have him killed?" And he just looked at us and said "you would never do that, because this was somebody that we knew and could deal with, and if we killed him somebody new, young, wanting to please would come in, so we would never do that." We asked "weren't you afraid he'd have you killed?" and he said "no, they would never have me killed, and we would never have him killed."[39]

But to Pearson, after almost nine months in dismal and deprived England an even greater thrill was the sun and the warmth and the fresh produce, "putting my hands around a glass of orange juice" and seeing "great stacks of fruit . . . pineapples, which I had not seen for a long time" in Lisbon's markets. (He brought some back for H.D. and Bryher.) He reveled in his laundered shirts and meals with "a whole week's meat ration on a plate at a single sitting."[40] And, always a traveler, he toured the Escorial and drove in the Guadarrama Mountains. Upon his return, Pearson was put in charge of the new "Iberian Desk" that he had just established. As the Allies continued to take back territory, X-2's rapid growth—from twenty-five employees in July 1943 to hundreds by early 1944—required a fundamental reorganization. Pearson was recalled to Washington on February 23 to plan the future of the branch. He remained there for three months, Susan joining him for part of that time.

Central to Pearson's philosophy of counterintelligence was not just gathering information but organizing it so it could be of use, a tenet he had adopted while working at Research and Analysis back in Washington. To Murphy and Donovan, he preached the gospel of notecards to which his British counterparts had evangelized him. (By the end of the war, Pearson's team had cataloged the information from eighty thousand documents and ten thousand cables onto a catalog of over four hundred thousand individual cards.)[41] Pearson had become so devoted to this method of record keeping and cross-referencing that one jocular X-2 employee, Jean Douglas, composed a ditty inspired by him:

X-2 Theme Song (to the tune of "I'll Be Seeing You")

I'll be carding you, in all those familiar old places
Everywhere, our long arm chases
    All year through . . . In that queer cafe
    That dive across the way
    The well-known underground
    The neutral port
    The suspect town

I'll be carding you, in every single move you make
And all your friends get carded too
I'll get their numbers for your sake
I'll watch you when you spill the beans
And give the files their cue.
I may leave when this war's through, but
They'll still be carding you![42]

Although comic, this song does convey something not just about the work but about Pearson's personality—his compulsive collecting, and the comfort he took in amassing and having control over sets of things, whether they were books or Hawthorne letters or people or, as in this case, information.

Pearson was delighted by how that song captured precisely the kind of environment he was trying to create. He wanted X-2's Ryder Street offices to offer the best of Yale and R&A—the bonhomie and witty banter among brilliant, cultured, and highly educated employees—without any of the petty rivalry and drudgery that plagued those workplaces. And despite the crushing workload that kept many of the agents and secretaries there until midnight, he generally succeeded.

But of course, that gallows joviality was also a necessary psychological defense against the fearful reality they all confronted daily. A typical note to Pearson from Alice conveys the "Keep Calm and Carry On" attitude that Londoners adopted to cope with the fear and deprivation: "2 bombs fell in Ebury Street [a block from Pearson's flat] somewhere near the church between 1 & 2. I was shopping, getting the flowers near the station. The air was full of grit. Good thing it was daytime or you might have been lifted out of bed. Have pork chops, no lamb this week. I have asked them to save something for you next Friday."[43]

A new weapon, first deployed just after the Normandy landings, ratcheted up the anxiety soon after Pearson returned from Washington. From June to October 1944, London was terrorized by German "buzz bombs" or "doodlebugs," the V-1 rockets that made an uncanny buzzing noise just before they reached their targets, then went eerily silent before exploding. Bryher described the barrage as "a great deal worse than the 1940 blitz, most destructive and unpredictable." Over six thousand Londoners died, and many more were injured, by the almost twenty-five hundred V-1s that rained on the city that summer. Pearson described the remnants of a rocket that killed 138 people who had just arrived for Sunday services at the Guards' Chapel, near Buckingham Palace, as "a thin tiny piece of metal, battered and thin like the mudguard of a wrecked Ford." (Perhaps this brought to mind his own totaled Model T, a lifetime earlier.) On July 5, a doodlebug hit Lowndes

Square and cleaved H.D. and Bryher's neighbors' apartment in two. Three weeks later, another landed just outside their flat; fortunately the women had fled to Cornwall. Pearson was also out of the office when one hit the street below, forcing him to work behind boarded-up windows for days. His friend Jerry Shay wasn't so lucky: one struck forty-five yards from his bedroom window, collapsing the house on top of him. After Shay dug his way out and took refuge in the house of an X-2 secretary, a doodlebug detonated one hundred yards away and "knocked out all their windows. He's now afraid to turn up anywhere," Pearson wrote in his diary. Alice couldn't sleep at night for fear of the rockets and stayed up until dawn sitting in a rocking chair under her stairs.[44] "No one will go out at night," Pearson remarked, "preferring, I suppose, to die at home."

The fear and danger seemed to stiffen Pearson's resolve. They also made him a better leader. Pearson was an inspiring boss, an insightful analyst, and a sophisticated strategist, appearing to one of his new recruits like "the epitome of a counterespionage chief"—quite a change from the tweedy freshman-comp instructor he had been just eighteen months before.[45] Yet he remained fundamentally a teacher, and it was that talent that made the greatest mark on his colleagues. His briefings were especially memorable, as he used all the tricks he'd learned for keeping the attention of sleepy undergraduates: he was in constant motion, from desk to window to filing cabinet; he modulated his voice so that the audience never knew when he was going to slow down or start a dramatic crescendo; and he deployed his sly wit and imposing intellect. That new recruit recalled Pearson as a "spectacular ham" who "savored every step in the unraveling of a plot and couldn't resist embellishing his presentation with wild gesticulations. . . . He would let his cigarette ash grow as he talked on. We sat there transfixed, wondering where the ashes would land when they finally fell off, and whether this habit of his was histrionics or sheer self-absorption with his briefing."[46] Although he had some of the character flaws that plague academics—name-dropping, occasional pomposity and self-importance, tunnel vision—he was rarely a bore. He made his briefings interesting because he genuinely found everything interesting.

Teaching, appropriately, became Pearson's most enduring legacy in counterintelligence. Of the four initial X-2 men, Pearson took the most interest not just in the practice of counterespionage but in the training of counterintelligence officers. One of his central responsibilities between July 1943 and February 1944 was to establish X-2's training program. Through the course of the war, Pearson at first personally and later vicariously (through his curriculum) trained every X-2 officer, and an order of June 30, 1944, designated him as "Training Officer for all X-2 Personnel."[47] His training program was particularly effective because Pearson's contacts gave him access to the much more highly developed British methods and assets. Beyond his own agency, in late 1944, Pearson took over the job of preparing counterintelligence officers for American embassies and legations. As the United States had never had its own counterintelligence service, his curriculum at X-2 quite literally established the basic practices of American counterintelligence and were implemented at the counterintelligence branch of the early Central Intelligence Agency. Many of the men he trained for X-2, moreover, became those first CIA officers.[48]

In January 1944 one of Pearson's actual students arrived in the Ryder Street offices. The aspiring poet and *Furioso* editor James Jesus Angleton had not thrived at Harvard Law. A few months after the war began, Angleton was drafted into the US Army and was preparing to be a specialist in the Military Government section when, in September 1943, he was plucked off his base in Michigan and sent to OSS headquarters. The transfer had been the result of a "friendly conspiracy" between James Murphy, Pearson, and Angleton's father, who was already serving as X-2's field representative in the North African theater. Seeing great talent in the ambitious young man, Murphy expedited his security clearance, specifying that Angleton was "very well known to Norman Pearson," and assigned him to London X-2.[49]

Angleton took over office 23-B, just down the hall from Pearson. Waiting for him in the tiny alcove was his secretary, Perdita Aldington. Perdita's new boss made a profound impression on her, as he did on everyone. With his "piercing eyes [and] emaciated good looks," Angleton was a captivating but somewhat unsettling sight, with a cadaverous, "ravaged" and "vulnerable" mien. Perdita described him as "a centrifugal force" with a "taut, lean, long-distance runner kind of build. Cavernous cheekbones, jet-black hair" and "marvelous hands: long, nervous, expressive."[50] He manifested the dark, tortured side of counterintelligence, and a later generation might have described him as a Goth.

Pearson worked long hours, but nothing seemed to distract Angleton from his work, and his wife, distressed at the tone of his letters, implored Pearson to make Jim "let up a little."[51] Pearson was affable and social while Angleton seemed haunted, prefiguring his later nickname, "the Ghost." (One of the few activities outside of the office that appealed to Angleton was paying social calls on his idol T. S. Eliot.) While working, he was indistractible. When a doodlebug exploded near the office, Perdita recounted, "my heart stopped, and my typewriter stopped too [but] Jim would inquire whether there was anything the matter." His incomprehension at Perdita's alarm was partly due to his focus, but also due to a common blind spot: as was true for so many men in the intelligence business, Angleton had little understanding of and much disdain for women.

Pearson, too, certainly had a male-centric view of the workplace, but he was always much closer to, and appreciative of, the work that women did. And his experience in the war only increased Pearson's respect for forceful and accomplished women, largely because of the time he spent with H.D. and Bryher. He came for lunch at Lowndes Square every Sunday and brought the women provisions from the US Army PX, such as (for H.D.'s fifty-eighth birthday) corn on the cob. Susan, too, sent them luxuries from Connecticut: cheeses, puddings, American cigarettes. "What we should have done without Norman Pearson I do not know," Bryher wrote in her memoir of the war years. "He rescued Perdita from a dreary job in the country to do far more interesting work in London and . . . kept up our spirits during that final difficult year when we were too exhausted to care whether or not we survived until the peace."[52] He also met and became friendly with the imposing Dame Edith Sitwell, another powerful woman. When she entered a room Sitwell resembled nineteenth-century Italian diva Eleanora Duse, Pearson recounted, "in her long black gown, studded with great Tibetan bracelets and a necklace like an order of the crown, behind all these flowing a great red cape." Sitwell also provided him with a means of meeting even more writers. After attending her birthday party he told his mother "it has been Sitwell all the way since! . . . This has given me a chance to at least catch a glimpse of some of the literary figures whose works I used to teach."[53] (In one October 1944 week, his calendar showed appointments with "Miss Sitwell" for tea on Sunday, tea on Tuesday, and attendance at her reading on Wednesday evening.)[54]

Pearson did spend much of his social life with men from work, Americans and British both. These were often less friendships than professional relationships. Apart from Cowgill, Pearson's closest British professional colleague was the infamous Harold Adrian Russell ("Kim") Philby, who also had offices in the Ryder Street complex. Philby, of course, was the center of the Cambridge ring of Soviet spies who passed British and, later, American secrets to the Soviets from the 1930s to the 1960s, and who all eventually defected to the USSR. (Many years later, Downes asserted that Pearson had suspected Philby was working for the Soviets, but Pearson dismissed this claim.) In London, Philby headed up the MI6 branch responsible for coordinating with OSS and so worked with Pearson every day. The canny Philby wanted to be Pearson's primary contact in British intelligence, but Pearson preferred Cowgill, and thus much information passed right over him. Philby resented this for professional reasons: he thought Cowgill was being buffaloed by this ingratiating X-2 tyro, and that Section V should be sharing its sensitive counterintelligence material only with the much more established and reliable FBI. He also wanted to make sure that he had access to everything that might be of use to his Soviet handlers.

But Philby's distaste was also personal. He could smell the middle classes on Pearson, who didn't even try to disguise his execrable Americanness. Like some sort of Rotarian with a government expense account, Philby felt, Pearson tackily invited his British counterparts to upper-class haunts like Claridge's, Quaglino's, or the St. James's Club where he had no business being. These invitations were, Philby was certain, a ploy to extract information from the notoriously sodden MI6 officers, but (at least according to one of these men) the "agile and cheerful if occasionally devious" Pearson tended to get inebriated first and thus outwit himself.[55] In his postdefection memoir, Philby sneers at "Normal" Pearson's "persistent and embarrassing offers of hospitality" and dismisses him as a "hail-fellow-well-met and have you heard the latest one about the girl on the train?" Even twenty years after the war, Philby's dander at being sidelined by the "notably bewildered" Americans is still elevated in this memoir, and he snipes that these amateurs couldn't even keep their file cabinets locked.[56] Philby was much fonder of Angleton, and quickly moved in to become Angleton's second teacher and mentor. Their decades-long friendship caused some of the gravest intelligence failures in American history, as Angleton disclosed innumerable secrets to Philby over their regular lunches in the 1950s, when Angleton was the CIA's head of counterintelligence and Philby MI6's liaison.[57]

The novelist Graham Greene also worked with Pearson at Ryder Street, where Greene helped run the enterprising Portugal-based British double agent GARBO. Although Greene shared Philby's contempt for the bumbling colonials, Pearson intrigued him, and they enjoyed talking literature. Greene also found Pearson much more savvy than Philby was willing to grant and so "guarded from his eyes my card-index of German agents working in Portugal," Greene remarked later. It was Greene, in fact, who was responsible for the unlocked-cabinet scandal that fueled Philby's scorn: after hours, Greene would walk down the hall to the American offices and wrest secret files out of a (locked) cabinet with a buckled drawer and strew them on the duty officer's desk, which would prompt a fine for the apparently careless officer.[58]

As the OSS began to outperform MI5 and MI6 in the last two years of the war, Philby successfully convinced his superiors that Cowgill was at fault, and his forced resignation in late 1944 hurt Pearson both professionally—he lost his closest contact at MI6—and personally. "I feel a kind of numbness at the pit of my stomach" at the news of his dismissal, Pearson wrote his old friend. In a more formal letter, he elaborated on how central this personal relationship was to his own accomplishments, and to those of X-2 more broadly.

> American counter-espionage will owe its maturity to your educa-
> tion. . . . This sharing of products in the way we have is something
> new in the history of intelligence. If it was not right to do so, then
> there was no point to the war and no hope for a future in which our
> two nations do not stand side by side. . . . You have believed from the
> start that such sharing was possible, and its proof, dear Felix, has been
> your gift. No one has given more towards the winning of the war or
> towards the holding of the peace.[59]

His crucial collaboration with Cowgill merely underscored the lesson that he had been learning for almost ten years now: personal relationships between people well-placed in their institutions were how things got done. X-2's success, in fact, can be attributed to this insight.[60]

In September 1944, Pearson received a significant promotion: he was made chief of X-2 for the European theater of operations, putting him in charge of all OSS's counterintelligence operations everywhere except China and Burma, thus making him "the most important American counter-intelligence officer in Europe."[61] (At the same time, the fast-rising Angleton was sent to newly liberated Rome as head of X-2's new Italian bureau.) In the month since D-Day, Allied territory had greatly expanded—providing much more area in which German stay-behind spies could operate—and X-2 units had been embedded with many of the forward troop positions to do counterespionage work in liberated areas. "The invasion of the continent . . . increased the necessities of our work a hundredfold," Pearson said.[62]

Characteristically, he threw himself into the work. One of his first priorities was a purely administrative one. In February 1945 Pearson personally designed, negotiated, and ushered into existence a body called "SHAEF [Supreme Headquarters, Allied Expeditionary Force] G-2 Counter-Intelligence War Room," which brought together MI5, MI6, OSS, and even Free French personnel to oversee and channel the flood of counterintelligence data now inundating the Allied forces.

This 175-strong committee "collected, collated, and analyzed all information about German clandestine activities" and almost immediately gained a reputation as the "best source for up-to-date information about the German intelligence services."[63]

By late 1944 Pearson supervised three hundred men in the European theater of operations, but even so many of them had to take on new responsibilities. One X-2 staffer working the French desk, Richard Cutler, remembers Pearson informing him that he would, in his evening hours, be learning German, and was expected to be sufficiently proficient after four months to chase down Abwehr and SD agents for General Omar Bradley as his Twelfth Army Group advanced. A typical week's harvest from the French front looked like this: "An important arrest in the South was that of a very active Tunisian W/T [wireless telegraphy] operator whose interrogations thus far have revealed few of the [German] contacts that are to be expected. Apparently violently anti-French, he is proving hard to deal with, but further reports are expected to be more fruitful. From the South also was reported the arrest of a Belgian in Menton whose mission was to contact an agent in Monte Carlo, having connections with a network operating behind the enemy lines over the Italian frontier."[64]

For all the satisfaction running American counterespionage provided, Norm often regretted that he could not be in the field. As agents returned to London for debriefing, then, Pearson reveled in the stories and gifts they brought him from exotic places. Among these transients were Yale friends and colleagues including Louis Martz and Don Gallup (who combined his intelligence work in France with attendance at Gertrude Stein's Thursday evening gatherings).[65] Eugene Waith, a Shakespeare scholar, ran double agents while assigned to the American units grinding east from Paris.[66] It could be hard to tell sometimes whether Ryder Street was hosting a Yale class reunion or Yale faculty meeting: the art historian Gerstle Mack, the future literary critic and biographer Richard Ellmann, and even Calvin Tenney, Pearson's childhood friend and grad school housemate, were all among the X-2 agents who reported to Pearson.

Pearson was responsible for overseeing not just the collection of information but its classification and use. Every agent name, every radio frequency, even every serial number on every piece of German equipment was recorded, tagged, and cross-referenced on those omnipresent notecards. By mid-1944, each advancing American or British Army group or headquarters had an OSS or MI6 Special Counter-Intelligence (SCI) team attached to it. X-2 London fed these men information drawn from ULTRA intercepts of German agents in their areas, and the SCI unit would hunt down the agent and offer a choice: death or doubling. It was a massive job: as of late 1944, the ULTRA intercepts indicated that 3,575 such agents were active between the Bay of Biscay and the German border.[67] X-2 also worked, at times, at cross-purposes with the local population, who would deliver justice to Nazi agents before the SCI team could get there to attempt to flip them, as in the case of a captured German stay-behind in Cannes who "enabled us to make numerous arrests" before he was "shot under circumstances not yet clarified." Pearson reported to Washington in proficient bureaucratese.[68]

His years of learning how to ingratiate himself with authority figures and manipulate institutions made him a formidable bureaucratic combatant. Although X-2 had sole control over the ULTRA intercepts, the Secret Intelligence (SI) branch of OSS recruited its own staff for covert activities and did not want X-2 to vet its agents. But after SI embarrassingly welcomed in an operative who was in fact working for the Germans, Donovan ordered Pearson's team to run the names of any new SI agents through his card file. Pearson assigned Cutler—another Yalie, who had been a junior associate in Donovan's Wall Street law firm—to oversee this vetting, knowing that his connection with Donovan would insulate him against any obstruction from SI.[69]

Pearson also headed at least two other major undertakings in the last year of the war. With sabotage a growing problem in liberated territory, he trained and sent to each SCIU a countersabotage team to advise the forward Army groups on protecting vital or vulnerable installations, as well as undertake on-the-ground investigations and find potential saboteurs. Retreating Nazis and stay-behinds were booby-trapping anything they could. In November 1944, Pearson reported to Washington that his "discussions" about such a countersabotage program had "been satisfactorily completed" and that he had detailed nine officers and eight enlisted men to counterespionage.[70] In a project that certainly thrilled the collector in Pearson, X-2 even helped establish the Museum of Sabotage Equipment on the Paris estate of the British intelligence officer Victor Rothschild.

Pearson was also in charge of the Art Looting Investigation Unit (ALIU) of the OSS. This unit should not be confused with the so-called Monuments Men, more properly known as Museums, Fine Arts, and Archives (MFAA), a US Army unit that hunted down the artworks that the Nazis had stolen and hidden in mansions and caves and salt mines across Germany. Seeing that the intelligence-gathering capabilities of OSS could greatly help the MFAA, in November 1944 Donovan created ALIU "to collect and disseminate such information bearing on the looting, confiscation and transfer by the enemy of art properties in Europe, and on the individuals or organizations involved in such operations or transactions, as well as be of direct aid to the United States agencies empowered to effect restitution of such properties and prosecute war criminals [and] to establish the pattern of looting and confiscation in its broader aspects, so as to be guided in the promulgation of plans for ultimate restitution."[71] The documents that ALIU unearthed and prepared became the databases that are still used to find looted Nazi art and return it to its rightful owners.

Oddly enough, Donovan situated ALIU under X-2's umbrella, rather than the seemingly more appropriate Secret Intelligence branch, on the logic that it would help the OSS find prominent and wealthy Nazis who might pose a threat to Germany's postwar stability. This meant, of course, that ALIU reported to Pearson, who stocked it with Yale men. In a clever bureaucratic move, Pearson overplayed its connection to X-2's mission. In December 1944, he stated that two "well-known museum directors" from the United States, currently serving in the US Army, would be put into civilian clothes and work with authorities in the liberated territories to "discover connections between the transmission of [the stolen] objects and the financing of espionage activities." While it's certainly possible that proceeds from selling these works might fund

Abwehr or SD spying, most of these works had simply ended up in the personal collections of high-ranking Nazis. Pearson seems to have had relatively little personal involvement in ALIU's work until the summer of 1945, when he and Gallup traveled to Stein and Toklas's apartment in Paris to take down a list of all the women's stolen treasures.[72]

Overwork kept him occupied, but Pearson deeply missed Susan and the domestic life he'd enjoyed before joining the OSS. She was with him some in Washington in early 1944, but he had not seen the girls much. And things at home were difficult. Fearing that New Haven might be bombed, and disliking the nightly blackouts, Susan and her daughters spent much of the war at the Bennett "Big House" on Johnson's Point, and it wore on the girls to be away from home. Tom Tracy began coming around more to see them when Susan was out of the house, causing friction. Then, in early 1945, Susan developed a tumor in the neck of her uterus, necessitating an emergency hysterectomy. Norm was upset that he was unable to get home in time to be with her, and devastated that he and Susan would now not be able to have any children of their own. And Susan was desperately lonely, which began to worry her family members. "Susan has never had the faculty of making intimate friends," Mrs. Bennett wrote Norm, "and I think it has been very forlorn for her with you away. I had not realized how all her life hung on you until she was ill and feeling particularly blue."[73]

As the war in Europe drew to an end, Pearson, who had long itched to see some sort of action, was finally able to get into the fray. On May 3, 1945, the day before the Germans surrendered in Denmark, Pearson parachuted into Copenhagen to help extract X-2 double agents in danger of retaliation from Danish civilians who knew them only as Nazis. He enjoyed telling this story to his daughters and colleagues, recounting that the reunion of these X-2 operatives and his agents was the only time he ever drank himself literally under the table. (Early the next morning, presumably with a brutal hangover, he then accompanied them back to England—by boat.)[74] Later that week he returned to Scandinavian soil, again by parachute, as he wanted to be the first American officer in Oslo after the German surrender. In the four days between these two drops, he celebrated V-E Day and shared Londoners' relief at the end of the long, terrible conflict, recounting to his mother that "I saw the king and queen late one night, when I was with a jovial group from the office. We wandered down the Mall to Trafalgar Square where everyone was snake dancing and singing and striking up friends for five minutes before passing on to new friends and more dancing. There was great joviality on the whole but the crowds were very orderly and I saw no one really drunk. There certainly wasn't any abandon, only happiness that for a while there could be freedom from worry."[75] What he did not mention was that he contributed to the "great joviality" by climbing on top of one of the lions in Trafalgar Square, a real feat for someone with a fused pelvis and femur. It might have taken him the entire war to prove to his colleagues that he was capable of physical bravery, but he finally had his chance. And he was proud that he had "led a merry dodge during the war . . . to keep the Army from knowing that I had an open lesion. That I was able to deceive them for so long was perhaps my only war triumph."[76] He finally came clean to his superiors when penicillin became available to military and OSS personnel, and immediately underwent a six-week course of antibiotic therapy.

In his almost three years of service overseas, Pearson played a small but key role in winning the war, particularly through X-2's protection of territory retaken by the Allies. The Army recognized him with a Bronze Star, and President Truman awarded him a Medal of Freedom; the Norwegians made him a Knight of St. Olaf, and the French named him a chevalier in the Legion of Honor. But since the nature of his work remained secret well after the war, he could never tell anyone about what he actually did. Especially on the Yale campus, he made the most of the mystery, enjoying his reputation as the small hunchbacked man who had been and possibly was still a top-ranking spy. When he did speak of his service, it was in the most elusive terms. To students and colleagues, he would merely say that he'd done some noncombatant work in the intelligence services during the war, knowing that others had dropped many hints and rumors about him. Inevitably, he downplayed his war experience and its impact on the conflict and on him. Certainly, having spent most of his time abroad in a nice London flat with a housekeeper and entertainment account insulated him from war's horrors, and he never saw combat. He still, though, had experienced hardships, and bombings, and danger. It was exciting, it was disorienting, and it certainly was at times frightening. But, sounding very much like the stiff-upper-lip Brits, it was mostly about a job well done. And, like those Brits, he was always self-deprecating. He told Susan that he'd like his war service, like his life in general, to be remembered as "médiocre avec éclat" (mediocre, but with style).[77]

As diffident as he could be about it, for Pearson as for so many other veterans, the war was a fulcrum in his life. When he entered the OSS, he was thirty-three, but despite all his professional accomplishments he was really just finishing the apprenticeship stage of life. He had been out of school for just over a year and married for about the same amount of time and was just starting his first real job. The war turned him into an adult, a leader, in a way that he had never been before. He had already cultivated, quite intentionally, a set of traits and skills that he knew he could use to achieve professional success: diligence, critical analysis, sociability, effective communication, the ability to read other people and motivate them, the ability to maneuver within institutions, personal bravery and resilience. His superiors immediately saw these talents and skills and quickly put Pearson in a position of significant responsibility. And in that position, he developed cross-cultural aptitude, organizational and personal leadership, subtlety, and the ability to manipulate or even create institutional structures to solve multidimensional problems. After the war, the men heading the nascent US intelligence services wanted Pearson to stay on and help them fight the Cold War, but he preferred to stay his prewar course. But those skills that he had developed proved themselves to be just as valuable in academia.

It took him longer than he hoped, though, to get back to his chosen career. Much to Pearson's and Susan's frustration, the end of the war in Europe didn't mean that Norman returned right away, although he was allowed to make a very quick visit home in September, when Susan was again hospitalized, this time for an intestinal obstruction. X-2 was crucial in denazification, in identifying and interrogating dead-enders and potential saboteurs or insurrectionists in Germany. Sent in November 1945 to Berlin, Heidelberg, Munich, Salzburg, and Vienna to oversee this work, Pearson was stunned at the destruction he witnessed. Munich was especially resonant to him: all through the center of the city every building was either "down or gutted," and the Lessing house, where he had boarded in 1932, was now an emergency telephone exchange, as the family had relocated to the country, where food was more plentiful. Seeing the ruined Circus Krone, he told Fanny, "more or less completed the cycle since the day I first heard Hitler speak in Munich."[78]

As he started to process the meaning of his experiences, he wasn't always so honest about the evolution of his feelings about the Nazis. Writing to William Carlos Williams, he slipped into the persona of the modest bureaucrat just happy to help, in his small way, defeat an enemy whose malevolence he had always recognized. But, perhaps understandably, Pearson effaced the fact that he had once felt the insidious appeal of Nazism. "I had the satisfaction of seeing tangible results to the work I did . . . the chance to satisfy my curiosity in seeing nations work with and against each other in a time of great stress . . . the chance to do something about a situation which I had hated almost from the first time I heard Hitler speak or saw him smugly at a Wagnerian opera. It was on all counts something that I had to do, and therefore I was lucky to be able to do it."[79]

What was true in this somewhat misleading reminiscence is that the war did make Pearson think much more deeply not just about Hitler's evil, but about the other judgments he had made about that long-ago speech: rationality was superior to emotionalism; messy pluralism to fascist unity; informed pragmatism to rigid idealism; duty and self-sacrifice to compulsion and force; dignity to madness. And through the 1930s, he had increasingly come to associate the positive terms in those dyads not just with the United States and Great Britain and the West, but specifically with the Puritans, and in this, his war experience added a new dimension to his personal philosophy and his scholarly work as well. The nascent American studies field of the 1930s had begun to rehabilitate the Puritans, redrawing them as intellectually serious, as moral models of a sort, as devoted to work and duty and community, as the precursors of a type of (limited) democracy, and—most important—as fundamentally humble, always aware of their own shortcomings. And while he had always thought and written about Puritans, during the war he increasingly started to refer to *himself*, only partly tongue-in-cheek, as a modern-day Puritan. "We are all Puritans, we Americans," he wrote to the son of an X-2 agent who had been killed in action. "And we know that we are our brothers' and our fathers' and our children's keepers."[80] During the war, Pearson and Bryher often joked about how their capacity for labor, their stubborn resistance, and their willingness to endure hardship made them fellow Puritans. "Curious how these old Puritan traits reassert themselves in our times. . . . Puritans are really only happy fighting!" she wrote him in the summer of 1944.[81] Few people then or even today would recognize his idea of Puritanism. But Pearson, with his work ethic and sense of duty and respect for the intellect and healthy awe at the mysteries of the universe, clearly was a Puritan—perhaps even, as he once called himself to Susan, "the Last Puritan."[82] His essential nature was so patent to everyone who met him that his OSS code name, from the time he left for England in March 1943 to the time he was mustered out of the service in 1946, was, of course, PURITAN.

+ 7 +

THE HOT PROPERTY

Just before Christmas 1945, Pearson finally received his orders to return stateside. At his farewell party, Norm's colleagues presented him with a gift of four elegant Crown Worcester teacups, while Bryher gave him several books of astounding value from Maggs: a first edition of John Milton's *Paradise Lost*, as well as early printings of other significant Milton works, including *Paradise Regained* and *Areopagitica*. This remarkable gift, of the most important works of the greatest of all Puritan writers, was perhaps a winking recognition of Pearson's code name (which she should not have known).

In order to get home in time for Christmas with Susan and the girls, Norm hitched a ride on an aircraft carrier for what turned out to be a harrowing crossing. The carrier, running without sufficient ballast, ran into rough weather in the North Atlantic, and as he described it to Bryher "the forward bulkheads were smashed in by the waves, and the water from 75-foot waves licked their way in; the steel plates on the bow were ripped open, and some of the guns were torn off." He was proud that he remained "hale and hearty."[1]

Docking on Staten Island early on December 24, Norm had to wait most of the day for his treasure-laden trunk to be extracted from the ship's hold, before he rushed up to New Haven just in time for Christmas Eve dinner with his family. It must have been disorienting to go from being tossed in rough seas aboard an aircraft carrier to putting presents in his stepdaughters' Christmas stockings, all within twenty-four hours. But it was also "sheer luxury," as he told Bryher, to be back home and resume the domestic life he'd had so little time to enjoy.

If the end of the war hadn't meant the end of Norm's counterintelligence work, neither did his return home. In September 1945, President Truman had signed an order dissolving the OSS. The Research and Analysis branch, where Norm had started, was transferred to the State Department, while the War Department took temporary possession of the espionage and counterintelligence divisions, naming them the Strategic Services Unit (or SSU). Norm was ordered to remain in Washington through the spring to help with the transition. So for the time being, he was an employee of the War Department.

The question was what would happen to these divisions, which now employed thousands. The United States hadn't needed a foreign intelligence service before the war, so would it now? If so, what was its purpose? Isolationists argued that this was the time to pull back, that a foreign intelligence service would just encourage the foreign entanglements that George Washington had warned against. But these isolationist voices had lost credibility during the war, and they seemed to want to deny the United States' new status as the unquestioned dominant world power. And with the Americans and Soviets, once allies but now rivals, uneasily facing each other, the answer as to whether the United States needed an intelligence service to discern the Russians' intentions seemed clear. Also important would be understanding the internal politics of the nations on the western side of that line that was not yet called an iron curtain. Moscow-aligned Communist parties were thriving in Greece, Italy, and France: how could the United States prevent them from winning elections and perhaps threatening the United States? How could the United States uncover and root out Soviet spies in those nations? X-2's remnants could be of particular use here. In Washington, Norm, now "Assistant Chief of X-2," helped plan the future of American counterespionage, while on the side, he taught aspiring counterintelligence agents, for the first time employing "British methods on American soil," in Naftali's words.[2]

The future of X-2, specifically whether it would remain independent or be folded into a larger government agency, was very much in doubt. Pearson and Murphy insisted that it should stand alone and superior, with access to "all operations information no matter from what branch," as it had during the war.[3] But the branch was being put up for auction. The director of SSU, General John Magruder, described X-2 as "the only operating American counter-espionage organization with coordinated coverage in both military and non-military areas outside of the Western Hemisphere." Magruder's description, importantly, was in the present tense: X-2 was still very much an active agency, one that also maintained, in Angleton's words, "friendly relationships with the counter-intelligence branches of indigenous Secret Intelligence and Security Services of those friendly countries in which SSU maintains official stations."[4]

If the United States was going to establish an independent intelligence service after the war, as seemed increasingly inevitable, Pearson—with his real-world experience, his comfort working in bureaucracies, his cultural competence, his impeccable communications skills, and his dogged determination and appetite for hard work—would be a strong candidate to head its counterintelligence branch. He had attained the equivalent military rank of lieutenant colonel, which would mean that he was qualified for high-echelon positions. In 1946, the State Department floated an offer to Norm to be the first special assistant for research and intelligence and chairman of the Advisory Committee on Intelligence, reporting directly to the secretary of state, with a salary of $8,000, and he was also on many people's minds for a deputy director position when the Central Intelligence Agency was created in July 1947.[5] These were tempting possibilities, certainly more glamorous and exciting than being part of Yale's freshman year teaching pool at $2,500 a year, a paltry salary even then.

But Norm had decided long ago that the world of books and letters was where he wanted to be. In April 1946, Yale College's Dean William DeVane informed Pearson that he was being promoted to assistant professor, which meant that he was now a college faculty member and on the tenure track, and would earn $4,600 a year, making him the highest-paid assistant professor in the department. Colleges didn't pay particularly well, and Yale especially had long been notorious for its low faculty salaries: well into the twentieth century, Yale faculty members assumed that they had to have either family money or a job on the side in order to make ends meet. Fortunately for Norm, in 1944 the Pearsons had bought out the Goodnows' interest in the Gardner store, and consequently Norm was now assistant treasurer of Goodnow Pearson's, with a $4,200 annual salary attached.[6] In addition, the Oxford anthology continued to sell—eleven thousand copies as of January 1, 1943, translating to thousands of dollars in royalties.[7] His outside writing and speaking jobs also brought in extra income, so money wasn't his main concern in making professional decisions.

DeVane was wise to move when he did, as Norm was still a hot property. Only a month later, DeVane received a personal letter from Alan Valentine, the president of the University of Rochester, stating frankly that his school, which was looking for "able young men . . . who do not define literature too narrowly nor separate it from the general development of American history and culture," sought Pearson to build its new American Studies program, and wanted to know how intent Yale was on keeping him.[8] DeVane frankly responded that Yale was "very keenly interested" in Norm, and then gave Valentine a full accounting of his character and achievements:

> His reputation in the country is far wider than his written works warrant. This is because Pearson has traveled over the country a great deal, has talked to young scholars in American literature where he went, and has a very great talent in stirring the imagination of young men and men his own age to do original and independent work of their own. This is his genius, and it is a considerable asset to him.
>
> He is widely known for his brilliant conversation. He is an extremely effective teacher of the intimate sort. He does his best in small groups of students and manages to light a fire in them. . . . He is a genuine intellectual force, and although I do not always agree with his opinions, he certainly starts people thinking. That is the best thing that one can say about a teacher.
>
> As you probably know, Pearson is a man of about thirty-seven years of age and is deformed. He has a humped back and walks a little like

a crab. I think his deformity has sharpened his mind and perhaps his tongue, as well, though I am certain there is not a more generous or public spirited person anywhere around here. . . . I think you ought to try to get Pearson for Rochester, but you will have a battle on your hands if you try to do so.[9]

Norm seriously entertained Rochester's offer and even took Susan and the girls to see the school, but he ultimately turned it down to stay at Yale.

But he needed a vacation before he would be ready to start his career. After reporting to Washington for a couple of weeks of OSS-related work, in late January Norm and Susan sent the girls to stay with their grandparents, and they set off on a long road trip, this one through the length and breadth of Mexico. He always loved a long driving excursion, but he saw this one also as therapy, feeling his way back to some kind of normalcy. "I want to see ruins made by something other than bombs," he wrote H.D., "and a civilization which has simply disintegrated, not [been] blasted to hell. It may restore balance."[10]

Driving briskly south via Baltimore and then down through the Southeast, they crossed the Mexican border near Monterey and slowed down to see the scenery: orchids growing in their natural state, the rugged and arid Sierra Madres, market days in Coahuilan villages. They used Mexico City as a base to explore the ruins of Teotihuacán as well as Taxco, Cuernavaca, Puebla, and the other colonial cities. The Pearsons then flew to the Yucatán to see the Maya ruins at Uxmal and Chichén Itzá, then upon returning to the capital drove south, to Oaxaca and its Monte Albán and Mitla ruins. Disappointed at not being able to add Guadalajara to their route back north—no paved roads and no gas stations, they were warned—they returned to the United States and drove home through Texas, Arkansas, Kentucky, and Cincinnati, revived and refreshed.

But though Norm was getting his "balance" again, the war had done much more serious damage to H.D., who along with Bryher had become one of the most important people in his life. Never particularly robust, over the last months of 1945, she had been wasting away, growing thinner and more psychically absent, even delusional at times. By January 1946 her condition had deteriorated to the degree that she was unable to leave her flat. In February, her doctor diagnosed her with meningitis and an "acute nervous breakdown," and friends feared she would plunge from the roof of the building, whether by accident or not. She needed to be attended at all times by a nurse and by someone else—and for the most part, this meant the otherwise peripatetic Bryher, who thus felt that such a life was "like being in a sort of prison," as she confided to Pearson.[11]

This enforced togetherness came, ironically, just as H.D. and Bryher had reached a turning point where each decided she no longer was the other's primary romantic partner. While their thirty-year relationship wasn't ending, precisely, they agreed to start living separately. Bryher intended to shuttle between London, Cornwall, and Kenwin, while H.D. would return to the States, where she would recuperate and regain her strength under Perdita's care. Norm had even managed to get her a teaching position at Bryn Mawr starting in spring 1946.[12] But her breakdown made this impossible, even though H.D. bravely tried, as Bryher reported to Norm, to draw on her "Puritan spirit." Bryher moved to a room in the basement at Lowndes Square and then, in April, departed for good, leaving H.D. in the care of Dr. Dennis Carroll. In mid-May, Dr. Carroll sent H.D. to the Küsnacht Nervklinic in Switzerland, where both James Joyce's daughter Lucia and the dancer Vaslav Nijinsky had been treated. H.D. would remain there until December, under the treatment of Dr. Theodore Brunner, who forbade any visits or letters between Bryher and H.D. for the first three months.[13]

As H.D. gradually returned to health, Bryher remained characteristically busy and reported her activities to Pearson on an almost weekly basis. She had started two novels inspired by the war. *Beowulf*, about the Blitz, excoriated the British government for failing to recognize the Nazi threat and was thus rejected by London publishers. It first appeared in a French translation in 1948 and was finally published in English—but not in England—by Pearson's friends Kurt and Helen Wolff's Pantheon Books in 1956. The other novel, *Fourteenth of October*, was ostensibly about the Norman invasion, with "the Normans being as it were, the Nazis," she told Pearson.[14] But like H.D., and so many others of her generation who had experienced both wars, she was also trying to recuperate. "Whether any of us will really recover from the war, I doubt," she told him. "The two wars, in my mind, merge together into eleven years of horror, misery, and above all, frustration."[15]

With his employment settled for the next year, and potentially for many years to come, Norm spent much of the summer preparing the new classes and starting to revise his dissertation for publication. In early August, he went to Chicago for a checkup with Dr. Hatcher, who was eager to try an intensive course of penicillin on Norm's hip, which still had an open wound. Dr. Hatcher discovered a small sequestrum on the pelvis to curette, extending Norm's stay for at least another week. After two weeks of recuperation, things looked good: better, in fact, than they had for decades. As a result of flooding his hip and sinus with penicillin, Norm reported to his mother in October, the wound on his hip, which had been open, infected, and seeping for over thirty years, was now closed and fully healed.[16] While this meant the active infection was finally resolved, the damage to his body from the injury and surgeries was permanent, and he would remain lopsided, hunchbacked, and unable to bend at the left hip for the rest of his life. But he had long come to accept this as just the way he was. "He did not talk about it," his stepdaughter Sue recollected. "And he never ever leaned on it or used it as an excuse for anything. He just fought it all the time—not in a scrambling, aggressive way, but it was just there."

The instructional side of his job, as well, had changed for the better. Norm's first year on the Yale College faculty gave him much more interesting classes, such as Literary Interpretation and Analysis and the first half of the American literature survey, which enrolled 190 students the first time Norm taught it, making it one of the largest classes at the university. It was an energizing time at Yale, which suddenly became a "dynamic, exciting place." The class that entered in the fall of 1946 was Yale's largest ever, swollen with returning GIs characterized by "industry, motivation and maturity."[17] They were met by a new curriculum intended to give students a broader general education and emphasizing the relationships between the arts and humanities, the social sciences, and the hard sciences. The English department even offered, for the first time, a literature class that went beyond the nineteenth century, taught not by Pearson but by Eugene Waith, who had worked under him at X-2.[18] The faculty were changing, too, becoming a "more diverse and intellectually engaged community" as Yale's departments recruited distinguished scholars.[19] Also new was the Scholar of the House program, which allowed a few outstanding seniors to spend their final year pursing an independent project under the supervision of a faculty member. Pearson was named the director of the program, which put him in direct contact with Yale's most brilliant and ambitious undergrads—the very kinds of men who might want to go into intelligence work.

In 1947, in fact, Norm quickly took on, or inserted himself into, almost all the so-called service responsibilities that would mark the rest of his career. It wasn't that he lacked big ideas about American literature, or American culture, or literary study, or the nature of contemporary poetry. But it was much more natural for him to put those ideas into *action*. So within two years he had shouldered side jobs that had him scouting for potential intelligence agents, shaping the Yale Libraries and building them into a major research center, and modernizing the Yale experience for the more ambitious undergraduates the college was attracting. Because of his people skills and deep knowledge of the university, Pearson became the default welcoming committee for celebrity professors like Cleanth Brooks who were recruited to bolster the department's scholarly profile.[20] Most important of all was his position as the first undergraduate director of Yale's American Studies program, to which he was named in 1947.

Pearson had always happily borne a taxing workload, but the effects of his willingness to volunteer for everything soon wore on him. As he wrote Bryher, 1948 was a

> kind of war year in peacetime. . . . In my lecture course on the history of American literature I had 300 students, who came three times a week to listen to me. This was the largest class in the department,

a kind of triumph I was often told, but a triumph which was appalling in the demands it made. I didn't have to read their exams, thank God, but each student did an original essay on any subject of criticism he elected and I approved. They came to my office in lines to talk about it; they were complimentary in wanting to linger when they came; they came back again and again. And then I had to read the papers. And I had to prepare the lectures. Men came to ask me what a sin was, and I became a kind of amateur analyzer of the sexual misadjustments of young married couples. One was helped and sent another. Then I had an advanced seminar on James, Hart Crane, Ezra Pound, etc. I had another advanced seminar on the theory of cultural analysis. I was in charge of the Division of American Studies, having to arrange the programs of all of the students who enrolled in it. I was put in charge of the Scholars of the House Program. . . . I was in charge of the visiting lecturers at Yale during the winter, and had to arrange for their visits and entertain them when they came. The university literary magazine fell into shambles of administration and pits of financial depression. I was in charge of the committee to reorganize them. I was made chairman of the English Institute. . . . I was made a member of a national committee on the teaching of American culture, another which supervised the annual meetings of teachers of American literature. I had to speak over the radio, speak at other colleges, talk at the college chapel.[21]

It can be trying to hear college professors, whose working conditions seem so cushy to many, bellyache about how hard they work, but in Norm's case it was true. He worked late most evenings, and when the family didn't go to the Branford cottage on the weekends he would be in the office much of Saturday and Sunday—preparing, reading, grading, researching, and writing endless letters. Susan and the girls disliked how much time he spent in the office so soon after an almost three-year absence.

Apart from this, his relationship with Lizzie and Sue had been quickly improving. One incident in particular earned Norm Sue's devotion: Susan and Norm had enrolled her in New Haven's Westover

School in 1945, and even though she was only fifteen, she requested that they give her formal permission to smoke at school. Although Susan refused, lifelong smoker Norm argued that little Sue should have the choice, and he prevailed. This really began to "warm things up" between them, Sue remembered.

And as she matured, Sue's respect and love for Norm, whom she called "Pop," grew. By the time she was in her first year at Smith College, Sue came to understand why so many of his students had such affection for him. When she asked him for advice on her term paper "Music in Poetry," she remembered, "he would say 'go take a look at this poem; it really is a fugue,' and I had enough music by that time so that I could do that myself. And he really did help with sources."[22] Although the two girls were not particularly close, Lizzie followed her sister's lead and grew more and more attached to him as well. But just as Sue started college, things with Lizzie got worse. Never a stellar student, Lizzie was struggling at the Emma Willard Academy in Troy, New York. When she was sixteen, she was diagnosed with schizophrenia, and her academic performance and behavior grew even more erratic and concerning. Upon turning eighteen, in the last term of her senior year, she announced that she had become engaged to a sixteen-year-old boy at another prep school. Because they couldn't legally prevent it, Norm and Susan resolved to make the best of it. "Fortunately," Pearson confided to Fanny, "the boy's parents are what you would call 'up-town,' and Susan has known the father for many years. . . . Although there is a little fantasy in this, it is of a kind which seems to stabilize her, may make her both more realistic and more serious." The engagement was soon broken, and Lizzie's mental stability only got worse. By age twenty-three she had suffered a full breakdown and was receiving long-term inpatient treatment at the Yale Psychiatric Institute.[23]

Outside of Yale, Pearson was developing a reputation as the kind of professor who could appear on demand and on time to communicate to an audience of nonacademics. Because of his connections in publishing, he was summoned to Washington in April 1947 by the Postal Committee for Books, a publishers' lobbying group, to argue against a bill raising the postage rate for books. "I was the only speaker for the ultimate consumer—teachers, etc.," he recounted to Bryher. "What particularly fascinated me was to see Congress at work, to share in the proceedings of a lobby, and to be trotted around the outside of the sessions of a committee to put the squeeze on individual members of the committee. One would never guess the democratic way of life to be what it is in practice," said the man who was simultaneously trying to figure out how to teach and instill devotion to that "democratic way of life" in the classroom.[24] He was a frequent guest on the *Yale Reports* radio program, and in 1947, his name made its way to the CBS Radio Network, whose long-running *Invitation to Learning* series was preparing a feature on Benjamin Franklin's *Poor Richard's Almanac*. In his appearance on that episode, Norm came across to CBS's broad audience as brilliant without being condescending or esoteric and after that often contributed to the show's segments on American novels. Where so many of his Yale colleagues were satisfied with talking just to other scholars, Norm had long wanted to be a kind of public intellectual as well.

He continued to keep his hand in trade publishing and had become a shrewd, confident, and in-demand operator. The royalties for the anthology had picked up ($2,300 in 1946, or more than half of his Yale salary), his Modern Library Hawthorne collection was going into a new edition, and he agreed to write the introduction for a new college edition of Thoreau's *Walden* and serve as a "special consultant" to Rinehart for further titles in the line. For some years, Norm had been toying with the idea of producing his own textbook for college poetry classes that would treat poems both as aesthetic works and as products of a particular culture and historical moment. In 1947 the Atlantic Monthly Press approached him and Dudley Fitts with a similar proposition. Norm responded that he'd take it on only if the press agreed to cover a full half of the permissions fees demanded by the authors, rather than putting that financial burden entirely on the editors as was customary. The press decided that was too much for them, but Norm was happy to walk away from the table.[25]

But the academy doesn't reward the kind of work that Norm had been producing. Most people know that professors must "publish or perish" but might not realize that often only one kind of publishing matters: original research in peer-reviewed scholarly journals or with university presses. To earn tenure and thus keep his job, Pearson would need to start publishing such work, and quickly, which he had never been able to do. So in the late 1940s, he began producing articles: one on Sherwood Anderson, another on Longfellow, another on Melville, another on American poets and science. The problem was that his major project, the one that could truly make his name in the academy, would take years to gestate. The complete edition of Hawthorne's letters would be invaluable to scholars, but if Pearson couldn't earn tenure he would never be able to finish it. In 1948, though, a tempting alternate possibility presented itself: Dixon Wecter, now at the Huntington Library in Pasadena, floated a nebulous offer to Norm to relocate to Southern California, where the Huntington and Pomona College would cobble together a kind of joint research and teaching appointment for him, at $5,000 a year. The Huntington owned many important Hawthorne materials, and "an appointment here at the library means complete freedom for writing," Wecter told Pearson.[26]

It was a tough decision. In California, Norm could build a career that would combine teaching, editing, writing, and building the Huntington's collections. The pay was better, and there would be no frantic scramble for tenure. On the other hand, it wasn't Yale, and as much as he loved travel, he and Susan both were deeply rooted in New England and New Haven. Norm and Susan chewed over the idea for several weeks, but in April, Pearson learned that he had been awarded a Guggenheim Fellowship for 1948–49. This meant that he would have a year to fully devote himself to the Hawthorne letters. He let Wecter know that he wouldn't be taking the Huntington job that year.

Disappointed, Wecter nonetheless offered his friend a summer fellowship, and the family jumped at the opportunity. Norm had to finish grading exams, so Susan and Sue shared driving responsibilities from New Haven to Pasadena via Santa Fe, where Norm flew to meet them. They hit the great sights of the Southwest: Zion and Bryce Canyon, Taos, the Grand Canyon, and finally Las Vegas, where even Lizzie played the slots. While Pearson worked in the library six days a week from 8:45 to 4:30, Pasadena provided a memorable summer vacation for Susan and the girls. In some ways it was like home — at the local equivalent of the Lawn Club, they played tennis and badminton daily — but unlike New Haven it seemed that everyone around them had a swimming pool, and of course they were an hour from the beach, the desert, the mountains, and Lake Arrowhead. They marveled at Southern California's famed gaudiness at Knott's Berry Farm, which boasted both an artificial volcano and an image of the Transfiguration of Christ that opened its eyes, and the over-the-top Forest Lawn Cemetery in Glendale. Susan described Forest Lawn's kitschy Great Mausoleum, complete with a stained-glass replica of da Vinci's *Last Supper*, as "so huge, and so corny, that it just staggers the imagination, and you don't know whether to laugh or weep for the silliness of humanity."[27] In early August, the family took an overnight trip to San Diego, Tijuana, and Ensenada, and a week later Norm drove Susan and the girls eight hours north, to Bridgeport (near Yosemite and Mono Lake), where they spent a week at a dude ranch while Norm toiled in the Huntington reading room.

Returning to New Haven in September, Norm felt confident that with the work he had accomplished, and a year's worth of effort funded by his Guggenheim Fellowship, he would be able to complete his edition of the Hawthorne letters before his "tenure clock" was up, ensuring that he could stay at Yale. But he didn't see his career unfolding like that of so many who earn tenure and then continue to teach their classes and produce more scholarship on the same narrow topics. He loved being in the world too much for this, and increasingly, he saw avenues through which he could make an impact on the literary scene outside the academy. For Pearson, the "ivory tower" would not be a refuge or a prison, but rather a home base that gave him the institutional credibility and status to venture into other worlds. And indeed, from his comfortable position, he would quietly and usually invisibly change the course of American literary history, shape a new academic field, and help broker the marriage pact between American universities and the growing national-security state.

GRAMPAW AND THE COMMAHUNTER

Everyone who has a relationship with a great man
ought to contribute something to the record.
PEARSON TO HARRY MEACHAM OF THE ACADEMY
OF AMERICAN POETS, 1962

When Pearson rejoined the Yale faculty in the fall of 1949 after spending his Guggenheim year working on the Hawthorne letters, he launched in earnest what would become a remarkable twenty-six-year career.[1] Almost all the memorable things he did in the literary, cultural-diplomatic, and educational spheres were accomplished through or because of his job. But the day-to-day or even year-to-year life of a professor doesn't have much of a "narrative arc" besides, perhaps, the attainment of tenure and promotion. Most years unfold in largely the same way, varying primarily in the names of the classes and students taught, committees served on, articles published. Moreover, it's difficult to illustrate chronologically Pearson's impact in the overlapping spheres of influence in which he moved.

For that reason, here this life of Pearson will shift away from the chronological structure it has used up to now and shift to a thematic organization, with each chapter detailing Pearson's activities in one of these spheres from the late 1940s until his death. Chapters 8, 9, and 10 all dig into how he established personal relationships with key modernist writers — especially Ezra Pound, William Carlos Williams, Marianne Moore, and above all H.D. — and used those relationships to shape not just those writers' reputations but also a new understanding of American modernism and American literary history. Chapter 11 examines how Pearson helped steer the nascent academic field of American studies into the informal coalition of cultural and political institutions that had come together to support the US side in the Cold War, and how in his own work he blurred the distinctions between professor, cultural diplomat, and spy. Chapter 12, then, returns to one key institution—Yale—and looks at the roles Pearson played as the university and its students experienced the early Cold War and then changed dramatically in the 1960s and early 1970s. Chapter 12 also explores how Pearson's stalled scholarly work made him a "man out of time" in his own department, and how as a result he left his mark on the university and in the academy not through his writing but rather through his teaching, mentoring, and collecting. Through these chapters, I hope to make the case that while the outward contours of Pearson's professional life might not appear notable, his achievements and impact in these several overlapping spheres were truly unique and extraordinary.

In the early 1940s, modernist literature was in a peculiar place. Great literary experiments like Virginia Woolf's *Mrs. Dalloway* or Eliot's *The Waste Land* no longer felt revolutionary to many readers. They had lost their fierce newness, their threat to middle-class society. Once a US district court had overturned its ban, Random House's Bennett Cerf even tried to teach Joyce to middle-class consumers in a magazine advertisement headed "How to Enjoy James Joyce's Great Novel *Ulysses*."[2] But even if it no longer seemed quite so challenging or innovative, modernist writing was still baffling to most readers and seemed intentionally obscurantist. Readers needed to be shown how to read it, what it meant, who was important in the movement, and why.

Institutions do this. Book reviews interpret and evaluate works. The publishing industry enshrines the "most important" writers in anthologies and textbooks that explain how to read their works. Libraries and museums preserve their papers and belongings. Boards and academies give them awards and honors. Eventually, universities teach classes in those writers and movements, and scholars write studies about them.

Together, these institutions don't just create writers' reputations; they shape the very process of reading. After the war, Pearson, through his institutions, did all these things for a set of American modernist writers and, in so doing, changed the common understanding of American literary history.

Certainly, this collector of people relished adding modernist writers to his network. But his love for experimental writing wasn't just a way to get in the mix. His work on Hawthorne had convinced him that that writer was experimental for his time, and that Hawthorne's narrative innovations—his use of gothic themes and atmospheres, his combination of realism and fairy-tale unreality, and above all his belief that the American experience was a unique one—had been perhaps the first important step forward in establishing an American literature. And even though their work might seem like an utter rejection of the tradition that Hawthorne represented, Pearson believed that the American modernists, from H.D. to Faulkner to William Carlos Williams, were actually carrying forth Hawthorne's project of moving American literature away from its English roots and embracing the New World. And finally, while he appreciated modernist writing's virtuosity and strangeness, Pearson believed that modernist writing's virtuosity and strangeness were a reaction to and reflection of the tumultuous modern world, and he wanted readers to see that.

For Pearson, science was the key to modernism's embrace of the new. "The modern American poet's concern with words," he wrote in 1949, "has at the very outset of his creative activity been profoundly affected by scientific thought."[3] The Enlightenment taught us that the world is fundamentally *ordered*: from Newton's laws of the physical world to the "Great Chain of Being" Alexander Pope described in his 1734 *Essay on Man*, everything was regular, expressing an underlying logic that implied a Designer. But the dawn of the twentieth century brought "an incredible disordering of old axioms and definitions." "Aristotelian logic had now been displaced. Euclidean geometry in respect to space had been overthrown. Newtonian physics had lost its primacy. Physical reality was constantly being redefined by geology, chemistry, physiology, physics, optics, and psychology. The older laws of the universe no longer obtained; they were insufficient to explain phenomena. . . . The world as we see it today through the mind's eye of the scientist is no longer a familiar and substantive mechanics but a helter-skelter of electronics out of which we can extract only equations of infinite variables."[4] For Pearson, artists and philosophers, not scientists, made sense of a world thrown off its axis. "Twentieth-century man learned to see differently, as Cézanne showed him. He learned to hear differently, as Schoenberg did. He learned to think differently, as Whitehead taught him." A frequent visitor to New York galleries and concert halls, Pearson knew modern music and art well. But as an expert in literature, he was most interested in how poets responded to this disorienting new world. In a 1961 Voice of America lecture, Pearson identified Stein, Pound, and Eliot as the poets whose work was "an expression not simply of the 20th-century mood but of the 20th-century mind." Stein, who "strives for the achievement of a constant present in her prose . . . is representing by the structure of her text what Bergson and Whitehead were asserting philosophically in regard to the nowness of time." And Pound—even though so much of his poetry is concerned with history—is also trying to express the "nowness" of all time. "History is not a past (that is, a concluded) event" for Pound. "It is present even by the very fact that the hero knows it in his own mind. . . . Actual and vicarious experience exist simultaneously."

Psychology was another current in modernism, Pearson argued. Stein had studied at Harvard with the father of psychology, William James, and his ideas deeply influenced her writing. Pound never read much in the field, but Pearson saw its influence in the structure of the *Cantos*, in which "cue leads to conscious and unconscious response in unpredictable sequence and constant flow. The apparent incoherences of the sequences of events in Pound's *Cantos* are in fact a representation of the flow of the hero's consciousness. There is no abandonment of logic; there is only the substitution of a logic of the imagination." Eliot, too, relies on the "same combining logic of the imagination for his vision of lost order and faded beauty."[5] In his most sweeping statement about the paradigm change from the mechanistic Enlightenment to the chaotic modern age, Pearson writes: "If the poet in response to the scientific destruction of the idea of a mechanical universe has filled the apparent void by a procedural logic, he has done so with a new logic of the senses, in which coherence in chaos is obtained by the cohesive force of the imagination itself."[6] Because of this, modernist writers are forced to return to their most basic of tools: words. "The paramount consideration of the writer . . . becomes words and their arrangement," Pearson wrote in 1949. But these words, and their relationship to meaning, have also changed their function because of all the century's other dislocations. "Even words, which have been our reliable source for the communication of experience, have been affected by science and are no longer valid in the older referential sense to which we were accustomed. . . . Old definitions of physical reality have lost validity. Their reference was to something which no longer exists in the same terms."[7] Pearson identifies in modernist poetry an attempt to capture, through the tools of language, this new reality, how modern science has dismantled our old understandings of the physical world. Quoting Archibald MacLeish's poem "You, Andrew Marvell," Pearson points to how because of MacLeish's rendering of the concept of "time, space, curvature" with "a new syntax . . . there is in the poem really no proper subject or predicate, and there are no commas to break up a flow of data which passes endlessly through a constant present of time."[8]

While writers like MacLeish, Stein, Dos Passos, James Joyce, Hart Crane, Virginia Woolf, and others tried to capture the new science and psychology through syntax and narrative voice, imagism—the movement associated with Pound and H.D. and Williams—proposed a different solution. Imagism radically pared back poetry: gone was the personal voice of the poet; gone was flowery language; gone were rhyme and meter. Instead, imagism exalted the image, or as Pound defined it in his 1913 imagist manifesto, "that which presents an intellectual and emotional complex in an instant of time."[9] For the imagists, the image was almost mystical in its power, and "it is better to present one Image in a lifetime than to produce voluminous works."

Pearson was especially drawn to Pound and H.D. because their work was the most essentially imagistic in using the image and the metaphor as the solution to this problem of the insufficiency of the word and the dissociation of language and the world. Words attempt to point to a concrete and unchanging reality that modern science has shown to be radically unstable and contingent, so meaning must combine words and imagination to "impinge . . . directly on the senses of the reader and become . . . a stimulus to knowledge." "If science took [away] from the poet of our century a complete reliance on the individual meaning of words," Pearson explained, "the loss only served to emphasize to the poet the vital importance and validity of the structured image. H.D. and Pound were reacting to the impact of science in the precision of their descriptions, but they were doing it in the way characteristic of poets."[10]

For Pearson, then, modernist art in general, and imagist poetry in particular, sought to *reconcile* a world broken apart by the modern age. Ironically, Pearson here diverges markedly from the most prominent of the modernist poets, Eliot. In his essay "The Metaphysical Poets," Eliot diagnosed a "dissociation of sensibility" beginning just after the Elizabethan period, when thought and emotion—which according to Eliot the great poets of the premodern era had experienced as one single complex—came to be expressed and experienced separately. The ensuring years had only deepened that "dissociation," until in the modern era all we have are fragments yearning for a wholeness that will never return.[11]

Pearson agrees with Eliot that in the modern era, the seemingly natural relationship between time, the material world, and the language we use to describe them had all been radically disrupted. But Pearson saw in imagism a *reintegration* of these now alienated aspects of consciousness. Metaphors and images didn't require the rational, empirical Enlightenment assumptions that the modern era had shattered, making imagist poetry "a religious and philosophical act as well as an aesthetic achievement." This fragmented era requires someone who can reconcile the *magisteria* of the "scientist and the poet," the creative and the rational. The modernist poet "has been the preserver of the Renaissance heritage. In his concept of total reality he has accepted what science has taught about this newest of new worlds, but in presenting it as a work of art he has encompassed an even wider sphere."[12]

Furthermore, this new way of seeing and describing the world, this response to the crumbling of Enlightenment and empirical certainties, that the modern poet has created has *not*, contrary to the pessimistic views of prominent critics of the time like Irving Howe and Lionel Trilling, created an abyss of meaninglessness and nihilism. Quite the contrary, in Pearson's view. This reconciliation of a broken time, this creation of a new reality from the shards of the old, came from the modernists' drive to revive community, their relentless questioning and self-examination. H.D. had been raised in the tight-knit Moravian community of eastern Pennsylvania, and although she had rejected that faith she still valued its communal feeling, and she used classical imagery and themes in her work to forge her own, deliberate community. Williams, especially in his long poem *Paterson*, wanted to tell the story of diverse American communities coming together to build a society in a new land. And Pound saw his own work as "the tale of the tribe," a counterhistory that exalted the values that should undergird a community and a state.[13]

No one would call the modernists "new Puritans," but in Pearson's mind, they had more in common with the Puritans than one might think, particularly in modernism's spiritual aspects. The divine the modernists strove for, though, was not the Christian God, but rather the mystical source of creativity itself, the eternal powers that ancient cultures pictured as gods or demons, or that the Romantic poets understood as the imaginative faculty, or that Freudian or Jungians saw as the psyche or the archetypal energies that predate the individual. In their thinking about the roots of creativity, the modernists drew on all these precursors, and Pearson shared their mysticism. "Art was a means of devotion," he wrote in 1948, "and the poem or tale was a form of prayer."[14]

Finally, Pearson also saw in modernist poetry a valorization of the individual, which was also an affirmation of the values of the West. "If we look at the psychological history of twentieth-century America," Pearson wrote, "it has been the poet who . . . has made the strongest public stand for the dignity and freedom of the individual."[15] Modernist literature had long celebrated the individual, especially against an oppressive or philistine society. This exaltation of the individual then gained a political inflection in the 1930s, when both fascism and Communism insisted that the collective—the state, or the party, or the people—was supreme. In the United States and the UK, the struggle against fascism was often figured as a fight for the individual against the faceless forces of Nazism. Early Cold War rhetoric, then, leaned heavily on this polarity, even as the enemy changed. And the Soviet Union obliged, with its excoriations of "bourgeois individualism." Modernist poetry, then, stood for the reintegration of consciousness, for the "Renaissance heritage," for the creation and maintenance of community (*not* collectivism), and for the fundamental importance of the individual: that is, for all the values the West was purportedly defending in the Cold War. And although almost all readers and critics at the time saw modernism as an essentially European phenomenon, native to Paris and London and Zurich and Berlin, Pearson found his modernist paragons much closer to home.

"No group in America's literary history," Pearson wrote in his 1938 anthology, "has proved so significant as that in which . . . Ezra Pound, Hilda Doolittle, William Carlos Williams, and Marianne Moore moved as friends."[16] For a few months in the first decade of the twentieth century, these future poets formed an informal personal and creative circle in Philadelphia, while Pound and Williams studied at the University of Pennsylvania and Moore and H.D. were classmates at Bryn Mawr. (Pound was even engaged to H.D. for a time.) In no small part because of Pearson, this tetrad is now widely regarded as the precursor compound of American modernist poetry, the unstable supercharged nucleus that would explode across the literary world and energize countless other poets and movements even today.

Pearson first became acquainted with each of them through the anthology and had met them all in person before the war. H.D. was so central to Pearson's life and career, and he to hers, that she will receive her own chapter in this book. But how he conducted his relationships with Pound, Williams, and Moore—as well as other prominent poets of the time including Wallace Stevens, W. H. Auden, Muriel Rukeyser,

John Gould Fletcher, and Horace Gregory—reveals not only Pearson's often invisible impact on American literary history, but also the pivotal and growing importance of *institutions* such as publishers, universities, foundations, and prize committees in creating that history in postwar America, and how Pearson expertly, if often invisibly, steered those institutions for the benefit of the writers he supported and the story he wanted to tell about links between modernism, American literature, and American culture.

And although he generally eschewed controversy, through this work Pearson found himself embroiled in one of the thornier literary episodes of the 1940s and 1950s: the case of Ezra Pound. The expatriate Pound, the first of this group to gain public attention, had been a prominent literary figure since before World War I. His work ranged from imagist gems of the 1910s such as "In a Station of the Metro" to the increasingly impenetrable *Cantos*, published in installments since the 1920s. He was equally well known, at least in literary circles, for his work on behalf of other writers as a networker and promoter. A strong case could be made that Pound created, or at the very least jump-started, American modernist poetry, first with his Philadelphia friends and then with dozens of others, such as Eliot.

Like Stein, his only rival as a modernist impresario, Pound left conservative America and decamped for Europe to pursue his muse. But where Stein had, a decade earlier, settled in among the painters of Paris, Pound went to London in 1908 to seek out what was happening in poetry. After a short apprenticeship immersed in Victorian and Georgian poets like Robert Browning and Lionel Johnson (and a brief encounter with Henry James), Pound reinvented himself as an avant-gardist, editor, and talent scout, and as a hype man for a series of short-lived poetic movements that he often created and named himself, such as imagism. Pound assembled its 1914 debut, the collection *Des Imagistes*, and even, in preparing one of her poems for submission to *Poetry* magazine in 1913, bestowed on his ex-fiancée Hilda the sobriquet that she would use the rest of her life.

Even if Norm hadn't liked Pound's poetry—and he did, very much—he knew that the Oxford anthology would need a large selection of Pound, whom he called "the most dominant personality of [the twentieth century's] first two decades."[17] Benét and Pearson included over a dozen of Pound's poems, as well as his imagist manifesto, "A Retrospect." Realizing that Pound's *Cantos* were daunting even for most followers of modernist poetry, Pearson also asked Pound for "another brief section [addressing] the technical problems behind the writing of the Cantos," but Pound, who had no patience with readers and critics who complained about the opacity of the *Cantos*, declined.[18]

Pound was enthusiastic, domineering, autodidactic, bombastic, loyal, and one of history's most florid mansplainers. (Stein memorably dismissed him as a "village explainer, excellent if you were a village, but if not, not.")[19] He refused to accept conventional opinion, which made him an effective leader for an artistic movement, but his oppositional character, and his unshakable confidence in his own ideas, led him to embrace and promulgate any number of fringe theories and ideas. By the 1930s, he had publicly committed himself to Mussolini's Fascist government in Italy and was increasingly expressing anti-Semitic conspiracy theories as well, including in his poetry. His books had stopped selling, and his American publisher dropped him in 1937, allowing James Laughlin's fledgling New Directions Books to pick him up. In 1939, he returned to the United States for a brief "lecture tour," and Pearson finally met him in person at a Yale reading organized by Angleton.

Pound only disgraced himself further in the following years. By 1943, he was making wartime radio broadcasts on behalf of Italy, and a grand jury indicted him for treason. After Mussolini fell, Pound was captured, held in a US Army detention camp, returned to the United States in 1945, avoided trial by a plea of mental incompetence, and was committed to a Washington, DC, mental hospital. The case of Ezra Pound bitterly divided the literary community, with many writers and critics arguing that Pound's service to literature outweighed his wartime offenses, and with others demanding that he pay for his crimes. When Pound's 1948 collection *The Pisan Cantos* won the inaugural Bollingen Prize—an award sponsored by the Library of Congress—the Pound furor reignited even more fiercely. The Bollingen controversy, ostensibly just about whether an agency of the US government should honor an indicted wartime traitor, became a proxy battle about much larger questions that pitted intellectual camps against each other: Was modernist literature a dangerous European import? Was anti-Semitism as unacceptable as treason? Did literature have a responsibility to express socially redeeming values, or should we read it apolitically? Had American elites become so disconnected from "ordinary" people that they couldn't see how offensive this prize was? In two inflammatory June 1949 *Saturday Review of Literature* articles, Harvard professor and traditionalist poet Robert Hillyer characterized the prize as a plot to force modernism on the American public, perpetrated by a cabal of anti-American poets, elite professors and critics, and shadowy plutocrats and intellectuals. This was "disheartening," Fitts lamented to Pearson, "because so many half-baked teachers & critics—the audience of *SRL*—will find in that article and in the frenetic supporting editorial a confirmation about all that they've feared and believed about modern poetry."[20]

Banding together to defend the prize was an unlikely alliance of the conservative New Critics and leftist (and largely Jewish) New York Intellectuals, who insisted that art should be judged solely on its own aesthetic achievements, not on any social or political criteria, as to do so would "deny the validity of that objective perception of value on which civilized society must rest," in the words of the Bollingen committee itself. If a fascist anti-Semite wrote the best poems of the year, they argued, his fascism and anti-Semitism detracted not a bit from how good the poems were. (Cynics such as Gregory took neither side and assumed that the committee had given the prize to Pound merely to "assure front-page publicity for a new Poetry Award," adjudging the combatants on both sides to be mere "tools.")[21]

Although he supported the prize committee's decision, Norm observed this spat from the outside. Yale had become the center of the New Criticism (an approach to literature detailed more fully in chapter 12 of this biography), and many of its major figures were now his friends and colleagues. He had no love for their method, but at the same time, he agreed with them that an artist's politics, no matter how reprehensible, should not determine one's opinion of the work. Writing to William Carlos Williams just after Pound was returned to face trial, veteran anthologist Pearson concluded that "he is not now much different from the recent years before the war. . . . I belittle him on his own terms by still admiring much of what he did as a poet while distinguishing his poetics from his ideology and from him as a man. He started, as I once wrote, as the Longfellow de nos jours; he ended up something much nastier. . . . But I wouldn't kick him out of anthologies—those splendid mausoleums of reputations."[22] Norm also deplored Hillyer's "philistinism," but the cautious assistant professor had no desire to pile on publicly and declined when a group including critic Cleanth Brooks and poets Allen Tate and John Berryman asked him to cosign a protest letter. Although he rejected Hillyer's implicit linking of "the 'new poetry' and the 'new criticism' . . . the controversy has already been dragged out beyond any useful purpose" and he didn't want to contribute to the "hysterical," name-calling tone of the protest letter. Recalling the advice C. S. Lewis gave him—"how easy it is to call a man a fool and a blackguard, but how difficult it is to do without naming those opprobrious terms"—he suggested that it would be wiser to try to "win back" the other side.[23] Such equanimity, along with a reluctance to take a strong public stand, typified Norm's approach to controversies. His OSS work had taught him the importance of not pinning oneself down to one position as it would limit one's maneuverability when circumstances changed, and might alienate someone who could possibly be of help later.

He had also reestablished contact with the Pound camp. Characteristically, this was also in service of the institutions Pearson served, and couched as an offer that would benefit his interlocutor. In 1947 he proposed to Pound's wife, Dorothy, that Ezra sell his papers to Yale to raise money for his defense and eventual living expenses. (Dorothy demurred, but Yale did end up with a considerable amount of Pound's correspondence when it purchased from the poet in 1949 thousands of carbons and microfilms of his letters that David Paige was using to compile his edition of Pound's letters.)[24] Pound also recognized the value of personal relationships, and so, as he was finishing the translation of Confucius's *Analects* begun during his detention in Italy, he asked Pearson to track down references in the Yale library. Seeing this as a way to ingratiate himself, Pearson happily agreed. But Pound was a demanding master, and within a few months, Pearson found himself serving as Pound's volunteer typist for this project, berated by an impatient and ungrateful Dorothy. "You say you want to be helpful," she griped, "but what possible help do you think it can be to sink a [manuscript] into oblivion for over two months? . . . A typing job in other countries from any normal agency is something done inside a week."[25]

Pound himself had kept publicly quiet during most of the Bollingen flap, but as his mental and physical health improved, he started writing again. (The *Analects* translation Pearson typed, for instance, appeared in two consecutive 1950 issues of the Pound-friendly journal the *Hudson Review*.) With some restrictions on his freedom loosened, he started to see visitors. Old friends Williams, Eliot, E. E. Cummings, MacLeish, and James Laughlin all came by. Other writers arrived, as well, including Tate, Elizabeth Bishop, Katherine Anne Porter, Stephen Spender, Conrad Aiken, and even Langston Hughes. The poet and American studies scholar Charles Olson visited regularly, until he could no longer stomach Pound's rantings about Jews. Professors, as well, made pilgrimages. Marshall McLuhan visited several times and in 1948 brought with him his protégé Hugh Kenner, who would later publish his Yale dissertation as the first book-length study of Pound. (Kenner had not met Pearson while at Yale—ironic, given that Pearson was actually teaching a grad seminar on the poet.) Even Pearson traveled down to Washington, in December 1952.

In addition to these guests, a loose-knit group of oddball admirers had formed a kind of salon around Pound, who held court in the hospital yard every afternoon. "He is the Socrates with his flock of unorthodox wanderers who drift into his fold," Pearson reported to H.D. "At precisely one o'clock they are at the gate of St. Elizabeths and walk to where Ezra is sitting out of doors under the trees." While Dorothy sits and listens, Pound "hears the lessons and gives out the next assignment."[26] Soon, Pound began an affair with one of these groupies, painter Sheri Martinelli.

More distasteful was the constant presence in this cohort of several young men attracted to Pound's anti-Semitism and conspiracy theories, including Eustace Mullins, T. David Horton, and John Kasper. Mullins, Horton, and Kasper, all active in far-right politics, saw Pound as a guru, and the poet's habit of ordering his followers to take up projects meshed with their youthful energy and entrepreneurialism. Mullins, a committed anti-Semite, eventually published a sloppy biography of the poet. Kasper had run a Poundian bookshop, then at Pound's urging started a publishing endeavor in 1950. Kasper and Horton's Square Dollar books, named for the cover price of each volume, reprinted texts in Pound's alternative economic, historical, and literary canon. There was poetry (Basil Bunting), literary criticism (Fenollosa's *The Chinese Written Character as a Medium for Poetry*, a touchstone of Poundian poetics), science (Louis Agassiz's anti-Darwinist work), and Pound's own work (his *Analects*). But it was mostly politics of the conspiratorial, anti–Federal Reserve stripe that so obsessed Pound.[27]

Pound wanted to get his ideas into American colleges, but he loathed the academy and especially professional literary scholars (or "commahunters" as he often called them). So to give the series the academic credibility he personally scorned, Pound assembled a board of university-professor advisory editors. "He does so, paradoxically, want the support of the professors against whom he always, and frequently rightly, screams in protest,"[28] Pearson told H.D. The advisory committee—consisting of Pearson, McLuhan, Otto Bird from Notre Dame, L. R. Lind from Kansas, and several others—was told they would oversee the selection of titles (it didn't; Pound did), would meet regularly (it never met), and would publicize and "assure the circulation and sale of books as they appear." The advisers' performance of this last, the real purpose of the committee, never satisfied Kasper, Horton, or Pound. "For shame, professor . . . the best ground-work accomplished thus far toward getting Square Dollar in the curriculum," Kasper badgered Pearson in 1952, "has come from persons NOT of the advisory committee. Hugh Kenner, Charles Olson, and William D. Hull have all placed Fenollosa and Pound's Analects in their classroom. Certainly Dr Pearson is not one to allow the 'utter and abject farce' of the American university to continue, is he?"[29]

For his part, Pearson confided to Pound that while he did assign Square Dollar books to his students, Kasper and Horton weren't particularly reliable on the distribution side of things "because of the twins' other jobs."[30] (Kasper was running his bookstore and then became active in the prosegregation movement after *Brown v. Board of Education*, and Horton worked part-time with a far-right group called Defenders of the American Constitution.) But Pearson's lack of hustle wasn't surprising, as he hadn't signed on because of any burning enthusiasm for the project but rather "as a gesture of friendship," he told H.D.[31] In addition to requiring his students to buy Square Dollar titles, Pearson pulled his weight on the publicity front. In an ethically iffy review of his own series in *Shenandoah* magazine, Pearson praised it as an innovative, outside voice: "Just as little magazines can provide a conspectus of what is fresh in contemporary clarity, so the little publishing houses, off the coastline, can, when imaginatively edited (and supported), recover what remains fresh from the past."[32]

"Imaginatively edited" it was, if one means solely by the imagination of Ezra Pound. More concerning, Pound and Kasper were increasingly of one mind, and that mind was going in darker and darker places. Asking Pound in 1953 for suggestions for new titles, Kasper specified that "I don't want any Jewish writers, composers, artists, etc., REPRESENTED unless the work is of such merit as to make it absolutely necessary."[33] As the series went on—it actively published until 1957, ultimately putting out ten books—Kasper threw himself into prosegregation work. And the student became, to some extent, the teacher: Kasper's own racism melded with Pound's anti-Semitism in a repellent symbiosis until the two came to share a virulent bigotry.[34] Never particularly concerned with America's racial issues before, at Kasper's urging Pound started to interpret the Constitution and the Fourteenth Amendment as not just allowing but mandating racial segregation, while Kasper eagerly adopted Pound's obsessions with sovereignty, national control over the money supply, and Jewish bankers. "Kasper regards Ezra as *cher maître* (and, to a real degree, vice versa)," Norm noted to H.D. with distaste.[35] And because of Pearson's eagerness to maintain his relationship with Pound, Pound was increasingly trying to drag Norm into this political morass.

In mid-1956, Kasper formed the Seaboard White Citizens' Councils with the motto "Honor-Pride-Fight: Save the White." (And unlike with the White Citizens' Councils in other states, Jews were excluded from Kasper's group.) In August, Kasper traveled to Clinton, Tennessee, to organize resistance to the integration of the public schools there. Pound coyly reported this to Pearson: "the excited Kasper off on something NOT universal, or at least superficially geared to local excitements."[36] Through the rest of 1956 and 1957, Kasper traveled the South agitating against integration and was a suspect in several bombings. He was acquitted of charges of sedition and inciting riot in November 1956, but national press coverage prominently identified him as a disciple of Pound's, complicating the campaign to get Pound released from St. Elizabeths. Later, Kasper served two short prison terms for his activities.

For his part, Pound was delighted that Kasper was preaching the Poundian gospel, and exasperated that the press misinterpreted their endorsement of segregation as a belief in white supremacy. The "jew press" was "furious that [Kasper] likes afro-americans but not kikes," he complained to Pearson.[37] (Influenced by Square Dollar author Agassiz, Pound believed that the races were anatomically distinct, and thus segregation was simply the justified separation of different species, not an expression of hatred or superiority.) He forwarded Pearson copies of Kasper's newspaper, the *Clinton-Knox County Stars and Bars*, and other racist material, while archly distancing himself. "[Kasper] is not acting on my orders, nor did he consult me / BUT I do not judge discretion of men acting in places I have never been," he told Pearson in a 1957 letter.[38]

Pearson hadn't signed on for any of this but chalked it up to Pound being "so hungry for attention and the sense of *being in* things that anything goes apparently."[39] Barraged by Pound's fulminating, racist letters, he tried to change the subject. "What the hell is [Kasper] doing [in Tennessee]?" he asked in 1956. "Much better if he'd keep to Square Buck series . . . , or to bookstore and pay me back the twenty bucks he still owes me."[40] A year later, he confronted Pound more directly on this: "Still can raise no enthusiasm for Kasper's rant. Can only see harm in what he tries to do. . . . Wish I could sense what you feel good in his rabbling."[41]

When he did respond to Pound's political rhetoric, Pearson's responses look like missives from an entirely different planet: his own establishmentarian New England Republican world. He was cautiously optimistic about Eisenhower's election in 1952, he told Pound, because it would bring about a "revolution"—specifically, a "revolution in the managerial sense and therefore well worth watching very closely. That is, the appointment of men who theoretically at least do know management; now we can see whether their kind of management can be turned over to govt. . . . I remember during the war being criticized by some big shots as being too 'professional.' But I don't admire the amateur per se in anything, whether in writing or statesmanship."[42] Pearson's faith in expertise epitomizes the postwar managerial/professional order that he himself embodied. Run by broad-based, interlocking, elite institutions, staffed by trained professionals and technocrats, this order was leading America into its new age of Cold War preeminence. Little, however, put Pound off more than this faith in bureaucrats and dismissal of uncredentialed amateurs. Pearson loathed Senator Joseph McCarthy because he was a populist and an ignoramus, while Pound, a passionate anti-Communist with a soft spot for demagogues, found him curiously appealing. Pearson also warned Pound away from the young poet and conservative thinker Peter Viereck for being a suck-up and "unclean physically as well as spiritually."[43] Viereck, son of a notorious Nazi sympathizer, rejected his father's politics and endorsed what he called "rooted liberty" and the "organic unity" of a people, ideas that would have been very appealing to Pound.

Although he refused to play along with his politics, Pearson indulged Pound's toxic ideas and language. He found Pound's bigotries largely benign, and certainly irrelevant to his actual accomplishments as a poet. "There was much talk of kikes and kikeressas," Norm recalled of a 1958 visit to Pound, "although not vicious."[44] Pearson may have been mildly liberal in this area by the standards of his milieu—"I do not approve," he reassured H.D., "of what Ezra says about the Jews"—but like Pound he also saw the world through the binary Cold War frame of communism versus freedom.[45] "Pound was never a Hitler man," Norm defended his friend to Bryher in 1958; "he was only violently anti-Communist."[46] Pearson and his peers might not have held, or at least expressed, Pound's and Kasper's poisonous prejudices, but they certainly didn't see them as disqualifying, or as evidence that these people, and the work they produced, were morally flawed.

Pound wrote and spoke in his own invented idiolect, combining faux down-home locutions and phonetic misspellings with a battery of key-words for his economic and anti-Semitic preoccupations. It was apparently hard to resist, and so like many of Pound's disciples and admirers, Pearson adopted a Poundian voice when writing to him, which is especially discordant given Pearson's usually elegant prose. When Pound demanded "what did you LEARN while in the 'intelligence' (end quote) service?" Pearson's response is initially cringeworthy: "What did I learn in the 'intellidunce' service? Waal, it warn't really that. My job was counter-'intelligence' (end quote), a task made much easier by the lack of such intelligence on the part of all services—German, wop, frog, eyetalian, usa, etc. . . . What did I learn? That nobody knows a half of what they think they do, and what they know ain't wuth knowing."[47] What seems on its face like an embarrassing attempt to mimic the master, though, is something much more telling about how Pearson moved through his institutions and circles, omnipresent and affable but never really trying to call attention to himself. He sidesteps here; he never answers the question directly because his OSS work was still secret, and frankly because he was, in a less direct way, still doing it, as we will see in chapter 11. "Once an agent, always an agent—for someone," Pearson once gnomically said about himself. Deflect, redirect, and flatter: like a good spy, always keep the focus on the target, and keep him talking.

But Pound and Pearson didn't correspond only about the Square Dollar series or racist politics in these years. A teacher by vocation and an editor by training and temperament, Pearson combined the two in the spring term of 1949 when he started teaching a graduate seminar on Pound and the *Cantos*, the first university class anywhere dedicated to the poet. Unlike Laughlin, whose publishing campaign framed Pound through New Critical lenses, Pearson didn't shy away from focusing on Pound's biography, unearthing long-forgotten facts about his early career. With access to the photocopies of his vast correspondence, Pearson had read through the poet's youthful letters with his parents and consulted with both Pound and H.D. about the real-world analogues to the literary figures depicted in early works such as "Hugh Selwyn Mauberley." His teaching, in fact, became some of the earliest scholarship on the poet.

Students responded. Pearson was always one of the most popular teachers at Yale, but in fall 1953, the second time he taught it, this class on one of the most difficult poems imaginable enrolled twenty-eight students—standing room only for a graduate seminar![48] "Wish there was something special to say about the way I teach Pound," he reflected in 1954, "but he makes such an open-door into the 20th-century, that almost anything is possible. . . . The best I can say is that it works."[49] This was partly because in using poems as a way to understand history and biography, and history and biography as ways to understand poetry, his class was so different from the others in Yale's now New Critical–dominated graduate program. Pearson was supremely confident in his approach, boasting that "I know perhaps even better than Pound does what he is really talking about, and I have no problem teaching the *Cantos* to Jews, when they understand him through me."[50]

The class was also a practical one. With the blessing of Pound and Laughlin, Pearson enlisted his graduate students to annotate and compile corrections to the *Cantos*. For their term project—interpreting and glossing all the references in a single Canto—most students turned in five- or six-page papers, but in 1952 the overachieving future journalist Tom Wolfe produced 105 pages on Canto 47![51] Pearson then compiled and mimeographed these into a samizdat reader's guide that he distributed among members of the small but growing network of Pound teachers and scholars. Pound, consumed with writing new Cantos, wasn't always supportive of this. He "fusses and fumes" at the idea that students were picking apart his references and "abhors a footnote," and "blows hot and cold" about the corrections but "is interested whenever we find a howler or a typographical error."[52] Pound did, though, immortalize Pearson in the poem: Norm's offhanded, typically anodyne comment to Pound about Istanbul's Hagia Sophia mosque (which he visited in 1954) appears in Canto 96: "'vurry,' said Pearson, N.H., 'in'erestin.'"

Throughout the mid-1950s, Pound and Pearson kept up a sporadic correspondence, focused partially on the editing work and partially on politics. Pound leaned on Pearson to find him publication outlets, and Pearson obliged by placing Canto 100 with the *Yale Literary Magazine*. In 1955, Pearson mounted an exhibition of Pound materials in the Sterling Library at Yale and helped a drama school group stage Pound's translation of Sophocles's *Women of Trachis* — which was, he assured Pound in a nod to the poet's hatred of bankers, "non-usurious in production" and "the first breath of fresh dramatic air in these here ivy-walled compounds in God knows how long."[53] Later, as Pound and Marcella Spann compiled the millennia-spanning anthology *Confucius to Cummings*, he sent Pearson long lists of poems to retrieve from the library.

Even though he rarely wrote on Pound himself, Pearson, like Kenner, created opportunities for critics and scholars to talk about Pound as a poet, not as an indicted traitor, which accelerated Pound's public rehabilitation and his entry into the canon of American literature. As chairman of the English Institute, he organized several panels on Pound's *Cantos* in 1953, signaling that the disgraced poet was indeed a legitimate, and even institutionally sanctioned, topic for scholarship. At the same time, Pearson was also helping the Berkeley grad student John Edwards with his *Preliminary Checklist to the Writings of Ezra Pound*. Pearson saw a little of himself in this serious and ambitious young man with "rather stern convictions about the importance of integrity in life but with no very strong directions as to where the point of view should lie."[54] Also like Pearson, Edwards was a collector, and he based his *Checklist* heavily on his own treasures, as no libraries were systematically collecting Pound materials. He counseled Edwards

not only on bibliographical minutiae but even on how to print, distribute, and price the *Checklist*, which eventually was published by a small
independent bookstore/printer in New Haven.[55] But Pearson's usually
reliable networks failed in Edwards's case: although he tried, he failed
to place Edwards in a top-rank academic job.

Particularly after his 1952 visit to Pound, Norm also became an
intermediary between Pound and H.D., who were reestablishing contact after many years of estrangement. Pound had always basked in the
hold he had over women—during the St. Elizabeths years, for instance,
Pound maintained his own marriage to Dorothy and his decades-long
romantic partnership with Olga Rudge, while also carrying on affairs
with at least two other women and engaging in flirtatious correspondence with exes. "Pearson sends an s.o.s. that I should send you a valentine," Pound coquettishly wrote H.D. in February 1953.[56] H.D., for
her part, sometimes felt that her life and career would have been easier
had she not realized she was bisexual, had she accepted Pound's offer
of marriage in 1907. So when a sheaf of poems he wrote for her back
then (eventually published as *Hilda's Book*) surfaced on the market,
Pearson had to navigate a delicate situation: attending to the feelings
of each friend, while also trying to obtain the book itself for Yale. (The
original manuscript went to Harvard's Houghton Library, but Yale did
obtain an early typescript.)

Unsurprisingly, given his own compulsion to make connections
and her desperate drive to be at the center of Pound's attentions, Pearson also was drawn into the orbit of Sheri Martinelli, a beatnik queen
who had become Pound's muse and lover, his "resident divinity" in the
words of his biographer. (In the *Rock-Drill* cantos, composed between
1949 and 1955, Pound figures her as Leucothea, Isis, Sybilla, Lux in
Diafana, and many other guises.)[57] But Pound grew bored with her
when the Texan teacher Marcella Spann entered his circle in 1957.
Martinelli, who already resented Pound's relationship with Dorothy,
burned with jealousy. When Pound was released and returned (with
Dorothy and Spann) to Italy, Martinelli left Washington for an aborted
stint at art school in Mexico, and then for the San Francisco area,
where she settled in Half Moon Bay. There, she painted, started a Poun-

dian magazine called the *Anagogic and Paideumic Review*, and became a fixture in the countercultural scene, befriending Allen Ginsberg, Jack Kerouac, Gary Snyder, and others. In her pre–St. Elizabeths days in Greenwich Village (where she had known Kasper) her circle included Anaïs Nin, Charlie Parker, Anatole Broyard, and Marlon Brando, and William Gaddis fictionalized her as "Esme" in his debut novel, *The Recognitions* (1955). She was an early champion of the work of Charles Bukowski and Clarence Major, as well, and Pearson saw in her, as in Pound, something of himself: a collector of people, a node in a network of artists. But she was also a link to the growing American counter-culture that had come to fascinate Pearson; through her, he learned about, and more importantly made contacts among, the underground poets of the West Coast whose work he read and whose artifacts he wanted to collect.

During but especially after her time in Washington, Martinelli wrote extensively to Pearson (whom she called "Boss"), mostly mooning about Pound's faithlessness, particularly after Spann supplanted her. In one typical lament, from just after Pound left the United States, she wailed that

> he promised for six years to take me to Italy so I could paint and just leave the drawings lying on the floor . . . but when Marcella went into the bushes with him . . . he threw me out into the street. . . . Why did he reward physical passion & throw divine and spiritual love into the gutter? . . . Marcella does not love grampa not that thrilling love which makes the female melt for the male. . . . She only loves to write letters home to Texas about how EP juwst lowves her and she cain't onderstand why.[58]

Typical of his own approach to people like this, Pearson was frank and analytical, writing her in 1960, after Pound had dumped Spann and fallen into silence, that "Ezra is, whatever you may like to think, an extremely difficult man to get along with—you couldn't have man-aged it. He has broken up with you, he has broken up with Marcella, he has broken up (hideously) with his daughter who has not had that easy a life either. He writes to people like myself only when he wants us to do something for him. We forgive him these things because of what he produces. But no one applauds his manner. All Ezra's life has been that of a spoiled only child."[59] Although his side of the correspondence often consisted of this—consoling her, explaining that Pound was unreachable, asking about the menagerie of bohemians and future artistic notables that orbited around her—the beautiful Martinelli's wild, artistic side was alluring to the devoted family man. Most of the female poets and writers that were part of Pearson's network, such as H.D. and Bryher, or Muriel Rukeyser, or Marianne Moore, also became friends of Susan's, but he was not interested in admitting Martinelli into his domestic world. She was something he could never have, and would never want, but at the same time he relished the vicarious bohemian experience and *frisson* of transgression she represented. Pearson wrote increasingly flirtatious or even lewd letters to her, addressing her as "Willow in the Wind" or "Queen of the Pacific," and sent her postcards of nudes and odalisques. (He lasciviously described to H.D. one "weird, appealing" Martinelli letter accompanied by "a self-photograph in a bikini, with the banner very much at half-mast.")[60] Ever the collector, he eagerly jumped at her offer to send him artworks and writings and, as he did with so many other artists and writers, sent her checks in return—$25 here, $50 there—for a "pad of paper" or "paint and potatoes." (She then began to send poems by Bukowski in the hopes that Pearson would fund him, as well.)[61]

Norm also connected Martinelli to H.D., whom Martinelli idolized, calling her "the real Isis." H.D., in turn, saw Martinelli as her doppelgänger, and identified with Martinelli's anguish at being spurned by Pound. She demanded that Pearson forward her Martinelli's letters and sent the painter money. In her analysis sessions with Erich Heydt, H.D. read Martinelli's current life as a recurrence of her own history. "[Heydt] felt she was intrinsically lonely—why? I want to work this out as it touches (very distantly) my own shock at Ezra leaving for Europe," H.D. mused, and she suspected that Martinelli's Mexican adventure was somehow a cosmic reverberation of her own writings about the Yucatán.[62]

After a concerted publicity campaign, coordinated by Laughlin and featuring literary A-listers including Hemingway, Eliot, and
MacLeish, in spring 1958 Pound was released and the charges against
him dropped, freeing him to travel. Always content to be a supporting player, Pearson wasn't central to this push to get Pound released
from captivity, but as with almost everything else in this story, he was
an interested participant, still convinced that Pound's poetic achievement outweighed any political crimes. He felt the odd man out among
the contributors to New Directions' 1956 pamphlet commemorating
Pound's seventieth birthday (which included Eliot, Auden, Stephen
Spender, and Edith Sitwell, and featured a Martinelli cover portrait of
Pound), but the press assured him that "even if you are not yourself a
writer . . . as a top representative of the academic world your inclusion
in actuality is a must."[63] He also helped produce a radio tribute to the
poet. Seeing an opportunity to crash the mass media, Pound implored
him to use Yale Radio to clarify that he and Hemingway had not in
fact had a falling-out: "The jew kikoRoose gang trying to make trouble
between Hem and me SINCE 1939 in the loathsome Jew York Herald,"
he complained.[64] Pearson, judiciously, declined.

Freed, Pound immediately began to embarrass himself with his blus-
tering gracelessness, sniping that Robert Frost—who had lobbied President Eisenhower and personally visited the attorney general to plead
for Pound's release—hadn't "been in much of a hurry" to help him
out, and laughing off his own venomous anti-Semitism as just "making
jokes about Jews." Interviewed by the *Washington Star*, Pound let loose
about Roosevelt, the "hell-hole" of St. Elizabeths, and the rest of his
grievances. "One or two more interviews like that and the government
will shanghai him out of the country," Pearson remarked to H.D.[65] His
departure, in fact, came soon after. Along with Laughlin, Pearson was
among the small number of Pound's circle who saw the poet and Dorothy off on their voyage back to Italy in June 1958. "Ezra was no different
than ever," Norm reported to H.D. "For a half hour he lectured me on
college entrance examinations, and his anthology, and what I must do
about it. He gave a dissertation on the Constitution, being corrected
by Horton who gave article and section and paragraph as authority for

each of Ezra's opinions."[66] And Pound brought it all full circle. As the *Cristoforo Colombo* docked at Naples ten days later, he announced his return by raising his right arm in a Fascist salute and announcing to the press that "tutt'America è un manicomio" [all America is a lunatic asylum].

With Pound back in Italy, Pearson's attention turned to more material things: Pound's materials. Pearson owned numerous rare Pound publications that he loaned to Yale, and along with Pearson's materials, Paige's copies of the letters had already made Yale's Pound collection the most extensive in the world. But Pound's own papers would complement those of Gertrude Stein, Carl Van Vechten, and James Weldon Johnson already at Yale. Like Pound, Stein and Van Vechten and Johnson were the centers of networks, and so their collections provided not just a view into their work but a broad portrait of twentieth-century literary culture. Pound's papers wouldn't just give Yale an unmatched breadth of modernist archival materials but would confirm that elite, conservative institutions certified the importance of modernism.

Pearson also wanted other archives with Pound-related materials, and he was creative in how he tried to get them. A 1953 appeal to Laughlin (who had a trove of modernist rarities) typifies how he approached anyone with treasures he wanted:

> Students here have been working on an annotation of the Cantos, and when they are finished Ezra has agreed to work out with me a truly definitive text of the Cantos. . . . He seemed pleased. The thing is to have *one* spot where people can go to find the whole of the toute ensemble. Yale has this now for Gertrude, Eliot, and Joyce. Pound should be alongside them. Would you consider depositing your things here, where they can be available. That doesn't per se mean giving them, although I wish you would (deducting for taxes), or letting us buy them (and we might be able to *try* to raise the money. . . . But simply to have them taken care of and available until you made up your mind would be something. I know what a loyal Harvard man you are, but in all honesty Yale has shown an interest in the 20th-century that Harvard is not likely to show. And since everything helps

everything else, your Pound would have its greatest service along the others, and would be filled out and maintained. What do you think?[67]

If one proposition didn't work, he had four more in his pocket. To Laughlin, he initially points out how these materials will be *used* by students and scholars, how Pound's papers and rarities will, along with Stein's and Eliot's and Joyce's, become the raw materials not just for the study of Pound but for the study of modernism as a movement — the very movement that Laughlin's own publishing house was founded to promote. In fact, these students were actually working pro bono for New Directions, which would eventually publish the corrected *Cantos*! Nor was Pearson suggesting that Laughlin's materials stay in New Haven indefinitely: this would just be a caretaking arrangement, until Laughlin decided where he really wanted them to go. (Of course, it would be difficult, practically and ethically, for Laughlin to yank his materials from Yale and transfer them to Harvard after a generation of students and scholars had come to rely on them.) Pound, he claimed, approved of this arrangement. And Pearson had already mastered the financial and legal practicalities of loaning, donating, or selling such collections.

Despite this entreaty, Laughlin didn't take Pearson up on his offer. Nor was Pearson being entirely honest in his assessment of Yale's resources at the time. While the university did hold the largest collection of Stein materials available anywhere, the Eliot collection was paltry, and the Joyce materials far from definitive, as the State University of New York at Buffalo already had an even larger collection.

The big prize, though, was Pound's archive. Within a few years of returning to Italy, Pound fell into a deep depression. He stopped writing, even the letters that had torrentially flowed from him for decades, even as a new generation of young poets started to credit him as their inspiration. With no personal contact with the poet — the two would only meet one more time, when a frail and aged Pound attended an Academy of American Poets dinner in 1969 — Pearson returned to his teacher-scholar-editor role with Pound's *Cantos*, working with Laughlin on the poems' texts. But he never lost sight of his quest to obtain the papers and eventually turned to Pound's daughter Mary de Rachewiltz, who was, according to Laughlin, "the only person who could influence him."[68] Although nominally a princess living in a Tyrolean castle, Mary was almost penniless, so Pearson offered her $1,500 to travel to the United States in 1958 to visit her father and work on an Italian translation of the *Cantos* and in 1962 conjured up a Yale Libraries stipend for her to catalog its Pound materials. He used State Department connections to untangle her convoluted passport situation. And from time to time he would just send her checks — $50 for travel expenses, $100 for a new washing machine.[69] Often, these checks and letters would also come with a suggestion that she sell *her* Pound materials to Yale. He also corresponded with and occasionally sent checks to Omar Pound, Dorothy's (but not Ezra's) son, who had less pull in the family affairs and mostly grumbled about how poorly Mary was treating his mother. Ultimately, Pearson's wrangling was successful, although other Yale officials helped him close the deal: in 1973, the first containers of the Pound collection came from Italy to New Haven, and $300,000 traveled in the opposite direction.

+ 9 +

THE NETWORKER

While working on a master's degree at the University of Pennsylvania in 1905, Pound had met a medical student from Rutherford, New Jersey, who like him wanted to be a poet. Despite their almost opposite personalities, political and social views, and poetic styles, Pound and William Carlos Williams developed a close friendship that would endure for the rest of their lives. And for a period in the 1950s, when the men maintained their mutual affection and respect but kept each other at arm's length, Norm became one of the few links between them. Pearson's relationship with the doctor-poet Williams was much more personal than the one he had with Pound. But through it, Pearson became entangled in one of the ancient personal imbroglios of this volatile group of friends. Rewriting the story of modernism, he learned, can be a messy thing.

Pearson had read Williams's poetry from the time he was an undergraduate, but while assembling the Oxford anthology, he came to find Williams's lesser-known works particularly appealing. The 1937 novel *White Mule*, for instance, was "keen sensitive prose by a man with a true ear and a superb sensitivity."[1] And for his part, Williams had long felt slighted by the public perception of him as only a supporting cast member in the drama of literary modernism. Joyce and Pound and Eliot were the headliners, and although he admired *Ulysses*, he found the *Cantos* obscure and increasingly distasteful, and he despised Eliot's work, which he found inhumane. He also resented the notion that the only Americans of consequence in the movement were those (like

Eliot and Pound and H.D.) who had made themselves into Europeans. Although he had lived, briefly, as an expatriate in Paris, his home was New Jersey, where he practiced medicine and was trying to create a uniquely American style of modernist writing, modest and rooted in the soil and people of the New World. Critics and publishers, though, were not interested in this: they wanted the grand gestures of the men of 1922. Norm greatly admired Williams's project of forging a native American modernism, showing how modernism was not a Continental import that American writers could only hope to imitate, that its had roots in earlier American literature. He saw this not just in Williams's familiar poetic works like *Spring and All* but in his stories and novels.

With the bravado of a young person experiencing his first professional success, in 1937 Pearson started plotting to compile (with Gregory's help) an edition that would make Williams's hard-to-find works available to the public. "It seems to me incredible that no commercial publisher will issue his work. . . . I'd like to talk to you and Williams about a volume. I haven't got a cent, unfortunately, to back it, but I am riding a wave with the publishers that is bound to recede once the initial impulse is over."[2] Williams felt vindicated by this young man's passion for this work and complained to Pearson that "I really can't understand why some publisher isn't interested because they publish book after book of verse, year after year, verse of all sorts of people from little children to lonesome old men and yet never mine."[3]

His frustration was at its height by the late 1930s. Random House had put out but barely promoted his last few books and showed no interest in compiling a collected or selected edition that could stir up more public attention. Fed up, Williams had signed an agreement with Laughlin to publish everything of his in perpetuity. (*White Mule* had been the first book New Directions ever published.) Pearson noted Williams's openness to working with an energetic young Ivy League hustler—although, creature of elite establishment institutions as he was, he found it a "desperate commentary on the arts" that Williams would be reduced to publishing with an undergraduate's shoestring startup.[4] "So help me God—and I say this with dead seriousness— I know that your stuff stands strong and secure. You have your audience; you always will have your audience. You'll see it grow before you kick off; and I'll see it grow (and help to shove it) for a little while longer than that."[5] Williams responded gratefully to Pearson's ardor. "Your taste is exceptional [and] the most remarkable thing is your enthusiasm. Where the hell you get that I don't know, but by God you have it."[6]

When they finally met in person in spring 1938, they immediately clicked. They exchanged warm letters during Norm's Chicago hospital stay, and Pearson continued to reassure Williams that the literary establishment snubbed him merely out of ignorance. Clifton Fadiman's lukewarm *New Yorker* review of Williams's 1940 novel *In The Money*, Norm remarked, was because "he simply didn't know what to say, and just pissed on the jacket blurb."[7]

Even this early in their friendship, Pearson was already nudging Williams to put his books and manuscripts somewhere they would be "safe from fire, from revolution, from loving executors." Pearson breathlessly described the little-magazine collection that he was starting to build (knowing that Williams had numerous copies of defunct and rare publications) and the exhibitions that he had already begun to organize "for Ezra, for Marianne, Stevens, Hilda, etc., etc. And yourself, and that pretty soon." "Yale is enthusiastic about" the central repository of modernism in New Haven that Norm planned to build, "and the English department are getting more and more so."[8] Williams, despairing of the clutter in his house, started to send Pearson bundles of his old magazines.[9]

After he returned from the war, Norm immediately rekindled his friendship with the poet and his wife, Floss, through letters and visits. In one letter, Williams remarked on "my dear friends, you first among them," and two years later he called Pearson something of a soulmate: "I have been closely attached to you since we met at Sarah Lawrence one evening many years ago. Something took place then which has to do with human dignity if not survival. Maybe it was love, who knows?"[10] But in the early 1950s, Williams fell on hard times, suffering debilitating strokes in March 1951 and again in August 1952. Money became tight after Williams pulled back on his medical practice. In 1950, Laughlin promised to pay Williams $250 a month for life, but

Williams declined and broke his agreement with New Directions to sign a three-book contract with Random House. But a publisher that big just didn't have much interest in promoting an aging poet whose books had never sold much. His 1952 appointment as poetry consultant to the Library of Congress fell through when he was accused of being a Communist (because he had donated to leftist causes in the 1930s), a fascist (because he was a friend of Ezra Pound), and physically unfit to serve (in the opinion of Librarian of Congress Luther Evans).[11]

Pearson did what he could to help. In 1947, he paid Williams to give a keynote talk to the English Institute, and in 1951 he brought the poet to Yale for a reading for a $150 fee. Pearson chose the poems for New Directions' *Selected Poems of William Carlos Williams* (1949), which served as the general-audience-aimed selected edition Williams had wanted for so long.[12] Doubling its prize money in 1953, the Bollingen committee gave $1,000 each to Williams and Archibald MacLeish, reflecting Pearson's influence after Yale Libraries became the official host for the award committee. And in 1954, Pearson arranged for Yale to purchase Williams's library and papers for $5,000: just one-sixtieth what the library would pay nineteen years later for Pound's archive.[13]

Although he was generally diplomatic and sure-footed in personal relationships, by insinuating himself into this group of forty-year friends Pearson also awkwardly stepped into one of their long-simmering feuds. Bryher had known Williams since 1921, when she had wed his close friend Robert McAlmon. Two days after the wedding, Williams received a postcard depicting several actors with their hands in a pot of money and signed "D.H." Williams interpreted this cryptic card as a derisive message from H.D., sneering at gold-digging McAlmon. H.D. denied this, but Williams "needed someone to blame for what he considered this travesty of a marriage, and he had come to believe that H.D. had masterminded the whole thing to get Bryher for herself," Williams's biographer Paul Mariani concludes.[14]

Williams nursed his bitterness alone for decades until briefly recounting the episode in his 1951 *Autobiography*: "Floss and I received a postcard . . . signed, obscurely, D.H., in bold capitals. I accused H.D. later of being the sender, but she violently denied it. I never believed her."[15] This public besmirching enraged Bryher, who resolved to force Williams to apologize. "I know that he is sick and embittered," she wrote Gregory, "but I really can't let his lies about H.D. and myself pass unchallenged."[16] It also impeded Pearson's plans. Only a few weeks before the *Autobiography* appeared, Pearson had suggested to Bryher that she give Williams $3,000 "for a year's rest at least in which he can write and not have to practice medicine." Once he read the passage, he tried to soften the blow: "he is a little snide," he told Bryher, "but I daresay [H.D.] will take it in her stride." But when Bryher saw the book, she resolved to take action—at the very least, a letter in the *TLS* demanding a public apology from Williams, and perhaps a libel suit on top of that. In his deliberate, pragmatic fashion, Pearson tried to convince her that it would be best to "act with truest dignity" and simply ignore it, for any reaction would draw more attention to what was "not even remotely a good book," and would bring embarrassing public attention to the intensely private Hilda. Furthermore, libel suits were much more difficult to win in the United States than in Britain, and if they wanted to punish him, what would hurt more than to deny the ailing, struggling Williams the $3,000 he was counting on? And it did hurt. Williams's financial hardships, the smears resulting from his Library of Congress appointment, his health problems (which now included the loss of sight in one eye), and his ongoing failure to receive what he felt was his due acclaim sent him into a deep depression in 1953. "He broods about death," Pearson worried.[17]

The episode even ended Williams's and Pearson's friendship. In her memoir *The Heart to Artemis* (1962), Bryher alleged that Williams had a "hatred of his native land" and, even worse, was "not particularly popular" among the Lost Generation crowd: "he apparently hated the lot of us." She also threw Pearson under the bus, albeit not by name. Alluding to the postcard flap, she remarked that "I wished to bring a legal action against [Williams]. My lawyers argued that this would only attract publicity to the book. I have always regretted taking their advice. All the survivors from the [Latin] Quarter should have joined together to refute his charges in open court. There is the danger otherwise that future historians of the period may believe them after we are dead."[18] Even though a savvy reader, acquainted with the players here, would easily recognize the cautious and deliberate Pearson as the "lawyer" who tried to cool Bryher down, the Williamses were outraged at what they saw as Pearson's betrayal. "Because I own the copyrights to Bryher's books," Pearson told Laughlin, "they feel I was responsible for what Bryher said about Bill in her memoirs."[19] At the time, though, Pearson was unaware of Williams's ire, as the two had not written or spoken for months before Bryher's book appeared. When Williams died in March 1963, Norm still did not know that his old friend had shut him out, and only learned of this from Floss's response to Gallup's condolence note: "Norman OK'd a passage in Bryher's book concerning Bill which is 100% false—and how Norman could do such a thing is beyond us.—Bill was so incensed—when he read that he said that he never wanted so see or have anything further to do with Norman. . . . So—when you plan to come here to collect the material you are entitled to—please remember that Norman Pearson is not to come with you."[20] This must have deeply hurt Pearson, but he handled it dispassionately. "I deeply regret this reaction on Floss's part," he wrote, "but I do not see that anything can be done about it. In no way does it alter my affectionate regard for them both."[21]

The oddest member of the Philadelphia tetrad might have been Marianne Moore. With her lapidary, lexicomanic poetry and unconventional domestic life—living with her domineering mother until she was in middle age—she had always evoked curiosity in the literary world, and of course Pearson wanted to meet her. He included almost a dozen of her poems in the anthology but was not able to tempt her into a correspondence at that time. Helen Neill McMaster brought Moore to Sarah Lawrence for a reading in 1940 and because he couldn't attend sent him a detailed, three-page report and character sketch of the poet: "The fleeting first impression is one of restraint, even coldness. She was wearing a nondescript black dress, exquisite collar of very fine lace close to the throat, and most delicate, almost microscopic lace point at the wrists. . . . She began talking about the making of [a new] poem in almost technical terms. Her language is like her verse, marvelous vocabulary. . . . I had expected something of an old maid with a

mother fixation. I found nothing of the sort; rather exceptional keen-
ness, intellectual curiosity of the first order, great understanding of
human beings regardless of sex."[22] (Moore's conversation, like her writing, was baroquely constructed and studded with recondite words, and
Pearson described it as being like "what must have run through Henry
James's head before he met the Queen.")[23]

Soon after, the two actually met, at a party in a New York apartment. Pearson's sly charm was one of his great weapons and almost, but
never entirely, masked his burning ambition. And Moore was certainly
charmed, as she told her brother:

> Mr. Pearson is a great wag, —as offsetting his lameness and invalid-
> ness, I infer. . . . He recited a limerick about the Van Dorens & the
> Morons to everyone's expected admiration. He said when he discov-
> ered my brother was a Yale man, that settled it, he was going to track
> me down. . . . He is wiry and thin, with a typical professor-writer
> alertness of eye & bookishness of bearing, rather short and lame of
> one leg. Looks like a dwarf tiger-cat & is always jesting. He is Ameri-
> can editor of the Oxford Press it seems & rather babbles of his ener-
> gies & activities there, though very pleasingly. He is not tiresome nor
> does he overrate himself.[24]

Pearson adopted his usual approach to befriending a literary eminence:
slathering on effusive praise while offering to *do* things for her, off-
handedly hinting that he had connections and that he'd be happy to
pull those strings. He dangled the possibility of Moore making a pho-
nograph recording, noting that Laughlin had put him in charge of New
Directions' audio-recordings division (in reality entirely speculative),
and volunteered to help smooth out any kinks in the correspondence
between Moore and Bryher. "Your willingness to make time, when
you really have none, for kindly deeds and renovating pursuits, I dwell
upon and wish I might imitate," she wrote him gratefully.[25]

Moore's mother's death in 1947 freed the poet from some psychological and personal restraints, and she became more of a public figure, adopting her quirky wardrobe of tricorn hat, cape, and nutria-fur

coat worn over discount dresses.[26] She also began, partly because of Pearson, to receive more attention from the literary establishment. In 1947, he cajoled her to endorse an exhibition of her books and papers at Yale, although she was reluctant: "I cannot imagine it. What is there to exhibit?"[27] After a March 1950 date was finally set, she then requested that it be postponed until she finished her translation of La Fontaine. But her 1951 Bollingen Prize, and the public attention it brought, provided an opening for Pearson and Gallup to mount the show in early 1952. In late 1962, in honor of her seventy-fifth birthday, Pearson and Gallup curated an even larger show toward which she was, again, ambivalent. She was more open to the other assistance that Pearson facilitated: money. Bryher had been providing Moore with regular checks since 1930, but after she and Pearson created the Bryher Foundation in 1949 Moore received the foundation's first grant: $2,500 to fund a trip to Paris to research the La Fontaine book.

Although Moore was conscious of, and always grateful for, Pearson's little tasks and favors, he could soon tell that she was not as susceptible to his charm as the other writers he had collected. She was more solitary and self-possessed, less avid for acclaim than Pound or H.D. or Gregory or Williams. He could never pry her open. She never admitted him to close friendship and did not even call him by his first name until 1955. This was partly because she knew what he wanted: access, proximity to literary fame, and her papers. She eventually grew impatient with Pearson's transparent solicitousness. Even in 1949 she mentioned "sourly opening 'another' letter from Norman Pearson" before being surprised by the unexpected Bryher Foundation check.[28] And Norm took note of her careful distancing. When Bryher shared with him a letter she had received from Moore, Pearson remarked on its "warm formality . . . so different from the manner of her [correspondence] to me." Whether as an unconscious backlash to her unavailability, or as a considered judgment, he admired her poetry less than he did that of the other members of the Philadelphia group, judging her a "most artful contriver of metrical effects, and a sparkling Imagist [but] there is nothing much in the way of thematic undercurrent."[29] "The feathers sparkle on her birds," he quipped to Pound, "but they are stuffed birds."[30] And while not stuffed, Moore herself was certainly an odd bird—one that Pearson, to his frustration, never quite succeeded in entrapping. (Her papers went to the Rosenbach Library in Philadelphia.)

Of all the poets and writers that Pearson surrounded himself with, Wallace Stevens was the most like him. Both were forty-year-plus company men—Pearson belonged to Yale, and Stevens to the Hartford Accident and Indemnity Company, where he rose to the position of vice president. A tall, stout, gray-haired man in a conservative three-piece business suit who looked precisely like the insurance executive he was, Stevens was also an extraordinary poet. There was nothing of the bohemian about Stevens. He had not, like most of his other modernist-poet coevals, fled to Europe to escape America's stultifying conventionality; he had, from his corner office, embodied it.

Pearson included him in the anthology, even though Stevens's intricate, playful, highly philosophical poetry (verging at times on verbal dandyism) lacks the mystical, oracular quality Pearson so admired in H.D. and Pound and is overwhelmingly concerned with the workings of the imagination and the relationship between the human mind and the outside world. "My intention in poetry," Stevens somewhat tautologically wrote in the headnote to his Oxford selection, "is to write poetry to reach and express that which, without any particular definition, everyone recognizes as poetry, and to do this because I feel the need of doing it."[31] Pearson's own headnote grants that he is not concerned with weighing in on politics or history and praises Stevens's "singularly sensitive imagination. . . . The impression it conveys to the reader is one of a subdued elegance created by his choice of the precise visual image and an equally distinguished vocabulary."[32] Stevens was no wild avant-gardist, in other words.

But he was, Pearson knew long before most of his colleagues, an exceptionally fine and sophisticated poet, someone whose work was of enduring importance. So once Pearson had established himself in a position where he could offer something to Stevens, he did. In early 1948, Pearson invited Stevens to give the annual Bergen Lecture at Yale and organized a dinner party for the visitor at his home.[33] Pearson

drew on that social connection a few months later to invite Stevens
to give a lecture at the English Institute, where he had become the
chairman. He felt that Stevens, who wrote thoughtfully about poetry,
would impress the attendees, which would include Cleanth Brooks,
René Wellek, Lionel Trilling, David Daiches, and other leading critics.
Fashioning his own persona to appeal to Stevens's reserve, Pearson's
request is almost embarrassingly obsequious:

> The committee was insistent that I ask you; and although I demurred
> strongly since I had already placed myself so much in your debt for
> the Yale talk, they would not let me off my duties as chairman. Of
> course I needn't say that I wish you might feel inclined to accept,
> perhaps out of a mating of Puritan and Pennsylvania Dutch instincts
> to do good. . . . Selfishly from my point of view, it would be a distinc-
> tion to the Institute. . . . I warm myself up genuinely in making such
> a request, and I shall pray as well as hope for its success.[34]

Stevens agreed, with some reluctance, to deliver a paper he called
"Imagination as Value." And although he enjoyed the experience, it
taught him that "my real job is poetry and not papers about poetry, so
far as I have any real job," as he told Pearson.[35]

A somewhat formal friendship between the two then arose, in which
Pearson maintained the subordinate role. The two exchanged letters
(always addressing each other as "Mr. Stevens" and "Mr. Pearson")
about art and travel and mutual acquaintances, dined at the Yale social
club Mory's with mutual friends like Thornton Wilder, and attended
Yale football games together. When Stevens expressed admiration for
a Hermann Hesse watercolor he saw at Pearson's house, Pearson got
Hesse (through his friend Bryher) to send Stevens a portfolio of paintings.[36]

Constant in Pearson's relation with Stevens was his fulsome praise
for the poet. Only late in life did Stevens receive widespread recognition by the literary establishment, so as with Williams, Pearson saw his
job as reassuring Stevens of his importance. "There is, I believe, only
one person in America today who is writing major poetry. You are that

one," he told him, in terms that might have made many of Pearson's other friends feel slighted.[37] If one knock against Stevens was that, for all his verbal filigrees and intellectual dexterity, he essentially was writing the same poem over and over again, Pearson knew how to turn that into a positive, as in this appreciation written in 1954: "He has, in a sense, believed in the poem as few poets of our time have done, believed in the poem as a thing in itself, but not isolated, not pure. And if he seems to have written the same poem many times—'x' ways of looking—he has shown not only that what is interesting in art is the way in which a poem is said, but that by saying it in many ways in many seasons he has always contrived something new."[38] He also relayed secondhand praise to the poet. After F. O. Matthiessen's suicide in 1950, Pearson informed Stevens that at the mention of his poetry Matthiessen "became suddenly illuminated with warmth and deep-felt admiration for all that you have done: the artistry, the powers of the imagination and the understanding."[39]

Stevens would also seek Pearson's advice and guidance. Did he need to furnish his own gown and hood when Yale gave him an honorary doctorate—and if so, where in New Haven could one find these items? (The key, Pearson told him, was a cap that fits in case one had to process in a windstorm.)[40] Stevens, a safely apolitical choice the year after the Pound imbroglio, won the Bollingen Prize in 1949 and after that attended the prize committee's meetings in New Haven, and served as a judge for the 1953 and 1954 competitions. He exchanged notes about these awards with Pearson, who had become an informal Bollingen adviser. Pearson advised Stevens on whether to put out a collected or selected poems and mounted an exhibition of his books and papers at Sterling. (The bulk of the Stevens archive eventually went to the Huntington Library.) When Stevens befriended Peter Lee, a young Korean American poet, Pearson did what he did best: read and evaluated the young man's poems, pulled strings and made connections and helped Lee get his book published with his own introduction.[41]

As with Horace Gregory fifteen years before, the relationship of master and student gradually become one of genuine friendship. "He is immensely good company," Pearson said of Stevens.[42] For his part,

Stevens came to admire this younger man with "one of the most generous spirits in the world."[43] "He has a character that has been made precious by all the difficulties he has had to overcome and merely pleasant chatter with him has a value because of his character that merely pleasant chatter does not always have with other people," Stevens told Lee. "His friendship is one of my better experiences."[44] Pearson attended Stevens's seventy-fifth birthday party that Alfred Knopf threw at New York's Harmonie Club, afterward strolling down Fifth Avenue with Stevens and Moore (who gloated to the bespoke-tailored men about finding a perfect dress for the event at the bargain price of $10).[45]

But not even a year later, Stevens was dead, and Pearson was one of only four mourners from the literary world at Stevens's funeral. "The other 75," he reported to H.D., "were all executives from the insurance business, or secretaries and a chauffeur. . . . One would never have guessed that it was a poet who lay in the half-open coffin. One would not have guessed it was anyone at all."[46] To Bryher he was even more melancholy:

> One would expect the funeral of a distinguished writer to be accompanied by the pomp of an equivalent Abbey. But it was not in a church, with stained-glass mellowing of light and the strains of a requiem choir. It was in a commonplace funeral home: a red-brick sprawling converted cottage from the end of the last century, but situated in the center of the city only around the corner from his insurance office. . . . It was an isolated ending, aloof as he had always been from the literary world in which his name was a planet. . . . I could not help saying "We have seen the funeral of the vice-president of the Hartford Accident and Indemnity Company; the other man will take care of himself."[47]

No one would have mistaken the English expatriate Wystan Hugh Auden, another of the stable of writers whom Pearson befriended, for an insurance executive. Unlike the others, he was of Pearson's generation, only two years older. Craggy-faced, droopy-eyed, and almost impossibly English-looking, Auden left his home country in 1939 to settle in the United States with Christopher Isherwood and live the life of a mostly out queer writer. At their first meeting, at Elizabeth Mayer's house in 1940, Pearson and Auden found they shared a deep interest in the history of English poetry. "Since I was not a poet and do not trade on my friendships, we enjoyed talking," he explained to Pound with an odd note of defensiveness about something—trading on his friend-ships—he in fact did all the time.[48] With other mutual acquaintances beyond the Mayers, and with both men seeking to establish themselves in the institutions of elite American literary culture, the two crossed paths often before the war. Auden asked Pearson to write his Guggen-heim recommendation because he quickly sensed that this young not-yet-professor had an uncanny sense for leveraging these institutions. Pearson also reached out to his contacts at the Universities of Iowa and Colorado to find a teaching position for Auden.

In 1947, the literary critic and editor Malcolm Cowley, who had helped to develop the Viking Portable series for Knopf, approached Auden with an ambitious idea: a massive anthology of English-language poetry, priced for a student market, that would outdo the venerable Oxford collection in scope and content, and still be cheaper. Royalties could be considerable, given that the college population was explod-ing. Intrigued, Auden turned to the experienced anthologist Pearson, and in April 1948 the two signed a contract to compile and deliver within eighteen months a four-volume *Poets of the English Language* in the Viking Portable series (it ultimately would include a fifth volume). Pearson was comfortable with Auden's homosexuality and had seen him in action charming the "nice young crocodiles" at any number of social events. But the poet wanted to make sure Pearson knew what kind of man he was metaphorically getting in bed with and so com-posed and shared with his coeditor "The Platonic Blow," a thirty-four-quatrain ode to cruising and fellatio. This didn't shock Pearson, among whose many book-collecting interests was vintage pornography. What did horrify the bibliophile Pearson was Auden's practice of scissoring out from his own books, rather than transcribing, the poems he wanted to include in the anthology.[49]

It was a genuinely collaborative effort, although Auden admitted in the end that Pearson had done the majority of the work. "We each read everything on both sides, got together once a week, and proceeded by dialectic," as Pearson described the experience.[50] Pearson made an initial selection of poems for each volume, which Auden would modify; Auden, the headliner of the team and in Pearson's own words "the better critic," wrote the introduction for each; and Pearson edited those at Cowley's request to emphasize content more and prosody less. But as it had an end date of 1914, Pearson couldn't use the anthology to promote his vision of American modernism, as he had done in his 1938 collection.

When the anthology appeared in the United States in fall 1950, it received warm reviews, even if most of them effaced Pearson. "The chief attraction offered by Viking's compact little five-volume set is the magic of W. H. Auden's name as co-editor," said the *Houston Post* in praising his "marvelously succinct, yet thoroughly comprehensive, introductions."[51] Louise Bogan, in the *New Yorker*, perceptively saw it as a "peculiarly modern achievement . . . a pioneer effort to put poetry in the midst of history and life, and to connect it to other arts with which it shares a common creative source."[52] (The first approach was Pearson's, the second Auden's.) In the *Observer*, Auden's friend Louis MacNeice declared "Mr. Auden has done it again," and the *Sunday Times* didn't even mention Pearson, treating the whole thing as Auden's work. The *Nation* wanted to know "what . . . does W. H. Auden do in his spare time? Here he comes now with a completed job which would take an ordinary mortal at least ten years hard labor."[53] But Pearson knew what he was getting into and didn't mind being publicly slighted as long as the right people knew that he was the one who could make things happen.

He wasn't in it for the money, either, which was fortunate, as the anthology wasn't the success that the editors and Cowley had hoped it would be. It took five years to earn back its $3,500 advance, and Pearson's own royalties—five cents on each copy—were paltry, rarely rising above $100 a year. Still, the anthology remained in print for over twenty years, and although only six thousand copies of the full set sold, individual volumes were much more successful, particularly the one covering the Romantics, which sold fifty thousand copies. After completing the anthology, Auden and Pearson remained friends and occasional collaborators. "We are good friends, correspond every other year, stay out of each other's hair and arms, and remain in common good grace," Pearson told Pound in 1957.[54]

After the war Horace Gregory continued to be an important part of Pearson's life, although as he grew more confident he went to Gregory less for advice. Instead, he became the poet's benefactor, even if much of the money ultimately came from Bryher. At Pearson's instigation, the Bryher Foundation granted Gregory $7,500, and Bryher personally gave him thousands of dollars a year until his death. Pearson used his influence with the Academy of American Poets on Gregory's behalf, as well, unsuccessfully suggesting him for one of their $5,000 fellowships in 1957 and then, in 1961, convincing Richard Wilbur to give that year's award to Gregory, who was struggling physically and financially with the aftermath of a stroke.[55] By the 1970s Gregory needed full-time nursing help, and Pearson covered his medical expenses, both with Bryher's funds and out of his own pocket. "My parents could never have had the medical attention they received had it not been for" this assistance, Gregory's son Patrick said.[56] Gregory was only one of dozens of writers, former students, and scholars to whom Pearson gave occasional or even regular financial gifts that made it possible for them to keep working and writing. "I am much luckier than most people," he explained, "and I can do good for other people which is a very small return for the good which has been done for me."[57]

Like Pound, H.D., Williams, and H.D.'s ex-husband Richard Aldington, the Arkansas native John Gould Fletcher had been part of the imagist group of poets, although his work had not appeared in the original *Des Imagistes* collection. Much like Gregory, Fletcher became something between a friend and mentor. Pearson included a number of Fletcher's poems in the Oxford anthology, and the poet had persuaded him to include works by Tate and John Crowe Ransom as well (after accusing Pearson of having a "grudge against the South").[58] Fletcher and his wife, children's-book author Charlie May, came to New York often, and Pearson saw them on these visits and corresponded with both regularly. In 1950, Fletcher drowned himself near his Little Rock home, and Pearson rushed down to help Charlie May deal with her late husband's papers (some of which he obtained for Yale, although the bulk went to the University of Arkansas).

Although Pearson mostly collected older writers—beyond those mentioned above, Pearson befriended, corresponded with, and visited Eugene O'Neill, Thornton Wilder, Katherine Anne Porter, Archibald MacLeish, Lola Ridge, Kay Boyle, and Ralph Hodgson, giving money to a few of these as well—he also kept a number of poets and artists closer to his age in his circle. He was on friendly terms with the sculptor Alexander Calder, who maintained his studio in nearby Roxbury, and who made a piece of jewelry for Susan in 1948 (charging Pearson only $50!). He was also an early supporter of younger poets like Richard Eberhart, Donald Hall, Gary Snyder, and Robert Duncan.

Muriel Rukeyser, one of the first baubles in his collection, remained a friend after the war. Before his marriage, they had seen each other often, and Pearson read (and provided frank commentary on) her new poems. Their relationship grew so close in 1940, in fact, that Pearson was "frightened at the thought of her now being in love with me. Too many women have been."[59] While it's doubtful that she was in love with Pearson, as most of her romantic relationships were with women, she relied on his help not just with her poetry but also with her 1942 biography of the American scientist Willard Gibbs. That the book was not primarily about science greatly troubled Gibbs's descendants, who lived in New Haven, and Pearson unsuccessfully tried to secure Rukeyser's access to family correspondence. Perhaps inappropriately, Pearson then reviewed the biography for the little magazine *Accent*, making what might seem a shortcoming—Rukeyser's scientific illiteracy—into an asset: "Certainly it is the poet's function, as it is that of the philosopher and the higher mathematician, to see things not merely in their literal features but also in their connotative fullness. Miss Rukeyser has indicated that it can be the biographer's function as well."[60] Her Gibbs biography, he told her at the time, was also influencing his teaching and scholarship, and he quoted it in his 1949 essay "The American Poet in Relation to Science."[61] "It makes the link for me between science and poetry and mathematics," he told her, "and over and over again students say to me: I hadn't thought about mathematics that way, and vice versa for poetry. . . . I'm having my reward for mixing up in the affair, returned a thousandfold."[62]

He wasn't able to befriend every poet he came across, though. T. S. Eliot, whom he had met during the war, remained distant and formal, if impeccably cordial, even when the Pearsons hosted a prereading cocktail reception for him in 1961. In preparation for the visit from the world's most prominent poet, the Pearsons cleaned their house "as though we were about to be inspected by the mother superior. He arrives, already in dinner jacket, a little before four by car from New York; lies down in dinner jacket for a rest, and then comes down for cocktails for a dozen guests who have all promised to leave by six-fifteen." But Eliot was a pro. Three thousand people bought tickets and, as Pearson reported to Bryher, got what they paid for. "Sitting behind him on the stage in my dinner-jacketed beauty, I could hear only a little of what he said; but I watched the audience and was surprised by their serious attention and quick response. He has become far better as a public performer, and earned his two thousand dollars to the last nickel."[63]

Sometimes the personalities just didn't click. The Welsh poet and wild man Dylan Thomas came to the United States in 1950 for the first of his raucous reading tours and made his second stop at Yale. Notorious for his drunken antics both after and during his appearances, Thomas seems to have ramped this behavior up for the benefit of American audiences, for whom "he behaved more extravagantly than he did in Britain . . . as if he wanted to shock everyone," according to his biographer.[64] It fell to Pearson to organize a reception for the bad-boy poet at Mory's, Yale's venerable canteen. Norm's considerable skills as a host failed him this time, as the guest was just not well matched for the "cold and aloof" party of academics, who only intensified Thomas's feelings of social and intellectual inferiority.[65] "During the dinner," Pearson remembered, "he spent a good deal of time explaining how he could have gone to university, to Cambridge. . . . He became very truculent [and] I believe it became as unhappy for him as for the group."[66]

Thomas's friend John Brinnin blamed Yale for this, describing the dinner as "so grim and stultifying as to become the standard against which [Thomas] would measure every awkward and unhappy event. With the exception of Cleanth Brooks, who conveyed by his presence more than by anything he said a sympathetic recognition of Dylan's dilemma, and of Norman Pearson, who was the talkative host to the party, all the professors sat around in a druidic circle apparently awaiting an oracle."[67] "The talkative host to the party": Pearson undoubtedly enjoyed being thought of as that, as the man who assembles and then catalyzes a lively group of creative people, without calling too much attention to himself. But as he started to become almost unavoidable in these small circles of writers and editors and publishers in the 1950s, many people started to think of him differently: as a sycophant, a groupie, a name-dropper, a suck-up, a hanger-on. And there is some truth to that accusation. For the collector, the collection becomes part of their cultural capital; and for Pearson, who was short on the most important kind of capital in the academic world—influential publications—this helped make up for it. But this collecting, this networking, was also instinctive as much as it was calculated, and even if transparent at times it genuinely was part of his larger aim to rewrite the story of American literature and culture.

+ 10 +

AN INTELLECTUAL MÉNAGE À TROIS

How good it is to sit down at a typewriter again,
and be with you.
PEARSON TO BRYHER, 1969

As central as he thought Pound and Williams and Moore, and to a
lesser extent Stevens and Gregory and Fletcher, to be in the story of
America and modernism and American modernism that he was formu-
lating, nobody in his pantheon of poets or even in his personal life had
anywhere near the importance of the final member of the Philadelphia
tetrad.[1] Unlike that with H.D., his relationships with the others were
structured and limited by his desire to be the intermediary connecting
them with his institutions. He certainly considered them friends, but
he did not open himself up to them or drop his persona as the "most
connected man" or "the young man who would and could do anything
to help." This guardedness, this hesitance to develop a close personal
relationship wasn't just true with the poets. He had friendly but not
deep relationships with many colleagues and throughout his adult life
stayed in touch with many of the friends from his youth.

The truly shaping connections of his adult life, though, were with
women. His closest relationship well into his teen years was with a
strong woman: Fanny. She was competent, reliable, talented, intelligent, and affectionate, and very much the most important person in
his life. Throughout college, his years abroad, and graduate school, he
wrote her multiple letters every week, and the flow of correspondence

slowed only when he was thirty-one, when he married Susan, another strong and independent woman. Then in London, the three-cornered bond between himself, Bryher, and H.D. developed new dimensions, and during the war they became the women on whom he grounded his day-to-day personal and emotional life.

Pearson's and H.D.'s relationship has often puzzled feminist literary scholars who have at times have been reluctant to recognize how central he was to her. "Pearson's relations with H.D. are mystifying," Barbara Guest says in her biography of the poet, speculating that he was "directed by his need for power," obtained "by devotion and loyalty to the object he desired."[2] That's partly true, but his relationship with H.D. was much less instrumental, much deeper and more reciprocal, despite their stark differences. She was a generation older, a bohemian pansexual whose romantic and family entanglements were almost impossibly complicated. He was a married college professor with two stepdaughters. She was Orphic and hermetic while he was, at least outwardly, utterly conventional. But their friendship would change both of their lives and alter the story of twentieth-century American literature even more than everything Pearson did for Pound, Williams, Moore, Stevens, Auden, and all the others combined. Pearson's labors for H.D. fundamentally shaped how readers understand her work and probably have ensured that readers still read it. But it also placed at the center of American modernism H.D.'s work and that of the other two members (Pound and Williams) of what he called the "most remarkable embryonic trio of American poets," a center where their work remains.[3]

It wasn't that they had nothing in common. Both were fascinated by early American history, and they both had family roots in Puritan New England, topics they discussed at their first meeting, in 1937.[4] She even signed an early letter to him "(your) Cotton Mather."[5] Both had a mystical side, although in inverse proportions. H.D. had less a mystical side than a small part of her personality that was not mystical. The pragmatic, rarely introspective Pearson felt that H.D., like Hawthorne, was a kind of embodiment of the Puritan "instinct of introspection" that allows one to see the "innate spiritual significance" of events. She became an outlet for his own mystical side. Donna Hollenberg sees the two sharing what Pearson often called "our mystery," a "mytho-poetic view of history that . . . regarded ancient myth as a repository of sacred revelation and substituted a metahistorical, spiritual defini-tion of truth for an empirical one."[6] Pearson also saw her as a kind of archetype of the feminine. "She impressed me chiefly . . . as a woman. I have never known a more womanly woman than she was or one who reacted as woman to men more than she did," he explained long after her death.[7] H.D. combined power, creativity, mystery, femininity, and intelligence with a willingness to depend on him. Susan was his life companion, Bryher his closest friend, but H.D. was his dream woman. While they engaged in romantic role-playing, and on occasion Pearson hinted (or perhaps joked) that he had had an affair with H.D., their bond was not fundamentally romantic or sexual. It was an asymmetri-cal relationship of master and servant, of queen and courtier, of artist and factotum, but also of dependence: hers on him.

But for all of that, it was an unlikely friendship. The war had some-thing to do with it. Clean and well-dressed where they were grubby and clad in threadbare clothing, unfailingly wry and chipper when they were worn down by years of war, Pearson brought H.D. and Bryher more than just variety on his Sunday visits. He was the promise of the world after the war, and the very American way it would look. And, according to their biographer Susan McCabe, after the war ended and Pearson took charge of both the business and the literary affairs of both of them in the United States—and began to collect and preserve their personal papers—they saw him as the man who would "weave their lives together" and tell their love story to future generations.[8] "Pearson offered H.D. and Bryher not an erotic attachment," scholar Annette Debo explains, "but an intellectual catalyst that spurred them both to write and publish."[9] They developed, Perdita concluded, a "cerebral ménage à trois" that lasted the rest of their lives.[10]

Bryher was a very different kind of woman from H.D., and her friendship with Pearson was a different kind of friendship. They were kindred spirits, doers, networkers, orchestrators, collectors, constantly in motion, constantly performing themselves through language. Pear-son revered H.D., and considered her one of the century's great artistic geniuses. Bryher, on the other hand, was just his kind of person, and he relied on her, prompting him to present her, in 1949, with a hand-printed mock "Award of Merit" for being "a paragon of guides and the best of friends." "What an alter ego I am for you," he told her in November 1973, when they were writing each other literally every day: "editor, agent, lover, husband, brother, and dear friend!"[11] She felt the same and often told him that she valued his opinion more than any other in the world.[12]

The erotic dimension of H.D.'s and Bryher's side of this ménage, although it had largely cooled by the 1940s, did not appear to faze him. Pearson, in his voluminous correspondence with and about both women, never expressed the slightest qualms about their sexuality—he never even addressed it but just took it for granted, whatever it was. Pearson might subconsciously have perceived echoes of his own blended family in the unusual kinship arrangement the two women had assembled. In fact, he became entwined in that expansive matrix and was named as a family member on H.D.'s death certificate.[13]

Given his stalwart Cold Warrior beliefs and the influential role he played in the postwar years in exploring and defining the American character, Pearson's tolerance for queerness and support of queer people is notable. It was a fraught stance to take at the time, even for someone with as much cultural and institutional capital as Pearson. As historians such as Alan Nadel, Elaine Tyler May, and David K. Johnson have shown, official homophobia in America intensified dramatically in the early 1950s as the nuclear family became crucial to the "American Way of Life"; and in the so-called Lavender Scare, gay men and lesbians were lumped in with Communists as security risks, or even as subversives who undermined the larger strategy of containment, both geopolitical and domestic.[14] But Pearson certainly had many close friends who were visibly queer: in addition to Bryher and H.D., this group would include Auden, Rukeyser, Robert Duncan, and Alice Hitchcock, his housekeeper in London. In addition, he was on friendly terms with other queer artists and writers such as Gertrude Stein, Alice B. Toklas, Benjamin Britten, Peter Pears, Kenneth Macpherson, Marianne Moore, Islay Lyons, Robert McAlmon, and Elizabeth Bishop and, importantly, made them a part of the story of twentieth-century art and literature that he was assembling. Debo, among others, has praised Pearson's "efforts to direct the evolving modernist canon toward an inclusive tradition that fairly represented women and queer writers," and he certainly did that.[15]

Being supportive, though, didn't mean naming what it was he was supporting. He almost never spoke openly or directly about his friends' sexuality, generally referring to Bryher and H.D. as "friends." And his unpublished biographical sketch of Bryher from about 1955, probably intended for an encyclopedia, doesn't mention H.D. once, although it discusses both of Bryher's marriages.[16] Pearson was similarly obtuse, or willfully blind, to the key role of queer sexuality in H.D.'s writing, arguing that "what she was searching for was through males . . . the principle of malehood and womanhood combined into a wholeness."[17] It was all very veiled, even among these three close confidants. To Pearson, H.D. called Bryher only her "most intimate friend," and Bryher, too, was always oblique about her sexuality, even in letters in which she railed at length against other lesbians such as Sylvia Beach, and once disingenuously told Pearson that the essential problem with her marriage to McAlmon was that she was not prepared for consummation as "Victorian girls were not instructed in" sex![18]

The end of the war and Pearson's return to the United States altered the dynamics and the structure of the three-sided relationship the three had built in London. He had always connected with them differently, but the disparity grew when H.D. was incommunicado while in her most intense period of convalescence and therapy. Bryher, who lived near H.D.'s clinic, attended to her needs as best she could, while Pearson mostly observed and offered moral support.[19] Both knew that after the stress and privation of the war, the women needed time apart. "You must escape," Pearson wrote Bryher when she was still in London, "and skip to the hills" in Switzerland. "Hilda I think too needs to be alone, to re-form herself."[20] As the two women led their parallel lives 130 miles apart, Pearson built very different but equally meaningful friendships with each one.

A legal shift also precipitated their changing relationship. When the war began, H.D. had empowered Marianne Moore as her literary agent in the United States, but soon after he arrived in London Pearson began advising her. In 1944, she published *The Walls Do Not Fall*, a set of poems about the resilience of London and the role of the poet in wartime. Osbert Sitwell persuaded Oxford to publish the book in the UK, and Pearson used his connections with their New York office to ensure that it would appear in the United States as well, with his blurb identifying him as the editor of Oxford's popular anthology.[21] She showed him poems from the second part of her wartime trilogy *Tribute to the Angels*, and he counseled her that although "the tone is right and the feeling is as sure as ever," it would probably be wisest until she completed the trilogy to publish it. (She did not heed this advice, and it came out in 1945.)

In December 1945, H.D. formally asked Pearson to "look after my literary affairs in the United States until I am able to cross myself," telling him that he should "just go ahead as YOU THINK BEST."[22] Without hesitation, he agreed.[23] She even transferred the copyrights to her American publications to him because "it was infinitely simpler for me to own the copyrights and to make her a gift of whatever earnings came in from them" than to file semiannual tax reports to the British government, Pearson explained later.[24] When she dedicated the third section of the trilogy, 1946's *The Flowering of the Rod*, to him, he made the transition from admirer to adviser. "It is my greatest honor from the war. No medal, nothing can compare to the pride I feel in seeing my name in it. . . . It gains even a new height in your poetry, so precise and meticulous, so beautifully controlled, so exquisitely and naturally formed," the fan said. "Now I am only anxious," the agent interjected, "to have the three parts appear together."[25] The agent in him was incensed, as well, that Oxford simply exported to the United States its British printings of *Flowering*, in cheap wartime paper wrappers noting a price of 3/6, and then marked the book up to $2 (a typical price for a nice hardcover at the time): "mind you," he reported to H.D., "I don't mean that a volume of your poems isn't worth two dollars; it is only because with the paper binding and the English price on the back it may lose something for gift sales in favor of the better format of other volumes of poetry."[26] He was blunter to Bryher: for Oxford to treat H.D. this way was "shameful" and amounted to "sabotage."[27]

Pearson mapped out a strategy to secure her due respect both in the contemporary poetry scene and in the history of twentieth-century American literature, where she invariably appeared as a minor figure. Readers had to see that she wasn't a martyred "virgin saint in the ruins of the [imagist] movement," that she hadn't stopped writing in 1914, and that her later work was in fact far richer than that early poetry. "My chief aim," he explained, "is to rid the public of the idea that H.D. is dead, or . . . a period piece. She has been praised so much as the poet who was loyal to the Imagist tenets that it has turned into no praise at all."[28] He needed new material to do this, though. Almost immediately, he began approaching publishers to publish her wartime work, and implored her that "any time you want to send a batch of mss over, do so by all means, and I will do my best with it."[29]

The problem was that others didn't share his lofty opinion of H.D.'s work and very much saw her as a period piece. Evaluating one of these manuscripts, Kurt Wolff bluntly told Pearson that "in view of the fact that only a very limited number of people are interested in H.D.'s poetry I am afraid that we would not find a large enough audience to even so much as break even with the publication costs."[30] He often had to resort to machinations that weren't completely aboveboard. In 1948, Gregory privately encouraged Pearson to submit *By Avon River*, H.D.'s multigeneric meditation on Shakespeare, to Macmillan, knowing that the publisher would ask him (Gregory) to review the submission and decide whether to recommend publication.[31] (He did, and they did.) With no small degree of chutzpah, after publication Pearson then tried to arrange for Marya Zaturenska to review the book for the *New York Herald Tribune*.

As Pearson started to successfully place manuscripts with publishers and journals such as *Poetry* and the *Yale Review*, H.D. began to trust him enough to expand his role beyond agent to proofreader. "Horace's part is over with having read the manuscript for the publishers, and all communications about the book will be with me," he told her after Macmillan offered a contract for *Avon River*, "and I will make no changes without consulting you." Some months later, putting on his scholar hat, he submitted to her an extensive list of queries and corrections regarding dates, spellings, accurate quotations, and even commas. But this work was solely copyediting and proofreading: nowhere does he make any suggestions about the substance of her writing, which he felt would be a presumptuous intrusion into her creative process.

Their personal relationship also became closer in the late 1940s. H.D. was still too fragile to travel, so Pearson proudly assumed the ceremonial parent role at Perdita's July 1950 wedding to literary agent John Schaffner, in effect standing in for H.D., Bryher (Perdita's legal mother), and Cecil Gray (Perdita's biological father) all at the same time. "She was really and properly 'given' and I am so deeply touched and grateful," H.D. told him.[32] The mock family relationship soon became real. In 1951, after five years of treatment at Küsnacht, H.D. finally felt strong enough to come to the US and see her daughter. She and Bryher spent most of the month of April in New York and attended the christening of Perdita's baby Valentine, who was H.D.'s grandson, Bryher's adoptive grandson, and Pearson's godson. "We are really related now—grand-mother and god-father!" she wrote him on March 2. With his devotion to her, Pearson and H.D.'s relationship become almost something out of medieval romance, even though—or, more likely, precisely because—they rarely saw each other. Pledging to ensure that her autobiographical novel *The Sword Went Out to Sea* would be published, he told her that "it has the seal of our fingers linked on it. Yours and mine." He became, she told him, "my chevalier," and for the rest of her life she addressed him—and he closed his letters to her—as "Chevalier."[33]

As their personal connections expanded, so did Pearson's campaign. Just after the war, he had proposed a joint Marianne Moore–H.D. exhibition at the Sterling Library much like the Stein one from 1941, but when that failed to materialize, he planned an H.D. solo show, to open on September 10, 1956, her seventieth birthday. Pearson had the materials—she had been sending him manuscripts and he had been assiduously collecting her rare editions for over a decade—but knew that the publicity-shy, ailing, and emotionally overwrought H.D. would not give a talk, attend any of the receptions or cocktail parties that would accompany the exhibition, or even attend the show with the crowds. But the chance to see Perdita's second baby as well as the exhibit finally swayed H.D. to come to the United States for the celebration, and she was visibly moved when Pearson privately escorted her and Bryher through this public assertion of her importance and accomplishments. The show "did greatly please her," Richard Aldington reported to Pearson some weeks later.[34] Pearson had made her a celebrity among Yale's literary crowd, and when she did meet one of her admirers, Guest says, she rallied enough to "exert her considerable magnetism."[35] Pearson also arranged for the *New Haven Register* to profile the visiting poet with a headline he likely suggested: "Poet Hilda Doolittle, on Yale Visit, Assails Imagist Label Used to Describe Her Work."[36]

FIGURE 8 H.D., Bryher, and Norm at H.D.'s seventieth birthday exhibition at the Sterling Library, Yale, 1956 (H.D. Papers, Yale Collection of American Literature, Beinecke Rare Book and Manuscript Library).

In terms of reshaping H.D.'s literary reputation, Pearson's most pivotal accomplishment was editing and finding a publisher for her *Selected Poems*. Collected or selected editions assert that a poet has had a career, a body of work worth considering in its entirety. Like an exhibition, publication of a hardcover selected or collected edition contends to reviewers, critics, and award committees that this is a major poet. In the 1950s, no such collection of H.D.'s work was easily available. Boni and Liveright's 1925 *Collected Poems* was difficult to find and didn't include any of her work from the last decades, thus presenting her as a fossilized imagist. Her work appeared in a few current literary anthologies (including, of course, Oxford's) and in scattered individual volumes, most of which were rare or out of print. Furthermore, at this time the so-called trade paperback format—physically larger and made with better quality materials than flimsy pocket paperbacks such as Penguins—was just beginning to emerge, targeting the growing student market. If a hardcover *Selected Poems* would be aimed at elites in the literary world and serious readers, a trade paperback would reach a market of young readers and students who might develop an enduring appreciation for her work.

Alfred A. Knopf had established its paperback division, Vintage Books, in 1954, but like Wolff, Knopf regretfully told Pearson that "I can't strike a spark of interest [for an H.D. collection], and I suspect my colleagues are right."[37] Two smaller American firms specialized in trade paperback editions of modern avant-garde writers, though: New Directions and Barney Rosset's more edgy Grove Press, which counted among its authors Samuel Beckett, Allen Ginsberg, and Jack Kerouac. Laughlin, focused at this time on Pound, passed, but in 1956, Rosset bit.[38] With Gregory's and Zaturenska's assistance, Pearson chose the poems and negotiated a contract specifying simultaneous hardcover and paperback editions, the latter priced at $1.25. The total print run would be thirty-eight hundred, with thirteen hundred of them hardbacks (and fifty of those signed collector's editions).[39] This would be the most ambitious and wide-reaching rollout for any book H.D. had ever published.

Grove's *Selected Poems*, which appeared in summer 1957, did its job, and 2,088 of the twenty-five hundred paperbacks sold in the first six months.[40] Pearson blanketed the literary world with complimentary copies, seeking not just reviews but to remind influential readers and writers that H.D. was still alive and not preserved (as he put it to Van Wyck Brooks, the great gray eminence of American literary historians) "in the amber cliche of Imagism in which most historians have buried her."[41] While her work was still too experimental to win either of the year's major awards, the National Book Award or the Pulitzer Prize (although it was a finalist for the NBA), it did urgently remind critics and readers that H.D. was still alive and still writing. Pearson capitalized on the attention to place poems in three wide-circulation American magazines—the *New Yorker*, the *Nation*, and the *Atlantic Monthly*—as well as in *Poetry* and Grove's own journal, the daring *Evergreen Review*.[42]

Frustratingly, though, Grove didn't follow the script Pearson had written and allowed *Selected Poems* to go out of print in early 1958. Pearson's response is worth quoting at length, as it demonstrates his expert understanding of how publishing and publicity create literary reputations:

> Word-of-mouth knowledge of the existence of *Selected Poems* is mounting, since reviews like the two in the January issue of *Poetry* have hardly had time to stimulate knowledge of its existence and quality, and because articles like Horace's forthcoming one in *The Commonweal* should help to continue the momentum. Again, the citation of her *Selected Poems* in my revision of *The Oxford Anthology of American Literature* as the source for many of the texts will be a further advertisement. . . . What is important to me in the building up of H.D.'s reputation is the fact that *Selected Poems* should remain in print [and] with this in mind I suggested to Horace the possibility of some business arrangement between the Grove Press and myself by which republication could be ensured.[43]

The logrolling here, invisible to most readers, is worth bringing into view. Pearson's and H.D.'s close friend Horace Gregory—whose reader's report on *By Avon River* for Macmillan had started the H.D. publishing revival in 1948, and who was now an editor at Grove—was reviewing *Selected Poems* positively in a wide-circulation magazine. Pearson, who represented H.D.'s financial interests in the United States, was using his position as editor of the Oxford anthology to promote sales of *Selected Poems*, and also offering to provide a subsidy to Grove in order to ensure that the book would remain in print.[44] As a former spymaster, Pearson was entirely comfortable with sub-rosa machinations that benefit the cause. There's not a great deal at stake in these conflicts of interest, and Pearson was not directly financially benefiting from this arrangement, but the ethics here do feel questionable.

And it worked. Only three days later Pearson received a one-line note from Grove: "WE WILL KEEP THE SELECTED POEMS IN PRINT!"[45] Grove didn't even accept the $1,000 subvention Pearson offered (although in 1963, with Grove again about to let the book go out of print, Pearson lent the company $500 to cover production costs for a new printing).[46] "It is a good title to have," he assured them, "and although the sales will never be spectacular I think they will prove steady. Two books on her are now being written and these should help to continue to draw attention to her."[47]

Just as he had hoped, *Selected Poems* spurred elite literary institutions to start paying attention to H.D., and after fifteen years of working on her behalf, Pearson was finally beginning to see the results he desperately desired. In February 1960, Pearson begged a "birthday present" from H.D.: would she consider making a trip to the United States that May? The American Academy of Arts and Letters, he informed her, had honored her with its Special Award of Merit for poetry, given only every five years and coming with a $1,000 prize. Knowing that she would be reluctant to travel, he appealed to the deepest aspects of their friendship. "Somehow, and I don't know why, I can't help feeling all this working out is part of the Mystery in which you have let me share. That it is somehow a means of bringing us together again just now, of letting you have a glimpse of [Perdita's] children . . . and in so many ways of being part of the cycle and circle. When it is the Mystery one follows it."[48] Pearson also sent a carbon of this letter to Bryher, noting that "to be the first woman to win the award is an honor to make Dame Edith swoon," as both Bryher and H.D. had always mildly resented the greater attention Sitwell received from the literary establishment.

Somewhat to Bryher and Pearson's surprise, H.D. agreed to come. Healthier and more confident than she had been in years, she wanted to "center herself" on this visit.[49] "I will come & fetch the gold medal, if only for the pleasure of handing it on to you," she told Pearson.[50] She flew to New York, where Rosset came to pay his respects to her. Also making the pilgrimage to see his idol was Robert Duncan, whom Pearson described as "a San Francisco poet but not really a beatnik . . . exceptionally well-read and well-housebroken, and with an uncanny understanding of what you are after."[51]

In his careful description for Bryher of the next day's award banquet, Pearson emphasized how strong, how self-assured H.D. appeared as she accepted the recognition that she had long felt she merited.

> She got out of the taxi to be greeted by Léonie Adams who had once called on her in London, and then—even before she got off the sidewalk—by Thornton Wilder and his sister. . . . She had a whirl, sitting in a corner of the room while people came up to salute her. I scurried and brought people I thought would interest her, and it was a pleasant melange for half or three quarters of an hour, while she drank several sherries, but had more vitality to begin with than she needed. Aiken came up, and Djuna Barnes and Kay Boyle, and Van Wyck Brooks, Marchette Chute, John Ciardi, Malcolm Cowley, Richard Eberhart, John Hersey, MacLeish. . . . We then went up to the terrace for the reception, and again Hilda was besieged but this time by the general public.[52]

Three thousand people were in the audience, Pearson reported, and another three hundred had to be turned away.[53] This was H.D.'s first public appearance since the 1943 London "Reading of Famous Poets" with Eliot and the Sitwells, and Pearson thrilled at knowing how much he had done to make it possible.

These honors and this acclaim didn't culminate Pearson's campaign on H.D.'s behalf; they just gave it more momentum. In the four years after *Selected Poems* appeared, Grove published *Bid Me to Live*, an autobiographical novel about the early years of her marriage to Aldington, in 1960, and *Helen in Egypt*, often considered her greatest work, in 1961. In addition to being H.D.'s most important work, *Helen* marked the zenith of Pearson and H.D.'s creative symbiosis, the point at which Pearson moved beyond agent and proofreader and began to contribute to the shaping of a work.

Most of H.D.'s postwar work had been prose, but Pearson continually, if gently, prodded her to send poems, new ones, because he knew that only new poetry could accomplish his goal of establishing her in the public and critical mind as a vital, living, practicing poet. And his encouragement motivated her to write. Finally, in 1952, a letter arrived with two sections of something called *Helen in Egypt*. "You asked for some poems," she wrote. "I have written nothing for five years, but somehow suddenly, this *Helen in Egypt* began; I have just finished 8 of these sections in 3 days." Pearson wasted no time: "IT IS SUPERB! KISSES ON BOTH CHEEKS, AND A DEEP BOW WITH A SWEEP OF THE PLUMED HAT. MAY I SEND IT OFF?"[54]

As she continued to compose new poems for the work, he advised her on how they might be published. "We will have a volume of the two series; they belong together," he proposed. "Perhaps there will be a third, so that it will be a triangle (like the war poems) rather than parallel lines."[55] When Pearson visited Switzerland in late 1954, the two extensively discussed how best to incorporate the notes and the poetry together—what they should look like on the page to best convey the effect that H.D. desired. Even before the poem was finished, he already had his mind on promotion. Sounding very much like the skilled press agent he had become, he leveraged the Academy of Arts and Letters award to pressure Rosset to accelerate the publication and promotion of *Helen in Egypt* and its accompanying audio recording. "The Academy's award . . . makes me wonder if the announcement of the publication of 'Helen' would not be appropriate," he suggested. "We could perhaps arrange also for the release of her recording of the poem before the book's actual publication, as a preliminary teaser."[56] As the poem neared completion, Pearson offered his suggestions on knitting the sections together, asking (for instance) "whether Part IV (Winter Love) needs some bridging paragraph at the beginning similar to what you have written for the other three sections. But not more than an opening one I should think; for after all it is a coda."[57] He never deigned to suggest any substantive alterations in her *texts* themselves but had a great deal to do with shaping the *books*: what was included, how it was presented on the page, what paratextual elements framed the texts, and what audiences they were intended to reach. And throughout the almost ten years she labored over *Helen*, he maintained his essential role of coach, supporter, devoted admirer, chevalier. T. S. Eliot once remarked that Ezra Pound's editorial interventions were a "caesarean operation" that helped birth *The Waste Land*, making Pound the poem's midwife; and if Pearson's maieutic contributions to *Helen* did not rise to that level, he might at least be considered the work's doula. "I asked for poems, and I got a masterpiece," he had told her in 1952.[58] It was indeed her masterpiece.

It would also be their last collaboration. In early 1961, Dr. Brunner's son decided to sell the Nervklinic, H.D.'s haven since she was evacuated from Britain in 1946. The disruption was damaging. In early 1961, Pearson, Bryher, and Perdita had discussed relocating H.D. to the United States, but worries about her psychological state convinced them that this was not the right time for such a move. And as is inevitable when dealing with aging family members, resentments were coming to the fore. "I suspect that [Perdita] and John secretly feel that" H.D.'s living arrangements were "none of my business," Pearson grumbled to Bryher, but "I have given really a good deal of my energy and life to helping Hilda not only in literary matters but in just those personal affairs where neither you nor I would have to worry if only they recognized some responsibility."[59]

Pearson was hoping to provide some support and counsel when he made his annual visit to Switzerland in July, after lecturing in Munich at the start of the month. But on June 6, Bryher telegrammed him that H.D. had suffered a serious stroke and minor heart attack. His visit to the frail and mute Hilda a few weeks later was his last, as she declined rapidly and passed away in September. Saddened at the loss of his great friend, Pearson nonetheless took comfort in the fact that his work over the last fifteen years had been successful, and that she had been able to see it. "I have tried," he told Bryher just a few weeks after H.D.'s death, "to help Hilda gain the rightful place in poetry that she deserved and that I think she so richly enjoyed at the end of her life with the prizes she got and the acclaim she had."[60]

But he wasn't done. Throughout the later 1960s and into the 1970s, Pearson stubbornly stuck to his strategy of deferring a full collected edition in order to showcase her later poems that, he insisted, should be published on their own, particularly because they were increasingly influential to contemporary poets. He wanted to make sure *Selected Poems* remained available, and "get into print a volume which reprints the war trilogy, the owl sequence, Sagesse, etc., which must appear separately without appearing first at the end of a Collected Poems," he told Bryher.[61] "The proper strategy," he explained in 1971, "is [to] assure attention to her later period. After that a selected or collected poems might appear, and obviously should, but if this were to be done now the reviews would rely on the old clichés."[62] The most pernicious "old cliché" was of course the reduction of H.D. to "the poet who remained true to Imagism, as though she were the Penelope," as he described it to Duncan.[63] Reviewers of a collected edition would "read up on the old reviews, and we'd have another 'quickie' on H.D. as the faithful Imagist."[64] But another misconception, typical of the androcentric assumptions of literary critics and historians who were starting to write the story of modernism, was that she was nothing more than a creation of the men who had surrounded her, Pound and Aldington in particular. Readers needed to realize, Pearson insisted, that rather than being a follower *of* Pound, she was instead a leader *like* Pound, with her own school of inheritors.

The initial choice of Grove Press, rather than the strongly Pound-associated New Directions, helped combat both clichés. Even though Rosset used "quasi pornography as a meal ticket," Pearson told Bryher, "there is a slight value in having her poems put out by even such a shady publisher as that of *Last Exit to Brooklyn*, which is the implication that she is interesting to the younger people and not a memorial wreath put out by Macmillan."[65] The nascent counterculture loved Grove's daring books. Moreover, Pound, Williams, and H.D. had spawned a panoply of antiestablishment inheritors and movements including the Beats, the San Francisco school, the Black Mountain school, and the New York Poets. Donald Allen's influential 1960 anthology *The New American Poetry 1945–1960*—published, naturally, by Grove—documented this lineage.[66] She may be dead, but she was not irrelevant or an antique, these movements proclaimed. Grove's fortunes fell in the late 1960s, in part because of Rosset's poor financial decisions (including investing in real estate and pornographic films), and in the early 1970s, New Directions, now that Pearson had demonstrated H.D.'s viability, began publishing her new titles and back catalog.[67]

Publishing was only one prong of Pearson's campaign. As a creature of the university, he knew that academic scholarship and research were ever more essential in creating and sustaining literary reputations. In the mid-twentieth century, universities were only just beginning to be sites for the study of contemporary literature, but Pearson had long sought to make Yale one of the most important of such locations. He did this through teaching, acquiring authors' papers, and organizing readings and exhibitions, but also through cultivating scholarship: helping graduate students find and access materials, reading their drafts, and using his connections to help them publish. He had done this as far back as 1941, in his first year on the faculty at Yale, for Robert Bartlett Haas (who was writing the first dissertation on Gertrude Stein); he had done this for Edwards and others writing about Pound; and in the 1950s, he started doing this for young scholars, most of them women, who were starting to write about H.D. In the early 1970s, for instance, he worked with Susan Stanford Friedman as she completed her dissertation on H.D., giving her access to the archives he kept in his own office.[68] Friedman and others established the field of H.D. studies and provided critical and scholarly reinforcement for the then-counterintuitive argument Pearson had been making for decades: that women writers were as central to American modernism as Pound, Williams, Stevens, and even Eliot.

But Pearson would not live to see the most unique critical work on H.D. published. Knowing that Pearson was H.D.'s gatekeeper, in 1958 Duncan sent him an unsolicited copy of his collection *Letters* and hinted that he wanted to write something about H.D. Pearson was "delighted" at Duncan's interest in writing on H.D. and encouraged him to write "a full-sized article, or a small book" to be published by the *Evergreen Review* or Grove.[69] This became a deal: in 1960 Pearson paid Duncan $1,000 to write this piece, which he intended to use as a Festschrift for H.D.'s seventy-fifth birthday.[70] Knowing the potential impact of a statement of H.D.'s current importance by one of the best-known avant-garde poets, Pearson did everything he could to bring it into being: he read Duncan's drafts, gave him access to H.D.'s archival material, and tried to arrange a publishing deal.[71]

Duncan's desire to evangelize for H.D. eventually caused Pearson and Laughlin some headaches. While she was writing *Helen*, H.D. was also composing a series of poems that she called, variously, *Hermetic Definition*, *Notre-Dame d'Amour*, and *Star of Day*. Always interested in Freud, she turned in this sequence to Jungian archetypes. "Freud gave her a sense of how to link the tribal myths with the personal dream. . . . This sense of 'ancient wisdom' is what 'hermetic definition' is," Pearson explained.[72] As she completed the poems in early 1961, she sent type-scripts to both Pearson and Duncan. She died, though, before she could give final approval for *Hermetic Definition*'s publication, and so for a decade the poems remained largely unread, held at the Yale Libraries where only Pearson could give permission to see them.

Duncan, though, had spoken highly of the collection, so the poets of his circle knew of it and wanted access to it. These avant-gardists grew impatient with Pearson, who seemed perversely or greedily unwilling to publish the poem. Pearson wanted the book out just as much as did H.D.'s other admirers, but since his target audience was scholars and critics, he wanted it to appear from a reputable and prestigious publisher so that it would contribute to H.D.'s academic literary reputation. But the poets weren't interested in Pearson's campaign or intellectual-property claims; they just wanted the poem. As the scholar

Michael Boughn remembers, "there was a great clamour among poets to have the poems made available so that they could work with them. From the point of view of many poets, the prestige of the publisher was less important than having the poems to work with."[73] By April 1971 Pearson and Laughlin had gotten wind that something was brewing, and by the summer, Frontier Press publisher Harvey Brown and designer Ron Caplan set and printed a pirated edition of *Hermetic Definitions* (giving it a plural title) in what Brown claimed was an edition of sixteen hundred, which he gave away for free.

In addition to monkey-wrenching their plans, a pirate edition also created legal and financial problems for Pearson and New Directions: whoever published the work first, authorized or not, could claim the copyright on the text. And the pirates knew this. Caplan said that "we simply wanted to force [Pearson] to publish it, knowing he'd have to do that to secure copyright. . . . God knows how long those fellows would have sat on that poem, and for whatever reason."[74] Laughlin was in fact already acquainted with the "wretched" Brown.[75] In 1965, Brown had run—without permission of the poet or his publisher—Pound's "Canto CX" and "Canto 116" in his *Niagara Frontier Review*, at a time when Laughlin was frantically trying to put a stop to unauthorized publication of Pound's last cantos, which were proliferating across Europe and the United States. Then, in 1970, Brown produced a pirated edition of Williams's 1923 *Spring and All* (originally published in Paris by Robert McAlmon's Contact Editions, his Bryher-funded press). Laughlin didn't hold all of Williams's copyrights at this time, but he did hold the rights to that book, and he was furious that Brown had put it out to compete with his own authorized editions of Williams's early poetry.

These "anarchistic" activities that Laughlin and Pearson condemned were to Brown and Caplan merely the 1960s equivalent of the internet-age slogan "information wants to be free." For them, copyright and ownership served the interests of the publisher, not the writer, and certainly not the community. This was particularly true in the case of a dead author like H.D. And Frontier achieved its aim: it did spur Pearson to move on an authorized edition of *Hermetic Definition*, which appeared the following year. Laughlin pushed Pearson, as the copy-right holder, to file suit against Brown, not just because of the damages but because Brown "deserves to be chastised, many times over."[76] Sus-pended between the establishment and the counterculture, Duncan urged Pearson not to bring an action against Brown, pointing out that the books "are not for sale" and his local bookstore — Serendipity, in Berkeley — was giving them away to H.D. collectors.[77]

It was a clash of orientations and fundamental worldviews that, in the late 1960s and early 1970s, Pearson was beginning to encounter everywhere in his life. His faith in and mastery of existing cultural and legal institutions had begun to encounter an increasingly widespread rejection of those institutions and ideals. Pearson stood for property, for respect, for the concept that America's strength inhered in the sometimes flawed but ultimately admirable institutions that structured the nation's society and culture. Brown and Caplan stood for *soixante-huitard* idealism and Prankster slipperiness in the service of art. Brown always acted as if his actions were perfectly legitimate, that the pur-pose of literary publishing was purely to circulate literature and foster artistic innovation. In fact, in 1973 an astonished Pearson reported to Laughlin that "Harvey Brown phoned my secretary to ask if, 'despite *Hermetic Definitions*,' she thought I would be willing to help him pre-pare a selection of the work of [Robert] McAlmon."[78] He declined.

If the *Hermetic Definition* episode was a glimpse of a future that appalled Pearson, his last intervention on behalf of H.D. brought him back far into her past, her genesis as a poet. For all that Pearson resolved to detach H.D. from Pound in the public mind, their stories began to parallel uncannily after the war, while Pound was hospitalized at St. Elizabeths and H.D. at Küsnacht. In the mid-1950s, then, both entered a highly productive stage of their careers, with Pound produc-ing three sets of Cantos (as well as other prose and editing projects) and H.D. composing *Helen in Egypt* and several other works. Laughlin and Pearson, their respective American publishers and representatives, were undertaking remarkably similar efforts on their behalf, as well: two-pronged campaigns to make available their earlier writings and at the same time showcase their new poetry, with the argument that these were both still vital poets, elders of the literary world.[79] But while Pearson was battling H.D.'s obscurity, Laughlin had the more daunting task of neutralizing Pound's infamy.

For that reason it seems almost overdetermined that the two—the poets he admired most, and also the vectors through which he most palpably exerted his influence over the history of American modernism—converged in Pearson's last editorial project. After Aldington sent her, in 1958, a sensationalistic *Nation* story on Pound's St. Elizabeths menagerie, H.D. composed a series of impressionistic short memoirs about Pound and their courtship. Bryher, who had never liked the grandiose and misogynistic Pound and despised anti-Semites and fascists, hated the idea, but Pearson encouraged it, hoping the process would be therapeutic. Pearson is everywhere in the resulting manuscript, which H.D. called *End to Torment*. (The "torment" in the title refers to Pound's incarceration.) The book is dedicated to him, and he is mentioned almost two dozen times in the short text. The book concludes with a long quotation from one of Pearson's letters to H.D. It also put Pearson, who had long stood invisibly by the side of these poets, discernibly at the center of modernist literary production for the first time.

Once it was complete, H.D. sent Pound the manuscript and then set it aside, not wanting (as Pearson relayed it) to "take advantage of Ezra's situation, or bring back too strong memories of Washington."[80] After H.D.'s death and the 1961 publication of *Helen*, Pearson didn't rush to publish *End to Torment*, and Laughlin just wanted to bury public memory of Pound's merry band of crazies and racists at St. Elizabeths. "Ezra really doesn't care too much," Laughlin told Pearson in 1971, but "it would be easier to 'present' this very unusual little book at a later date."[81] A few years later, the two moved to get the book into print, but Pearson would not live long enough to prepare the final text. Even so, Pearson knew by then that his work on behalf of H.D. had succeeded. Indeed, the lifelong chain smoker had lit a metaphorical victory cigar back in 1967, writing Bryher with satisfaction that "at long last my campaign for her recognition is beginning to take hold, and my hunch is that she will soon be the focus of much critical attention."[82] He was right.

The long, extraordinarily close and sustaining friendship between Pearson and Bryher didn't have the same tangible effects on the career of a major author or on public understanding of American literature. While Bryher was an author, and Pearson did for her many of the things he did for H.D., her talents and accomplishments did not rank with those of H.D. and she was not a significant writer in any literary movement. (She wasn't American, either.) But that's not to say that it didn't impact the larger literary world. When Bryher met Pearson in 1937, she found someone who would eventually become a partner in her project to financially support *other* writers and artists and help them build an alternative aesthetic and sexual world separate from the conventional, strictly gendered one in which she had never fit.

What was first a relationship of mentor and student became more balanced during the war, when it was Pearson who could do things for the women. After the end of the war Pearson and Bryher's collaboration truly commenced. As they lived on separate continents, they conducted their friendship and partnership largely through the mail, seeing each other once or twice a year. And unsurprisingly for two people who approached and understood the world through language, they exchanged a truly staggering number of letters, comprising close to a million words. From the end of the war until H.D.'s death, Bryher and Pearson wrote each other at least once a week. After H.D.'s death, that correspondence accelerated to multiple letters a week and, in the late 1960s and early 1970s, one or two letters a day. They are full of gossip, of literary opinions, of Pearson groaning about his workload, of Bryher reporting on her travels and her personal relationships. Their relationship, and their letters in particular, also provide one of the most candid and unguarded perspectives on the very cagey Pearson's personality, character, and even political views, and on the beliefs and activities of a woman whose role in twentieth-century art and literature has been vastly underappreciated because, like Pearson's, it was largely invisible.

Bryher and Pearson were affectionate and devoted and adored spending time together, but their friendship was grounded on shared values and priorities—above all, their drive to use their capital to help writers and serve the cause of literature. Pearson's capital was social, cultural, and institutional, and he not only had access to prestigious institutions but, by the later 1940s, held positions of influence within them. Bryher's capital, on the other hand, was capital. She had money. Her family's wealth gave her some access to elite institutions, but she refused to present herself in the conventional ways that would make her welcome in them. Instead, as queer people have often done, she built her own. Her money funded films, magazines, architecture. Rather than working through existing institutions she assembled networks of like-minded people, of artists and writers and photographers and filmmakers and psychoanalysts. Pearson used his position in institutions to construct his networks; Bryher used her money to build hers.

It made for an effectively complementary partnership. Their first beneficiary, of course, was H.D., for whom Bryher was empowered to make personal and medical decisions, matters in which Pearson was mostly a supportive observer. But Pearson was aware of Bryher's long history of giving financial gifts to writers and artists in need, something that he, too, had wanted to do but lacked the means to. Bryher had long wanted to extend her philanthropy to writers located in the United States, but US tax laws and the British Foreign Exchange Control regulations were an obstacle. She didn't want to deal with red tape; she wanted just to give money away. After Pearson explained to her that in the United States, nonprofit foundations enjoyed great latitude, in 1949 she created the Bryher Foundation and endowed it with about $14,000 (later adding another $2,500). Although in reality the money would be at Pearson's personal disposal, he advised her that it would be necessary, legally as well as in terms of appearances, for a duly constituted committee—ultimately consisting of Pearson, Fitts, Harvard's Harry Levin, and Princeton's Willard Thorp—to make award decisions. Their first grant, $2,500, went to H.D., and another soon went to Bryher's old friend Moore. "I am touched to learn how poor [Moore] is," Levin told Pearson, expressing a hope that these Bryher grants would "sweeten the air" for poetry awards, which generally came with very little money.[83] In the end, the Bryher Foundation awarded almost half ($7,500) of its total of $16,783 in assets to the penniless Gregory and Zaturenska, with its only other considerable gift going to Conrad Aiken.[84]

But this was a far too formalized and distant means of giving for Bryher, and she dissolved the foundation after only three years. She had settled on a much easier and more direct solution: regular disbursements directly to a Swiss bank account Pearson opened under the code name "Winson" (Winifred and Pearson), that he could use to distribute the funds. Like "Kenwin," this portmanteau name represented one of Bryher's greatest creative achievements, one in which she characteristically concealed her own involvement. Like Pearson, she much preferred to work behind the scenes. She didn't want to publicize her generosity: those who received it would know about it, and those in the know understood that she had funds for those in need. Nor did she want to embarrass the recipients of her generosity. And ultimately, for a literary woman whose accomplishments were always overshadowed by her partner's, she also wanted to be known as an *author*, not just a rich dilettante with a checkbook. But in its twenty-five years, "Winson" disbursed over $100,000 to dozens of writers and scholars and students, allowing them to continue their work and, often, just pay their bills.

"Winson" also made it seamless for Bryher to continue to fund Pearson himself, as she had started doing in 1949 when, pitying his brutal workload, she gave him money to hire a part-time secretary (an expense that she covered for the rest of Pearson's life).[85] The endless and expensive task of hunting down and obtaining Hawthorne's letters for his collected edition got much easier once Bryher got involved. When he wanted to publish the 1953 English Institute proceedings as a collected volume, Bryher covered the printing and binding; and despite her loathing of Pound, she even approved a $500 subvention for Edwards's *Preliminary Checklist*.[86] She didn't just fund professional expenses, either. After he complained about car trouble in 1955, she gave Pearson $3,000 to purchase a brand-new cherry-red Oldsmobile

Super 88, and in 1967 she replaced that car and bought Susan a dishwasher as well. Often, when she deposited several thousand dollars intended for another one of her beneficiaries—Gregory, for instance—she would insist that he take $1,000 off the top for himself, as a "gift."[87]

But Pearson regretfully declined her most substantial attempt to underwrite his work. In 1952, she offered him a commission to take a leave of absence from Yale and write a comprehensive history of modern American poetry, a project she would support by doubling his Yale salary and hosting him at Kenwin. But this was asking too much. In a long, earnest, grateful letter, Pearson explained that he was only beginning to rebuild his relationship with little Susan and Elizabeth after their "cruel and thoughtless" father "did his best to break things up between them and me during the war"; in addition, he had at least four other books he was committed to complete, and it would be "catastrophic" for Yale's English and American Studies programs if he were to leave.[88] (As much as he loved Bryher and craved such focused time for work, he likely also realized, if only subconsciously, that without being actively involved in all the institutions and boards and committees that made his life so exhausting, he might lose his base of power.)

Bryher also made Pearson's astonishing collection of rare books and manuscripts possible. Her 1945 Christmas gift—that array of John Milton first editions—marked the start of decades of boxes full of untold treasures regularly arriving at Goodrich Street. Pearson received the catalogs of every rare-book dealer and auction house in Britain and the United States, and sent wish lists that she would fulfill through the convenient fiction that she was buying these for *herself*, and storing them at his house temporarily. But they were in truth his books. A 1967 list of the collection they had amassed just of early English literature and manuscripts runs to ten pages and includes early editions of Ben Jonson, Marlowe, Dryden, Sir Walter Raleigh, and especially Beaumont and Fletcher, who were a particular passion of both Bryher and Pearson. The most valuable book on the list was a precious Shakespeare First Folio, appraised at $20,000. (Only 235 of these books are known to exist.) Like young Norman, as a child Bryher had reveled in the boys' adventure stories of Victorian authors R. M. Ballantyne and

G. A. Henty and in retrospect interpreted her passion for them as an early indication of her genderqueerness, and so the two gleefully collaborated on obtaining complete runs of both authors' first editions, a collection that they nicknamed their "Dusty Diamonds." All these books eventually went to Yale.

Almost as soon as he took over H.D.'s, Pearson also began to handle Bryher's authorial business in the United States. He approached Pantheon about publishing her novels, but the Wolffs were reluctant because of their poor sales prospects. Pearson persuaded them to accept Bryher's subventions of over $3,000 per book to pay for printing and marketing *The Fourteenth of October* (1952), *The Player's Boy* (1953), and *Beowulf* (1956). These were investments, he told Bryher—she was trying her hand at a new genre of writing, and the public needed the opportunity to get to know her new voice. And it's hard not to detect Pearson's hand behind Pantheon's 1956 joint advertisement for *Beowulf* and H.D.'s *Tribute to Freud*, headlined "The meeting of two creative minds," that ran in the *New York Times* and *Saturday Review of Literature* and delighted the women when they saw it.[89]

Their deep friendship was grounded on shared interests and temperamental similarity; Sue Addiss called Bryher Norm's "intellectual mistress."[90] But despite their very different orientations, it did have an erotic charge. To Pearson (and H.D. as well), Bryher's nickname was "Fido," and she often closed her letters with "Love and barks!" In what was likely just a safe form of displacement for the happily married man and the confirmed lesbian, Pearson would often take this canine imagery into flirtatious or even sexual territory—in 1953, for instance, he wrote that he wished he "could have taken my Fido for a run, rub her ears and pat her tail, rough up her fur and then smooth it down again, so that we could forget everything in the clean air." "I have always thought of you as an erotic being," he told her years later, "a highly erotic one who managed by strict decorum to maintain yourself as a Puritan. To outer appearance, that is; within you tumesce." (He even did some wingman work for Bryher, it seems: when she inquired about Marie Borroff, who became in 1959 the first female professor in the Yale English department, Pearson reported that Borroff was "unmarried, could be a little that way I think in a stiff fashion.") As he did with Sheri Martinelli, Pearson certainly enjoyed some flirtatious playfulness with Bryher, but there was no risk of any boundaries being crossed, as even Susan, who "laughed when she read of a possible scandal of us traveling à deux," knew.[91]

Pearson and Bryher's close bond in the early 1950s did, though, arouse jealousy—not from Susan, but from H.D. In London, Pearson had known them as a couple, but in Switzerland after the war they lived separately, and so he conducted his friendship with them separately, and increasingly differently. He was *friends* with Bryher, while he *served* H.D. Although he was much more strategic and farsighted in his campaign for H.D. than in his more ad hoc work for Bryher, H.D. sometimes felt that she was the one being slighted. Pearson and Bryher were logorrheic, while H.D. was much more compressed, which made for many more letters between the former. He always visited both women when he came to Europe but saw Bryher much more frequently, as she often traveled to the United States. He adored them both, but reality determined that he would see Bryher more. Both Bryher and Pearson had to be in constant motion, and thus their paths often intersected, while H.D.'s mental and physical health compelled her to remain in place. Pearson was well aware of H.D.'s hurt. "I'm afraid she feels I've neglected her," he confided in Bryher in 1953, "though I have always felt that I constantly walked with an arm about each of you."[92]

Perhaps only second to collecting was their shared passion for travel. They regularly met to explore Italy, Denmark, France, even Turkey, but both craved more rugged experiences. For most of her life, Bryher had been fascinated by the culture of the native people of northern Canada and Greenland, and so in 1957—when Bryher was sixty-three!—she and Pearson journeyed together first to Churchill, Manitoba (on the west coast of Hudson Bay), and from there to Chesterfield Inlet, in what is now the Nunavut Territory. It was not luxury travel. "We pitched camp on top of a headland of rocks and shivered for a week or so during nights that started at 35 and were stirred up by winds as high as 60 mph," Pearson excitedly reported.[93] "It's the craziest thing I ever did," Bryher told a reporter afterward. "I'm lucky to come back alive!"

Both remarked on the "extinction of culture patterns" they witnessed among the Inuit.[94] Just as Bryher wanted to learn more about the Inuit, in the late 1950s Pearson was developing an interest in Leif Erikson, and so Greenland became their next destination. In July 1958, they met in Copenhagen and sailed from Elsinore to the populated southwestern coast on a cold but exhilarating two-week trip. Bryher was not able to join Pearson on his return to Greenland in 1962, which caused him to "weep a few dry tears."[95] He tried to organize a final Greenland excursion in 1967 to Gardar and Brattahild, to "go way in the Eriksfjord to the other settlements, to feel the fjord as Erik did," but by then Bryher, at seventy-three, was simply too old to make such a taxing journey.[96]

The two were also in sync politically. A sponge for information, Pearson had followed British politics since his Oxford days. His heritage predisposed him to Anglophilia, and in the run-up to World War II he felt more British than American in his insistence on the necessity of confronting Hitler early and forcefully. His OSS years in London had sharpened his perceptions even further, which he generally approached as an observer whose moderate New England Republicanism didn't precisely map onto the British political spectrum but often rhymed with the Conservative Party. Spying also gave him a respect for what he felt was the UK's greater maturity and cold-eyed realism in geopolitics and intelligence work.

Bryher was a die-hard Conservative and Churchill idolizer but more than that reviled the Labour Party and especially anything that smelled of socialism, and she detested the changes that Labour brought to the country after their 1945 election victory. "They have destroyed the centuries-old tradition of voluntary service in England, they have brought down the level of education and training, set up class warfare where it scarcely existed, and thrown away wantonly most of our economic resources," she grumbled to Pearson. In the run-up to the 1950 election she even made half-serious attempts to prepare to apply for Swiss citizenship, but the Tory resurgence that year gave her hope that there would be "a brake at least for a while on the wilder economic schemes."[97] The always probusiness Pearson was right there with her, diagnosing the postwar Labour government as "a kind of weakened Fabian socialism. . . . England's public-school socialists seem to think they understand the workers, that government ownership really changes things, that there is enough to go around and that the whole problem is still how to distribute it. They don't realize that, for them, with the passing of the Empire, the surplus has vanished. They've lost their Tory guts, and believe all that is necessary is to take Marxism on their knees for a fondle."[98] Like Bryher, he was incensed at Labour's expansion of welfare and social services, and here his anti–New Deal- ism aligned seamlessly with her Toryism: "all they want to prove is that no private individual ever has a sense of responsibility, and make the voters eat from their hands." Private employers, he felt, should handle this, pointing to how at Goodnow Pearson's, his father would just "pen- sion the oldsters himself, much better than any of the new old-age ben- efits do."[99] (He wasn't entirely wrong: Goodnow Pearson's did offer gen- erous retirement benefits and even profit sharing as early as 1914.)[100]

For all her bohemianism and refusal to accept conventional gen- der roles, she had every bit of the rigid snobbishness of the British upper classes to which her own family had only recently ascended. "My unpopular view is that the masses cannot take too much educa- tion," she haughtily pronounced after seeing a 1968 anti–Vietnam War protest in front of the American Embassy in London. "And it is forced on them now in the English schools." Norm offered a lukewarm agree- ment, colored by his own experience of twelve years in a factory town's public schools and forty spent among the most privileged students in the United States: "most might disagree with you but a very large num- ber would agree. And say that education was not only a panacea, but a way of keeping people busy when the world does not provide enough work for them to do, and off the streets until post-puberty."[101] She was appalled when Yale's faculty, in solidarity with student demonstrators in 1970, voted in support of a moratorium on classes. "How safe are say Hilda's papers, collections of books etc going to be in the University," she asked rhetorically. "I don't feel particularly inclined to say let them have papers and Elizabethan books if [the faculty is] going to side with the strikers."[102]

If Pearson didn't always agree with her staunchly conservative (and

Conservative) views, the two were of one mind when it came to the Cold War and Churchill. "Poor Bulldog was so right in that Fulton speech of his that was so criticized at the time," she wrote in the wake of the Chinese entry into the Korean War.[103] (Churchill had declared in a 1946 speech in Fulton, Missouri, that "an iron curtain has fallen across Europe.") A March 1949 speech was "splendid, as always," Pearson proclaimed, and he felt that it was "unusually fortunate" for Britain that Churchill was in power when King George VI died, as "it is time for Bulldog and tradition. And despite all the inevitable sadness of the British people, I have a feeling that they will look on the second Elizabeth as a good omen. . . . It will seem like a return to the older strengths of character, the bulldog tradition and that of Bess."[104] Never a fan of Eisenhower, in 1960 the normally controlled and arch Pearson uncharacteristically fulminated about how the president "offended" and "embarrassed" him by his "confusion and maladroitness" in response to the U-2 incident and communist revolution in Cuba. "One can say flatly that never in America's history has its prestige been so low," he concluded.[105] Unusually, the two split politically in 1972, when Pearson reviled the shameless and "psychopathic" Nixon, while Cold Warrior Bryher insisted on the need to project strength above all, and thus refused to support McGovern.[106]

Age—she was fifteen years older than Pearson—slowed Bryher down by the mid-1960s and shrunk her world. She traveled much less, although after H.D. died she came often to America to visit Perdita and her children, always seeing Pearson when she did. Pearson, on the other hand, began to travel much more, and his adventures became hers. On his trips to Australia, Japan, South Korea, the South Pacific, Denmark, Ireland, Trinidad, and elsewhere he wrote her constantly, allowing her to vicariously experience what had once given her such sustenance. By the early 1970s they wrote each other briefer letters daily, the equivalent of an evening telephone check-in at a time when transcontinental calls were for emergencies only. As he had been for H.D., he became a lifeline for her. She began to experience memory problems in the mid-1970s, but Pearson died in 1975, before Bryher lost her ability to communicate and retreated to a single room at Kenwin, where she lived until January 1983. Age did nothing to attenuate their connection or their banter, which lasted literally until the end. "I still tingle with the pleasure of hearing your voice on the phone," Pearson told her only weeks before his death; and in his last letter to her, spinning out a fantasy in which she scolded him for buying a custom-tailored shirt in expensive Tokyo, he joked that "I am too much the crooked old man, in the nursery rhyme crooked old house, to want crooked little shirts. You must learn to forgive me, and simply to accept my love."[107]

+ 11 +

AMERICAN STUDIES AND
THE AMERICAN CENTURY

Describe and compare the final dinner parties of The Age of Inno-
cence and A Lost Lady in terms of the symbolic value of each to the
novel in which it appears.

This midterm exam question, for Pearson's 1950–51 American Studies 35 course, might seem notable because it asks students to write
about two novels by women (Edith Wharton and Willa Cather) at a
time when Yale's English curriculum included vanishingly few female
authors. But what makes this midterm truly worth remembering is
on the back of the page. On the verso of several copies of this brief
test, Pearson drafted a four-page memo that surprisingly remains,
whether intentionally or through an oversight, in his otherwise thoroughly scrubbed archive at Yale's Beinecke Library. Titled "Intelligence
Training in Service Schools," Pearson's memo to William H. Jackson,
the first deputy director of central intelligence and Pearson's former
X-2 subordinate, urged the CIA to ensure that intelligence training
was included in the curriculum of the service academies, since officers
trained at West Point and Annapolis would eventually be responsible
for handling intelligence. "This is an academic question which is not
an 'academic' question," he told Jackson.[1]

While it's not surprising that a former intelligence chief would have
some ideas about intelligence training, the second, untitled part of

the memo is even more provocative. In eleven bullet points, Pearson offered Jackson ideas for recruiting CIA officers in American colleges and universities *beyond* the service academies. Schools such as Yale were fertile grounds for harvesting potential spies, Pearson explained, because they were full of young men with "some intellectual training and social presentability, as well as particular language qualifications [and no] fixed professional interests." Moreover, the four years of college provided an "extended time for their observation on the part of those aware what characteristics and abilities are needed." Expressed here in exquisitely detached and abstracted bureaucratese, he is referring here to "spotters," faculty members tasked by CIA with identifying promising spy candidates. This identification and recruitment process, he stressed, should remain completely veiled from the student: "No direct approach should be made to such persons by the spotters, but their names and qualifications, permanent addresses, and the like, plus a permanent file should be at headquarters." (Ever the X-2 chief, Pearson never lost his faith in archives and catalogs, in indexed and cross-referenced information.) Pearson concludes by granting that he has been—again, in consummate governmental prose—"openly known to have associated with such work in the past."[2]

This was true. Many veterans on the Yale campus knew that Professor Pearson had done something important in OSS, and it soon became conventional wisdom that if Pearson wasn't an actual CIA officer, he was certainly freelancing for the agency. "Pearson's involvement in the world of spies continued" well after the war, Daniel Horowitz writes in his profile of his Yale class of 1960, and Jesse Lemisch, another student from the same era, simply calls Pearson "an actual CIA man."[3] "The CIA does not run Yale," a 1969 article in the Yale student publication the *New Journal* portentously begins. "It does not need to," because so many Yale professors and administrators such as Pearson had or have CIA links.[4] Pearson thoroughly enjoyed and milked the legend that grew about him. He often dropped oblique hints about his wartime adventures, knowing that the undergraduates would run with them. "Once an agent, always an agent—for someone," he would teasingly tell students brave enough to ask him about his spying. But his activities promoting American geopolitical interests after the war were by no means limited to whatever spying or recruiting he might have done. As this chapter will show, from the end of the war to the end of his life, Pearson wove his beliefs about the American character and his work as a scholar and a teacher into the United States' burgeoning cultural-diplomatic campaign to win over foreign audiences in the Cold War, making himself into a central figure in the collaboration between academia and the national-security state.

"No other American university, it seems," Gregory Hodgson wrote in 1987, "has sent so many of its graduates into" espionage—a number that includes America's first spy, Nathan Hale, whose statue stands in Yale's Old Campus.[5] But although Yale was undoubtedly a cradle of spies, the myth of Pearson vastly overstates the reality. Certainly, Pearson did talent spot for the CIA in its first years until sometime in the early 1950s. But as he advised Jackson, he rarely made direct contact with these students. Instead, he sent their names and personal information data to a Washington, DC, post office box rented to a "Ray L.," who would contact the potential candidate. Over those few years, dozens of Pearson's referrals made the trip south for an interview. A rare exception to his generally secondhand practice was the writer Peter Matthiessen, who recounted that Pearson, his favorite professor, approached him in person about joining the CIA. Matthiessen did just that and was working for the agency in France in the early 1950s while he was founding the *Paris Review*. (Pearson might have broken with his usual practice in this instance because he considered the young man part of his network: Peter Matthiessen's first cousin was F. O. Matthiessen.)[6]

So Pearson definitely was a CIA talent scout, and in those early years of the agency even proposed to Jackson an informal group of like-minded X-2 veterans who could be asked to spot talent on their campuses. Among these men were Eugene Waith, his colleague in the Yale English department; Calvin Tenney, his Gardner and Yale friend who had headed X-2's Paris office and taught at nearby Wesleyan; and Edward Weismiller, who worked at Pomona College in California.[7] Rumors of his talent spotting—grounded in fact—over the years became a mystique, a suspicion, and eventually a certainty not just that Pearson was the CIA's main man at Yale, but that he also moonlighted as an overseas agent during the many foreign trips he would take in the 1960s and 1970s. Because of this, Pearson became and has remained a cynosure for those who decry how the infiltration of the national-security state into higher education turned universities into arms of American military imperialism. But as far as I or any other scholar or journalist or friend or even family member knows or can actually document, his talent spotting was the extent of his involvement in the Central Intelligence Agency, and all available evidence indicates that it ended in the early 1950s.

That's not to say that Pearson wasn't a key figure in the Cold War alliance between higher education, the national-security state, and US propaganda operations. On the contrary: Pearson was one of the most important such operators, even an architect of that alliance. And his involvement came from genuine and considered belief. In the 1930s, his studies had shown him the uniqueness of American civilization and the American character, and his experience in Germany and Britain showed him the evil of Nazism. In the 1940s, his war service convinced him that this civilization was genuinely threatened by totalitarianism, not just Nazi but communist, and that America needed to use every tool at its disposal to counter its enemies and spread what was positive and affirming about our "way of life." Then, after the war, he saw how America's institutions of soft power—universities, literature, foundations, publishers, professional societies, and trade organizations—could supplement our economic and military might in protecting our society, explaining its virtues, and stopping the spread of communism. He was an unabashed Cold Warrior without being a nationalist or an American chauvinist and in the postwar period used his unique combination of talents and positions of influence to convert American studies itself into a weapon in the Cold War. And none of this was secret or covert. Even a spy can do his most important work out in the open.

In a February 1941 *Life* magazine editorial, ten months before Pearl Harbor, publisher Henry Luce had urged the war-reluctant people of the United States to abandon isolationism. We were already in the conflict, Luce insisted, because of our material and moral support of Great Britain. Americans needed to realize that this was a defensive struggle to protect our democracy and way of life, and that the world's democracies were looking to the United States to lead them. The increasing interrelatedness of the peoples of the world, and the United States' material wealth and spiritual example, made it imperative that the twentieth century become "to a significant degree an American Century." Only America, Luce added, could "make the society of men safe for the freedom, growth, and increasing satisfaction of all individual men." Free enterprise and free trade, the rule of law, technological innovation, individual rights, protection from violence, and ending hunger: the United States not only could but had an obligation to use its power to advance these causes and ideas. The United States was the "most powerful and the most vital nation in the world. . . . America as the dynamic center of ever-widening spheres of influence, America as the training center of the skillful servants of mankind, America as the Good Samaritan, really believing again that it is more blessed to give than to receive, and America as the powerhouse of the ideals of Freedom and Justice — out of these elements can surely be fashioned a vision of the 20th Century to which we can and will devote ourselves in joy and gladness and vigor and enthusiasm." "The complete opportunity of leadership is *ours*," Luce insisted, and we needed to "exert upon the world the full impact of our influence, for such purposes as we see fit and by such means as we see fit."[8] And while Pearson did not express it in quite such messianic terms, he had also pushed for the United States to join the war. His OSS service, then, had strengthened his conviction that America's commitment to individual rights, democratic governance, and free enterprise gave it a mission to spread these values as a counter to fascism and, later, Communism. And his scholarly research and teaching in the field of American studies were giving these convictions an even stronger intellectual foundation.

In the 1940s and 1950s, universities became part of the United States' strategic infrastructure. The A-bomb — a project funded by the government, but "completely dependent on the efforts of university scientists"—suggested that military technology would be the most crucial battlefield in the Cold War, and after the USSR detonated its own bomb in 1949, President Truman resolved that the US government needed to bolster the nation's capacity for scientific research.[9] America needed more scientists and engineers, and more and better-equipped universities where they could study and conduct research. A 1947 federal report, *Higher Education for American Democracy*, called to double postsecondary enrollments, expand the number of university campuses, and provide "vastly increased public appropriations" to basic research funding.[10] Although the initial influx of funding and administrative support for university-conducted research dwindled by the mid-1950s, *Sputnik* then shook the American establishment out its complacency that the private sector would keep America ahead of the Soviets in technological development. Significantly increased sums for research poured in beginning with the National Defense Education Act of 1958, and the universities ready to do this research thrived: Chicago, Berkeley, Wisconsin, Michigan, MIT, Caltech, Carnegie Tech (later Carnegie Mellon), and other large state and private schools. Even the Ivy League got into the act, with Harvard and Columbia receiving significant government funding for scientific research.

Yale, though, was missing out. Unlike Harvard and Columbia, Yale had never emphasized science and engineering, and in fact until 1945 the science departments were separate from Yale College, in the Sheffield Scientific School. After the war, Yale's science and engineering programs lagged well behind their counterparts in Cambridge and New York and even Princeton in terms of fueling the push for Atomic Age discoveries and patents (and, perhaps more importantly, in terms of federal grant money received). Because Yale still saw itself as fundamentally a liberal arts college, it tended not to attract students who showed talent in those areas or faculty who conducted that kind of research. This didn't mean, of course, that Yale was absent from the nation's Cold War leadership; Yalies were vastly overrepresented in the upper echelons of government, national security, and diplomacy, thus its major contributions to the Cold War came from the boardroom and classroom, not the lab.

And unlikely as it sounds, chief among these contributions was American studies. Beginning almost immediately after World War II ended, the field of American studies, and Yale's program in particular, signed on to the project of fighting communism. At home, American students would be taught that the American character was fundamentally incompatible with "totalitarianism" and collectivism; abroad, American Studies programs would put a positive face on American civilization to generate goodwill for US policies among intellectuals and opinion makers. Universities, the State Department, the United States Information Agency, the Central Intelligence Agency, professional groups like the American Studies Association (ASA) and American Council of Learned Societies (ACLS), and nonprofit foundations all joined in this effort. Pearson, entirely supportive of the liberal-centrist vision of the nation that the new field was elaborating and disseminating, viewed this not as an ethical capitulation or intellectual compromise but rather as a calling, and he answered. He may have turned down offers to work in the State Department and CIA, but he would serve his country through American studies. Because of his experience in the OSS, his extensive professional networks, and his ability to communicate with audiences beyond the academy, Pearson became one of the most important academic figures in the collaboration between academia and the national-security state.

That he would help with matchmaking and shaping this joint venture was appropriate, as, in keeping with his uncanny knack for being present right when important things were happening, he had been around American studies from its start. He had been a student in the first "American studies" class ever offered, earned one of the first PhDs in the program that later became American Studies, and was now that program's first undergraduate director. He was among the first editorial-board members of the field's flagship journal, *American Quarterly*, and spoke and wrote frequently on the practicalities of starting American Studies programs at universities. And in 1968, he would serve as president of the ASA. His term as president would appropriately mark the end of American studies' first era, which ended with the field's reversal from providing scholarly cover for the American Cold War project to bitterly opposing it.

American studies began as an effort to understand the nature of the civilization of the United States through its history, society, and literature. (The field's name uncritically asserted "America" to be synonymous with the United States, rather than referring to the nations and cultures of the Western Hemisphere more broadly.) The bureaucratic structure of the research university, which silos off fields of knowledge into departments into which faculty members must fit, impeded the institutional development of American studies, but the field met little of the intellectual resistance that American *literary* studies had encountered. In fact, the legitimation of American literary studies made possible the genesis of American studies.

Back then, it had taken an aesthetic argument to get the academic establishment to accept American literature: *the great works of American literature are the match of any other nation's in terms of their artistic achievement, and thus they are worth teaching, studying, and researching.* Throughout the nineteenth and early twentieth centuries, whether stated as a fact or expressed as a complaint, the proposition that American high culture wasn't up to snuff was almost universally accepted by Americans (with the notable exception of Ralph Waldo Emerson). In Henry James's novels, for example, Americans aspiring to culture had to go to Europe to get it, and the East Coast ruling class slavishly modeled their new boarding schools on English counterparts. But around the time of the First World War, a group of young US "literary radicals" emerged, insisting that America had nothing to be ashamed of. Randolph Bourne, along with Van Wyck Brooks, Waldo Frank, John Macy, and others insisted that America had created its own culture and civilization and had definitively broken with the English tradition. As Harold Stearns said in 1922's *Civilization in the United States,* "whatever else American civilization is, it is not Anglo-Saxon, and . . . we shall never achieve any genuine nationalistic self-consciousness as long as we allow certain financial and social minorities to persuade us that we are still an English Colony."[11] And Americans needed to have pride in what they had created: in a well-known 1914 essay, for instance, Bourne lamented Americans' "cultural humility," their instinctive tendency to genuflect to European artistic achievements and denigrate their own.[12]

By incisively zeroing in on the very word "culture," Bourne's argument became a cornerstone of American studies itself. Americans, Bourne insists, are too willing to acquiesce to the English concept of "culture," especially as defined by the influential nineteenth-century English writer and educator Matthew Arnold. Culture, for Arnold, is "the best that has been thought and said"; it is the crowning aesthetic and philosophical achievements of a people. Of course, Bourne says, by that measure European culture would be superior to ours; they've had two thousand more years to generate it, and to refine and propagate their judgments about what is "best"! But Americans shouldn't truckle to Europeans just about their time-venerated art, Bourne continued. Recalling 1913's Armory Show, which brought modernist art and sculpture to the United States for the first time, Bourne decries its "avowed purpose of showing American artists how bad they were in comparison with the modern French," and that Americans' "groveling humility" to our European betters "can only have the effect of making us feeble imitators."[13]

Instead, Bourne proposes, Americans should approach culture differently, not as "an acquired familiarity with things outside"—that is, simply affirming and reiterating the judgments of the past—but rather as "an inner and constantly operating taste, a fresh and responsive power of discrimination, and the insistent judging of everything that comes to our minds and senses." Americans, he insists, have the unique ability, indeed responsibility, to do this, if they would only look at their homegrown artists and writers with "a keen introspection into the beauties and vitalities and sincerities of our own life and ideals." He provocatively calls for a "new American nationalism." Praising Whitman, Emerson, sculptor Auguste Saint-Gaudens, and others as the equal of any Europeans, Bourne concludes that "we shall never be able to perpetuate our ideals except in the form of art and literature; the world will never understand our spirit except in terms of art."

A couple of Bourne's points are worth emphasizing here. First, of course, is the claim that one cannot limit "culture" just to those works that have existed for centuries and have accumulated generations of praise and esteem. Rather, a new civilization can produce works of the imagination that are just as accomplished and valuable as the older ones. The second is his accusation that Americans are willfully but unjustifiably self-deprecating about their own culture. We shouldn't be ashamed of what we produce because it doesn't match up to Europe's on Europe's own self-serving terms; we should celebrate our work on its own merits. Bourne also contends that a civilization expresses itself most honestly and directly in its art and literature, and that one can understand a civilization best by looking at its cultural products, even if those products don't attain the aesthetic standards established by the world's dominant nations. This final point provided a powerful justification for American literary studies. American literature didn't have to prove that it was the equal of English masterworks in order to justify studying and teaching it; American literature was the best evidence for, and way to understand, the uniqueness of American culture and the American experience, thus making studying it worthwhile. As literary historian David Shumway puts it, "The principal cultural work of the new field of American literary studies [was] to demonstrate the existence of an American civilization."[14]

Bourne and the other literary radicals' rejection of "culture" or "civilization" as a value judgment then meshed with another development emerging from an entirely different field. In the Arnoldian view, "culture" meant the intellectual and artistic achievements of a people, and these could be graded. National cultures were arranged on a ladder, and the United States' was nowhere near the top. But in the early twentieth century, anthropologist Franz Boas was building a new science of culture. Boas had long rejected the pseudoscientific ranking of human races common in Victorian times, but in his fieldwork, he expanded this idea beyond races to cultures and in so doing redefined the term.

"Culture," he argued, wasn't a commendation conferred on the greatest artistic and intellectual accomplishments (as Arnold would say) or even a term describing all the artistic and intellectual products of a people, no matter how aesthetically distinguished (as Bourne would have it). Instead, for Boas and his followers "culture" was the entire set of practices of daily life and assumptions about the universe held by a group of people. And in a radical break from previous anthropology, Boas and his group insisted that no culture was superior to any other. Cultures, Boas and his students argued, needed to be understood as discrete, harmonious wholes, and the job of the anthropologist was to articulate the unique wholeness of the culture that he (or she, as Ruth Benedict and Margaret Mead helped develop these ideas) studied as a "participant-observer." Malinowski, whose fieldwork had been in the western Pacific, brought these ideas to Yale in the late 1930s, and Pearson drank them in when he audited Malinowski's class in 1939. He would in fact call Malinowski his most important intellectual influence, and claim repeatedly that his approach to American studies—melding "socio-anthropology and psycho-sociology"—drew almost entirely from Malinowski.[15]

Boas, Mead, Benedict, and Malinowski wrote about cultures that most Americans would find exotic, such as the Hopi, the First Nations of British Columbia, and the peoples of Samoa and Papua New Guinea. But to Pearson, their method applied just as well, and just as urgently, to the United States. "I wanted to find out from the Trobriand Islanders what questions to ask of the Long Islanders," Pearson joked about why he was drawn to study with Malinowski.[16] Bourne urged readers to look at what was unique and individual in American art and literature (rather than comparing it, unfavorably, to Shakespeare and Milton); at the same time, the anthropologists were demolishing the assumption that there even *was* a hierarchy of cultures.

American studies, then, took this idea and ran with it. American studies was not about justifying American culture; it was about identifying how all the elements of American life and thought were "bound together into a significant whole," to quote Edward Sapir's influential definition of culture. Yale embraced the anthropological approach when it began to build its program. Anthropologists "brought to the undertaking the concept of culture, a concept which includes much more than art and literature."[17] "In American Studies at Yale we attempt to use the anthropologist's approach and outlook," faculty member Ralph Gabriel explained.[18] And although there is no explicit nod to anthropology in such early American studies classics as Parrington's *Main Currents* or Miller's *The New England Mind*, both sought to elucidate the worldview of this people, without value judgment. Literature was perhaps the richest evidence for this, Pearson believed. "If one were going to study the life of a people they should know something about their literature," Pearson said when asked to explain the relationship of American studies and literary studies. "A literary man is a man who lives in his age and cannot escape it, and . . . he reflects his age as much as he guides it and brings it forward toward new goals by what he writes."[19]

Although it was one of the nation's first, Yale's American Studies program wasn't always "American Studies." When Pearson became one of its first faculty members, it was an offshoot of the History, Arts, and Letters (HAL) program in which Norm had earned his PhD. The purview of HAL wasn't just limited to America, but it had produced what is now generally considered the first American studies PhD dissertation, written by future Yale president A. Whitney Griswold in 1933. But by 1946 Yale was playing catch-up. In the late 1930s, Harvard, Pennsylvania, and Minnesota all offered graduate degrees in "American Studies" or "American Civilization," and by World War II there were almost thirty BA-level tracks in "American studies," "American history and literature," or "American civilization" at schools from California to Texas to Massachusetts.[20] In January 1946, Yale president Charles Seymour approved the HAL faculty's proposal for an "'American Studies Group' the purpose of which will be to train at the undergraduate and graduate level selected students whose primary purpose is to achieve a broad understanding of American civilization—its origins, evolution and present world relationships."[21] Flush with postwar confidence, that fall the university undertook a survey of the competing programs so that the leading one could be built in New Haven. None of these schools,

Dean DeVane asserted in a funding request to the Ford Foundation, had succeeded in "knitting together and synthesizing the elements of American studies into a comprehensive view of the nation as it has become through its history and as it is to-day." With $25,000 annually from Ford as seed funding to attract further donations, DeVane proposed, Yale would build just such a program.[22]

DeVane put the touch on Ford because it, along with the Rockefeller Foundation and the Carnegie Corporation, had started to nurture the development of American studies in the belief that it could help prepare the nation for its new leadership role. Younger Americans, foundation officers worried, didn't know enough about their country and, worse, in the words of historian Inderjeet Parmar, "lacked conviction in America's heritage, in what America stood for, and how that might hinder the rising superpower in aggressively facing down the challenges of European dissent, Third World nationalism, and Soviet power." American studies could be an answer. The Carnegie Corporation, in the late 1940s, put almost a million dollars into developing American studies in universities and creating the American Studies Association.[23] Rockefeller had been there even earlier: in 1935, a $100,000 Rockefeller grant underwrote the Yale Institute of International Studies (a training ground for future diplomats and strategists) that quickly became the leading international-relations program in the nation. In 1946 Yale added a summer school of American studies where foreign students could "study, in close contact with American life, the institutions and principles of American democracy . . . mak[ing] a major contribution to the mutual understanding among the peoples of the world so necessary for the securing of the peace."[24] Pearson, in his first weeks back on campus, became an enthusiastic participant in this program.[25] The Ford Foundation, the newest and richest of the three major foundations, would begin funding such area-studies and international-relations programs after the war and ultimately have the greatest impact of any of them.[26]

In a larger sense, the foundations were part of the cement for the state-private networks that characterized elite American culture in the postwar period, and that became Pearson's habitat. The Rockefeller money behind the Yale Institute of International Studies didn't just train students; it paid for conferences at which governmental officials and scholars met, exchanged ideas, and forged ties with each other. The Carnegie Corporation provided seed money for universities to start American Studies programs, which gave employment to these scholars. And Ford's assets — an order of magnitude greater than those of the other foundations — didn't just bolster the position of these university departments but also funded professional organizations like the ACLS, which in turn provided travel and research support for American and foreign scholars and students, many of whom would go to work for government agencies. American cultural diplomacy had long been characterized, far more than that of other nations, by extra-governmental partnerships, but the resources that these foundations poured into such partnerships after the 1930s, and especially in the 1950s and 1960s, turned them into diverse, enduring, and much wider-ranging networks than they otherwise could have been.

And while the field's scholars continued to approach American studies as disinterested scholarly inquiry, those building these networks — government, foundations, professional societies, universities — gently pushed for the field to be a weapon in the ideological Cold War and a tool for building the American Century. As the United States assumed the mantle of global leadership, elites in government, academia, and foundations concluded (in the words of a congressional report on the topic) "that it was in our national interest that other peoples in the world understand the United States — its history, literature, ideals, civilization."[27] And this wasn't in just self-interest. "The United States," OSS veteran and American studies scholar William Langer wrote in his report for the 1960 Presidential Commission on National Goals, "should exert its influence and power on behalf of a world order congenial to American ideals, interests, and security . . . [because] such a world order will best fulfill the hopes of mankind."[28] Such programs sprung up not just at home but abroad. The 1946 Fulbright Act sent scholars of American studies abroad to promote research on America and foster American Studies programs at foreign universities.[29] University, foundation, and government funds underwrote the creation, in 1947, of the Salzburg Global Seminar, which brought Matthiessen, Mead, and literary critic Alfred Kazin to Austria to teach war-ravaged European students about American civilization.[30] (In its second year, Salzburg asked Pearson to be on its faculty, but he declined because he was in Los Angeles on his Huntington Fellowship.)[31] The same thing was happening on the other side of the globe in another former enemy land: in 1950 Rockefeller and Stanford University created a Salzburg-style annual American Studies Seminar in Tokyo, and then, a year later, a similar program in Kyoto, programs that ultimately shaped American literary and cultural studies in Japan.[32] The State Department was intensely interested in these American Studies programs abroad, and in fact three separate governmental bureaus—Educational and Cultural Affairs and International Education at State, and the United States Information Agency (USIA)—all produced separate reports on American studies programs abroad just in 1962.[33]

A striking number of the people involved in American studies and other "area studies" fields after the war had served in the OSS or other intelligence services during the war: Pearson, of course, but also Perry Miller, R. W. B. Lewis, and even the anthropologist Gregory Bateson. These men then returned to their universities to shape not just American Studies departments but also programs in international studies, Russian studies, African studies, Asian studies, and the like. "The first great center of area studies in the United States," National Security Advisor McGeorge Bundy attested in 1964, "was not located in any university but . . . in the Office of Strategic Services. In very large measure the area study programs developed in American universities in the years after the war were manned, directed, or stimulated by graduates of the OSS."[34]

Ford, though, turned down DeVane's request, prompting a fundraising campaign for a stand-alone American Studies department.[35] This department, DeVane proposed, would be unique. It would not be, like Harvard's or Penn's, merely a center for disinterested scholarly inquiry, a conventional academic silo. Instead, it would use scholarly inquiry to bolster America's Cold War resolve. As he put it, "We ought to utilize all the resources that we can mobilize to teach our students the facts of Communism and the implications of Russian ideology and foreign policy. . . . The Communist threat must . . . be met vigorously and in a positive sense. The most direct means of confronting it is through a fundamental understanding of American principles."[36] Such a department at the United States' "most native university," DeVane continued, would "convince the wavering peoples of the world . . . of the merits of our way of thinking and living in America . . . that we have something better than Communism to offer them." It would be "a weapon in the 'cold war.'"[37] The program had *urgency*, clear relevance to the world beyond Yale, and links to the growing diplomatic, national-security, and foundation-funded Cold War infrastructure. By 1948, American studies had become the second-most-popular "intensive" (or honors) major in the college. It also was fueled by a sense of shared mission. Like Pearson himself, many of the students who enrolled in the program had served in the war and viscerally believed in American leadership.

In 1950, the British-born corporate executive and fervent anticommunist William Robertson Coe answered DeVane's call and endowed this program with half a million dollars. Coe wanted more than just his name on a chair, though. For Coe, communism didn't just come in the guise of the Red Army or foreign subversion. He wanted any program he funded to take a stand on *domestic* politics. Like many conservative businessmen, he reviled the New Deal as creeping collectivism and hoped Yale's program would help arrest this development. As a condition of his gift, Coe insisted the program's head be someone who "firmly believes in the preservation of our System of Free Enterprise and is opposed to the system of State Socialism, Communism and Totalitarianism," and he wanted veto power over Yale's choice.[38]

President Seymour and Dean DeVane had to walk a fine line. A university jealously guards its privileges, one of the most cherished of which is the appointment of faculty members. But a deeper issue here affected not just the administration of the program but its intellectual content. Coe, the Yale administrators, and the Yale American Studies faculty all agreed that the program should instill in students an understanding of "the fundamental principles of American freedom in the field of politics and of economics" and "the privileges which have molded our development as a nation." They all believed that doing so was essential to combat "the illiteracy of our citizens in regard to the most vital aspects of America's past," which had led to the present "menace of foreign philosophies."[39] Coe saw that "menace" in very particular present terms. For him, the program should explicitly instruct students that New Deal liberalism was a manifestation of these "foreign philosophies," and gird them to combat their infiltration into American society. It should be a kind of political boot camp.

But the faculty understood these issues in the more abstracted way of scholars. For Potter and Gabriel and Pearson, "freedom," perhaps the key ideological concept of the Cold War, didn't self-evidently mean laissez-faire economics, as Coe insisted. Rather, it was "a force as broad as society itself—a force whose economic, social and political aspects are inseparable." "Democracy," too, went beyond the simple Election Day ritual, and the Yale American Studies student "must be educated to think of democracy not in narrow or formalistic political terms, but as a germinal impulse with profound bearings upon every range of human activity."[40] As David Potter explained it, "There is a distinction . . . between having a primary purpose to teach American history, with the faith that from such teaching an appreciation of the principles of individualism and free enterprise will result, and a purpose to teach the principles of individualism and free enterprise, using American history as the medium of instruction. One actually involves teaching . . . the other involves indoctrination."[41]

Ultimately, Yale's administration and faculty resisted Coe's pressure to make the program a center for "indoctrination"—at least of Coe's economic principles. (This disappointed at least one well-known undergraduate: William F. Buckley Jr., class of 1950, carped in *God and Man at Yale* that the American Studies department refused to honor the spirit of Coe's gift.)[42] But even though they resisted some of his demands, Yale's administrators were happy to trumpet that the Yale American Studies program expressly served geopolitical, not just scholarly, purposes. In announcing the gift, Seymour described the department as a means by which "the Communist threat could be met vigorously and in a positive sense."[43] Yale American Studies thus made itself perhaps the first academic department at a major American university to put itself openly at the service of government political objectives. Many would follow, and much more lucratively so, but the Yale American Studies program sent an important early signal to the nation: elite academia was going to sign on to the US Cold War effort.

Because of its reach and prominence, the program also gave intellectual heft to the growing "vital center" understanding of American politics and society, as adumbrated most clearly in Arthur Schlesinger Jr.'s 1949 book of that name. Schlesinger proposed that America's political and social order was grounded on a "freedom" defined by liberal individualism, democratic governance, and moderately regulated capitalism; rejecting "extreme ideologies" such as Communism, fascism, monarchism, and theocracy, and embracing pragmatism and realism; and overseen by an interlocking set of governmental, philanthropic, corporate, religious, and educational institutions led by disinterested technocrats disproportionately drawn from the elite levels of society.[44] This liberal-individualist, "free" society, Schlesinger acknowledged, faced significant threats from those "extreme ideologies," and pragmatism and realism might demand that it would have to curtail some civil liberties at home and engage in military action abroad to protect itself. Schlesinger's book elucidated the loose postwar consensus that had arisen among the most powerful institutions in American society—government, academia, cultural institutions such as museums, mainstream religious organizations, foundations, business, labor, the military, and print and broadcast media.

The idea of a "center" arising from a pragmatic, flexible response to real-world conditions rather than unbending ideology was crucial to this consensus and seen as an inoculation against extremism and totalitarianism.[45] Elites from government, academia, foundations, and the business world had forged this consensus in boardrooms, faculty meetings, and policy retreats as the United States quickly retooled to lead the so-called Free World that had become one side of a bipolar standoff. Pearson had long been at this pragmatic political and cultural center, as in his 1937 comment to Horace Gregory that he and his entire generation rejected the ideological extremes of left and right because "our hope is based on facing complexity and resolving if possible a solution."[46] The political environment, in other words, was moving to where Pearson already was. He appreciated the important guiding and structuring role played by society's enduring institutions. Hierarchy and class distinctions did not trouble him, and he knew where he fit. As a pragmatist, he understood that one had to cross party lines at times: he supported Roosevelt in 1932 and 1936 (but not 1940). He preferred eastern establishment candidates who had been educated and trained in respectable institutions, and he mistrusted outsiders. He thus disliked the rube Truman, whose 1952 whistle-stop tour was "a revolting spectacle, especially since he so blithely sacrifices himself to an intelligent audience in proving himself either a fool then or a fool now." In 1964 he reported with horror to Bryher of the "hatred of the east coast by westerners" such as Barry Goldwater, who were wresting control of the Republican Party from East Coast establishmentarians such as himself. (His revulsion at the populism and barely veiled racism of the Goldwater candidacy, in fact, drove him to vote for Lyndon Johnson.)

Although they barely changed over the course of his life, his politics increasingly became informed by his academic thinking about the nature of the American character, which for Pearson was fundamentally and essentially Puritan. But in the early twentieth century, "Puritan" had taken on negative connotations of prudery, self-righteousness, closed-mindedness, fanaticism, hypocrisy. As a result the Pilgrims, as well as Puritan dissenters such as Anne Hutchinson and Roger Williams, became the popular heroes of the American seventeenth century, and Jonathan Edwards and Cotton Mather the villains.[47] The popular image of the Puritan became even worse in the liberalizing cultural atmosphere of the 1920s. You didn't have to be a flapper to hate Puritans, either; influential writers like H. L. Mencken saw residual Puritanism in the small-town philistinism he so loved to lambaste, and Harold Ross's famous 1925 mission statement for the *New Yorker*— "not edited for the old lady in Dubuque"—was a sideways swipe at the same heartland Puritanism.[48]

But Pearson's Puritanism wasn't the cartoonish prudery and censoriousness of stereotype. For him, the essence of Puritanism—and thus America itself—was the desire for purification and improvement through relentless self-criticism and self-examination. "The Puritan instinct," Pearson explained, "was one of honest and sober introspection. It penetrated the sham of man's exterior to his more animal nature beneath."[49] They reached for the divine and the transcendent in new and difficult ways, rejecting conventionality and conformity and constantly striving for renewal. They recognized the sanctity of labor and the dangers of idleness. They wanted to build an ideal community on earth, but one that would give each individual maximum freedom to determine his or her own path and responsibility for his or her own actions. This drive for self-examination and renewal were always in a dialectic with the conservative force of the institutions Pearson trusted to structure society. For Pearson, this desire for a productive tension between conservative institutions and purifying individuals wasn't just a political orientation, it was his literary taste: not only Ezra Pound and H.D. but also Hawthorne and Melville, Santayana and Sherwood Anderson, and even J. D. Salinger and Ken Kesey all exhibited this most American of dynamics, as Pearson explained in articles like "Anderson and the New Puritanism," where he characterized Anderson as "a reformer rather than a revolutionary, a revitalizer rather than a cynic. He could find again and again the joy of rediscovery and of crashing down the old barriers encrusting belief and power of feeling."[50] Pearson saw himself in exactly the same way.

And he would promulgate these ideas about America at home. In *The Vital Center*, Schlesinger had argued that liberal societies fostered a dynamism that energized and renewed, rather than overthrew, their structuring institutions, and the most dynamic of these institutions was business. The advertising industry had long promoted the idea that business was an essential player in a free society, and as the Cold War opened, the Advertising Council began to explain to Americans *why* business was so central to freedom and prosperity not just at home but abroad. For the 1947 "Our American Heritage" campaign, the council produced print, billboard, and broadcast advertisements and pamphlets that (in the words of historian Robert Griffith) "stressed freedom of enterprise and expanding productivity through mechanization and increased efficiency, recognized labor's right to organize and bargain collectively, acknowledged the need to protect the individual against those 'basic hazards of existence over which he may have no control,' and endorsed limited state intervention 'when necessary to ensure national security or to undertake socially desirable projects when private interests prove inadequate to conduct them.'"[51]

The committee behind the Our American Heritage initiative, moreover, perfectly embodied the ideal of a well-meaning technocracy led by representatives of enmeshed, collaborating institutions. It included Studebaker Motors president Paul G. Hoffman (who would go on to administer the Marshall Plan and later head the Ford Foundation), Boris Shiskin of the American Federation of Labor (who would also work with the Marshall Plan), and George Shuster, president of Hunter College (who had strong connections to the Catholic hierarchy in the United States, and had served in the American military government in Germany). Business, government, labor, the military, religion, education, and foundations, all in three men: this was the vital center in microcosm.

But not everyone joined in America's embrace of business. The United States' new position of unquestioned world leadership had intensified European skepticism about American culture. Many European intellectuals and leaders simply believed that the United States had none, apart from the most vulgar and venal consumer capitalism. And advertising, whose first principle was that fulfillment in life came from buying the right products, was especially implicated in the Europeans' charge. So, to brainstorm responses to European skepticism about American culture, in 1953 the council convened a series of high-minded roundtables under the title "Culture in the United States" and asked Pearson to address how America's art "compares with the arts of other countries." In his talk, Pearson hit on many of his familiar themes: the Puritan roots of American self-criticism, the interdependence of American institutions, the vibrancy provided by capitalism. In twentieth-century America, "both industrial and cultural institutions come into dynamic relationships with each other, and are inter-involved," he continued. And the introduction of the mass media into this matrix "provides the true excitement to the American scene."[52]

But in this talk, he also elaborated on a key argument of the vital-center consensus: that these powerful institutions, rather than dominating what Pearson called "the common man" as was the case in communist societies, actually served to allow ordinary Americans to more fully express their individualism, while preventing the nation from declining into a commercially driven mass culture. He stressed the responsiveness of American institutions, including business, to aesthetic demands; the crucial role these institutions play in making high culture "accessible to practically everybody"; and how these institutions elevated the public taste rather than, as Europeans argued, simply churning out lowest-common-denominator entertainment. America's capitalistic, "common-man"-driven society hadn't produced a vast cultural wasteland: instead, we had just experienced our most "distinguished half-century" of poetry, our painters set the tone for avant-garde art, the rest of the world looked to our architects and playwrights for inspiration. Our peculiar combination of democracy, powerful cultural institutions, and commerce had produced almost a new Renaissance.[53] The scholarly veneer Pearson applied to the advertisers' pitch convinced at least one important European. The British radio commentator and roundtable attendee Alistair Cooke, in his influential "Letter from America" that week, told his listeners that he had come away from Pearson's talk convinced at the "enormous stirring and ferment of the arts today" and that "this America is so unlike the grotesque Babylon so confidently pictured by the smarting propagandists of Europe."[54]

With the election of Dwight Eisenhower in 1952, the vital center came to the White House. In addition to his military experience, Ike had served as president of Columbia University for over four years and fully endorsed an economy and society dominated by large and powerful institutions, so long as they were led by "enlightened and disinterested" men such as himself.[55] Eisenhower was also much more attuned to the importance of information in a global conflict than Truman had been, and in 1953 his administration created the United States Information Agency to coordinate so-called public diplomacy abroad. The USIA immediately joined forces with the council in a high-minded initiative called "People's Capitalism," at first in the form of a traveling exhibition refuting Soviet accusations about the cruel and exploitive nature of capitalism. In American "people's" capitalism, the exhibit asserted, gains were equally shared by management and labor, and class lines in America were gradually disappearing.

This echoed Pearson's own beliefs, and he soon joined the team. By 1955, "People's Capitalism" had become an ongoing publicity campaign aimed at a domestic audience as well, trying to persuade Americans that they had "high cultural standards" and a "destiny to serve mankind."[56] Steering committee chair and advertising executive Chester La Roche was particularly intent on closing the gap between the worlds of business and education, because only with those two in league, he believed, could we "lick the Russians." And Pearson seemed to be the man who could close that gap—as his 1953 talks had expressed, in much more erudite terms than the ad men could employ, the central philosophy of People's Capitalism. Once on the steering committee, Pearson gave the People's Capitalism campaign academic credibility. He genuinely believed that capitalism was elevating the cultural level of America and of individual Americans: he and his own family, who two generations before had been struggling farmers in northern Vermont, proved this.

And he agreed, as well, with the Luce-ian argument that Americans need to spread the good news about themselves and be a model to the rest of the world, as he had said in his keynote address at the City of New Haven's gala Columbus Day 1951 celebration, which was attended by most of the local worthies as well as a delegation of eleven minor Hollywood stars on a publicity tour of Connecticut. "Given the position in the world which we possess today," Pearson orated, "we are called to be Columbuses ourselves" and open passages to the rest of the world's people. It was a heady experience for this junior professor to be the main speaker at an event like this. "I felt like the boy who made good," he told H.D., "when some people came for autographs."[57] The fact that he was asked, when Yale had no shortage of skilled toastmasters and lecturers, attests to the reputation he was building.

By the 1960s, that reputation was formidable. He was promoted to full professor in 1962, had built a distinguished record as a scholar and editor, and sat on numerous boards and committees and advisory councils. Sabbaticals also come to senior faculty, and Pearson spent his first, in the fall of 1963, in Japan, as a scholar in residence at the Kyoto Seminar in American Studies, the long-running Rockefeller-funded summer program. Although he told one of his Japanese correspondents that "my real reason for going to Japan is not on behalf of American Studies but so I can learn about Japan," Pearson was well aware of the geopolitical importance of his presence, and that this work was as much cultural diplomacy as it was academic outreach, especially when he ventured beyond Kyoto to speak in places like Sendai, Taipei, and Seoul. Many of these side engagements were arranged and funded not by the institutions themselves, but instead by the US State Department or the Fulbright program, who found that he was not only an effective ambassador for American studies but a talented cultural diplomat.[58] Official State Department reports praised Pearson's "amazing ability to enter empathetically" into discussion of any topic his Korean hosts brought up and his ability to shift rhetorical gears, "seemingly without effort," to speak to different kinds of audiences. His visit "will have a definite influence on the development of American Studies programs."[59] For the remainder of the 1960s and 1970s, Pearson became one of the most in-demand academic ambassadors in the Pacific region and made numerous trips to Japan, South Korea, Taiwan, and elsewhere in the region to promote American studies on behalf of multiple institutions: the Department of State, Yale University, the Fulbright program, the American Studies Association, and the American Council of Learned Societies. In a restive region in an increasingly volatile time, against the backdrop of Vietnam, growing tensions in Korea, and increasing anti-Americanism in Japan, Pearson spread the message of American cultural benevolence and sophistication to audiences of intellectuals and future opinion makers.

Interest in American studies was growing in Australia, as well, and

FIGURE 9 Pearson and Japanese students and teachers, Sendai, Japan, 1963 (Norman Holmes Pearson Papers, Yale Collection of American Literature, Beinecke Rare Book and Manuscript Library).

the State Department was keen to strengthen cultural ties between the two nations as the Vietnam War was intensifying. In 1968, the Australian-American Educational Foundation (which administered Fulbright grants in Australia) and the ACLS invited Pearson, recently elected president of the American Studies Association, to tour the universities in Canberra, Adelaide, Brisbane, Newcastle, Melbourne, Sydney, and New England that had received funding from the council.[60] Norman Harper of the University of Melbourne, the leading American studies scholar in Australia, piggybacked onto this trip to book Pearson as the keynoter for the meeting of the Australia–New Zealand American Studies Association (ANZASA) in late August. Officially, Pearson wore three hats on this trip Down Under, representing the Fulbright commission, the ACLS, and Yale itself. But he knew that the Department of State was also paying close attention: as he told the head of the Australian-American Educational Foundation, "I need to learn as much as I can about Australia to be of use to the ACLS and to Washington."

The year 1968 was much tenser than 1963. January brought the threat of a rekindled Korean War when, in the so-called Blue House

FIGURE 10 Pearson giving the opening keynote to the 1968 ANZASA conference in Sydney, US ambassador William Crook immediately behind him (Australian and New Zealand American Studies Association).

raid, a team of North Korean commandos in South Korean Army uniforms nearly infiltrated President Park Chung-hee's official residence to assassinate him. Two days later, North Korea captured an American spy ship, the USS *Pueblo*, further increasing tensions. Vietnam, as well, only got more urgent in early 1968. On January 30, a week after the *Pueblo* capture and nine days after the Blue House attempt, the Tet offensive began, prompting an increase in US and Allied troops and making it clear that the war was nowhere near its end. Tet also prompted widespread doubt in the United States that the war was winnable, or even worth fighting.

Australians across the political spectrum had long embraced the United States, but there as elsewhere in the world public opinion was beginning to turn against the war. Vietnam, thus, was going to be a particularly touchy subject for an American cultural/academic diplomat. But one wouldn't know from the ANZASA conference program that any such controversy was raging. After US ambassador William Crook officially convened the conference, Pearson provided his own thirty-year perspective in a talk called "The Nature and Possibilities of American Studies." In his address, he reiterated the central Cold War–era message that the United States valued intellectual diversity and freedom of conscience; that centralization and control from above were anathema to American culture; and that nations and peoples should determine their own destinies and express their own cultures. Praising the fact that each nation's scholars would pursue American studies differently, he suggested that "at some future biennial conference . . . a representative from the American Studies Association of Great Britain and a representative from the similar organization in Canada" might compare "methods of instruction as well as . . . scholarly conclusions." Not, he emphasized, because this would reveal "unanimity." Rather,

> Australians and New Zealanders would not and could not look at the United States through British or Canadian eyes. You have your own eyes and they are part of your strength, just as the others find their strength in their eyes.
>
> The question might well be asked whether unanimity of method and conclusion is an essential part of the nature of American Studies. I should myself, I think, answer no. I look on the strength of American Studies as lying both in its openmindedness and its openendedness. Only with this strength can one approach the American experience which in itself is still so openended, so flexible, so pragmatic.[61]

Openness, flexibility, pragmatism: there is scarcely any daylight here between "America" and "American studies," but Pearson's is an extremely light touch, with none of the dramatic "either freedom or totalitarianism" rhetoric that typified much of American public messaging of the period. As Neville Meaney, one of the organizers of this conference, remarked, Pearson "tended to quite gently promote the Cold War cause."[62] This isn't surprising, because Pearson truly believed in the virtues of American civilization, while seeing his own work and his field as a critical analysis—not a celebration—of that civilization. In this, according to another American studies scholar in Australian,

Elaine Barry, he was typical of the Fulbright Scholars sent to Australia, who never seemed "overtly political. They were simply examples of the best kind of American intellectual life. There certainly wasn't anything of the creepy subtext of Government intrusion."[63]

Pearson could also afford to be gentle because of the power he personified. Barely notable in the text of his address is how the audience would have perceived him as invested with the aura of the US institutions that were blessing and underwriting American studies on the other side of the world. He represented not just Yale University, but also its American Studies department—which he had helped build and whose resources he had tapped to bring a number of the conference's attendees to New Haven—and the authority of the ASA itself. He represented the Fulbright program and its model of collaboration between governments and universities. He was an emissary from the ACLS, which was funding not only this conference but many of the universities represented there, and whose grants had gone to many Australian academics. And as a sometime contractor for the US Department of State, he was another reminder—along with the presence of Ambassador Crook—that the government of the most powerful country on earth was avidly interested in this small corner of scholarship and learning.

If Australian public opinion about Vietnam was starting to change in mid-1968, it had decisively turned by 1970, when Pearson made his second and final visit to the country. "Vietnam was on everyone's mind at the time," William Breen of La Trobe, the organizer of ANZASA's 1970 conference, remembered. "The left was outraged already, and even the right wing within academia . . . had turned against the war."[64] On May 8, 1970, the Vietnam Moratorium brought two hundred thousand people into the streets—the largest protests in Australian history to that point—with another massive demonstration held in September.[65] That year was also pivotal in terms of Australia's sense of itself in the world. Queen Elizabeth II arrived for a monthlong royal tour at the end of March, underscoring Australia's ties to the Commonwealth even as the country was increasingly expressing its cultural and political independence. But Pearson carried on much as he had two years before. He attempted to strengthen the links between foreign universities and American institutions, even as students and even their professors were, like their American counterparts, repudiating the American government. It was an "intensely social" several weeks, he reported to Bryher, with dinner parties, shopping for art, tours of the cities, a visit to Ayres Rock (Uluru), and one memorable plane ride from Sydney seated next to a seven-foot-tall wax figure of Captain Cook, bound for the new Captain Cook Motel in Canberra. Later, he traveled to Korea and Taiwan to assess and meet the faculty of several American Studies programs in those Cold War flashpoints. But it wasn't all cultural diplomacy: just before returning to the United States, he flew to New Zealand / Aotearoa to meet and interview H.D.'s girlhood companion Margaret Pratt. (Pearson promised to buy Pratt a television with funds from H.D.'s royalties, as a posthumous present from her old friend.)[66]

Pearson's primary responsibility abroad in 1970, though, was as dean of the Kyoto Seminar in American Studies. In that role he delivered a series of ten lectures on twentieth-century American poetry: two talks on Pound, one each on Eliot, H.D., Williams, Stevens, Hart Crane, E. E. Cummings, and Frost, and a final lecture on "the 1960s."[67] Together, these laid out the emerging canon of American modernism that he had been so instrumental in establishing, identifying how a movement that was assumed to be entirely European in character actually drew just as much from the American literary and philosophical tradition. They also, importantly, linked the themes and techniques of American modernist art and poetry to the terms of the Cold War consensus. While he wasn't claiming that H.D. or Frost or Crane or the others were anti-communists (even though many were), here and elsewhere he read into their work some of the key ideas of the vital center: the insistence on the primacy of the individual, freedom of conscience, and the right to choose and build one's community, all of which made possible artistic fertility and the conditions to choose and build one's own community.

Pearson's contribution here was actually a late entry into a much broader argument about literary and artistic modernism. As early as 1947, the State Department assembled a group of modern American paintings that included many modernist and abstract canvases and proposed to tour it around Europe, as a representation of American artistic achievement. Then, over the course of the 1950s American critics and curators and publishers and even cultural diplomats started to argue that modernist art was not, as it was widely perceived to be, nihilistic and anarchistic and antibourgeois and obscurantist. Instead, they claimed that modernism's wild experimentation was the product of the freedoms afforded to artists in the West, as opposed to the programmatic, tendentious, and simplistic "socialist realist" art and literature demanded by Communist authorities. Rather than an attack on middle-class society, modernism was actually proof of the triumph of middle-class society. As he rarely wrote on modernist art and literature, Pearson was not an important figure among those making this "Cold War modernism" argument in the 1950s, but his Puritan interpretation of American modernist poetry rhymed in many ways, and of course his personal advocacy for modernism was further proof that the movement could be compatible with American values.[68]

But the real battle here wasn't over whether modernism could be compatible with US institutions: that had largely been decided. Instead, it was about those institutions themselves, and whether the new generation of Americans saw a place for themselves within them. Even such a creature of the establishment as Pearson could see that something was changing in youth culture in the United States. In Kyoto, his concluding talk, entitled "Three 'Bibles' for the Young," covered the triad of novels he felt gave the best insight into the mindset of postwar youth: J. D. Salinger's *Catcher in the Rye*, Joseph Heller's *Catch-22*, and Kesey's *One Flew over the Cuckoo's Nest*. "I feel somewhat hippie about it," Pearson remarked about this talk, "but there seems to be little point in reproducing the orthodox survey of recent American literature."[69] Significantly, he identifies these three sacred texts of the counterculture as further iterations of the Puritan strain in American literature going back through Sherwood Anderson, the modernists, and Hawthorne, all "linked to a tradition of self-examination and self-criticism in American literature."[70] But they were also of their moment, as these blackly humorous novels taught their young readers that institutions, the very foundation of postwar American society, were corrupt, fallible, and ultimately absurd. Pearson explained that Salinger's Holden Caulfield felt that "all institutions are man-made, hence suspect, phonies like men themselves," and in *Catch-22* "the absurd, the black humors play through a gallery of individuals and then through a series of institutions, of which the army itself of course is an extrapolation of the ordinary condition of life." And then in Kesey, the institution is literally an *institution*—a mental hospital for the criminally insane—and what was derided or absurd in the other two novels is now sinister and oppressive.[71] This Organization Man saw that the children of the 1960s were rejecting the institutions that had formed and nourished him.

Instead those students were, he saw, envisioning a different and more inclusive American democracy. In Kyoto, he also noted that his Yale students were "intensely interested" in Black and Native American literature, and he speculated that "ethnic writing has taken the place of regional writing in our literature." (In fact, he requested that a potential faculty member for the following year's Kyoto Seminar develop sessions on "Negro and Jewish writers.")[72] Although the development of a curriculum doesn't seem political on its face, the way that Pearson envisioned Kyoto's literature offerings were of a part with his larger outlook on American culture in the Cold War: its institutions of criticism, literature, and higher education showed their dynamism in how willing they were to change in response to the times, to fully embrace the modern, and to welcome the voices of marginalized communities. This adaptability, openness, and rejection of rigidity, he believed and his lectures argued, were America's key attributes, and even, counterintuitively enough, a legacy of the Puritans.

Although he was an emissary between institutions and a representative of American culture on these journeys abroad, his instinctive personal networking resulted in dozens of new professional relationships and even friendships. After his 1963 trip to Japan, he became close to Fumio Ano and Shinji Takuwa, both of whom would become prominent American studies scholars in Japan. But these friendships also advanced the cause. Pearson contributed an introduction to Takuwa's 1963 *History of American Literature*, a Japanese-language anthology that

helped form Japanese understanding of American literature and culture with not just cultural but political ramifications. Pearson's institutional connections made this happen at several levels: Takuwa had
studied with Pearson at Yale; Pearson's status and contribution ensured
that a Japanese publishing company would publish the book; in part
because of Pearson's prominence, the book was made available at USIA
cultural centers and libraries, and the book spurred many other Japanese students to study American literature and, eventually, to apply for
Fulbright and ACLS Fellowships to come to America (which Pearson
helped them obtain). Pearson wrote dozens of fellowship and travel-
grant recommendation letters for young scholars from Japan, from Taiwan, from South Korea, even from South Vietnam, and then when they
would come to the United States, he would host them at his house,
connect them with the most prominent American studies scholars,
and provide them with entry into his professional networks. But he
wasn't trying to mold clones. Hiroko Sato remembers him pushing
her to bring a specifically Japanese perspective to her work on Willa
Cather, and praising her after she presented "a paper written from the
point of view of a Japanese and with the immense advantage of being
Japanese. This no native American could accomplish." For so many of
these young scholars, who would themselves become influential teachers or writers in the near future, Pearson's welcoming face became a
metonym for America itself. "We in the Orient revere him," Korean
scholar Sungkyu Cho wrote after his death, "because he was a good
American and a good human being. He was a good American in the
sense that he was deeply rooted in America."[73]

He operated the same way in Australia. In Melbourne in 1970, for
example, he met Brenda Niall, a young and as-yet unpublished lec-
turer at the new Monash University. Niall hosted Pearson and Susan
at her family's beach house at Mount Martha, where he surprised his
hostess by eagerly going for a swim despite his "crippled" and "frail"
appearance.[74] A few years later, funded by a short-term ACLS grant,
Niall came to the United States to revise for publication her thesis on
Edith Wharton. Pearson invited her to Yale for a six-week stay and used
his friendship with R. W. B. Lewis to secure Niall special access to the

Wharton archive that Lewis had embargoed just for his own use. With his connections in the New York literary world, Pearson also reached out to publishers on Niall's behalf. It was "remarkable and worth noting," Niall recalled forty-five years later, that he would go out of his way to help someone who really could not have been any use to him. "He could open doors and liked doing it," she concluded.[75]

Niall's personal experiences of Pearson mesh with what struck so many others who worked with or even briefly encountered him. More than anything, he relished being in the middle of things, being *connected* (in both senses of the word). For him, networking wasn't a chore or a duty; it invigorated him. The Australian scholar and poet Chris Wallace-Crabbe noted that Pearson loved "oiling the hinges" for people and wanted to be a "fixer," a "combination of a networker and an aesthetic intellectual." Barry fondly remembered his "personal engagement with students from many countries and the generous friendship he extended to so many of them, including me." "His gift was that of questioning and making you feel brilliant. . . . He was a listener rather than a talker," Niall recalled, "and his attentive manner was part of his charm." But for all his warmth, Pearson liked to keep the focus on the person he was talking *to* and was cagey and cautious about himself. He didn't "flick at balls outside the off stump," Wallace-Crabbe observed with a cricket metaphor.[76]

Putting people at ease, learning about people, connecting those people with institutions, and fading into the background: these are the skills of a spy. Many, in fact, have speculated that after a period of dormancy between the early 1950s and his first visit to Japan in 1963, Pearson returned to doing piecework for the CIA on these foreign trips. (This included many of those who knew him well such as Richard Ellmann, William Goetzmann, and Avril Winks, wife of Pearson's colleague and friend Robin.)[77] One dark rumor, believed by many close to Pearson, even holds that his 1975 death, soon after a trip to Seoul for yet another American studies gathering, was a North Korean assassination in reprisal for Pearson's spying. No available hard evidence, however, supports this speculation. Although in his correspondence, Pearson muses on the intelligence trade and often criticizes what he saw as the CIA's missteps, the one memo to Jackson quoted at the start of this chapter is the only document in his huge archive that suggests he was working with CIA at any point. And those who have studied his life most closely—Winks, Tim Naftali, Donna Hollenberg, Michael Holzman, and now me—are the least likely to claim that Pearson maintained actual CIA ties.[78] A spy as experienced and meticulous as Pearson would certainly have covered his tracks, and it is possible that Pearson, ever attentive to the power of archives, so thoroughly cleansed his papers (before the CIA itself did after his death) that he erased all trace of thirty years of freelancing for the agency. But he was just as effective in a professor and diplomat's gray suit as in a spy's trench coat—probably more so. Like Rome's, like Britannia's, the pax Americana was built on its functionaries.

+ 12 +

ODD MAN IN

While Pearson's work outside the university and abroad was consequential for the alliance between higher education and US foreign
policy, and pivotal in the evolution of American studies, his real job
was always at Yale. There, he forged a curious career, for even as his
profile rose outside of the English department, he grew increasingly
peripheral within it. But being the headliner had never been Pearson's
primary aim. He had long known the value of knowing the channels
through which power and resources and prestige are allocated, and
being one of the men (always *men* at the time) who did the allocating.
He didn't crave fame, but he did want to be known as the person to
go to if you needed something done. For almost thirty years he was
that person, not just at Yale but in the literary world. Through this, he
helped manage what scholar James English has called the "economy
of prestige": the distribution of status and awards and recognition and
institutional support to students, scholars, and writers who would in
turn shape elite American culture.

But as the 1970s approached, this consummate Organization Man
watched as faith in the Cold War order, particularly among his students, began to crumble. Even at elite and elitist Yale, the vital-center
consensus came to seem to many like a pact to shut vast segments of
American society out of full participation in society, and to generate
complacent citizens who would produce for the military-industrial
complex and consume for the benefit of capitalism. Gradually, Yale
opened up its curriculum, administrative structure, and even student

body in response to demands for greater inclusion and relevance. While he was ever cagey about his personal opinions of these changes, Pearson outwardly accommodated and even welcomed them. Puritans know when they have to change with the times. This final thematic chapter of Pearson's biography will chronicle how Pearson grew in influence and importance in the contemporary American literary world even as he failed to fulfill the brilliant scholarly promise he had shown in the 1930s, and how these developments took place against the backdrop of the dramatic social changes of "the Sixties," both on the Yale campus and in American society more broadly.

The Yale to which Pearson returned in 1946 was much like the Yale where he had matriculated in 1928. Above all, it remained extremely clubby. This hadn't changed a bit since his undergraduate years, and in some ways it became even stronger, as it reflected the 1950s American imperative to *belong*, to *be part of the group*. The archetypal "Yale Man," in other words, wasn't dead, even after the curricular and admissions reforms that President Griswold instituted after the war. Asking "does this image still obtain in the light of modern admissions and scholarship policy?" the *Yale Daily News* explained in 1960 that

> the Yale Man of the image is an enthusiastic follower of the success ethic . . . quietly and graciously smooth, not a back-slapper. . . . Extracurricular activities are an integral part of his life—he is concerned with not just one or two aspects of his Yale career, but broadens himself by working on a campus publication or political organization. Because he ambitiously hopes for success in business or a profession, he tries to blend the intellectual and practical parts of his education, usually stressing the latter. . . . The Yale Man overlaps many worlds in his activities and interests—the intellectual, the extracurricular, the social.[1]

In the 1950s, the Yale Man started to look very much like another emerging archetype: the Organization Man. In his groundbreaking 1956 sociological study of that name, William Whyte posited that postwar Americans had come to believe that organizations and groups, not individuals, were best equipped to make decisions and lead society. This was leading, Whyte worried, to conformity, groupthink, and the loss of individual creativity. While Whyte's book focused most on sub-elite organizations like large corporations or government, on the elite level the vital-center consensus was pushing society in precisely the same direction. If the road to fulfillment for ordinary Americans was to join the organization, the path to success for more ambitious Yale men was to find their place in elite institutions.

But as a neo-Puritan, Pearson felt that the stability and meaning provided by institutions had to be balanced with the dynamism and fertility of the creative individual mind, and he was wary of the conformity that an organization-dominated society engendered. Asked by *Time* magazine in 1957 to describe the current generation of college students, Pearson responded that the "mass media and technology" have "broadened the danger" of conformity, but the state of the American arts in the 1950s—which he characterized as "creative output of a high order"—indicated that conformity had not triumphed. He did, however, discern a quiescence and self-satisfaction in the students of the time:

> They constitute a "comfortable" generation even when they hardly realize it [is] because they have no other circumstance with which they can make comparison. They are cushioned by the immediate inflationary prosperity, cushioned by the increased scholarly aid which they now look upon as their due, and deferred to in what is now a traditional American reverence for youth. . . . If they haven't anything much to say besides an affirmation of conservatism it is because they want to keep what they have. . . . They like to talk about almost anything, but to commit themselves to very little except the status quo.[2]

In his sly, institutionalist way, Pearson had long tried to nurture non-conformity and individualism in an environment that encouraged group identity. Sometimes this was through literature, such as backing Angleton's *Furioso*, orchestrating the staging of Pound's *Women of Trachis*, or testifying for the defense in the 1962 obscenity trial of a Hartford bookseller prosecuted for selling Henry Miller's *Tropic of Cancer*.[3] In addition to serving as the first faculty adviser for the Scholars of the House program, in 1951 he became the faculty adviser to the Pundits senior society. (Cole Porter, Stephen Vincent Benét, McGeorge Bundy, *Hiroshima* journalist John Hersey, *New Yorker* writer Calvin Trillin, *Harper's* editor Lewis Lapham, Supreme Court justice Lewis Powell, and Yale presidents Griswold and Kingman Brewster had all been Pundits, but Pearson hadn't.) The Pundits billed themselves as "Yale's ten funniest men" and engaged in elaborate pranks, including an annual lobster-and-champagne initiation dinner on the first day of final exams that traditionally culminated in a brief, often nude, run through Sterling Library's nave. The 1958 Pundits took this too far when, naked and fueled with Dom Perignon, they attempted to move the glass case containing Yale's Gutenberg Bible. Pearson archly but sincerely apologized to the librarians for his charges' "exaggeration of what is usually only a moment of gay indecorum."[4]

As Pearson had observed to *Time's* reporter, Yale's pressure for conformity and group belonging, along with the generally privileged personal circumstances most Yalies enjoyed, created a politically conservative environment. In that sense it is unsurprising that 1950s Yale reflected the establishmentarian political consensus of the time—probably more so, and more importantly so, as the school trained the very elites who were forging the terms of that consensus.[5] A 1960 poll of Yale upperclassmen found a split of 41 percent Republican and 17 percent Democratic, with a surprising 42 percent calling themselves independents. Horowitz describes the late 1950s political atmosphere as largely quiescent, with a conservative lean. For one Yale undergraduate of that era, Jesse Lemisch, it was a "dreadful time . . . when the institution endorsed bigotry of every kind: anti-Semitism, anti-Catholicism, racism, nativism, homophobia, sexism, class contempt."[6]

In such an environment, Pearson was a liberal. This certainly didn't prompt him to make any public stands against McCarthyism when the Yale Political Forum withdrew its invitation to leftist screenwriter Howard Fast for a speaking engagement, or when the law school denied

FIGURE 11 Norm with the Yale Pundits in the 1950s (Norman Holmes Pearson Papers, Yale Collection of American Literature, Beinecke Rare Book and Manuscript Library).

promotion to Vern Countryman because of his progressive advocacy. Pearson was a strident anti-communist and likely found himself nodding along with President Seymour's 1949 pronouncement that "there will be no witch-hunts at Yale because there will be no witches. We do not intend to hire communists."[7] But when the occasion called, he could lose his reticence. In January 1949, William F. Buckley Jr. editorialized in the *Yale Daily News* that Lafayette College in Pennsylvania was foolish to refuse a $140,000 bequest providing scholarships for "American-born students, Catholics and Jews excepted." "If someone leaves a bequest to go strictly to Negro scholarships," Buckley archly pronounced, "he becomes a great democrat; if the bequest excludes Negroes, the thirty pieces of silver are righteously (with front-page fanfare in leading NY papers) turned down." Yale should certainly, Buckley insisted, go after that "restricted" money if Lafayette didn't want it. "The reasoning behind the editorial argument is as twisted as the morality of its writer," Pearson shot back in a letter to the editor, "disavow[ing]" the piece as a Yale graduate and faculty member. In print, Buckley dismissed Pearson as expressing "unenlightened opposition" more suitable for a "George Babbitt" than a member of the Yale faculty.[8]

When Pearson joined the Yale English department in the 1940s, it was widely considered one of the best in the world. At the time, its renown was due to philological and historical scholars like Pearson's teachers Williams, Phelps, Frederick Pottle, Chauncey Brewster Tinker, and Frederick Hilles. But a textbook published in 1938 would dramatically change not just Yale's English department, but literary study across the nation. Cleanth Brooks and Robert Penn Warren's *Understanding Poetry* expressed as a practical teaching method the emergent approach to literature called the "New Criticism." Brooks, Warren, and their colleagues John Crowe Ransom and Allen Tate had developed the New Criticism in the 1920s and 1930s through their subtle and incisive close readings of poems, while theorists set out New Criticism's philosophy in works like Ransom's "Criticism, Inc." (1937), René Wellek and Austin Warren's *Theory of Literature* (1948), and W. K. Wimsatt's landmark essays "The Intentional Fallacy" (1946) and "The Affective Fallacy" (1949). To perhaps oversimplify the idea, the New Criticism insisted that meaning in literature lay only in the *text*: not in the intention or biography of the author, not in the response of the reader, not in the historical or cultural events surrounding its creation. The job of a critic, according to the New Criticism, is to tease out all the elements of that text (metaphors, ironies, ambiguities, symbols, themes, images, even the sounds of words and the rhythms of sentences) and elucidate—the more elaborately and with the more virtuosity, the better—how they all worked together to create an ingenious little organism of meaning and feeling.

The New Criticism insisted that its aims and method were apolitical, but its roots were in reaction. Before becoming New Critics, Brooks, Warren, Tate, John Gould Fletcher, and others (including, at times, even Randall Stewart) made up a group of southern intellectuals calling itself the "Fugitives." They were fugitives, they said in their 1930 manifesto *I'll Take My Stand*, from contemporary industrial America; they sought to revive the ostensibly more refined, more humane agrarian culture of the antebellum South, which had its roots in the aristocratic English Renaissance society that T. S. Eliot (one of the New Critics' great heroes) venerated. When practicing literary analysis, the New Critics left out the politics, but New Criticism is a deeply conservative project, insisting that literature has no role to reflect or motivate social or economic change.

What started in political conservatism then became entangled, like modernist literature, in Cold War ideology. The New Criticism saw itself as objective, empirical, and reasonable, just as Cold War liberalism imagined itself to be. In New Criticism's self-imagining, the critic is (in the words of William H. Epstein) "the encircled, non-ideological defender of the vital center's middle style."[9] Its claims to being grounded on rigor and objectivity, rather than "taste" or "sensibility," also gave it, and literary study in general, institutional legitimacy at a time when the natural and applied sciences were taking primacy in elite higher education. Finally, New Criticism's intricate interpretations also had an analogy in spy craft, counterintelligence in particular. Like the New Critic, the intelligence analyst must look at a "text"—a stolen document, a side remark, a furtive observation—and tease out every possible nuance of significance. (James Angleton was obsessed not just with poetry but with New Critical interpretation.)[10]

Pearson did not believe that a poem was an intricate artifact to be described or a subtle puzzle to be solved, although he granted that New Critical close-reading techniques and analytical exactitude influenced him. But like many others, he saw the logical holes in their principles: how could they claim to be excluding history, for instance, when they used the *Oxford English Dictionary*'s documentation of the historical evolution of a word's definition as a cornerstone of their interpretations?[11] In their methodological dogmatism, he was convinced, they were missing something essential about what makes literature live and give life. "They have . . . limited taste and sensibility," he told Bryher.[12] What he saw in the poets he particularly admired—Pound and Stevens and Williams and above all H.D.—was how they expressed the spirit of a particular time and place. "No writer, no matter what his genre of expression, can altogether escape his age," he once wrote,[13] and giving readers the experience of another age is one of the great powers of literature. But the best poetry also channeled a sort of timeless mystic energy. A true work of art is always changing, becoming something new and different to new generations of readers even as it carries the traces of the time of its creation. Poems were not ingenious and static machines to be appreciated, "well-wrought urns" (to use one of Brooks's favorite metaphors) to be apprehended. They were a source of vitality, of life itself, and an almost Jungian connection to the consciousness of the human race.

But the New Criticism became uniquely influential in those years. It gave young scholars the chance to show off their close-reading chops, and was easily implemented in high school curricula as well. It spread quickly among scholars and critics tired of the 1930s arguments between Marxists and so-called New Humanists who thought literature should serve the Aristotelian purpose of improving one's soul. Let's just judge literature *as literature*, New Critics said, and stop assuming that it has to serve some outside purpose. And New Criticism's conservative agrarian identity faded when many of its most prominent writers left their southern homes for perches in the North. Ransom came to Kenyon College in Ohio; Tate to Princeton, New York City, and Minneapolis. But mostly they gravitated to New Haven. Wellek was the first, founding Yale's Comparative Literature department in 1946, and was soon followed by Brooks in 1946 and Robert Penn Warren in 1961, both of whom joined the English department. And they came to a school that had already embraced the New Criticism. Wimsatt had joined the department in 1939, and in 1940, Maynard Mack made *Understanding Poetry* the center of Yale's revamped freshman English curriculum.[14] "The most popular and powerful teachers of literature at Yale by 1950," recalled literary critic Alvin Kernan, "were leading New Critics all."[15]

As New Critics flocked in, the old guard got gently pushed aside, their own historical and cultural approach dismissed as "reconstructionism." Pearson, still untenured, was sidelined even more than he had been before. He had long felt overshadowed by Mack, a fellow member of the class of 1932 who completed his PhD and joined the Yale faculty in only four years—"the real climber among my acquain-

tances, a real man on the make," Pearson described him in his journal.[16] But it wasn't just Mack who sprinted past Pearson. Other faculty
members of his generation such as Louis Martz, Charles Feidelson,
and R. W. B. Lewis became prominent scholars and earned tenure and
promotion while Pearson seemed stuck in place. "With the growth of
an exceptionally brilliant faculty, many of them associated with New
Critical methods," former Duke University president and Yale graduate student Richard Brodhead remembered, Pearson was "cast into
deep shade" and had become "effectively a non-person in the department by the 1960s."[17] (Although Brodhead wrote his dissertation on
Hawthorne, it never even crossed his mind to work with Pearson.)
His Harvard American Studies friend Daniel Aaron was disgusted at
how Pearson's Yale colleagues "shamelessly patronized" him.[18] A 1967
formal portrait of the department poignantly figures his marginalization, with Pearson relegated to the very edge, while in the center the
imposing, six-foot-eight Wimsatt looms over the only woman on the
faculty, Marie Borroff.

But Norm tried not to let his bruised ego color his personal rela-

FIGURE 12   Yale English department, 1967, Norm in the back row, extreme right (Yale University Department of English).

tionships with his colleagues and eschewed the "backbiting and gossiping" endemic to academic departments.[19] He was particularly close with Eugene Waith as well as Lewis, Martz, the Shakespearean Charles Prouty, and even Brooks and Warren. And because he had been in Yale's English department so long, he was also a link between these younger men and department elders like Tinker and Stanley Williams. Inevitably, though, he became one of those elders, seen by new and younger colleagues as the odd but amiable man with a mysterious past who never seemed to have lived up to his potential. To Harold Bloom, the wunderkind who joined the department in 1955 at the age of twenty-five, Pearson was a "good friend . . . courtly and charming," and widely admired for how he had "triumphed over his physical disabilities and behaved as though they had never existed." Alan Trachtenberg, his American studies colleague from 1969 on, remembers him as being comfortable with his peripheral position in the department. "Once the Yale English department developed its own intellectual character because of Martz, Mack, Warren, and others, he was not part of that," Trachtenberg commented. "People didn't identify Norman in any other way than as a nice old guy who was very generous, loved to take people to lunch, and had his own table at Mory's." He was as "an odd man out who was deeply in," Trachtenberg concluded.[20]

But even as his relevance to the English department, and to the field of literary studies in general, shrank over the 1950s, Pearson became more and more central to American studies. He was involved in many of the innumerable self-studies that the field conducted in its early years and served on the editorial board of two of the field's major journals, *American Quarterly* and *American Literature*. An editorial-board member can affect the direction of his or her field, as the articles appearing in those journals indicate where the real energy in a field is. It's a largely invisible but potentially consequential role, and thus perfect for Pearson. He also used his profile in the field to promote its growth. When the University of Alabama opened its American Studies program in 1962, for instance, Pearson gave the formal inaugurating lecture, which was then printed up as a commemorative keepsake.[21] A few years later, Pearson's protégé William Goetzmann brought him in to headline a University of Texas American Studies conference, where he gave a similar lecture. These talks were often less about specific topics in the field than about the field itself: they were, in a sense, metalectures, and at times his were uncharacteristically impenetrable, such as when, in a bolus of jargon, he explained the purpose of American studies as "to determine a socio-anthropological framework of cultural and societal structures against which both a general field of abstract ideas and a particular field determined by the individual physiologically and psychologically considered can be said to operate in mutual tension." Most of the time, thankfully, he toned things down, but the subject was often "what can American Studies do?" rather than "what makes Americans the way we are?"[22]

In this, he was just reading the room, for despite his prominence, by the 1950s his type of scholarship was passé. As Gene Wise has shown in an influential history of the field, Pearson's founding cohort practiced what might be called "intellectual history": they posited that there is something unique about the American mind that was fundamentally shaped by the experience of the "New World" and identified a number of characteristics of this unique American mind (including Puritanism, progress, pragmatism, optimism, and liberalism) in the works of the major US writers. In practice, then, American studies consisted of reading and studying Roger Williams, Jonathan Edwards, Thoreau, Emerson, Fenimore Cooper, Mark Twain, Walt Whitman, and the like. The little scholarly work Pearson had produced up to this point fell securely into this box.[23]

Soon after World War II this intellectual-history approach refined itself, and a new group of scholars posited that a number of "myths" and "symbols" actually drove Americans' thinking. One could find these myths and symbols not just in the work of the major writers but everywhere: in popular fiction and poetry, in newspapers, in architecture and entertainment and every form of cultural production. (Curiously, although he was fascinated by the workings of myth and symbol in the work of poets, Pearson rarely applied this approach to his own field.) Henry Nash Smith's *Virgin Land*, from 1950, is generally credited as the first such work, followed by John William Ward's *Andrew Jackson:*

Symbol for an Age (1953), Lewis's *The American Adam* (1955), and many others, perhaps concluding with Trachtenberg's *Brooklyn Bridge* (1965). Directly and indirectly, this "myth and symbol" school was the product of the Cold War cultural consensus and the foundation and government support it provided to American studies.[24] And although none of these men saw themselves as propagandists, and these books still hold up as intellectual and scholarly achievements, they were certainly underwritten by the Cold War environment of (as Wise calls it) "patriotism and consensus."[25] So although American studies was intellectually moving away from Pearson's scholarly work, its role in the Cold War infrastructure aligned with Pearson's own feelings about his field. His work as cultural ambassador, journal editor, conference organizer, and committee stalwart reinforced the alliance of government and academia built on the work of these scholars. And what they didn't say, he often would. His lectures about "what American Studies can do" always carried a tacit predicate of *"for America?"* — if not in the text itself, then in the concatenation of status and influence and principled Cold Warrior anti-communism that he personally represented. He didn't need to say it: his bearing made it clear.

He carried in that bearing not just his academic and perigovernmental authority, but also his new standing in the literary world. During the 1950s and 1960s, he kept a close eye on contemporary poetry, even the most countercultural and avant-garde. In 1963, he struck up an odd friendship with the literary provocateur Ed Sanders. Sanders had begun publishing a mimeographed underground magazine called *Fuck You: A Magazine of the Arts* in 1962, and after Lawrence Ferlinghetti had told him about it Pearson wanted a full run of the magazine for Yale's collection. "Many thanks for the vigorous Bugger," he wrote Sanders upon receiving the copies. "My church deaconess secretary may have found them a little hard going," but the magazines were "like shots of life." He sent letters of support when Sanders was arrested at his Peace Eye bookstore in 1965 for selling obscene materials such as the magazine. And as he did with Martinelli, Duncan, and other struggling young artists, Pearson also gave small checks, $25 here and there. In fact, in his responses to a 1964 questionnaire about *Fuck You*, Sanders said that the magazine was funded in part by "a leading Ezra Pound scholar at Yale."[26]

He liked slumming, at times, but Pearson was always a creature of the establishment. In 1958, he became a judge for Wesleyan University Press's new Poetry Series, which published book-length manuscripts by younger poets not yet ready to be honored by the American Academy of Poets or the Bollingen committee. Pearson was a Wesleyan series editor for well over a decade, championing the early work of future eminences such as John Ashbery, Galway Kinnell, Denise Levertov, and Robert Bly. Carefully reading dozens of manuscripts a year was taxing, he told Bryher, but "they pay reasonably well . . . [and] I get a feeling of what is being written currently."[27] From this position he also observed the steady migration of young poets into the academy, which now needed to fill jobs in new creative-writing programs. Pearson had helped catalyze the academy's embrace of contemporary writing and, in so doing, influenced at least one poet—John Hollander, a Yale professor and fellow Wesleyan board member, whose 1976 *Reflections on Espionage* featured a Pearson-like spymaster character named, inevitably, "Puritan."[28]

While Wesleyan's series was for emerging writers, Pearson was also active at the pinnacle of the literary scene. In 1953 he was asked to be one of the judges for the new National Book Awards, which had begun in 1950 as the publishing industry's version of Hollywood's Academy Awards. He and fellow judges Richard Wilbur, Delmore Schwartz, John Crowe Ransom, and Katherine Garrison Chapin voted to give the 1954 poetry prize to Conrad Aiken's *Collected Poems*, a career retrospective of the early twentieth-century author. Generally, only writers occupied these positions (all four of Pearson's fellow judges were poets), so Pearson's presence on the committee attests to the prominent place he had already taken in the American poetry world. And while Wallace Stevens, whose own collected edition would win the prize the following year, had gained the acceptance of the poetry establishment by this time, it's hard to imagine that Pearson didn't have some effect on that decision, if only through informal politicking. He continued to exercise his influence over those awards throughout the 1960s, when he served for several years on the Advisory Awards Committee, the group that actually chose the judges, and served again as a judge in 1965, when Theodore Roethke's final collection was the winner.

The Advisory Awards Committee provided another chance for Pearson to cross paths with a man with a similar portfolio in twentieth-century literature. Like Pearson, Malcolm Cowley was a bit of everything: writer, teacher, editor for both magazines and publishers, talent scout, public intellectual situated "at the center of an extensive web of literary, political, and intellectual relations," in the words of Hans Bak.[29] After serving as an ambulance driver in World War I Cowley migrated to Paris for almost a decade as part of the "Lost Generation." (His *Exile's Return* is one of the best memoirs of the time.) Active in the 1930s literary scene as both a poet and a critic, Cowley had positioned himself firmly on the Marxist side and was one of the founders of the leftist League of American Writers, resigning in 1940 in protest of the Communist Party's commandeering of the group.

Obviously the two didn't meet through their political activities. Rather, Norm had initially encountered Cowley soon after the war, when Cowley was helping develop the Viking Press's Viking Portable anthologies — sturdy, small-format hardcover collections of an author's most important works. (Cowley's 1946 *Viking Portable Faulkner* is widely credited for sparking the revival of interest in William Faulkner.) Cowley admired Pearson's Modern Library edition of Hawthorne and so in 1947 asked his advice on compiling a *Portable Hawthorne*. Wanting to help, and no doubt seeing Cowley as a potential jewel in his network, Pearson drove the ninety minutes to Cowley's house in Gaylordsville to bring him some books — including his precious photostats of the *French and Italian Notebooks!* — and give him a crash course on Hawthorne. (Having sold the rights to the 1937 anthology outright to Random House, he had nothing to lose, at least financially, if Cowley's book supplanted his.) In return, of course, Pearson begged and received something: the letters that Faulkner had sent Cowley from the editing process for the *Portable Faulkner*, and an introduction to the man himself. "For God's sake," Malcolm implored, "don't tell him that I gave his letters to the library."[30]

They soon became friends and frequent collaborators. Cowley edited Auden and Pearson's *Poets of the English Language*, while Pearson tried to secure Cowley contracts to edit volumes for the Rinehart series. Pearson obtained Yale Library privileges for Cowley and brought him in to lecture at several hundred dollars an appearance. Pearson put Cowley in touch with the poets he knew, while Cowley returned the favor with his stable of writers. In the 1960s and 1970s, when Cowley was teaching in university creative-writing programs, he would often call Pearson's attention to promising students such as Ken Kesey, Larry McMurtry, and M. Scott Momaday, which helped Pearson preserve his status at Yale as the professor most in touch with contemporary writing. Pearson wrote a recommendation for Cowley's (unsuccessful) 1961 Guggenheim Fellowship application, and Cowley sponsored Pearson's candidacy for membership in New York City's Century Club. They performed for each other, in other words, the services needed to attain and maintain status within America's elite cultural institutions. But for all the parallels of their careers, their philosophies were fundamentally opposite. While Pearson was most comfortable as a creature of institutions, Cowley saw himself as an oppositional intellectual and preferred what Benjamin Kirbach has called "institutional itinerancy"—maintaining his independence and constantly moving among institutions, never fully joining any of them.[31] Apart from the brilliance of *Exile's Return*, it is perhaps for that reason that Cowley is so much better known than Pearson.

Being a creature of institutions means that one is subject to their rules. If the never-completed Hawthorne letters project, and the knowledge that he had untold treasures stashed away in his office, added to Pearson's mystique, it didn't help him earn promotion. Yale was familiar and patient with such extended undertakings, as its press published many such multivolume, decades-long editions of major authors. Pearson's OSS rival Lefty Lewis had overseen the Horace Walpole papers project since 1937, and Pearson himself was on the editorial board for Yale's Works of Jonathan Edwards series, which commenced in 1957 (and as of 2008 had reached volume 26). But Pearson's own project was stalled. He couldn't finish it during his 1948 Guggenheim

Fellowship year and in 1956 was one of the few people to receive a *second* Guggenheim Fellowship for the same project, with the same result. "I have been sucking blood out of that corpse for twenty years," he ruefully told an interviewer in the 1950s.[32] And as he sat for decades on his collection of original letters, which technically belonged to Yale but for which he was gatekeeper, other Hawthorne scholars began to resent him.

Given how hard he worked and how productive he could be, why he couldn't ever complete this project is a bit of a mystery. Certainly, he lost a bit of steam as he saw American literary studies and American studies moving away from his approach in the 1940s and 1950s, and he would often grumble to graduate students enthralled by the New Criticism that Yale didn't value his kind of old-fashioned scholarship. (After Pearson's death, in fact, nobody at Yale took on the project, and it fell to Thomas Woodson of Ohio State University to eventually complete and publish the letters.) It was also solitary work, which didn't suit this intensely social man well. Gallup thought that Pearson never completed the Hawthorne letters because "he put the interests of other scholars and of Yale over his own immediate ones," which is flattering but only partly true.[33] Pearson relished working on behalf of others, but he needed this work to be recognized and appreciated. A beautiful hardbound multivolume set of Hawthorne's complete correspondence would be evidence only of his accomplishments as an editor and collector. It wouldn't showcase the interpersonal skills and cultural capital in which he took the most pride.

Teaching, though, could do that, and as a result he was long one of Yale's most beloved teachers. Wry and ironic, moving deftly from technical discussions of poetry to disquisitions on the American character, his classes always sagged with waiting lists, and his students, long after they graduated, remembered his erudite, wide-ranging lectures. In an oblique dig at colleagues like Mack who had never left Yale's ivy once they matriculated, Pearson credited his success as a teacher in part to the experiences he had had *outside* academia. "I am like a bear who has come out of hibernation, but who is still living off the fat he has accumulated," he told a *Yale Daily News* profiler in 1954.[34] As he had been in the OSS, he was a brilliant performer who made his misshapen body part of the show, as his student, the future literary biographer Scott Donaldson, remembered: "At the first meeting . . . Pearson would limp across the platform, reassemble himself into a sitting position, and announce that 'when God made me, he made me incomplete.' *Pause as students stared in embarrassed silence.* 'He gave me a terrible memory,' Pearson said, 'and I probably won't be able to call on most of you by name.' *Smiles of relief from the audience, then delight as Pearson delivered his customary sparkling lecture.*"[35] "He was the most superbly theatrical teacher I have ever seen," the journalist Tom Wolfe (who knew something about theatricality) remembered, describing how Pearson would masterfully deploy a cigarette pack as a stage prop. By the end of the term, another student recalled, Pearson had kindled devotion in his students.

> The last words of Norman Pearson's final lecture had hardly been spoken when the assembled student body, some two hundred strong, broke into applause. The clapping grew louder until it reached almost unbelievable intensity, then remained constant at this point. This black-browed, black-mustached man with the grotesquely hunched back, whom many of his pupils had pitied at the beginning of the term but who had gradually and completely forgotten his deformity and had grown to marvel at the brilliance of his delivery and the sincerity of his teachings, gathered together his books and notes, and limped hurriedly out of the auditorium. The thunderous applause continued for a full minute, unabated by the departure of the person for whom it was intended.[36]

His theatricality was only part of his appeal as a teacher. He also became a personal mentor for many of his students and "shrewdly saw in people not just their lives but their promise," one concluded.[37] Pearson had come into his adulthood as a Yale student, and thus for him a Yale education was most essentially about moving into maturity. And in this all-male environment, "maturity" meant "becoming a man." "If you walk freely and easily with this tradition," he would often say at the conclusion of his yearlong American Literature course, "it will help you become a man." Dozens of his former students attested that this was the most important lesson they took from him. "I can honestly say you have taught me by example what it means to be a man in the fullest sense of the word," one member of the class of 1970 wrote him.[38] (Not everyone saw this as a positive: Lemisch complained that Pearson's American Lit syllabus "oozed male privilege, sexual mystique, etc.")[39] Yale's New England Protestant-rooted idea of what it meant to be a "man" amalgamated piety, honesty, integrity, patriotism, and leadership with the aristocratic values of not striving too hard or being excessively intellectual. So for Pearson, an ideal Yale "man" combined the university's traditional "God, country, and Yale" notion of masculinity with the values he felt were necessary for the Cold War era and that he prided himself on embodying: resoluteness, intrepidity, hardiness, and resilience, but also intellectual curiosity and an openness to new or strange or even frightening experiences.

Graduate students, on the other hand, don't come to school to be shaped into men (or women—Yale's graduate programs had long been coeducational). Graduate school is job training. But it can be an even more intensely developmental or even parental experience, as students often come to a department to be mentored by particular professors, and professors often seek to mold their students into junior versions of themselves. Even though he was never the kind of scholarly star who drew a legion of students, Pearson always had his share and directed dozens of dissertations, often on topics far removed from his own home turf of Hawthorne. Charlie Fenton, already an accomplished teacher and scholar even as a graduate student, wrote a study, "Ernest Hemingway's Literary Apprenticeship," for Pearson in 1951, and after Fenton committed suicide in 1960, Pearson worked with his widow to prepare his manuscript for publication. The next year, Robert Bone, a World War II conscientious objector and radical socialist, produced a dissertation, "The Negro Novel in America," that became a foundational critical text for African American literature when it was published in 1958. (Pearson actually codirected this dissertation with the famed African American poet Sterling Brown, who was teaching at Howard University at the time.)

But Pearson's most famous doctoral student never went into the academy. The patrician Virginian Tom Wolfe was one of the first students to enroll in Yale's American Studies graduate program and, as he would throughout his career, quickly showed himself to be a brilliant, and fulsomely opinionated, overachiever. His dissertation on the League of American Writers relied on dozens of interviews with prominent authors, including Cowley, Gregory, and James Farrell, and argued that so many of them had joined the league seeking status, not because of genuine political commitment. It is an impressive piece of work, written with flair (although not the flamboyance that would later characterize his journalism). But it wasn't, at least in the eyes of the Yale American Studies faculty, acceptable. While it was "original" and "frequently brilliant," and displayed "considerable ingenuity" in the research, the review committee deemed it a tendentious piece of "polemical journalism." "That he has a book which certain publishers would accept as it stands, I have no doubt; but that it fulfills the final requirement for a doctoral degree, I cannot believe," one of the three readers pronounced. But they threw Wolfe a lifeline: if he would rewrite it to seem more scholarly and objective, and modify the slanted way he had used some of his evidence, he could resubmit.[40]

Enter Pearson. Wolfe had originally worked with Ralph Gabriel but lost faith in Gabriel after this debacle and asked the misfit-collecting Pearson to get him across the finish line. Pearson had been patient with Wolfe in classes, indulging not just his 105-page research project on Pound's Canto 105 but a 193-page term paper titled "Hemingway's Oral-Narrative Use of the Word *And*." Like Wolfe, Pearson crossed the scholarly/general-interest divide, shared the adamant anti-communism that colored Wolfe's dissertation, and even knew many of the writers that Wolfe interviewed. Also, Wolfe knew that Pearson would rubber-stamp the project once he managed to "strike out all the laughs and anti-Red passages and slip in a little liberal *merde*." Within a year Wolfe had his degree, forever relieved of his desire to be a professor. Pearson, who stayed in contact with Wolfe for the rest of his life, is likely the only person who was close to both of American literature's Thomas Wolfes.

To an uncommon extent, likely because of his compulsion to network, Pearson opened his life and his house to writers, fellow academics, and even students like Wolfe, making Susan an essential collaborator in Pearson's professional accomplishments. For all his fascination with literary bohemianism, Norman and Susan's marriage embodied the most traditional gender and class roles. He worked, traveled, and had a full social and professional life outside of the house, mostly with other professors and writers. Susan's sphere was domestic and social: she took care of the children, was active in the Junior League and the Lawn Club, and was president of the Garden Club of New Haven. Like her mother, she was an expert flower arranger whose arrangements won awards in national competitions. Studying *Gourmet* magazine made her an accomplished cook, and she understood how important it was for her to be a charming, well-dressed hostess at the couple's constant dinner parties. When she accompanied him to the banquets and award ceremonies and readings, Susan was the ideal faculty wife. Knowing that he could bring people home for dinner or host them at his cottage on the shore gave Norm the confidence to expand his networks. But while they genuinely loved and were devoted to each other, and shared interests such as travel, theater, and music, Norm also needed the intellectual and artistic stimulation that relationships *outside* of his marriage provided.

This very conventional marriage, and Norm's immersion in his work and networking, meant that it fell to Susan to manage the traumas and challenges that the family experienced in the 1950s. Winchester Bennett died in 1953, and Chester Pearson in 1956. Burglars broke into the Pearson house in April 1957, making off with most of Susan's jewelry. Most serious was Lizzie, who barely graduated from Emma Willard. She just didn't seem to be getting any better even with intensive treatment for her schizophrenia and remained at the Yale Psychiatric Clinic for much of 1958 and 1959. Her erratic and frightening behavior continued after she was released and moved to Florida, with heavy

FIGURE 13 Fanny, Susan, Norm, and Chester in the 1950s (Norman Holmes Pearson Papers, Yale Collection of American Literature, Beinecke Rare Book and Manuscript Library).

self-medicative drinking, snap engagements that were just as quickly broken, and a number of suicide attempts.

Sue, on the other hand, was fulfilling her parents' high expectations, making her society debut at the New Haven Assemblies in 1949 as a Smith sophomore, and graduating in 1951. While studying at the Yale School of Music in 1953, Sue became engaged to Rowland Lippincott Mitchell Jr., a Yale history professor with a social pedigree. But realizing "I couldn't live with the guy," as she said later, she broke off the engagement, withdrew from music school, moved to New York City, and soon announced her engagement to Jim Addiss—whom she did marry, in 1956, at home on Goodrich Street just as Norm and her mother had done. For a time, their marriage was idyllic, and Susan and Norm adored being grandparents. Norm especially doted on Sue and Jim's first child, Justus, who at his 1958 birth became the son he had always wanted, and he blatantly favored the boy over his little sister

FIGURE 14 Norm on his back porch in Branford. After his 1938 surgery, he was unable to bend his left hip and so had to sit on chairs with his leg hanging off (Norman Holmes Pearson Papers, Yale Collection of American Literature, Beinecke Rare Book and Manuscript Library).

Susan. "It was unfair partisanship. . . . He just spoiled Justus rotten," his mother remembers. (Sue and Jim would divorce in 1967.)

Age brought its usual ravages. Penicillin had finally cleared up Norm's tuberculosis in 1946, but the lingering repercussions of the injury and infection affected him for the rest of his life. His hunchback compressed one lung, making him more susceptible to colds and respiratory ailments, and his heavy smoking didn't help. In early 1959, he was hospitalized for over a week with a serious bleeding ulcer, what he described to Pound as a "vesuvian eruption of the duodenum." It took a long time to bounce back, and he was still too weak even to drive much for weeks afterward, although he still made it to the office almost every day. Utterly dependent on Susan's cooking, when she went to visit her mother in Florida, Norm was forced to eat out at Mory's and the Lawn Club every night. "Since one of every ten persons has an ulcer," he assured her, "restaurants are like dieticians in these matters and know even better than I do without consulting my list what is allowed and not." He even had to quit smoking for several months. After experiencing relatively few health problems in the 1960s, things got worse in the early 1970s. He experienced terrible back spasms from the compressed nerves in his spine, a major infection of the foot, and an excruciatingly painful case of shingles in 1971 that prompted him to grow a beard.

Yale changed more slowly than the society around it, but eventually the strange and disorienting effects of "the Sixties" arrived even there. A 1962 report, commissioned by President Griswold, prescribed a more meritocratic approach to admissions, and a shift to a research-university model for undergraduate education.[41] (This "Doob Report," named for its lead author, also recommended admitting women, but that was a nonstarter for Griswold.) Some of the changes precipitated by the Doob Report were small, such as the 1967 elimination of the requirement that students wear coats and ties in the dining halls. But others fundamentally changed Yale's population—and, conservative alumni feared, its character. In the early 1960s, Yale belatedly began to open its doors a bit wider to Jews and public-school graduates, and 1967's entering class was, for the first time, composed of roughly equal numbers of prep school and public school students. (Harvard had reached this milestone in the 1940s, and Princeton a decade later.)[42] Even African Americans were finding somewhat easier access to Yale, even if they were not precisely welcomed. Fourteen Black students matriculated in 1964, the greatest number Yale had ever seen, and these students founded the Black Student Alliance at Yale, which brought their concerns about the racial climate at the university to President Kingman Brewster.[43] The patrician Brewster was largely oblivious to the racist markers everywhere at Yale: Confederate flags and bullwhips in Calhoun College, racist caricatures in the nineteenth-century paintings adorning Payne Whitney Gymnasium, constant campus-police stops of Black students while white people passed unnoticed.[44] Most dramatically, in 1969, Yale College went coeducational, and 230 female first-year students and almost 350 transfer students enrolled that fall.

It's telling that Pearson, by then a forty-year Yale man, left no trace of his feelings about what so many alumni saw as tectonic changes to Yale's very essence. Temperamentally circumspect, he didn't want to damage his standing in the institution by taking a stance that ended up being controversial or unpopular. He supported increasing Jewish, Black, and public-school students' access to Yale so long as they had "earned it" through meritocratic measures. Restricting admission to legacies and members of one social class would result in "intellectual death," he believed.[45] And he had long worked with and supported women in Yale's graduate programs. Coeducation at Yale College, though, was a different thing, and the molding of Yale *men* so central to his understanding of his job, that it is possible he opposed it. But although he served on several committees with Sam Chauncey, the influential assistant to President Brewster who coordinated the move to coeducation, Pearson never tipped his hand to Chauncey. He never brought it up to his stepdaughter Sue either, or wrote about it to Bryher.[46] The only public statement he made on the matter was typically elliptical. In a 1969 *Yale Reports* radio program installment titled "Thinking about Writing by Women," Pearson said only that "the Yale undergraduates are always saying the great advantages [of the imminent move to coeducation] will be to them. Now I am happier, of course, to say that this is a gesture toward the freedom of women."[47]

He also stayed remarkably quiet about the dramatic changes roiling American studies, which had for twenty years enjoyed a lucrative symbiosis with the institutions of US cultural diplomacy. But this marriage began to crack in the mid-1960s. What was the point, graduate students in the field asked, of antiseptically dissecting the roots of the American character when very real Americans—often the friends and family of these students themselves—were being sent to Vietnam to kill and die? Had the self-satisfied Cold War consensus brought us this bloodshed and imperialism? Or were they in fact baked into American civilization? American studies, young faculty and graduate students increasingly insisted, needed to undo this consensus, to "assume an adversary role against the culture," and perhaps even train its students to become activists rather than scholars.[48]

This revolution started small. In 1966, University of Michigan professor Robert Sklar proposed "American studies as a form of dissent" at a Detroit conference, and within three years Sklar, Betty Ch'maj, Robert Meredith, and others founded the Radical Caucus within the ASA. The caucus started publishing its own newsletter in November 1969, demanding that the association's executive committee formally recognize the caucus, transform *American Quarterly* into a "vanguard journal," and—most provocatively—endorse the upcoming anti-Vietnam march on Washington. While this caucus's membership represented the new generation of American studies scholars, and included far more women than one usually saw on an ASA conference or journal lineup, even some of Pearson's era, such as Carl Bode of the University of Maryland, signed on.[49]

Pearson observed these developments from an especially privileged position. In 1962, he had become a member of the ASA's Executive Council and in 1968, just as the radical energy was intensifying, became president of the ASA. The year was a particularly turbulent one in student life across the United States, but one would not discern that from reading Pearson's personal and professional correspondence, which was just as even-keeled and apolitical as ever. As ASA president, rather than worrying about the dramatic events happening not only on campuses but in his own organization, Pearson was concerned primarily with promoting the field, as he did in his address to the Australian conference that year. To a niece who wrote him excitedly about participating in the October 1969 Vietnam Moratorium Day at the University of New Hampshire and wanted to know his perspective on student activism, Pearson merely said that "as it happened I was speaking that day at Hartwick College in Oneonta, NY, where the classes did not shut down but were attended voluntarily and were mostly given over to discussions of the issues. Students were very alert and eager in their questions and I enjoyed that as much as addressing them at night."[50] But of course, this scholarly insistence on remaining "apolitical" was its own form of politics, serving to reinforce existing structures of power. Only to Bryher did he let the affable and nonpartisan mask slip. He sniped at the anti-American demonstrators at the London embassy, complained that his only problem with the CIA's infiltration of student and cultural groups was how "unprofessional" the agency was about it, and grumbled about the United States' "humiliating defeat" in Vietnam if Robert Kennedy were to be elected president.[51]

Although much of the energy fueling the ASA's Radical Caucus came from outside of the elite universities—its organizers worked at schools like Wayne State and the University of Miami—Pearson's students felt much the same way. One wrote in 1971 that "standing at the window-slits in the upper stacks of Yale's Sterling Memorial Library, American Studies graduate students can see beyond the New Haven ghetto that begins only two blocks away. . . . The American Studies program invites them to gaze instead at an academic middle landscape where the word 'problems' refers to intellectual conundrums, where young acolytes come to receive priestly secrets and the King's touch, where publishability is the highest good and tenure is the Grail, the reward for research so dazzling that it teaches itself."[52] Yale students increasingly wanted to connect what they were studying with the world outside of the campus, and the world was coming ever closer to their campus. Beginning in the mid-1950s, New Haven had become a laboratory for so-called urban renewal and slum removal. Per capita, the city received more urban renewal funding than any other in America, but it only seemed to exacerbate the tensions between lower-income groups and further disadvantage the city's African American population.[53] Only two weeks after Pearson wrote Bryher that "we are wondering when New Haven will have its first Negro rioting," four days of racially charged violence broke out on August 19, 1967.[54] Like so many of his class, despite his liberalism when it came to sexual identity and women's roles and even ethnic diversity, Pearson was largely blind to or dismissive of the deep-seated structural racism of northern cities and of his own university. Discrimination was, in his mind, a southern practice, even though New Haven was highly segregated and its Black residents relegated to low-skilled jobs and substandard housing in a "ghetto" that began on Dixwell Avenue, just a few blocks from Yale.

There was growing tension on campus as well. In 1969, Yale's Students for a Democratic Society (SDS) chapter insisted that ROTC be ejected from campus. The Black Student Alliance at Yale demanded an African American cultural center and an Afro-American studies major. Pearson was more sympathetic to the Black students, whose concerns were largely educational, than to the student radicals. "We have new confrontations daily from the Blacks and the SDS," he told a colleague on leave overseas in late 1969, "but fortunately the latter seems to be losing ground."[55] But Yale wasn't seeing the kinds of mass protests and disruptions that were going on in Berkeley, at Michigan, or at Columbia. Writing a French colleague in early 1969, Pearson assured him that Yale was "not having any real turmoil" of the type that had convulsed France the previous year, although "there is a kind of uneasiness on the part of young faculty members as well as students."[56]

This didn't last. On and around May Day 1970, the murder trial of several Black Panthers brought tens of thousands of activists to New Haven Green and to the campus itself, which was largely shut down by a student strike.[57] For once, though, Pearson wasn't where the action was but rather on the other side of the globe, at the American Studies Seminar in Kyoto. Everyone was in a "state of anxiety," Pearson's secretary wrote him, dealing with the "tense, nightmarish atmosphere" of a city preparing for the worst.[58] (She and Bryher both feared that arson would destroy the treasures in Pearson's office.) But the worst didn't come. Brewster issued a statement sympathetic to the Black Panthers, infuriating conservatives on the faculty and prompting US vice president Spiro Agnew to call for his ouster. But thanks to the efforts of Brewster and Chauncey, the university and city largely avoided the large-scale unrest that many New Haven residents feared, and in anticipation of which Connecticut governor John Dempsey had deployed National Guard troops to the city.

Although he supported American involvement in Vietnam and had no love for student radicalism of the SDS type, Pearson was surprisingly patient, even indulgent, with the dramatic changes that his 1960s students wanted in their education. He was, after all, a pragmatist who understood that institutions had to evolve to serve their constituents, and an American studies scholar who had long seen the demand for change as an essential component of the American character. And where he had long been the professor most responsible for bringing avant-garde literature to Yale, he now looked to his students for guidance. Responding to their enthusiasm for the genre, he had started reading science fiction in the late 1950s and often trotted out a lecture called "Science Fiction as Myth" on his tours abroad. He also began teaching a popular undergraduate class, Literature of the 1960s, which in its various incarnations over the years had the students reading Kesey, Thomas Pynchon, Tillie Olsen, William Gass, Joyce Carol Oates, Vladimir Nabokov, and Bernard Malamud. The class always included at least one work by an African American author (most often Paule Marshall's *Brown Girl, Brownstones* or Ishmael Reed's *Mumbo Jumbo*), and *House Made of Dawn* by the Native American novelist M. Scott Momaday. In this sense, his teaching in the late 1960s and early 1970s mirrored Yale itself: still overwhelmingly white and male, but cautiously open to 1960s youth culture and gradually beginning to include women and people of color.

His understanding of America was evolving, as well. In September 1975, he received an invitation to attend the Asia and Pacific Conference of Regional American Studies Specialists in Fujinomiya, Japan, and speak on the state of American studies in that country. "To have a conference on American Studies in Japan without Norman Holmes Pearson, is like apple pie without ice cream," organizer Robert Forrey told Pearson.[59] The Department of State offered to pay his travel expenses, and proposed that he also come to Korea for a week to meet with academic and professional groups there.[60] And although he usually chose his own topic for these lectures, the Seoul organizers asked him specifically to address "changing concepts of American democracy" as the bicentennial approached. His talk advocated the pragmatic view of American society and institutions expressed by, among others, Pearson's distant relative Oliver Wendell Holmes. Ideas change, interpretations change, populations change, and the nature of American society and government is to respond to these changes as they exist in the real world. Rather than consistently looking back to preexisting and unchanging "rights" and principles, one must take society as it is and people as they are. This "Whig" model "is flexible, pragmatic, slow-moving, highly political," he explained, quoting political philosopher Alexander Bickel. Its end goal was "perfectibility," the impossibility of ever reaching which did not "invalidate the pursuit."

And Pearson's proof of how this had historically worked in America drew not just from his study of American history and literature, but also from what he had seen as a teacher and diplomat, and what he had learned from his students. The present moment was characterized by an expansion of the idea of who was an American beyond the "relatively homogenous population of the Eastern Seaboard" to encompass the inhabitants of other regions, women, "so-called minorities" such as "Jewish Americans, Afro-Americans, and American Indians." If this meant that he could no longer consider his own heritage as the essence of Americanism, so be it. "A WASP like myself," he continued, "has now become ethnic by definition. I should blame democracy if I didn't like it; on the contrary, I have democracy to thank." And as they entered into full political citizenship, these "so-called minorities" were starting to express their unique experiences of life in the United States in literature, thus expanding the possibilities of what literature could do, just as Hawthorne and Whitman and Pound and H.D. had done before them. What some of his conservative colleagues in academia were already starting to disparage as "identity politics" he saw as a welcome development, and much in keeping with American literary history. "If I were to involve all aspects of selfhood, enlarging the Jeffersonian 'assumption of a responsible self,' I should include recent writing by women *qua* women, and ethnic writing as they have developed in response to changing concepts of American democracy." And he concluded by gesturing back to what Puritanism meant and how its heritage manifested itself today. "American literature has always had a strong Puritanical thrust of self-examination, an examination of the state of the world and of one's soul within the world. American self-criticism is not normally a matter of cynicism but an inverse consequence of idealism, of the pursuit of perfectibility. For those to whom everything seems possible, any alternative seems failure. One can read American writing . . . as though it rendered an absolute realism. I myself prefer to read it as an ironic reminder of an ideal which is often violated but remains a democratic dream."[61]

To an audience of South Koreans who certainly had on their minds America's battered image after the chaotic withdrawal from Vietnam, Watergate and the pardoning of President Nixon, oil shocks and urban decay and crime, Pearson here brought together his long-standing interest in the Puritan legacy with his newfound enthusiasm for "ethnic" literature, and even science fiction, and expressed his liberal pragmatism and optimism. He stressed the eternal possibility of self-renewal through the expansion of the community and the citizenry, and through the revivifying power of self-examination and literature. If his career was to have a capsule summary, he could do worse than this.

CONCLUSION

"Changing Concepts of American Democracy" was in fact to be the last thing he ever wrote, and the last lecture he ever delivered. Soon after returning to the United States in mid-September, Pearson developed a respiratory ailment that developed into pneumonia. It worsened quickly, as many of his health problems did in the 1970s. His curved spine made it impossible for him to clear one of the lungs, and smoking-related emphysema had already weakened his respiratory system. After a brief hospitalization, he died on November 5, 1975.

Even in death, Pearson remained both omnipresent and overshadowed by his more famous colleagues. The *New York Times* ran an obituary for him on page 40, but Lionel Trilling died on the same day, and the jump from Trilling's front-page obituary dwarfed Pearson's own.[1] It's hard to imagine that this would have bothered him much. "If the conventional world had concerned me," he wrote Bryher once, "I should certainly not have led the life I have led. . . . I should have gotten on the ladder and been a full professor, had my honorary degrees, published innumerable stupid books as tokens on the academic exchange for which I would have been handed out little prize-packages on the house."[2] Instead, he lived his life surrounded by the things that gave him pleasure: his family, his collections, his connections, and the institutions that nurtured him and that he helped build. And even in death, he remains tethered to those institutions. He is buried in New Haven's eighteenth-century Grove Street Cemetery, only a quarter mile

FIGURE 15 Norm on Lake Toya, Japan, 1975. This is one of the last images of Pearson before his death (Norman Holmes Pearson Papers, Yale Collection of American Literature, Beinecke Rare Book and Manuscript Library).

from his office in Yale's Hall of Graduate Studies, and barely one hundred yards from the Beinecke Library.

His family carried on without him. Susan survived Norman for almost twelve years, passing away in 1987. The financial difficulties that she had endured before marrying him returned after his death, when the "Winson" Swiss bank account—now worth almost a million dollars—came to light, and the tax liability almost bankrupted her. After many years of struggle with mental illness and alcoholism, Lizzie's schizophrenia went into remission when she was in her forties, and she was finally able to hold a job and maintain a marriage. Tragically, she was killed in a gas-station robbery in 1991. "Everyone says life is unfair," her sister, Sue, remarked, "but to have schizophrenia all of your adult life and come out of it at age 40 . . . and then to get murdered, that's the height of unfair. Every time I look at her picture I think 'boy, you were cheated.'" For her part, Sue earned a degree in public health at Yale in 1969 and enjoyed a distinguished career in that field, serving both as the president of the American Public Health Association and as the Connecticut state health commissioner in the early 1990s, and was deeply involved in what became 1998's Tobacco Master Settlement Agreement—a somewhat ironic achievement with regard to this story, for Pearson had fully won her over because of his insistence that she be allowed at age fifteen to smoke at school.

Pearson's memory lingers at Yale almost as a curiosity, an amusing anecdote from the Cold War world when professors could be spies. If his role in American studies has been largely forgotten, particularly after the field repudiated its previous partnership with the US government, he can still be felt at the Beinecke, which he helped build into one of the greatest collections of manuscripts and rare books in the world through bringing writers' archives to Yale and through decades of service on the Yale Library Associates (its fundraising arm). And he of course donated his own massive personal collection of books and manuscripts, containing everything from the "Dusty Diamonds" to his Shakespeare First Folio to Hawthorne's letters and H.D.'s manuscripts. The twentieth-century materials he brought, and that researchers then used, reshaped the story of modern writing. Melissa Barton, a curator of the Yale Collection of American Literature, said in 2022 that "it is impossible to measure Norman Holmes Pearson's impact on our understanding of 20th-century American literature. [The] collections Pearson helped Yale to acquire have seen frequent, continuous use into the 21st century."[3] But too often during his life, he was the only one at Yale using these treasures. "Except for Norman," Gallup wrote in 1998, "outside scholars invariably showed far more interest in the archives of contemporary writers than members of the Yale faculty."[4] He'd likely be happy to know, though, that his quirky "Art for the Wrong Reasons" collection gets trotted out on occasion. "Art for the Wrong Reasons" consists of dozens of paintings that he obtained from the writers he knew: an abstract by Sherwood Anderson, a self-portrait by Henry Miller, Katherine Anne Porter's caricature of Elinor Wylie, a watercolor by John Dos Passos. These paintings are "glimpses of reality as the writers see it," he explained to the *Yale Alumni Magazine*.[5] The paintings, and the oddness of the collection itself, convey a bit of his angular, idiosyncratic, and ironic view of the world.

Literary study today would be utterly unrecognizable to Pearson, but

I like to think that he would welcome the changes, which he seemed to see on the horizon in his "Changing Concepts" lecture and in his later teaching. (The same cannot be said for American studies, which has become perhaps the most uncompromisingly leftist of all American academic fields; he would, I dare say, distance himself from the organization he once led.) After the New Criticism faded in the 1970s and was supplanted, at Yale and elsewhere, by esoteric theoretical approaches such as deconstruction, English departments today seem most interested in how literature, and storytelling in general, express and can help construct the identity of individuals, of communities, of ethnic groups and gender identities, and how literature and literary study can give marginalized communities a voice. In essence, this is the approach that the early American literature scholars like Stanley Williams had taken to the writing of the United States, and that Pearson had started to adopt in including works by Jewish, Native, and Black authors in his courses. Nor would he, I suspect, have any problem with welcoming so-called multimodal texts (films, television, web texts, digital literature, etc.) into literary study, a development that many conservatives decry: just as modernist literature created new techniques of expression and representation to capture the disorienting changes of the early twentieth century, these texts do the same for the ages of mass media and the internet. Pearson's advocacy for women writers was well ahead of its time, and the significance of his (and Gallup's) collecting shouldn't be underestimated. The Stein and Bryher and H.D. papers have been foundational to feminist literary studies and, even after Pearson's death, prompted Yale to collect additional archives of American women modernists, advancing feminist literary study even more. His masculinist tendencies as a teacher and scholar, and especially his indulgence of Ezra Pound's abhorrent views, haven't aged as well, nor have his occasional personal expressions of casual bias. He was, in every way, a man of his time and milieu, even if just slightly ahead of both.

Despite Luce's hopes, the "American Century" lasted only about twenty-five years. For all their high-minded intentions, the men who ran the interlocking elite institutions of the liberal establishment could not transcend their own blindness and occasional arrogance, concocting disasters such as the American involvement in Vietnam and ill-conceived urban renewal that mars New Haven. While it held fast against the Communism against which it was a bulwark, the vital center could not withstand the pressures from the student left, the civil rights and feminist movements, and the New Right that would eventually take power in 1980. Whatever romance lingered in Pearson's professor-spy image began to curdle with the 1967 exposure of the CIA's involvement in cultural groups like the National Student Association and then putrefied with the 1975 revelations of Philip Agee and the Church Committee about the agency's dirty tricks. Cultural diplomacy, the Fulbright program, and academic exchange still exist, although both Democratic and Republican administrations from Reagan on have deemphasized and defunded them. And even the modernist literature that he loved so well came under attack when Pound's fascism and anti-Semitism, Eliot's Anglo-Catholic royalism, and the pervasive misogyny of many of these writers began to seem a lot less irrelevant to their poetry (while the reputations of other writers he championed, from H.D. to Stein to Moore, rose). But for all that quarter century, Pearson was not just a true believer in an American liberal society, informed by the best elements of its Puritan heritage, led by its benevolent institutions, and with a mission to bring that liberalism to the world; he was perhaps its emblematic figure.

ACKNOWLEDGMENTS

A book like this isn't just the product of the writer. Many people provided assistance that made this work possible. Among the most crucial of these were three members of Pearson's family I had the immense pleasure to meet and who provided invaluable assistance: Pearson's stepdaughter Susan Addiss twice sat for long interviews in the house where her parents had lived; his niece Elizabeth Rice Smith, charged with enthusiasm for this project from the beginning, toured me around Gardner, Massachusetts, and East Jaffrey, New Hampshire, and frequently sent me valuable tidbits and ideas; and his late niece Joan Pearson hosted me at her Concord, Massachusetts, house and showed me the doll he had sent her from Germany in 1933.

Among the many friends, colleagues, and generous people who have helped with this project with advice, perspective, anecdotes, and encouragement have been Richard Brodhead, Genny Buxton, Debbie Cohn, Annette Debo, the late Scott Donaldson, the late Susan Stanford Friedman, William Goetzmann Jr., Michael Gorra, Ezra Greenspan, Justina and Patrick Gregory, Brenda Helt, Archie Henderson, Donna Hollenberg, Michael Holzman, Geoff Kabaservice, Peter Kalliney, Linda Kinnahan, Ira Nadel, Tim Naftali, Hiromi Ochi, Lance Richardson, Harry Stecopoulos, the late William Stott, Steve Weinberg, Michael Winship, and Yukari Yoshihara.

The bulk of the research for this book took place at Yale University and the Beinecke Library, which holds Pearson's archive. Over the years I worked on this book I visited Yale many times in short bursts until 2021–22, when I was named a Visiting Fellow in the Yale English department for the year, allowing me to spend the extended time there necessary to get the project done (and, in those COVID times, even to access the library). I am grateful to Jean-Christophe Agnew, Melissa Barton, Jessica Becker, the late Harold Bloom, Jessica Brantley and the Department of English, Sam Chauncey, Michael Forstrom, Basie Gitlin, Jay Gitlin, Lanny Hammer, Michael Lotstein, George Miles, John Monahan, Adrienne Sharpe-Weseman, Joel Silverman, Amber Suess, and Alan Trachtenberg for all their help.

But materials relevant to a Pearson biography are present in dozens of other archives across the country, as my list of archives consulted indicates. While my visits to these repositories showed me yet again that archivists' and librarians' reputation for helpfulness and solicitude is if anything understated, a number of these professionals went above and beyond: Zachary Bodnar, archivist, Congregational Library and Archives; Alison Fraser, associate curator of the Poetry Collection, University at Buffalo Special Collections; Marion Knoll, coordinator of the Gardner Museum; Kathleen Leslie of the Levi Heywood Memorial Library; Tal Nadan of the New York Public Library Manuscripts and Archives Division; Paige Roberts, director of Special Collections and Archives, Philips Academy Andover; Eric van Slander, archivist, United States National Archives at College Park; and the volunteers at the Gulf Beaches Historical Museum in Pass-a-Grille Beach, Florida. I couldn't travel to every library, though, and Natalie McGartland, Corinna Norrick-Rühl, Annie Page, Keaton Studebaker, and my niece Ellie Colbert all provided additional research assistance.

A brief trip to Australia proved quite fruitful in fleshing out chapter 11, and I'm grateful to Amanda Laugesen and the Australian National University for inviting me, and to Elaine Barry, William Breen, Beth Driscoll, Nicole Moore, Simone Murray, Brenda Niall, and Chris Wallace-Crabbe for their help.

A National Endowment for the Humanities Fellowship in 2021–22 quite literally made it possible to complete this book, and I am more grateful than I can say for the NEH's support of my work over the years, for this project and others.

Many thanks to Duquesne University for its unstinting support—financial and logistical—of this project, and especially to Provost David Dausey, McAnulty College deans Jim Swindal and Kris Blair, and English department chair Danielle St. Hilaire.

The University of Chicago Press and my editor Tim Mennel have been a joy to work with throughout this project. I am grateful to Tim for believing that this is a story that would interest people, and for helping me shape the manuscript so that it does (I hope). Reviewers Eric Bennett and Hugh Wilford also provided invaluable suggestions, and the final book reflects their guidance. Editorial associate Andrea Blatz was very helpful in preparing the manuscript for publication, and Kathleen Kageff gave it a meticulous copyedit, and me a robust course in Chicago style. Steven Moore went above and beyond the duties of an indexer.

Quotations from the correspondence of Norman Holmes Pearson used by permission of the Yale Collection of American Literature, Beinecke Rare Book and Manuscript Library (© Yale University). Unpublished correspondence from Bryher used by permission of the Schaffner family. Quotations from the correspondence of Horace Gregory and Marya Zaturenska used by permission of Patrick Gregory. Quotations from the correspondence of Ezra Pound, H.D., and James Laughlin and Robert MacGregor used by permission of New Directions Publishing Corporation. Unpublished correspondence by Dorothy Pound used by permission of Elizabeth Pound. Quotations from the correspondence of William Carlos Williams used by permission of the William Carlos Williams MD Estate, care of the Jean V. Naggar Literary Agency, Inc. Quotes from materials from the Yale Office of the President and Office of the Yale College Dean used by permission of Yale University Manuscripts and Archives. Quotations from the correspondence of officers of the Australian and New Zealand American Studies Association used by permission of ANZASA. Quotations from the correspondence of Sheri Martinelli used by permission of Steven Moore.

Portions of chapter 11 appeared in a different form in the *Australasian Journal of American Studies*. Portions of chapters 8 and 10 appeared in a different form in *Post-45*.

Finally, my greatest gratitude is to my wife, Alison, and sons, Jack and Beckett, who showed endless love and patience through many years of travel, inconvenience, distraction, colonization of the dining room, and having to listen to far too many stories about Norman Holmes Pearson.

NOTES

INTRODUCTION

1 American Studies Association, "Carl Bode–Norman Holmes Pearson Prize."
2 "Getting well," Norman Holmes Pearson to Fanny Pearson, July 1931 (Beinecke Library, Yale University, Norman Holmes Pearson papers, hereafter NHP; also used for Pearson himself, e.g., in citations of letters); "not tiresome," Moore to John Warner Moore, October 6, 1940, in M. Moore, 402; see also "MELUS," unpublished talk (1974?) (NHP). "MELUS" may stand for *Multi-ethnic Literatures of the United States*, a journal that began in 1974, but in the document NHP doesn't indicate that specifically.
3 Santayana, 7.
4 On the "City on a Hill" speech and how American studies scholar Perry Miller drew links between the Puritans and the Cold War, see Rodgers, esp. 200–230.
5 Richard B. Sewall, untitled "Theme" (1948) (NHP).

CHAPTER ONE

1 Baltzell, *Puritan*, 197.
2 E. Johnson, 129–30; Winthrop, 122.
3 Crane, 130; Cutter, 1902–3; *History of Orleans County*, 57; Blodgett and Jewett; Currier, 571; Jeffrey, 100–101.
4 Crane, 130.
5 Kittredge, 4–5.
6 Baltzell, *Puritan*, 75, 92, 199.
7 Crane, 123.
8 Gardner employed a form of government typical of New England towns, with no mayor but a council of three selectmen and an elected town treasurer and clerk, from its founding in 1785 until 1922, when it converted to a city model with a mayor and council. E. Moore, 147–51; Massachusetts Municipal Management Association.
9 Crane, 123.
10 W. R. MacAusland, "Resume in Case of Norman Pearson," June 13, 1932 (NHP).

11 Brand, "Biographical Sketch."

12 Alfred Pearson to NHP, 1921 (NHP).

13 All quotes from Pearson's diary (NHP). Gardner demographics from US Census, 1920, Massachusetts State Compendium, 25, https://www2.census.gov/prod2 /decennial/documents/06229686v20-25.pdf.

14 Becker, "Book Letter Contest."

15 Norm is not named as the author of this quote, but given the letter Becker sent him, it seems clear that she is quoting from his letter.

16 George W. Ludlow to NHP, May 29 and August 12, 1925 (NHP).

17 Ostby Photo Service to NHP, November 28, 1921 (NHP).

18 NHP to Joan Pearson, April 20, 1938 (NHP).

19 NHP, "Ivy Oration," 90.

20 NHP to Chester Pearson, August 15, 1928 (NHP).

21 NHP academic transcript from Phillips Academy (Phillips Academy Andover Archives).

22 NHP, "Development of Modern Poetry" (essay for English class at Andover) (NHP).

23 Phillips Academy, 109.

24 NHP, "The Problem of Assimilation," original declamation, 1928 (NHP, Personal Papers, "Class papers 1927 and undated" folder).

25 *Decennial Census, State Compendium, 1930*, https://www2.census.gov/library /publications/decennial/1930/population-volume-3/10612963v3p1ch08.pdf.

26 NHP to mother, May 1928 (NHP).

27 Mary Guyton to Chester Pearson, September 28, 1928 (NHP).

CHAPTER TWO

1 Fitzgerald, 31.

2 Pierson, *Yale: The University College*, 65.

3 Horowitz, *Consuming Pleasures*, xix.

4 Thelin, 166–67.

5 Canby, 50.

6 Karabell, 53–54.

7 Qtd. in Oren, 53.

8 Oren, 55.

9 Thelin, 166–67.

10 Kelley, 373, 389–90.

11 Pierson, *Yale: The University College*, 402.

12 Oren, 90.

13 Qtd. in Oren, 56.

14 Canby, 127–29.

15 On this topic, see Karabell, 207; Oren, 54; Synnott; Soares.

16 Alfred Pearson to Joseph Ellis, August 23, 1928 (NHP).

17 Elizabeth Rice Smith, email to the author, January 31, 2022.

18 Bowen, 226.

19 Black, 139, 271–73; Bowen, 135–36; Gelb and Gelb, 213–14.

20 NHP to Fanny Pearson, April 1930.

21   Mary Lib Thomson to NHP, July 28, 1930 (NHP).
22   Mary Lib Thomson to NHP, July 20, August 18 and 19, 1930 (NHP).
23   Mary Lib Thomson to NHP, October 5, 1930 (NHP).
24   Dr. W. R. MacAusland, "Resume in Case of Norman Pearson," medical memo, June 13, 1932 (NHP).
25   NHP to Mary Lib Thomson, July 20, 1930 (NHP).
26   NHP to Fanny Pearson, January 25, 1932 (NHP).
27   NHP to Fanny Pearson, February 8, 1932 (NHP).
28   Chester Pearson to NHP, May 10, 1932 (NHP).
29   Zimmerman, 2.
30   "How Did You Choose," 13. He earned a 380, or 96 percent, for his work with Williams the following year, but we'd probably consider that an "independent study," not a class per se.
31   See Herbst, 214.
32   Graff, 22, 36, 37.
33   Jones, 118. Also see Gross; Shumway, esp. ch. 1; Vanderbilt.
34   S. Smith, 79.
35   Hubbell qtd. in Shumway, 149.
36   Vanderbilt, 446.
37   Shumway, 132.
38   See F. Turner.
39   Lecture notes, 1925 (Yale University Manuscripts and Archives, Stanley T. Williams papers).
40   Winks, 252.
41   Tuition for 1931–32 was $450 (Pierson, *Yale Book of Numbers*, 590).
42   NHP, "Story by Hawthorne."
43   "How Did You Choose," 13.
44   Braestrup, 4–5.
45   NHP to Fanny Pearson, July 1931 (NHP).
46   Gene O'Neill Jr., telegram to NHP, June 15, 1931, and letter to NHP, August 5, 1931 (NHP).
47   NHP to Fanny Pearson, spring 1932 (?) (NHP).

CHAPTER THREE

1   NHP to Fanny Pearson, June 1932 (NHP).
2   NHP to mother, August 1, 1932 (NHP).
3   The text here is from what appears to be a typed journal entry made at the time, saved among his contemporaneous papers. He recounted this same story, in substantially the same words, in a September 13, 1932, letter to his mother (both in NHP). The fact that he set this experience down twice attests to the significance he gave it.
4   NHP to his mother, September 13, 1932 (NHP).
5   NHP, "Introduction," in *Complete Novels and Selected Tales of Nathaniel Hawthorne*, ix.
6   NHP to mother, October 12, 1932 (NHP, letters).
7   Sayer, 198, 205.

8   NHP to mother, March 25, 1933 (NHP).

9   NHP to mother, November 10, 1932 (NHP).

10 NHP to mother, November 3 and 18, 1932 (NHP).

11 NHP to mother, December 13 and 29, 1932 (NHP).

12 NHP to mother, January 29, 1933 (NHP).

13 NHP to Stanley Williams, September 18, 1933 (NHP).

14 NHP to mother, January 29, 1933 (NHP).

15 NHP to mother, April 16, 1933 (NHP).

16 NHP to mother, March 1, 1933 (NHP).

17 NHP to mother, June 15, 1933 (NHP). In that year, ownership of the German film production company Universum-Film Aktiengesellschaft (UFA) was transferred to the Nazi Party.

18 NHP to Fanny Pearson, August 1933 and July 23, 1933 (NHP).

19 NHP to Fanny Pearson, August 5, 1933 (NHP).

20 Speech to Rotary Club of Gardner, MA, n.d. (NHP).

21 NHP to mother, August 25, 1933 (NHP).

22 NHP to mother, September 18, 1933 (NHP).

23 NHP to Stanley Williams, September 18, 1933 (NHP).

24 NHP to mother, September 29, 1933 (NHP).

25 Steve Morris to NHP, April 5, 1935 (NHP).

26 NHP to mother, November 7, 1933 (NHP).

27 NHP to mother, December 14, 1933 (NHP).

28 NHP to mother, February 9, 1934 (NHP).

29 Pierson, *Yale: The University College*, 265.

30 Kelley, 390.

31 Stanley Williams to NHP, December 15, 1933 (NHP).

CHAPTER FOUR

1   NHP to mother, August 18, 1934, and October 1934 (NHP).

2   NHP to mother, October 1934 (NHP).

3   NHP to mother, June 9, 1935 (NHP).

4   Notes on Gertrude Stein lecture, misdated January 12, 1934; NHP, letter to mother, misdated January 13, 1934; NHP, letter to Stein, July 31, 1936 (all NHP).

5   Journal entry on Stein lecture, misdated January 12, 1934 (NHP).

6   NHP to mother, January 25, 1935 (NHP); NHP, "Robert William Wright," 565.

7   Elizabeth Mayer to NHP, October 28, 1935 (NHP).

8   NHP to Chester Pearson, December 8, 1935 (NHP).

9   NHP, affidavit signed at New Haven (CT) County Clerk, February 2, 1936 (NHP).

10 John Fulton to NHP, December 11, 1935 (NHP).

11 Beata Mayer to NHP, February 28, 1936 (NHP).

12 Gailey, 1.

13 NHP to mother, November 3, 1935 (NHP).

14 NHP to mother, January 6, 1936 (NHP).

15 NHP to mother, January 6, 1936 (NHP).

16 NHP to mother, September 22, 1936 (NHP).

17 NHP to mother, September 22, 1936 (NHP).

18 NHP to mother, September 22, 1936 (NHP).

19 NHP to mother, October 16, 1935 (NHP).

20 Gates, 31; also see Tompkins.

21 Price, 3.

22 Csicsila, 8.

23 Raff, 597–98.

24 NHP to mother, 1937 (NHP).

25 NHP to Howard Lowry, January 10, 1936 (NHP, Oxford Anthology materials).

26 Blackwood, 117.

27 NHP to Howard Lowry, January 10, 1936 (NHP, Oxford Anthology materials).

28 NHP to mother, fall 1936 (NHP).

29 Stanley Williams to Howard Lowry, February 12, 1937 (NHP, Oxford Anthology materials).

30 NHP to Benét, February 11, 1936 (NHP); Stanley Williams to Howard Lowry, February 12, 1937 (NHP, Oxford Anthology materials).

31 Blackwood, 117.

32 Howard Lowry to NHP, December 4, 1936; Stanley Williams to Howard Lowry, December 8, 1936 (NHP, Oxford Anthology materials).

33 Lowry to NHP, February 2, 1937; NHP to Benét, February 11, 1936 (NHP, Oxford Anthology materials).

34 NHP to Bryher, December 19, 1938 (Beinecke Library, Yale University, Bryher papers).

35 Blackwood, 117.

36 "Washington Irving" headnote, in Benét and Person, 1599.

37 Price, 3.

38 NHP to Howard Lowry, May 3, 1937 (NHP, Oxford Anthology materials, box 161).

39 NHP to Bryher, December 19, 1938 (Bryher papers).

40 NHP to Van Wyck Brooks, November 8, 1950 (Kislak Center for Special Collections, University of Pennsylvania, Van Wyck Brooks papers).

41 NHP to mother, February 2, 1938 (NHP).

42 NHP to mother, March 17, 1938 (NHP).

43 NHP to Saxe Commins, January 20, 1937 (misdated 1936) (NHP, Hawthorne Editorial).

44 NHP to mother, March 2, 1937 (NHP).

45 Saxe Commins to NHP, June 11, 1937 (NHP, Hawthorne Editorial).

46 NHP, "Introduction," in *Complete Novels and Selected Tales of Nathaniel Hawthorne,* xiv.

47 NHP to Horace Gregory (HG), October 17, 1937 (NHP).

48 NHP to Elizabeth Mayer, July 28, 1937 (Beinecke Library, Yale University, Elizabeth Mayer papers).

49 NHP, diary entry, 1937 (NHP, "Notebooks, Journals, and Notes").

50 Hicks, 22–23.

51 NHP to HG, October 17, 1937 (NHP).

52 NHP, "Introduction," in *Complete Novels and Selected Tales of Nathaniel Hawthorne,* xv.

53 NHP to John Gould Fletcher, June 25, 1937 (NHP).

54 Wecter, v.

55 NHP to mother, December 4, 1937 (NHP).
56 NHP to mother, March 2, 1937 (NHP).
57 Thomas Wolfe to NHP, December 18, 1936, in Nowell, 567; Benét and Pearson, 1537–53.
58 Thomas Wolfe to NHP, January 21, 1938 (NHP).
59 NHP to mother, spring 1938 (NHP).
60 See Thomas Wolfe.
61 NHP to Benét, September 30, 1938 (Beinecke Library, Yale University, William Rose Benét papers).
62 NHP to Dixon Wecter, October 10, 1938 (NHP).
63 All NHP poems from NHP, Personal Papers, series 8, Notebooks, 1932–64.

CHAPTER FIVE

1 NHP to Bryher, October 30, 1938 (Bryher papers).
2 NHP to mother, July 8, 1938 (NHP).
3 NHP to mother, July 25, 1938 (NHP).
4 NHP to Dixon Wecter, October 10, 1938 (NHP).
5 NHP to mother, September 26, 1938 (NHP).
6 Mertens.
7 NHP to William Carlos Williams, November 7, 1940 (Beinecke Library, Yale University, William Carlos Williams papers, hereafter WCW Beinecke); WCW will be used for Williams himself, e.g., in citations of letters.
8 NHP to mother, probably September 25, 1938 (NHP); NHP to Henry C Badger, December 12, 1938 (NHP).
9 NHP to Fanny Pearson, probably September 25, 1938; Ingelfinger to NHP, October 10, 1938; NHP to mother, September 26, 1938 (NHP).
10 NHP to mother, November 1, 1938 (NHP).
11 NHP to Dudley Fitts, November 1, 1938 (NHP).
12 NHP to H.D., November 21, 1956 (Hollenberg, *Between*, 191–92); NHP to John Gould Fletcher, November 1, 1938 (NHP).
13 NHP to Fanny Pearson, October 24, 1938 (NHP).
14 William Sweet to Fanny Pearson, October 18, 1938 (NHP).
15 Howard Lowry to NHP, October 29, 1938 (NHP, Oxford Anthology materials).
16 NHP to Bryher, December 19, 1938 (NHP).
17 NHP to John Gould Fletcher, November 12, 1938 (NHP).
18 Bryher to HG, October 24, 1938, and June 20, 1939 (Special Collections Research Center, Syracuse University Library, Horace Gregory papers, hereafter HG; as noted earlier, HG is also used for Gregory himself, e.g., in citations of letters).
19 NHP to the Gregorys, December 22, 1938 (HG).
20 Patrick Gregory, email to the author, August 9, 2023.
21 NHP to HG, December 22, 1938 (HG).
22 NHP to Bryher, October 30, 1938; NHP to mother, November 20, 1938 (NHP).
23 NHP to Stanley Williams, December 18, 1938 (NHP).
24 NHP to Chester Pearson, January 2, 1939 (NHP).
25 William Sweet to Fanny Pearson, October 18, 1938 (NHP).

26 NHP to mother, December 23, 1938 (NHP).

27 NHP to mother, January 30, 1939; Marya Zaturenska to NHP, January 17, 1939 (NHP).

28 NHP to WCW, February 3, 1939 (WCW Beinecke).

29 Marya Zaturenska to NHP, February 23, 1939 (NHP); HG to NHP, April 4 and 6, 1939 (NHP); Bryher to Zaturenska, June 20, 1939 (HG).

30 NHP to Bryher, December 18, 1938 (NHP).

31 NHP to HG, April 9, 1939 (HG).

32 NHP to mother, April 14, 1939 (NHP).

33 NHP to the Gregorys, December 22 and 7, 1938 (HG papers).

34 NHP to Bryher, October 16, 1961. He was actually twenty-nine at the time of the Chicago surgery.

35 *New York Times*, December 17, 1938; *San Diego Sun*, December 4, 1938; *Chicago Tribune*, December 17, 1938; *New Masses*, December 13, 1938; *Rocky Mountain News*, December 25, 1938; *Dallas News*, December 11, 1938. I have cited a number of periodical items that were clippings from archives and for which page numbers are no longer available; where page numbers are available, I have included them.

36 NHP to mother, March 17, 1938 (NHP).

37 NHP to Daniel Aaron, April 8, 1940 (Houghton Library, Harvard University, Daniel Aaron papers).

38 NHP to mother, January 3, 1940 (misdated 1939, NHP).

39 Caplow and McGee, 110.

40 H. N. Hillebrand to NHP, April 25, 1938 (NHP).

41 Ben Abramson to NHP, October 12, 1940 (NHP).

42 NHP to mother, March 17, 1938 (NHP).

43 NHP, "Surveying," 588.

44 NHP to mother, September 15, 1940, and March 17, 1938 (NHP).

45 "MELUS," unpublished talk, 1974? (NHP).

46 Kirk, 561.

47 NHP, "Literary Forms," 65, 66.

48 Pearson, "Literary Forms," 67, 68. For comparison, see esp. the essays in Malinowski.

49 NHP to Fanny Pearson, September 1940 (NHP).

50 Eric Bentley to NHP, December 16, 1941, and March 6, 1943 (NHP).

51 Stanley Williams to NHP, November 16, 1938 (NHP).

52 Winks, 331; Zaturenska to NHP, April 20, 1939 (NHP).

53 NHP recommendation letter qtd. in Holzman, *Spies and Traitors*, 63.

54 Gallup, *Pigeons*, 19.

55 NHP to Robert Stein, January 15, 1941 (NHP).

56 Gallup, "Gertrude Stein," 30; NHP to WCW, November 7, 1940 (WCW Beinecke).

57 Knollenberg to NHP, April 11, 1941 (NHP). On the 1941 and 1947 Stein exhibitions, see Debo, *American H.D.*; Debo, "Norman Holmes Pearson"; Gallup, "Gertrude Stein."

58 NHP to John Gould Fletcher, May 29, 1940 (NHP).

59 Joe Gould to NHP, May 18, 1943. By this time Pearson was already in England, so the letter did not reach him until after the war. On Gould, see J. Mitchell, "Joe Gould's Secret"; J. Mitchell, "Professor Sea Gull"; Lepore.

60 NHP to Frances Steloff, October 2, 1939, Archives and Manuscripts Division, New

York Public Library, Astor, Lenox, and Tilden Foundations (hereafter NYPL Astor), Gotham Book Mart papers (hereafter Gotham).

61 NHP to Frances Steloff, October 31 and November 6, 1939 (Gotham); "We Moderns," Gotham Book Mart Catalogue no. 42 (1940).

62 Josef Scharl to NHP, January 31, 1940 (NHP).

63 NHP, biographical statement to George K. Bowden of OSS, February 20, 1943 (United States National Archives II at College Park, Maryland, Office of Strategic Services [RG 226], [hereafter RG 226], Central Files, box 173).

64 NHP, Guggenheim Fellowship recommendation letter for W. H. Auden, n.d. (1941?) (NHP).

65 NHP to mother, February 1, 1938 (NHP).

66 NHP to Rukeyser, July 29, 1940; December 3, 1941; October 8, 1942 (all NYPL Berg, Rukeyser papers); Rukeyser to NHP, August 9, 1941 (NHP).

67 Matthiessen to NHP, August 8, 1939 (NHP).

68 All quotes from NHP, "Review of *American Renaissance*," 107–11.

69 NHP to Matthiessen, November 25, 1941 (Beinecke Library, Yale University, F. O. Matthiessen papers).

70 NHP to mother, May 17 and May 26, 1940 (NHP).

71 Hotchkiss, 258–59.

72 Henshaw, 13–22.

73 "Father of the Modern Firearms Business."

74 "Bennett Quits Board of Winchester Arms," 33; Ward; Trevelyan, 115.

75 "Obituary Notice, Arthur William Wright," 309; Yale Graduate School of Arts and Sciences.

76 NHP to mother, July 21, 1940 (NHP).

77 See Woloshyn.

78 Interview with Sue Addiss, Branford CT, September 3, 2021.

79 Interview with Sue Addiss, Branford CT, September 3, 2021; NHP to Fanny Pearson, October 6, 1940; Susan Bennett Tracy to NHP.

80 Susan Silliman Bennett to NHP, October 11, 1940 (NHP).

81 NHP to Fanny Pearson, December 10, 1940 (NHP).

82 Braestrup, 4–5.

83 NHP to Fanny Pearson, December 10, 1940, and January 13, 1941 (NHP).

84 NHP to mother, January 31, 1941 (NHP).

85 NHP to mother, February 11, 1941 (NHP).

86 *Phillips Bulletin*, July 1941, 45.

87 NHP to WCW, November 20, 1940 (WCW Beinecke).

88 NHP to mother, December 10, 1940 (NHP).

89 NHP to Fanny Pearson, December 10, 1940 (NHP).

90 NHP to Tom Tracy, February 19, 1940 (NHP).

91 John Tracy to NHP, April 2, 1940 (NHP).

92 NHP to Bryher, February 6, 1952 (Bryher papers).

93 NHP to Bryher, March 27, 1946 (NHP).

94 Kelley, 396.

95 NHP to Bryher, November 25, 1938 (NHP).

96 NHP to HG, January 31, 1939 (HG).

97 NHP to Gregory, November 21, 1938 (NHP).

98 NHP, untitled journal entry, September 3, 1939 (NHP).

99   Bryher to NHP, May 31, 1938 (NHP).

100   Bryher to NHP, May 2, October 14, December 5, 1940, January 19, 1941 (NHP).

101   NHP to John Gould Fletcher, May 29, 1940 (NHP).

102   Quoted in Kelley, 396.

103   "Inevitable" NHP to mother, December 12, 1941; NHP to Elizabeth Mayer, December 18, 1941 (Mayer papers).

104   Kelley, 396.

105   NHP to mother, December 12 and 23, 1941 (NHP).

106   NHP to Muriel Rukeyser, August 14, 1942 (NYPL Berg, Rukeyser papers).

107   NHP, undated 1942 form letter to English departments (NHP).

108   NHP to mother, July 9, 1941 (NHP).

109   NHP to mother, October 21, 1942 (NHP).

CHAPTER SIX

1   NHP to mother, December 12, 1941 (NHP).

2   Naftali, 55.

3   NHP to mother, July 9, 1941 (NHP).

4   Winks; for more on Downes, see Kirchik, 66–76.

5   NHP to Donald Downes, August 11, 1942 (RG 266, Downes papers, box 6).

6   Naftali, 27–28.

7   NHP to mother, October 12, November 8, and December 12, 1942 (NHP); David Seifeheld to NHP, December 2, 1942 (RG 266, OSS Personnel Files, box 592); Security Office Investigation Report to Donald Downes, November 20, 1942 (RG 266, Downes papers, box 6).

8   Winks, 100.

9   NHP to mother, February 7, 1943 (NHP).

10   Winks, 256.

11   Winks, 259.

12   See the CIA website: https://www.cia.gov/static/7851e16f9e100b6f9cc4ef002028c e2f/Office-of-Strategic-Services.pdf, accessed December 3, 2023.

13   Holzman, "Ideological Origins," 74–75.

14   Katz, 9, 13, 25; Donovan qtd. in MacDonald, vii. Also see Central Intelligence Agency.

15   Naftali, 30.

16   Memo from NHP to George K. Bowden, February 20, 1943 (RG 266, COI/OSS Central Files, box 173).

17   Handwritten note by OSS evaluator on memo from NHP to George K. Bowden, February 20, 1943 (RG 266, COI/OSS Central Files, box 173).

18   General Donovan to Office of Selective Service, March 1, 1943 (RG 266, COI/OSS Central Files, box 173); Winks, 262.

19   NHP to mother, March 4, 1943 (NHP).

20   W. H. Auden to NHP, March 23, 1943 (NHP).

21   MacPherson, 193; "thrilling," NHP to mother, April 29, 1943 (NHP); Winks, 263.

22   Holzman, *Spies and Traitors*, 14.

23   Naftali, 31.

24   MacPherson, 192–93; see also Winks, 260–62; Central Intelligence Agency.

25   Winks, 266.

26   NHP to mother, April 29, May 15, June 11, 1943. Pearson's colleague Donald Gallup, a second lieutenant in the US Army stationed in Cheltenham, also noted the over-abundance of brussels sprouts among the local produce (Gallup, *Pigeons*, 41).

27   NHP to Bryher, May 15, 1943 (Bryher papers); Bryher to NHP, May 11, 1943 (NHP); NHP to H.D., May 14, 1943 (Beinecke Library, Yale University, H.D. papers, hereafter H.D.; also used for H.D. herself, e.g., in citations of letters).

28   Schaffner, "Keeper," 32–33.

29   Schaffner, "Running," 10–11.

30   Winks, 297.

31   OSS War Diary, Preamble to January 1944, pt. 3, "Supervising Policy, Plans and Operations: Control of the Branches," 33–34 (RG 226, Entry A1 147, container 3).

32   MacPherson, 194.

33   Cutler, 13. The street numbering has changed; 14 Ryder Street is the current address.

34   Kahrl, 3.

35   NHP to mother, December 5, 1943 (NHP).

36   Masterman, 3; NHP, "Introduction," in *Double-Cross System*, xii.

37   Kahrl, 3.

38   Qtd. in Pearson, "Introduction," in *Double-Cross System*, xi.

39   Susan Addiss, interview with the author, September 2021.

40   NHP to mother, January 13, 1944 (NHP).

41   History Project, 197.

42   War materials (NHP) (ellipses in the original).

43   Alice Hitchcock to NHP, 1944 (NHP).

44   Bryher to Susan Pearson, September 12, 1944; Bryher to NHP, July 27, 1944 (NHP); Winks, 300–301; NHP war diary, July 3, 1944 (NHP); NHP to H.D., August 2, 1944 (H.D.).

45   Cutler, 13.

46   Cutler, 22–23.

47   X-2 Branch, European Theatre of Operations, US Army (ETOUSA) Branch Order 17, June 30, 1944 (RG 226, New York and London Records, Entry 147, folder 48).

48   Naftali, 40.

49   Winks, 339–41; Holzman, *Spies and Traitors*, 83–84; Mangold, 38.

50   Winks, 346; Schaffner, "Glass," 16.

51   Cecily d'Autremont to NHP, October 17, 1944 (NHP).

52   Corn anecdote from Hollenberg, *Winged*, 209; Bryher, *Days of Mars*, x.

53   NHP to mother, September 16 and 20, 1943 (NHP).

54   NHP appointment calendar 1944 (NHP, "OSS materials").

55   Milne, 148–49. This account by Milne—A. A. Milne's son—might also be colored by his long friendship with Philby.

56   Philby, 74–75.

57   Of the similarly innumerable accounts of Philby and Angleton, particularly useful is Holzman's *Spies and Traitors*.

58   Shelden, 255; Sherry, 172–75; Greene.

59   Qtd. in Naftali, 41.

60   History Project, 198.

61   "ETO X-2 Branch Progress Report, 1–15 September 1944" (RG 226, New York, London, and Paris Field Station Files, boxes 1–10); Naftali, 37.

62   Naftali, 37.

63   "ETO X-2 Branch Progress Report, 1–15 February 1945" (RG 226, New York, London, and Paris Field Station Files, boxes 1–10); Naftali, 39.

64   "ETO X-2 Branch Progress Report, 1–15 December 1944" (RG 226, New York, London, and Paris Field Station Files, boxes 1–10).

65   Wynne, 16.

66   Winks, 302.

67   Cutler, 21.

68   "ETO X-2 Branch Progress Report, 1–15 November 1944" (RG 226, New York, London, and Paris Field Station Files, boxes 1–10).

69   Cutler, 37–38.

70   ETO X-2 Branch Progress Reports, November 1–15 and 16–30, 1944, February 1–15, 1945 (sabotage museum) (RG 226, New York, London, and Paris Field Station Files, boxes 1–10).

71   ALIU mission qtd. in Rothfeld; on ALIU see also Hussey et al.

72   On ALIU activities, see John Philips and Charles Sawyer's report on the Art Project sent to NHP on January 4, 1945 (RG 226, Entry NM 54-76, Correspondence of the Biographical Records Division, container 1); the ETO X-2 Branch Progress Reports, December 1–15 and February 16–28, 1945 (RG 226, New York, London, and Paris Field Station Files, boxes 1–10); Naftali, 39; and Salter, 306–512.

73   Susan Bennett to NHP, February 1, 1945 (NHP).

74   Susan Addiss, interview with the author, September 2021.

75   NHP to mother, May 14, 1945 (NHP).

76   NHP to WCW, January 9, 1946 (WCW Beinecke).

77   Winks, 303.

78   NHP to mother, November 12, 1945 (NHP).

79   NHP to WCW, January 9, 1946 (WCW Beinecke).

80   Winks, 306.

81   Bryher to NHP, May 20, August 5, 1944 (NHP).

82   In a September 1944 letter, qtd. in Winks, 278.

CHAPTER SEVEN

1   NHP to Bryher, January 9, 1946 (Bryher papers).

2   Naftali, 42.

3   Qtd. in Naftali, 43.

4   Holzman. *Spies and Traitors*, 112, 114.

5   Holzman, "Ideological Origins," 77.

6   Alfred Pearson to NHP, January 1, 1944 (NHP).

7   Oxford University Press to NHP, February 4, 1943 (NHP).

8   Alan Valentine (president of University of Rochester) to William DeVane, May 28 and June 14, 1946 (Yale University Manuscripts and Archives, Office of the President records).

9 William DeVane to Alan Valentine, June 11, 1946 (Yale University Manuscripts and Archives, Office of the President records).

10 NHP to H.D., January 23, 1946 (H.D.).

11 Bryher to NHP, March 7, 1946 (NHP).

12 McCabe, 256; Hollenberg, *Winged*, 213.

13 Bryher to NHP, March 7, 1946 (NHP); McCabe, 259–68; Hollenberg, *Winged*, 215–20.

14 Bryher to NHP, December 6, 1946 (NHP).

15 Bryher to NHP, May 1, 1946 (NHP).

16 NHP to mother, August 17 and September 1, 1946 (NHP).

17 Kelley, 410.

18 "Contemporary English Literature," covering "Joyce, Woolf, Huxley, Yeats, Lawrence, Maugham, Shaw, Coward, and Auden." Like Pearson, Waith was a Yalie (BA 1935, MA at Cambridge, then PhD 1939 at Yale, after which he was appointed as an instructor). According to Winks (315), he served under Pearson in X-2 during the war, and when he returned he became assistant professor. Ironically for the first person to teach contemporary literature at Yale, Waith was a specialist in Elizabethan and Jacobean drama.

19 Gillette, *Class Divide*, 5.

20 Cleanth Brooks to NHP, November 24, 1946 (NHP).

21 NHP to Bryher, October 28, 1948 (Bryher papers).

22 Interview with Susan Addiss, Branford CT, September 3, 2021.

23 NHP to mother, April 19 and June 2, 1952; NHP to Ezra Pound (hereafter EP; will also be used for his papers, Beinecke Library, Yale University), January 15, 1957 (NHP).

24 NHP to Bryher, April 2, 1947 (Bryher papers).

25 Atlantic Monthly Press to NHP, October 29, 1947; NHP to Atlantic Monthly Press, October 31, 1947 (NHP).

26 Dixon Wecter to NHP, January 25, 1948 (NHP).

27 Susan Pearson to Fanny Pearson, July 19 and 26, 1948 (NHP).

CHAPTER EIGHT

1 The chapter epigraph, Pearson to Harry Meacham of the Academy of American Poets, is from a letter of June 5, 1962 (NHP).

2 C. Turner, esp. 173–214.

3 NHP, "American Poet" 118.

4 NHP, "Escape from Time," 60.

5 NHP, "Escape from Time," 67.

6 NHP, "American Poet," 123.

7 NHP, "American Poet," 117.

8 NHP, "American Poet," 120.

9 Pound, "Retrospect," 4.

10 NHP, "American Poet," 124.

11 Eliot, 64.

12 NHP, "American Poet," 126.

13 Pound, *Guide to Kulchur*, 194.

14 NHP, "Anderson and the New Puritanism," 59.

15 NHP, "American Poet," 126.

16 Benét and Pearson, 1660.

17 NHP, "American Poet," 119.

18 NHP to EP, August 9, 1937.

19 Stein, 246.

20 See Hillyer, "Poetry's" and Hillyer, "Treason's"; Fitts to NHP, June 21, 1949 (NHP).

21 HG to NHP, 1949 (NHP).

22 NHP to WCW, January 9, 1946 (WCW Beinecke).

23 Unsigned draft protest letter to *Saturday Review*; NHP to John Berryman, November 5, 1949 (both NHP).

24 Gallup, "Ezra Pound Archive," 162.

25 Dorothy Pound to NHP, March 21, 1949 (NHP).

26 NHP to H.D., December 20, 1950, December 22, 1952 (Hollenberg, *Between*, 134).

27 For the full story of the Square Dollar series, see Barnhisel, "Hitch."

28 NHP to H.D., November 11, 1951 (NHP).

29 John Kasper to NHP, August 2, 1952 (NHP).

30 NHP to EP, February 4, 1955 (EP).

31 NHP to H.D., November 11, 1951 (NHP).

32 NHP, "Square Dollar," 81.

33 John Kasper to EP, August 26, 1953 (EP).

34 The definitive account of Pound's relationship with Kasper is Marsh.

35 NHP to H.D., March 31, 1957 (Hollenberg, *Between*, 205).

36 EP to NHP, August 30, 1956 (NHP).

37 Moody, 382.

38 EP to NHP, 1957 (NHP).

39 NHP to H.D., March 10, 1957 (Hollenberg, *Between*, 203).

40 NHP to EP, September 1956 (EP).

41 NHP to EP, March 10, 1957 (EP).

42 NHP to EP, February 22, 1953 (EP).

43 NHP to EP, January 31, 1954 (EP).

44 NHP to H.D. March 30, 1958 (Hollenberg, *Between*, 213).

45 NHP to H.D., April 8, 1958 (Hollenberg, *Between*, 219).

46 NHP to Bryher, April 15, 1958, qtd. in Hollenberg, *Between*, 251.

47 NHP to EP, September 1956 (EP).

48 NHP to John Edwards, November 5, 1953 (Special Collections and University Archives, University of Tulsa Library, Jonathan Edwards Hamilton papers).

49 NHP to John Edwards, January 31, 1954 (Hamilton papers).

50 NHP to H.D., April 8, 1958 (Hollenberg, *Between*, 219).

51 Thomas K. Wolfe Jr., "An Annotation of Canto XLVII," 1952 (NYPL Astor, Tom Wolfe papers).

52 NHP to John Edwards, July 11, 1955; "abhors" from NHP, introduction to Edwards, 2; NHP to Richard Ellmann, March 30, 1953 (Special Collections and University Archives, University of Tulsa Library, Richard Ellmann papers).

53 NHP to EP, January 28 and March 24, 1955 (EP).

54 NHP to H.D., December 20, 1950 (Hollenberg, *Between*, 100).

55 NHP to John Edwards, April 12, 1951 (Hamilton papers).

56 EP to H.D., 1953, qtd. in Hollenberg, *Between*, 171.

57 "Resident divinity": Moody, 315; on Martinelli, see S. Moore *Beerspit*, S. Moore, "Sheri Martinelli."

58 Martinelli to NHP, June 28, 1958 (NHP).

59 NHP to Sheri Martinelli, August 14, 1960 (NHP).

60 NHP to H.D., May 10, 1958 (Hollenberg, *Between*, 225).

61 NHP to Martinelli, June 4 and 29, 1962 (Beinecke Library, Yale University, Sheri Martinelli papers); also see S. Moore, *Beerspit*, 2001.

62 H.D. to NHP, June 3 and 26, 1958 (Hollenberg, *Between*, 226, 227).

63 Robert MacGregor to NHP, January 17, 1956 (NHP).

64 EP to NHP, September 23, 1957 (NHP). "KikoRoose" was a Poundian portmanteau slur expressing his belief that Franklin Roosevelt and his administration were controlled by Jewish bankers.

65 NHP to H.D., May 4, 1958 (Hollenberg *Between*, 224).

66 NHP to H.D., July 8, 1958 (Hollenberg, *Between*, 229).

67 NHP to James Laughlin (hereafter JL), August 4, 1953 (Houghton Library, Harvard University, New Directions Publishing Company records, hereafter ND).

68 In Moody, 335.

69 NHP to Mary de Rachewiltz, October 20, 1957; December 11, 1961; November 21, 1962; Mary de Rachewiltz to NHP, January 2, 1962 (all NHP).

CHAPTER NINE

1 NHP to Elizabeth Mayer, 1938 (NHP).

2 NHP to HG, September 7, 1937 (HG).

3 WCW to NHP, November 13, 1937 (NHP).

4 WCW to NHP, January 10, 38; NHP to John Gould Fletcher, November 12, 1938 (both NHP).

5 NHP to WCW, November 7, 1940 (NHP).

6 WCW to NHP, October 3, 1938 (NHP).

7 NHP to WCW, November 7, 1940 (NHP).

8 NHP to WCW, November 7, 1940 (NHP).

9 See NHP, "People Who Use," 33.

10 Gallup, "William Carlos Williams Collection," 54.

11 Leibowitz, 414–15, 418.

12 JL to NHP, March 20, 1947 (NHP); NHP to JL, April 1, 1947 (ND). The actual list is in the "Subject Files: People: William Carlos Williams" file of the NHP.

13 For the full story of Pearson and Yale's purchase of the Williams papers, see Gallup, "William Carlos Williams Collection."

14 Mariani, 179. After consulting the actual postcard in the Poetry Collection, University at Buffalo Library, William Carlos Williams collection (consisting of those materials Craig Abbott obtained in the early 1950s before Pearson made the deal for the rest of the lot), Mariani notes that Williams didn't even read the initials correctly: they are actually "A.H." (see also Ahearn).

15 W. Williams, 177–78.

16 Bryher to HG, October 16, 1951 (HG).

17 NHP to Hannah Josephson of the American Academy (NHP).

18 Bryher, *Heart to Artemis*, 221–22.

19 NHP to JL, July 20, 1963 (ND).

20 Gallup, "William Carlos Williams Collection," 55.

21 NHP to Stanley Koehler, June 14, 1963 (NHP).

22 Helen McMaster to NHP, May 1, 1940 (NHP).

23 NHP to H.D., July 5, 1949 (H.D.).

24 Moore to John Warner Moore, October 6, 1940, in M. Moore, 402.

25 Marianne Moore to NHP, October 12, 1940 (NHP).

26 Leavell, 350–51.

27 Qtd. in Debo, "Norman Holmes Pearson," 453.

28 Moore to John Warner Moore, July 1, 1949, in M. Moore, 472.

29 NHP to Bryher, January 21, 1957 (Bryher papers).

30 NHP to EP, February 2, 1958 (EP).

31 "A Note on Poetry," in Benét and Pearson, 1325.

32 Benét and Pearson, 1666.

33 Stevens's talk, titled "Effects of Analogy," was later collected in *The Necessary Angel*. Richardson, 295.

34 NHP to Wallace Stevens, July 8, 1948 (Huntington Library, Wallace Stevens papers).

35 Stevens, "Imagination as Value," in *Necessary Angel*, 131–56; Stevens to Pearson, December 19, 1948, in H. Stevens, 627.

36 NHP to Stevens, May 31, 1951 (Stevens papers).

37 NHP to Stevens, October 12, 1950 (Stevens papers).

38 NHP, "Wallace Stevens and 'Old Higgs,'" 35–36.

39 NHP to Stevens, May 17, 1950 (NHP).

40 NHP to Stevens, February 7, 1951 (Stevens papers).

41 Stevens died before Lee's book, *Anthology of Korean Poetry*, came out in 1964.

42 NHP to H.D., January 9, 1954 (H.D.).

43 Stevens to NHP, December 22, 1954, in H. Stevens, 860.

44 Wallace Stevens to Peter Lee, December 10, 1954, in H. Stevens, 856.

45 NHP to Bryher, January 2, 1965 (Bryher papers).

46 NHP to H.D., August 11, 1955 (H.D.).

47 NHP to Bryher, August 6, 1955 (Bryher papers).

48 NHP to EP, January 15, 1957 (EP).

49 "Crocodiles" from NHP to Bryher, February 22, 1951 (Bryher papers); Carpenter, 358–59, 367.

50 Cowley to NHP, July 19, 1949 (NHP); NHP to EP, January 15, 1957 (NHP).

51 "Poets of the English Idiom."

52 Bogan, 127, 128.

53 MacNeice; "Revolution in Taste"; Humphries, 293.

54 NHP to Bryher, December 7, 1967 (Bryher papers); NHP to EP, January 15, 1957 (NHP).

55 Bryher to NHP, 1952, April 18, 1961; NHP to Richard Wilbur, August 5, 1961 (both NHP).

56 Patrick Gregory, email to the author, August 9, 2023.

57 NHP to Bryher, February 6, 1952 (Bryher papers).

58 NHP to John Gould Fletcher, February 5, 1938 (NHP).

59 NHP, journal entry on Rukeyser, September 16, 1940 (NHP, "Notebooks, Journals, and Notes").

60 NHP, "Among," 186.

61 NHP, "American Poet," 121.

62 NHP to Rukeyser, August 12, 1942 (NYPL Berg, Rukeyser papers).

63 NHP to Bryher, November 29 and December 4, 1961 (Bryher papers).

64 Ferris, 234.

65 M. Mitchell, 247.

66 Ferris, 235.

67 Brinnin, 38.

CHAPTER TEN

1   The chapter epigraph, Pearson to Bryher, is from a letter of November 6, 1969 (Bryher papers).

2   Guest, *Herself Defined*, 267.

3   From an unpublished introduction to William Carlos Williams prose pieces (Poetry Collection, University at Buffalo Library, Robert Duncan collection).

4   Hollenberg, *Between*, 2.

5   H.D. to NHP, February 5, 1938 (NHP).

6   Hollenberg, *Between*, 120; Hollenberg, *Winged Words*, 244–45.

7   Dembo, 436.

8   McCabe, 280.

9   Debo, *American H.D.*, 201.

10 Schaffner, "Keeper," 33.

11 NHP to Bryher, November 10, 1973 (Bryher papers).

12 As in, for instance, Bryher to NHP, September 1, 1950 (NHP).

13 Debo, *American H.D.*, 201.

14 Nadel; May; D. Johnson.

15 Debo, "Norman Holmes Pearson," 458.

16 NHP, "Bryher" biographical sketch (NHP, "Writings").

17 Dembo, 445.

18 Bryher to NHP, December 22, 1948 (NHP).

19 Guest, "Intimacy," 66.

20 NHP to Bryher, March 27, 1946 (Bryher papers).

21 NHP to H.D., August 31, 1944 (H.D.).

22 H.D. to NHP, August 8, 1948 (NHP, "H.D. publication materials").

23 H.D. to NHP, December 10, 1945 (NHP).

24 Dembo, 436.

25 NHP to H.D., August 28, 1946 (H.D.).

26 NHP to H.D., December 8, 1946 (H.D.).

27 NHP to Bryher, October 31, 1948 (Bryher papers).

28 NHP to Bryher, December 10, 1948 (Bryher papers); NHP to HG, February 4, 1949 (HG).

29 NHP to H.D., November 27, 1946 (H.D.).

30 Kurt Wolff to NHP, December 2, 1946 (NHP, "H.D. publication materials"). Pearson

had known the Wolffs, through Elizabeth Mayer, since their arrival in the United States in 1942.

31   NHP to HG, March 22, 1948 (HG).

32   H.D. to NHP, July 2, 1950 (NHP).

33   Hollenberg, *Between*, 98.

34   Aldington to NHP, November 20, 1956 (NHP).

35   Guest, *Herself Defined*, 319.

36   "Poet Hilda Doolittle."

37   Alfred A. Knopf to NHP, June 17, 1954 (NHP).

38   HG to NHP, December 8, 1956 (NHP).

39   NHP to HG, August 20, 1956 (HG); NHP to Barney Rosset, February 14, 1958; NHP to H.D., January 26, 1957 (both NHP, "H.D. publication materials"); Boughn, *H.D.*, 48–51.

40   Royalty statements, December 31, 1957, and June 30, 1958 (Special Collections Research Center, Syracuse University Library, Grove Press Records).

41   NHP to Van Wyck Brooks, July 22, 57 (Kislak Center for Special Collections, University of Pennsylvania, Van Wyck Brooks papers).

42   The poems are "The Moon in Your Hands" (*New Yorker*); "The Revelation" (*Nation*); sections 4, 5, and 37 of "Vale Ave" (*Poetry*); "Do You Remember?" (*Atlantic Monthly*); and "Sagesse" (*Evergreen Review*). The *New Yorker* contribution is not listed in Michael Boughn's bibliography.

43   NHP to Barney Rosset, February 14, 1958 (NHP, "H.D. publication materials").

44   NHP specified the $1,000 amount in a July 26, 1963, letter to Judith Schmidt of Grove (NHP).

45   Barney Rosset to NHP, February 17, 1958 (NHP, "HD publication materials")

46   Barney Rosset to NHP, July 30, 1963 (NHP, "H.D. publication materials").

47   NHP to Judith Schmidt of Grove Press, August 5, 1963 (Grove Press Records).

48   NHP to H.D., February 10, 1960 (NHP).

49   McCabe, 308.

50   H.D. to NHP, February 14, 1960 (NHP).

51   NHP to Bryher, April 23, 1960 (Bryher papers); to H.D., April 24, 1960 (H.D.).

52   NHP to Bryher, May 29, 1960 (Bryher papers).

53   McCabe, 308.

54   H.D. to NHP, September 23, 1952; NHP to H.D., September 26, 1952 (NHP).

55   NHP to H.D., September 17, 1953 (H.D.).

56   NHP to Barney Rosset, February 23, 1960 (NHP, "H.D. publication materials").

57   NHP to H.D., October 4, 1960 (NHP, "H.D. publication materials").

58   Eliot qtd. in Paige, 170; NHP to H.D., December 22, 1952 (H.D.).

59   NHP to Bryher, May 15, 1961 (Bryher papers). Also see John Schaffner to NHP, May 14, NHP to John Schaffner, May 17, 1961; Perdita Schaffner to NHP, May 22, 1961 (both NHP).

60   NHP to Bryher, October 16, 1961 (Bryher papers).

61   NHP to Bryher, January 2, 1965 (Bryher papers).

62   NHP to JL, October 11, 1971 (NHP, "H.D. publication materials").

63   NHP to Robert Duncan, August 7, 1960 (NHP).

64   Dembo, 442.

65   NHP to Bryher, January 2, 1965 (Bryher papers). The "pornography" Pearson refers to were several controversial titles that Rosset published, including D. H. Law-

rence's *Lady Chatterley's Lover*, William S. Burroughs's *Naked Lunch*, and Henry Miller's *Tropic of Cancer*.

66 For more on Grove, see Glass.

67 JL to NHP, November 19, 1971 (NHP, "H.D. publication materials").

68 Susan Stanford Friedman, email to the author, November 10, 2021.

69 NHP to Duncan, September 12, 1959 (Poetry Collection, University at Buffalo Library, Robert Duncan papers).

70 Jarnot, 193.

71 *The H.D. Book*, which neither Pearson nor Duncan lived to see actually published, became a strange and capacious project that Duncan described as "a tapestry or collage book; unfolding the story of my adventure and vocation in the art; and at the same time, interwoven, imagining what another generation will have to work at." Robert Duncan to NHP, September 12, 1960 (NHP). The University of California Press finally brought it out in 2011 to a limited but rapturous reception, such as that of Jed Perl, in the *New Republic*, who called it "the book that could save American art."

72 NHP, "Foreword," in *Hermetic Definition*, v–vi.

73 Michael Boughn, email to the author; Jarnot, 485n14; Boughn, "Olson's Buffalo."

74 Boughn, "Preliminary Bibliography."

75 JL to NHP, April 26, 1971 (NHP, "H.D. publication materials").

76 JL to NHP, June 22, 1972 (NHP).

77 Jarnot, 300.

78 NHP to JL, January 22, 1973 (NHP).

79 On Laughlin's publishing campaign for Pound, see Barnhisel, *James Laughlin*.

80 H.D. quote from NHP to James Laughlin, March 11, 1961 (NHP, "H.D. publication materials"). The *Nation* article in question was Rattray's "A Weekend with Ezra Pound."

81 JL to NHP, April 26, 1971 (NHP).

82 NHP to Bryher, April 23, 1967 (Bryher papers).

83 Harry Levin to NHP, June 23, 1949 (Houghton Library, Harvard University, Harry Levin papers).

84 Bryher Foundation balance sheet upon dissolution in 1952 (NHP).

85 NHP to Bryher, March 16, 1949 (Bryher papers).

86 NHP to Bryher, September 13, 1952 (Bryher papers). The payment was to be to Yale University Press, but in the end the foundation didn't spend that money as Yale declined to publish *Checklist*.

87 Binding reference in NHP to Bryher, November 3, 1953 (NHP). For gifts, see, for example, Max Rüegg of FIDES Union Financiaire to NHP, December 23, 1974 (NHP).

88 NHP to Bryher, February 6, 1952 (Bryher papers).

89 McCabe, 304.

90 Susan Addiss, interview with the author, September 21, 2021.

91 NHP to Bryher November 1953 ("fur"); August 4, 1972 ("erotic"); May 29, 1965 ("unmarried"); May 17, 1949 ("laughed") (all Bryher papers).

92 NHP to Bryher, January 26, 1953 (Bryher papers).

93 NHP to EP, September 14, 57 (NHP).

94 Sands, "Mrs. Bryher"; Sands, "At Last."

95 NHP to Bryher, June 28, 1962 (Bryher papers).

96 NHP to Bryher, April 23, 1967 (NHP).

97   Bryher to NHP, September 1, 1950, and September 1950 (NHP).
98   NHP to Bryher, January 9, 1950 (Bryher papers).
99   NHP to Bryher, February 23, 1951 (Bryher papers).
100 "Local News."
101 NHP to Bryher, June 4, 1968 (Bryher papers).
102 Bryher to NHP, May 3, 1970 (NHP).
103 Bryher to NHP, December 3, 1950 (NHP).
104 NHP to Bryher, March 31, 1949, February 6, 1952 (Bryher papers).
105 NHP to Bryher, July 13, 1960 (Bryher papers).
106 NHP to Bryher, October 21, 1973 (Bryher papers); Bryher to NHP, November 18, 1972 (NHP)
107 NHP to Bryher, September 3 and 9, 1975 (Bryher papers).

CHAPTER ELEVEN

1   Memo on recruiting, 1950 (NHP, "OSS materials").
2   Memo on recruiting, 1950 (NHP, "OSS materials").
3   Horowitz, *On the Cusp*, 137; Lemisch.
4   Kahrl, 3.
5   Hodgson.
6   Naftali, 44; Matthiessen background information is from the author's correspondence with Lance Richardson.
7   Memo on recruiting, 1950 (NHP, "OSS materials").
8   Luce, 168, 169, 165, 171, 165.
9   Lewontin, 13.
10   President's Commission on Higher Education, 94.
11   Stearns, vii.
12   Bourne.
13   Bourne, 504, 505, 507.
14   Shumway, 132.
15   He expressed this, among other places, in a talk he gave at the Archives of American Art (at the time based in Detroit, before it became part of the Smithsonian Institution) in May 1961. Also see his unpublished lecture "Changing Concepts of American Democracy" given in Seoul, September 1975 (NHP).
16   "Yale Reports 115," 3 (NHP).
17   Sapir, 6.
18   "Brought to the undertaking the concept of culture" is from Ralph Gabriel, "The Yale Program in American Studies," unpublished lecture, May 1953 (see correspondence in NHP, "American Studies 1946–75" folder). "In American Studies" is from an interview of Gabriel and Pearson by Bernard Mullins, "Yale Reports 115," 3 (NHP).
19   "Yale Reports 115," 3 (NHP).
20   Walker, *American Studies in the United States*, 158–59; Dorson, 1.
21   Gabriel, "Recommendation to the President" January 11, 1946 (Yale Manuscripts and Archives, Records of President Charles Seymour; also qtd. in Holzman, "Ideological Origins," 78).

22 Holzman, "Ideological Origins," 81.

23 Parmar, 100.

24 Kaplan, 21; "A Prospectus of the Yale School of American Studies for Foreign Students" (Yale Manuscripts and Archives, Records of President Charles Seymour, RG 2A15, series 1, box 15, folder 127).

25 Holzman, "Ideological Origins," 81.

26 Wallerstein, 208.

27 W. Johnson, 3.

28 Qtd. in Berman, 113.

29 Scott-Smith, 89.

30 Matsuda, 158; on Salzburg, see Blaustein, esp. 122–71.

31 NHP to mother, March 29, 1948 (NHP).

32 Matsuda; Ochi.

33 USIA, "Programs in American Studies" report, June 1962; State Department Office of International Education, "Programs in American Studies" report, June 1962; State Department Bureau of Educational and Cultural Affairs, "American Studies Abroad" report, May 1962 (all in Manuscript Division, Library of Congress, American Studies Association records, box 190).

34 Bateson material from RG 226, "Monthly Report OSS China Theater," Entry A1 147; Bundy, 2–3.

35 Ahlstrom, 512.

36 DeVane qtd. in Holzman, "Ideological Origins," 87.

37 William DeVane, "American Studies at Yale" (Yale Manuscripts and Archives, Records of President Charles Seymour, RG 2A15, series 1, box 15, folder 127).

38 Holzman, "Ideological Origins," 87.

39 Language from Seymour's 1950 public announcement of Coe's gift, qtd. in Holzman, "Ideological Origins," 87.

40 "Yale Reports 115" 4 (NHP).

41 From a 1955 letter from Potter to Coe's son, Yale University Manuscripts and Archives, Office of the President records, Presidency of A. Whitney Griswold.

42 Buckley, 103.

43 Qtd. in Oppermann, 61.

44 Schlesinger.

45 Kabaservice, 110.

46 NHP to HG, October 17, 1937 (NHP).

47 Rodgers, 197.

48 See Mann, the subject of which is an NYPL exhibition on the *New Yorker*, and within which is reproduced the original prospectus for the magazine.

49 NHP, "Hawthorne's Fiction," 14.

50 NHP "Anderson and the New Puritanism," 58.

51 Griffith, 400.

52 NHP, talks on "Cultural Aspects of the American Society," January 21, February 23, 1953 (NHP, "Writings" series).

53 NHP, talks on "Cultural Aspects of the American Society," January 21, February 23, 1953 (NHP, "Writings" series).

54 Alistair Cooke, transcript of "American Letter no. 310," recorded February 26, 1953 (NHP).

55 Griffith, 404.

56 C. J. La Roche to People's Capitalism steering committee members, February 26, 1957 (NHP).

57 "City's Greatest"; NHP to H.D. October 16, 1951 (H.D.).

58 Shinji Takuwa to NHP, August 8, 1963 (NHP); also see, for instance, an August 14, 1963, invitation from the US Educational Commission in Korea, or a May 27, 1968, State Department memo regarding an invitation to New Zealand (both NHP).

59 William Phipps, report on NHP's visit to Korea, December 9, 1963 (NHP).

60 NHP to H. F. Willcock, July 19, 1968 (NHP).

61 NHP "Nature and Possibilities," 2–3.

62 Neville Meaney, email to the author, February 20, 2018.

63 Elaine Barry, email to the author, June 21, 2018.

64 William Breen, interview with the author, Melbourne, August 12, 2019.

65 "Defining Moments."

66 NHP to Bryher, July 21 and 27, and August 5, 1970 (Bryher papers).

67 NHP to "Otis" at Kyoto Summer Seminar, May 13, 1970 (NHP, correspondence, "Kyoto miscellaneous," folder 4).

68 See Barnhisel, *Cold War Modernists*, for a further explanation of this argument; on the 1947 show, see Littleton and Sykes.

69 NHP to Lewis Jones of the State Department, March 12, 1969 (NHP).

70 NHP, notes for lecture "Three 'Bibles' for the Young" (NHP, Teaching Materials).

71 NHP, notes for lecture "Three 'Bibles' for the Young" (NHP, Teaching Materials).

72 C. E. Eisinger to NHP, November 3, 1970; NHP to Eisinger, November 16, 1970 (both NHP).

73 Sato, 35; Cho, 25.

74 Niall, 151.

75 Brenda Niall, interview with the author, August 17, 2019.

76 Niall, 151; Christopher Wallace-Crabbe, interview with the author, Melbourne, 2019; Elaine Barry, email to the author, September 2018.

77 Avril Winks, individual communication with the author, June 2022; William Goetzmann Jr., interview with the author, June 21, 2018.

78 Winks, in fact, actually denies that Pearson was even a talent spotter and reads the Jackson memo merely as guidance to potential spotters such as Tenney and Waith; but Winks also based his portrait of Pearson as much on his own friendship and conversations with Pearson as on the documents, and Pearson's practice was always to deny or deflect any particulars about his intelligence work, whether for OSS or CIA. I would go so far as to say that Winks, almost as savvy about Yale as Pearson himself was, not only knew that Pearson was talent spotting but probably could also name many of the young men he picked out.

Susan Pearson's travel diary from the 1970 trip, when they spent February to August abroad, also suggests that Norm was not working for the CIA at that point. Detailed almost down to the hour, her description of their activities and the people they met would leave little time for Norm to slip away to meet with CIA associates or foreign assets, unless many of the young scholars and university administrators and Fulbright program bureaucrats and State Department officials she names were themselves those associates and assets, which is certainly possible.

Predictably, my efforts to use the Freedom of Information Act to wrest information out of the CIA or FBI about Pearson's intelligence work resulted in only a "can neither confirm nor deny" form letter (in the case of CIA) or a flat, albeit quite implausible, denial that the Bureau has any information whatsoever on him, with the stipulation that it is required by law to deny holding any information on people with intelligence connections.

CHAPTER TWELVE

1   Boyer, A12.
2   NHP to Edward Barthelme of *Time*, October 30, 1957 (NHP).
3   Demeusey. The poet Richard Wilbur of Wesleyan University had recommended Pearson to the defense team as an expert witness.
4   NHP to Dorothy Bridgewater, May 26, 1958 (NHP).
5   It would exhaust the reader's patience to list the Yale graduates who occupied powerful and influential positions in government, business, education, and the nonprofit world in 1960. But just the few hundred graduates of the class of 1960s counted among them future pillars of the national-security establishment as Senator John Heinz, Defense Secretary Les Aspin, CIA director Porter Goss, and Director of National Intelligence John Negroponte (Horowitz, *On the Cusp*, 218).
6   Horowitz, *On the Cusp*, 181–93; Lemisch.
7   Countryman criticized McCarthyite persecution of suspected Communists and suspected that he was denied promotion at Yale because of it. See Schrecker, 92, 115.
8   "Theatrics," 2; NHP, letter to the editor of *Yale Daily News*, January 6, 1950 (NHP). Pearson also referenced another article he found offensive, a piece entitled "Ode to a Bigot" that had appeared in a campus publication called *Et Veritas* and was written by Buckley's brother Reid.
9   Epstein, 76.
10 See, for example, Morley.
11 NHP to Harry Levin, February 25, 1950 (Houghton Library, Harvard University, Harry Levin papers).
12 NHP to Bryher, June 16, 1949 (Bryher papers).
13 "Changing Concepts of American Democracy," unpublished lecture (NHP).
14 M. Mitchell, 250.
15 Kernan, 62.
16 NHP, journal entry, November 12, 1941 (NHP).
17 Richard Brodhead, email to the author, June 29, 2017. Like Pearson thirty years previously, Brodhead was a Yale undergrad, PhD, and faculty member.
18 Daniel Aaron to Robin Winks, July 11, 1985 (Houghton Library, Harvard University Daniel Aaron papers).
19 S. Donaldson, 75.
20 Harold Bloom, email to the author, May 28, 2019; Alan Trachtenberg, interview with the author, May 31, 2019.
21 Such reports included that of the Committee on Curricula in American Civilization and Robert Walker's 1957 *American Studies in the United States: A Survey of College Programs.* NHP, *American Writer and the Feeling for Community.*
22 NHP to Harry Hayden Clark, April 15, 1948 (NHP).
23 Wise, 306; NHP, "Anderson and the New Puritanism"; NHP, "American Poet"; NHP, "Hawthorne's Usable Truth."

24 Wise, 309.

25 Wise qtd. in Davis, 355–56.

26 NHP to Ed Sanders, May 10, 1963, August 2, 1964; Sanders, 1964 questionnaire about *Fuck You* (all Archives and Special Collections, University of Connecticut Library, Ed Sanders papers). Like Harvey Brown did with Williams and H.D., Sanders would later publish a pirated edition of Ezra Pound's last poems, earning him as well James Laughlin's fury.

27 Willard Lockwood of Wesleyan University Press to NHP, March 25, 1958; NHP to Bryher, November 18, 1970 (Bryher papers).

28 NHP, *Decade*, xxi; Hollander.

29 Bak, xxv.

30 Cowley to NHP, July 20, 1948 (NHP).

31 Kirbach, 40.

32 Zimmerman, 2.

33 Gallup, *Pigeons*, 132.

34 Zimmerman, 2.

35 S. Donaldson, 41; see also Richard Sewall, reminiscence of Pearson's class, 1948 (NHP). I am grateful to the late Mr. Donaldson for speaking with me about Pearson in St. Paul in 2017.

36 Richard B. Sewall, untitled "Theme" (1948) (NHP)

37 Ault, 27.

38 Bronwell Ault to NHP, July 5, 1948; see also Joseph Fincke to NHP, June 4, 1970 (both NHP).

39 Lemisch's title: "History at Yale in the Dark Ages."

40 David Potter, letter to Tom Wolfe, May 19, 1956; unsigned faculty evaluations of Wolfe's dissertation, May 14 and 17, 1956 (both NYPL Astor, Tom Wolfe papers, box 71); Horowitz, *Consuming Pleasures*, 275–77.

41 Doob et al.

42 Horowitz, *On the Cusp*, 65.

43 "Afro-American Cultural Center: History," Yale University, https://afam.yalecollege .yale.edu/about-house/history, accessed December 5, 2023; Kabaservice, 329.

44 Kabaservice, 328–29.

45 Ebiike, 3.

46 Interview with Sue Addiss, September 8, 2021; Sam Chauncey, email to the author, April 8, 2022; "Women Who Changed."

47 Transcript of *Yale Reports*, no. 514, "Thinking about Writing by Women," May 4, 1969.

48 Wise, 312.

49 Membership list in the newsletter *Radical American Studies* 1.1 (November 1969), 14–15 (Manuscript Division, Library of Congress, American Studies Association Records, box 42); memo to ASA Executive Council from Robert Sklar of Radical Caucus, November 3, 1969 (NHP, "American Studies" folder).

50 NHP to Grace Pearson, October 20, 1969 (NHP).

51 NHP to Bryher, February 21, 1967, March 18 and April 1, 1968 (Bryher papers).

52 Leach.

53 Zaretsky.

54 NHP to Bryher, August 2, 1967 (Bryher papers); O'Leary.

55 NHP to Robin Winks, November 26, 1969 (NHP).

56 NHP to Jean Joubert, January 27, 1969 (NHP).
57 Yale University Libraries; Kabaservice, 403–12.
58 Wilda Hamerman to NHP, April 29, 1970 (NHP).
59 Forrey to NHP, December 20, 1974 (Yale University Manuscripts and Archives, Bicentennial Committee for International Conferences of Americanists records).
60 Albert Ball of Department of State to NHP, April 24 and May 28, 1975; US-Japan Conference on Cultural and Educational Interchange (CULCON), "Who We Are," https://culcon.jusfc.gov/about-us/, accessed December 5, 2023.
61 NHP, "Changing Concepts of American Democracy," unpublished lecture (NHP, "Research and Teaching Files").

CONCLUSION

1 "Norman H. Pearson," 40.
2 NHP to Bryher, October 16, 1961 (NHP). Pearson was, though, a full professor when he wrote this.
3 Melissa Barton, email to the author, June 6, 2022.
4 Gallup, *What Mad Pursuits!*, 211.
5 NHP, "Double Sense," 9.

BIBLIOGRAPHY

ARCHIVAL COLLECTIONS

Archives and Manuscripts Division, New York Public Library, Astor, Lenox, and Tilden Foundations (NYPL Astor)
Gotham Book Mart
Tom Wolfe
Archives and Special Collections, University of Connecticut Library
Charles Olson
Ed Sanders
Archives and Special Collections, University of Melbourne Library
Norman Denholm Harper
Beinecke Library, Yale University
William Rose Benét
Bryher
Henry Seidel Canby
Wilda Hamerman
H.D.
Sheri Martinelli
F. O. Matthiessen
Elizabeth Mayer
Eugene O'Neill Jr.
Norman Holmes Pearson
Ezra Pound
Olga Rudge
Gertrude Stein
William Carlos Williams (WCW Beinecke)
Kurt and Helen Wolff
Gardner (Massachusetts) Museum
Goodnow Pearson

Harry Ransom Humanities Research Center, University of Texas at Austin

John Gould Fletcher

Alfred A. Knopf Photographs

Edith Sitwell

Eric White

Houghton Library, Harvard University

Daniel Aaron

Harry Levin

New Directions Publishing Company

Huntington Library, San Marino, California

Wallace Stevens

Kislak Center for Special Collections, University of Pennsylvania

Van Wyck Brooks

Theodore Dreiser

Louis Mumford

Levi Heywood Memorial Library, Gardner, Massachusetts

Local History Collection

Manuscript Division, Library of Congress, Washington, DC

American Studies Association

Archibald MacLeish

Muriel Rukeyser

National Archives of Australia

Australian Association for Cultural Freedom Files

Fulbright Program Records

Norman Denholm Harper

National Library of Australia

Alec Derwent Hope

Newberry Library, Chicago

Sherwood Anderson

Malcolm Cowley

Morton Dauwen Zabel

New York Public Library, Berg Collection (NYPL Berg)

W. H. Auden

James Joyce Society

Muriel Rukeyser

William Carlos Williams

Philips Academy Archives (Andover, MA)

Poetry Collection, University at Buffalo Library

Contemporary Manuscripts

Robert Duncan

William Carlos Williams

Rubenstein Library, Duke University
   American Literature (journal)
   Arlin Turner
Special Collections and University Archives, University of Tulsa Library
   Richard Ellmann
   Jonathan Edwards Hamilton
Special Collections Research Center, Syracuse University Library
   Horace Gregory
   Grove Press Records
Special Collections, University of California at Davis Library
   Gary Snyder
Special Collections, University of Maryland Library
   Djuna Barnes
   T. S. Eliot
   Katherine Ann Porter
United States National Archives II at College Park, Maryland
   Office of Strategic Services (RG 226)
Yale University Manuscripts and Archives
   American Studies Program
   Bicentennial Committee for International Conferences of Americanists
   Donaldson Family
   Donald Downes
   Elizabethan Club
   Ralph Gabriel
   Wallace Notestein
   Office of the President
   Office of the Provost
   Pundits Collection
   Records of President Charles Seymour
   Stanley T. Williams
   Yale in World War II Collection

UNSIGNED WORKS

American Studies Association. "Carl Bode–Norman Holmes Pearson Prize."
   https://www.theasa.net/awards/asa-awards-prizes/carl-bode-norman-holmes
   -pearson-prize. Accessed August 22, 2022.
"Bennett Quits Board of Winchester Arms." *New York Times*, May 15, 1926, 33.
Central Intelligence Agency. "Julia Child: Cooking Up Spy Ops for OSS." March 30,
   2020. https://www.cia.gov/stories/story/julia-child-cooking-up-spy-ops-for-oss/.

———. "The Office of Strategic Services: America's First Intelligence Agency."
https://www.cia.gov/static/7851e16f9e100b6f9cc4ef002028ce2f/Office-of
-Strategic-Services.pdf. Accessed December 3, 2023.

"City's Greatest Columbus Day Observance Closes with Dinner." *New Haven Evening Register*, October 13, 1951.

"Defining Moments: Vietnam Moratoriums." National Library of Australia.
https://www.nma.gov.au/defining-moments/resources/vietnam-moratoriums.
Accessed April 9, 2020.

"Eugene O'Neill Jr. Is Found a Suicide." *New York Times*, September 26, 1950, 21.

"Eugene O'Neill Jr. Marries at Yale." *New York Times*, May 26, 1937, 29.

"Eugene O'Neill's Son Is Married Secretly." *New York Times*, June 27, 1931, 24.

"The Father of the Modern Firearms Business." Winchester Repeating Arms
Company. June 1, 2016. https://www.winchesterguns.com/news/articles/happy
-fathers-day-oliver-winchestesr.html. Accessed December 3, 2023.

History of Orleans County Vermont: Civil, Ecclesiastical, Economic, Military. White
River, VT: White River Paper, 1882.

History Project, Strategic Services Unit, Dept. of War. *War Report of the OSS.* New
York: Walker, 1976.

"How Did You Choose Your Academic Field?" *Yale Alumni Magazine*, October
1973, 13.

"J. P. Morgan Buys Rare Manuscripts." *New York Times*, October 27, 1909, 1.

"Local News." *Gardner News*, April 11, 1914.

Massachusetts Municipal Management Association. "Form of Government."
http://www.massmanagers.org/home/pages/form-of-government. Accessed
October 10, 2016.

"Mayors of Gardner." City of Gardner, MA. http://www.gardner-ma.gov/428
/Mayors-of-Gardner. Accessed October 7, 2016.

"Norman H. Pearson, an English Scholar." Obituary. *New York Times*, November 7,
1975, 40.

"Obituary Notice, Arthur William Wright." *Monthly Notices of the Royal Astronomical Society* 77 (February 1917): 309.

"Poet Hilda Doolittle, on Yale Visit, Assails Imagist Label Used to Describe Her
Work." *New Haven Register*, September 16, 1956, 10.

"Poets of the English Idiom." *Houston Post*, October 1, 1950.

President's Commission on Higher Education. *Higher Education for American
Democracy.* New York: Harper and Brothers, 1947.

Proceedings of the New Hampshire Medical Society at Its Eighty-Ninth Annual Meeting. Concord, NH: Evans, Sleeper, and Evans, 1879.

"The Revolution in Taste since 1880." *Sunday Times* (London), August 31, 1952.

"Theatrics." Unsigned editorial by William F. Buckley Jr. *Yale Daily News*, January 4, 1950, 2.

Twelve Southerners. *I'll Take My Stand: The South and the Agrarian Tradition.* New York: Harper and Brothers, 1930.

"The Women Who Changed Yale College: Sam Chauncey Interview." *Yale Alumni Magazine*, September/October 2019. https://yalealumnimagazine.com/articles/4959-the-women-who-changed-yale-college-sam-chauncey-interview.

Yale Graduate School of Arts and Sciences. "Mission and History." Yale University. https://gsas.yale.edu/about/mission-history. Accessed December 3, 2023.

Yale University Libraries. "Bulldog and Panther: The 1970 May Day Rally and Yale." Online exhibit. https://onlineexhibits.library.yale.edu/s/black-panther-may-day/page/home. Accessed December 3, 2023.

SIGNED WORKS

Ahearn, Barry. "Williams and H.D., or Sour Grapes." *Twentieth-Century Literature* 35.3 (Autumn 1989): 299–309.

Ahlstrom, Sydney E. "Studying America and American Studies at Yale." *American Quarterly* 22.2 (Summer 1970): 503–17.

Allen, Donald, ed. *The New American Poetry 1945–1960.* New York: Grove, 1960.

Auden, W. H., and Norman Holmes Pearson, eds. *Poets of the English Language.* 5 vols. New York: Viking, 1950.

Ault, J. Burchenal. "An Aura of Mystery, Knowledge, Existence, and Spirit." *Pembroke Magazine* 8 (1976): 27–28.

Bak, Hans, ed. *The Long Voyage: Selected Letters of Malcolm Cowley 1915–1987.* Cambridge, MA: Harvard University Press, 2014.

Baltzell, E. Digby. *The Protestant Establishment: Aristocracy and Caste in America.* New York: Random House, 1964.

———. *Puritan Boston and Quaker Philadelphia.* Boston: Beacon, 1982.

Barnhisel, Greg. *Cold War Modernists: Art, Literature, and American Cultural Diplomacy.* New York: Columbia University Press, 2015.

———. "'Hitch Your Wagon to a Star': The Square Dollar Series and Ezra Pound." *Papers of the Bibliographical Society of America* 92.3 (September 1998): 273–96.

———. *James Laughlin, New Directions, and the Remaking of Ezra Pound.* Amherst: University of Massachusetts Press, 2005.

Becker, May Lamberton. "Book Letter Contest." *Wellspring*, January 30, 1927, 1.

———. "Now the Results of the Book Letter Contest!" *Wellspring*, June 12, 1927, 8.

Benét, William Rose, and Norman Holmes Pearson, eds. *The Oxford Anthology of American Literature.* New York: Oxford University Press, 1938.

Berman, Edward. *The Influence of the Ford, Carnegie, and Rockefeller Foundations on American Foreign Policy: The Ideology of Philanthropy.* Albany: State University of New York Press, 1983.

Black, Stephen A. *Eugene O'Neill: Beyond Mourning and Tragedy*. New Haven, CT: Yale University Press, 1999.

Blackwood, James R. *Howard Lowry: A Life in Education*. Wooster, OH: College of Wooster, 1975.

Blaustein, George. *Nightmare Envy and Other Stories: American Culture and European Reconstruction*. New York: Oxford University Press, 2018.

Blodgett, George Brainard, and Amos Everett Jewett. *Early Settlers of Rowley, Massachusetts*. Rev. ed. Rowley, MA, 1933.

Bogan, Louise. Review of *Poets of the English Language*. *New Yorker*, March 17, 1951, 126–28.

Boughn, Michael. *H.D.: A Bibliography 1905–1990*. Charlottesville: University of Virginia Press, 1993.

———. "Olson's Buffalo." In *The World in Time and Space: Towards a History of Innovative American Poetry in Our Time*, edited by Edward Foster and Joseph Donahue, 34–48. Jersey City, NJ: Talisman House, 2002.

———. "A Preliminary Bibliography of the Publications of Frontier Press." http://individual.utoronto.ca/amlit/a_preliminary_bibliography_of_th.htm. Accessed December 4, 2023.

Bourne, Randolph. "Our Cultural Humility." *Atlantic Monthly*, October 1914, 503–7.

Bowen, Croswell. *The Curse of the Misbegotten: A Tale of the House of O'Neill*. New York: McGraw-Hill, 1959.

Boyer, Willis. "Academia and the Old Blue." *Yale Daily News*, May 12, 1960, A12.

Braestrup, Peter. "Pearson: Teacher by Choice." *Yale Daily News*, March 8, 1950, 4–5.

Brand, Richard A. "Biographical Sketch: William Russell MacAusland MD, 1882–1965." *Clinical Orthopedics and Related Research* 469.1 (January 2011): 3–4.

Brewster, Kingman. "Admission to Yale: Objectives and Myths." *Yale Alumni Magazine*, October 30, 1966.

Brinnin, John. *Dylan Thomas in America: An Intimate Journal*. Boston: Little, Brown, 1955.

Bryher. *The Days of Mars: A Memoir 1940–1946*. New York: Harcourt Brace Jovanovich, 1972.

———. *The Heart to Artemis*. London: Collins, 1963.

Buckley, William F., Jr. *God and Man at Yale: The Superstitions of "Academic Freedom."* Chicago: Henry Regnery, 1951.

Bundy, McGeorge. "The Battlefields of Power and the Searchlights of the Academy." In *Dimensions of Diplomacy*, edited by Edgar Augustus Jerome Johnson, 1–15. Baltimore: Johns Hopkins University Press, 1964.

Canby, Henry Seidel. *Alma Mater: The Gothic Age of the American College*. New York: Farrar and Rinehart, 1936.

Caplow, Theodore, and Reece J. McGee. *The Academic Marketplace*. New York: Basic Books, 1958.

Carpenter, Humphrey. *W. H. Auden: A Biography*. Boston: Houghton Mifflin, 1981.

Cho, Sungkyu. "My Professor Norman Holmes Pearson." *Pembroke Magazine* 8 (1976): 21–26.

Coursey, O. W. *Biography of Senator Alfred Beard Kittredge*. Mitchell, SD: Educator Supply, 1915.

Cowley, Malcolm. *Exile's Return: A Literary Odyssey of the 1920s*. New York: W. W. Norton, 1934.

Crane, Ellery Bicknell, ed. *History of Worcester County, Massachusetts*. New York: Lewis Historical, 1924.

Csicsila, Joseph. *Canons by Consensus: Critical Trends and American Literature Anthologies*. Tuscaloosa: University of Alabama Press, 2004.

Currier, John J. *History of Newbury, Mass. 1635–1902*. Boston: Damrell and Upham, 1902.

Cutler, Richard. *Counterspy: Memoirs of a Counterintelligence Officer in World War II and the Cold War*. Washington, DC: Brassey's, 2004.

Cutter, William Richard. *Genealogical and Personal Memoirs Relating to the Families of Boston and Eastern Massachusetts*. New York: Lewis Historical, 1908.

Dahl, Robert A. *Who Governs? Democracy and Power in an American City*. New Haven, CT: Yale University Press, 1961.

Davis, Allen F. "The Politics of American Studies." *American Quarterly* 42.3 (September 1990): 353–74.

Debo, Annette. *The American H.D.* Iowa City: University of Iowa Press, 2012.

———. "Norman Holmes Pearson: Canon-Maker." *Modernism/modernity* 23.2 (April 2016): 443–62.

Dembo, L. S. "Norman Holmes Pearson on H.D.: An Interview." *Contemporary Literature* 10.4 (Autumn 1969): 435–46.

Demeusey, Gerald. "Yale Professor Defends 'Tropic of Cancer.'" *Hartford Courant*, February 17, 1962.

Diamond, Sigmund. *Compromised Campus: The Collaboration of Universities with the Intelligence Community, 1945–1955*. New York: Oxford University Press, 1992.

Donald, David Herbert. *Look Homeward: A Life of Thomas Wolfe*. New York: Little, Brown, 1987.

Donaldson, Frances. *Edward VII: A Biography of the Duke of Windsor*. Philadelphia: Lippincott, 1974.

Donaldson, Scott. *Death of a Rebel: The Charlie Fenton Story*. Madison, NJ: Farleigh Dickinson University Press, 2012.

Doob, Leonard, et al. "Report of the President's Committee on the Freshman

Year." Yale University. April 13, 1962. https://www.yale.edu/sites/default/files
/files/freshman_year.pdf.

Dorson, Richard M. *The Birth of American Studies*. Bloomington: Indiana University Press, 1976.

Duncan, Robert. *The H.D. Book*. Berkeley: University of California Press, 2011.

Ebiike, Shunji. "An Interview with Prof. Norman Holmes Pearson." *Study of English* (Japanese magazine), April 1964, 2–6.

Edsel, Robert. *The Monuments Men: Allied Heroes, Nazi Thieves, and the Greatest Treasure Hunt in History*. New York: Center Street, 2009.

Edwards, John. *A Preliminary Checklist to the Writings of Ezra Pound*. New Haven, CT: Kirgo Books, 1953.

Eliot. T. S. "The Metaphysical Poets." In *Selected Prose of T. S. Eliot*, edited by Frank Kermode, 59–67. New York: Farrar, Straus and Giroux, 1975.

English, James. *The Economy of Prestige: Prizes, Awards, and the Circulation of Cultural Value*. Cambridge, MA: Harvard University Press, 2008.

Epstein, William H. "Counter-intelligence: Cold War Criticism and Eighteenth-Century Studies." *ELH* 57.1 (Spring 1990): 63–99.

Ferris, Paul. *Dylan Thomas*. New York: Dial, 1977.

Fitzgerald, F. Scott. *This Side of Paradise*. 1920. Edited by James L. W. West III. New York: Cambridge University Press, 1995.

Fry, Philip. "A Very Brief History of the Yale English Department." September 2019. Yale English Department. https://english.yale.edu/about/history-department.

Gabriel, Ralph H. *The Course of American Democratic Thought*. New York: Ronald, 1940.

Gailey, Amanda. *Proofs of Genius: Collected Editions from the American Revolution to the Digital Age*. Ann Arbor: University of Michigan Press, 2015.

Gallup, Donald C. "The Collection of American Literature." *Yale University Library Gazette* 48.4 (April 1974): 241–52.

———. "The Ezra Pound Archive at Yale." *Yale University Library Gazette* 60.3/4 (April 1986): 161–77.

———. "The Gertrude Stein Collection." *Yale University Library Gazette* 22.2 (October 1947): 21–32.

———. *Pigeons on the Granite: Memories of a Yale Librarian*. New Haven, CT: Beinecke Library, 1988.

———. *What Mad Pursuits! More Memories of a Yale Librarian*. New Haven, CT: Beinecke Rare Book and Manuscript Library, 1998.

———. "The William Carlos Williams Collection at Yale." *Yale University Library Gazette* 56.1/2 (October 1981): 50–59.

Gates, Henry Louis. *Loose Canons: Notes on the Culture Wars*. New York: Oxford University Press, 1992.

Geiger, Roger. *The History of American Higher Education: Learning and Culture from the Founding to World War II*. Princeton, NJ: Princeton University Press, 2015.

Gelb, Arthur, and Barbara Gelb. *By Women Possessed: A Life of Eugene O'Neill*. New York: Putnam, 2016.

Gillette, Howard, Jr. *Class Divide: Yale '64 and the Conflicted Legacy of the Sixties*. Ithaca, NY: Cornell University Press, 2015.

Gitlin, Jay, and Basie Gitlin. *Mory's: A Brief History*. New Haven, CT: Mory's Preservation, 2014.

Glass, Loren. *Counterculture Colophon: Grove Press, the "Evergreen Review," and the Incorporation of the Avant-Garde*. Stanford, CA: Stanford University Press, 2013.

Graff, Gerald, *Professing Literature: An Institutional History*. Chicago: University of Chicago Press, 1987.

Greene, Graham. "Security in Room 51." *Sunday Times* (London), July 14, 1963.

Griffith, Robert. "The Selling of America: The Advertising Council and American Politics, 1942–1960." *Business History Review* 57.3 (Autumn 1983): 388–412.

Gross, Robert "Building a National Literature: The United States 1800–1890." In *A Companion to the History of the Book*, edited by Simon Eliot and Jonathan Rose, 315–28. Oxford: Blackwell, 2007.

Guest, Barbara. *Herself Defined: The Poet H.D. and Her World*. Garden City, NY: Doubleday, 1984.

———. "The Intimacy of Biography." *Iowa Review* 16.3 (1986): 58–71.

Halberstam, David. *The Best and the Brightest*. New York: Random House, 1972.

Hammer, Langdon. "Shadows Walking: With Wallace Stevens in New Haven." *Los Angeles Review of Books*, July 3, 2021. https://lareviewofbooks.org/article/shadows-walking-with-wallace-stevens-in-new-haven/.

Hardy, Michael. "A Brief History of the English Institute." Yale University. https://englishinstitute.yale.edu/about-institute.

Hawthorne, Nathaniel. *The Centenary Edition of the Works of Nathaniel Hawthorne*. Vols. 15–18. Edited by Thomas Woodson and Norman Holmes Pearson. Columbus: Ohio State University Press, 1987.

H.D. "Do You Remember?" *Atlantic Monthly*, April 1958, 42.

———. *End to Torment: A Memoir of Ezra Pound*. New York: New Directions, 1979.

———. *Helen in Egypt*. New York: Grove, 1961.

———. "The Moon in Your Hands." *New Yorker*, July 20, 1957, 29.

———. "The Revelation." *Nation*, August 31, 1957, 94.

———. "Sagesse." *Evergreen Review*, Summer 1958, 27–36.

———. "Vale Ave," sections 4, 5, and 37. *Poetry*, December 1957, 149–51.

Heim, Stefania. "'Another Form of Life': Muriel Rukeyser, Willard Gibbs, and Analogy." *Journal of Narrative Theory* 43.3 (Fall 2013): 357–83.

Henshaw, Thomas, ed. *The History of Winchester Firearms, 1866–1992*. 6th ed. Clifton, NJ: New Win, 1993.

Herbst, Jurgen. "The Yale Report of 1828." *International Journal of the Classical Tradition* 11.2 (Fall 2004): 213–31.

Hicks, Granville. "Review and Comment." *New Masses*, September 28, 1937, 22–23.

Hillyer, Robert. "Poetry's New Priesthood." *Saturday Review of Literature*, June 18, 1949, 7–9, 38.

———. "Treason's Strange Fruit: The Case of Ezra Pound and the Bollingen Award." *Saturday Review of Literature*, June 11, 1949, 9–11, 28.

Hodgson, Gregory. "Yale: A Great Nursery of Spooks." *New York Times*, August 16, 1987. https://www.nytimes.com/1987/08/16/books/yale-a-great-nursery-of -spooks.html.

Hollander, John. *Reflections on Espionage*. New York: Atheneum, 1976.

Hollenberg, Donna Krolik. *Between History and Poetry: The Letters of H.D. and Norman Holmes Pearson*. Iowa City: University of Iowa Press, 1997.

———. *Winged Words: The Life and Work of the Poet H.D.* Ann Arbor: University of Michigan Press, 2022.

Holzman, Michael. "The Ideological Origins of American Studies at Yale." *American Studies* 40.2 (Summer 1999): 71–99.

———. *Spies and Traitors: James Angleton, Kim Philby, and the Friendship and Betrayal That Would Shape MI6, the CIA, and the Cold War*. New York: Pegasus, 2021.

Horn, Jonathan. "Yale: An Arsenal of Democracy in World War II." *Yale Daily News*, February 21, 2001. https://yaledailynews.com/blog/2001/02/21/yale-an -arsenal-of-democracy-in-world-war-ii/.

Horowitz, Daniel. *Consuming Pleasures: Intellectuals and Popular Culture in the Postwar World*. Philadelphia: University of Pennsylvania Press, 2012.

———. *On the Cusp: The Yale College Class of 1960 and a World on the Verge of Change*. Amherst: University of Massachusetts Press, 2015.

Hotchkiss, Fanny Winchester. *Winchester Notes*. New Haven, CT: Tuttle, Morehouse, and Taylor, 1912.

Humphries, Rolfe. "Verse Chronicle." *Nation*, September 20, 1950, 292–93.

Hussey, Michael, Michael J. Kurtz, and Greg Bradsher. "Art Looting Investigative Unit Reports." National Archives and Records Administration. https://www .archives.gov/research/holocaust/art/oss-art-looting-investigation-unit-reports .html. Accessed December 4, 2023.

Jackson, Russell Leigh. "The Pearsons and Their Mills." *Historical Collections of the Essex Institute* 66.4 (October 1925): 345–60.

Jarnot, Lisa. *Robert Duncan: The Ambassador from Venus*. Berkeley: University of California Press, 2012.

Jeffrey, William H. *Successful Vermonters: A Modern Gazetteer of Caledonia, Essex, and Orleans Counties*. East Burke, VT: Historical, 1904.

Jewett, Willard. *Rowley Revisited: An Updated History from the Early 1800s to the Present*. Rowley, MA: Rowley, 1989.

Johnson, David K. *The Lavender Scare: The Cold War Persecution of Gays and Lesbians in the Federal Government*. Chicago: University of Chicago Press, 2004.

Johnson, Edward. *A History of New-England: From the English Planting in the Year 1628; To the Year 1652*. London: Printed for N. Brooke, 1654. Beinecke Library call number Ch6 29.

Johnson, Owen. *Stover at Yale*. 1912. With new introduction by Kingman Brewster. New York: Macmillan, 1968.

Johnson, Walter. "A Special Report on American Studies Abroad." Congressional report. 88th Congress, 1st session. July 11, 1963.

Jones, Howard Mumford. "American Scholarship and American Literature." *American Literature* 8.2 (May 1936): 115–24.

Kabaservice, Geoffrey. *The Guardians: Kingman Brewster, His Circle, and the Rise of the Liberal Establishment*. New York: Henry Holt, 2004.

Kahrl, William L. "'Yet Time and Change Shall Naught Prevail / To Break the Friendships Formed at Yale.'" *New Journal* 2.6 (February 9, 1969): 3–7.

Kaplan, Fred. *The Wizards of Armageddon*. New York: Simon and Schuster, 1983.

Karabell, Jerome. *The Chosen: The Hidden History of Admission and Exclusion at Harvard, Yale, and Princeton*. Boston: Houghton Mifflin, 2005.

Katz, Barry. *Foreign Intelligence: Research and Analysis in the Office of Strategic Services 1942–45*. Cambridge, MA: Harvard University Press, 1989.

Kelley, Brooks Mather. *Yale: A History*. New Haven, CT: Yale University Press, 1974.

Kernan, Alvin. *In Plato's Cave*. New Haven, CT: Yale University Press, 1999.

Kirbach, Benjamin. "Institutional Itinerancy: Malcolm Cowley and the Domestication of Cosmopolitanism." In *After the Program Era: The Past, Present, and Future of Creative Writing in the University*, edited by Loren Glass, 39–52. Iowa City: University of Iowa Press, 2016.

Kirchik, James. *Secret City: The Hidden History of Gay Washington*. New York: Henry Holt, 2022.

Kirk, Rudolf. "The English Institute." *College English* 2.6 (March 1941): 558–68.

Kittredge, Mabel Thorndike Hodges. *The Kittredge Family in America*. Rutland, VT: Tuttle, 1936.

Leach, Gene. "Yale: Trimming the Ivy." *Connections*, Fall 1971.

Leavell, Linda. *Holding On Upside Down: The Life and Work of Marianne Moore*. New York: Farrar, Straus and Giroux, 2013.

Lee, Peter H. *Anthology of Korean Poetry*. New York: John Day, 1964.

Leibowitz, Herbert. *"Something Urgent I Have to Say to You": The Life and Works of William Carlos Williams*. New York: Farrar, Straus and Giroux, 2011.

Lemann, Nicholas. *The Big Test: The Secret History of the American Meritocracy.* New York: Farrar, Straus and Giroux, 2000.

Lemisch, Jesse. "History at Yale in the Dark Ages, 1953–1976." History News Network, 2006. https://historynewsnetwork.org/article/33300.

Lepore, Jill. *Joe Gould's Teeth.* New York: Knopf, 2016.

Lever, Jane, and Pepper Schwarz. *Women at Yale: Liberating a College Campus.* Indianapolis: Bobbs-Merrill, 1971.

Lewontin, Richard. "The Cold War and the Transformation of the Academy." In *The Cold War and the University: Toward an Intellectual History of the Postwar Years,* edited by André Schiffrin, 1–34. New York: New Press, 1997.

Littleton, Taylor D., and Maltby Sykes. *Advancing American Art: Painting, Politics, and Cultural Confrontation at Mid-century.* 2nd ed. Tuscaloosa: University of Alabama Press, 1999.

Luce, Henry. "The American Century." *Life,* February 1941. Reprinted in *Diplomatic History* 23.2 (Spring 1999): 159–71.

MacDonald, Elizabeth. *Undercover Girl.* New York: Macmillan, 1947.

MacNeice, Louis. "A Poet's Choice." *Observer* (London), September 21, 1952.

MacPherson, Nelson. *American Intelligence in War-Time London: The Story of the OSS.* London: Frank Cass, 2003.

Malinowski, Bronislaw. *A Scientific Theory of Culture, and Other Essays.* Chapel Hill: University of North Carolina Press, 1944.

Mangold, Tom. *Cold Warrior: James Jesus Angleton, the CIA's Master Spy Hunter.* New York: Simon and Schuster, 1991.

Mann, Meredith. "'Not for the Old Lady in Dubuque': Read the Original Vision for *The New Yorker.*" *Gothamist,* September 7, 2021. https://gothamist.com/arts -entertainment/not-old-lady-dubuque-read-original-vision-new-yorker.

Mariani, Paul. *William Carlos Williams: A New World Naked.* New York: McGraw-Hill, 1981.

Marsh, Alec. *Ezra Pound and John Kasper: Saving the Republic.* London: Bloomsbury, 2015.

Masterman, John. *The Double-Cross System in the War of 1939–1945.* New Haven, CT: Yale University Press, 1972.

Matsuda, Takeshi. *Soft Power and Its Perils: US Cultural Policy in Early Postwar Japan and Permanent Dependency.* Washington, DC: Woodrow Wilson Center Press, 2007.

May, Elaine Tyler. *Homeward Bound: American Families in the Cold War Era.* New York: Basic Books, 1988.

Mayer, John C. Interviewed by Sandra Stewart Holyoak, August 11, 2005. Rutgers Oral History Archives. Rutgers University. http://oralhistory.rutgers.edu /interviewees/30-interview-html-text/401-mayer-john-c.

McCabe, Susan. *H.D. and Bryher: An Untold Love Story of Modernism*. New York: Oxford University Press, 2021.

McDowell, Tremaine. *American Studies*. Minneapolis: University of Minnesota Press, 1958.

Mertens, Richard. "Letter by Letter." *University of Chicago Magazine* 93.6 (August 2001). http://magazine.uchicago.edu/0108/features/letter.html.

Milne, Tim. *Kim Philby: The Unknown Story of the KGB's Master Spy*. London: Biteback, 2014.

Mitchell, Joseph. "Joe Gould's Secret—1." *New Yorker*, September 11, 1964, 61–124.

———. "Professor Sea Gull." *New Yorker*, December 4, 1942, 28–43.

Mitchell, Mark Royden. *Cleanth Brooks and the Rise of Modern Criticism*. Charlottesville: University Press of Virginia, 1996.

Moody, David. *Ezra Pound: Poet*. Vol. 3, *The Tragic Years 1939–1972*. New York: Oxford University Press, 2015.

Moore, Esther Gilman. *History of Gardner, Massachusetts*. Gardner, MA: Hatton, 1967.

Moore, Marianne. *Selected Letters*. Edited by Bonnie Costello. New York: Penguin, 1997.

Moore, Steven, ed. *Beerspit Night and Cursing: The Correspondence of Charles Bukowski and Sheri Martinelli, 1960–1967*. New York: Ecco, 2001.

———. "Sheri Martinelli: A Modernist Muse." In *My Back Pages: Reviews and Essays*, 535–66. Los Angeles: Zerogram Press, 2017.

Morley, Jefferson. *The Ghost: The Secret Life of CIA Spymaster James Jesus Angleton*. New York: St. Martin's, 2017.

Nadel, Alan. *Containment Culture*. Durham, NC: Duke University Press, 1995.

Naftali, Timothy. "Yale Ph.D., O.S.S., CIA: Sherman Kent, Norman Holmes Pearson, and the Development of an American Intelligence Profession." Senior essay, Yale University, 1983.

Niall, Brenda. *My Accidental Career*. Melbourne, Australia: Text, 2022.

Nowell, Elizabeth, ed. *The Letters of Thomas Wolfe*. New York: Charles Scribner's Sons, 1956.

Ochi, Hiromi. "The Reception of American Literature in Japan during the Occupation." *Oxford Research Encyclopedia of Literature*, September 2017. https://doi.org/10.1093/acrefore/9780190201098.013.163.

Ohmann, Richard. *English in America: A Radical View of the Profession*. New York: Oxford University Press, 1976.

O'Leary, Mary, Ed Stannard, and Shahid Abdul-Karim. "1967 Riots: 4 Tense Days." *New Haven Register*, August 12, 2017. https://www.nhregister.com/new-haven/article/1967-riots-4-tense-days-that-began-11813921.php.

O'Neill, Eugene, Jr. "The Song of the Freight." *Helicon* 1 (December 1928).

Oppermann, Mattias. *American Studies in Dialogue: Radical Reconstructions between Curriculum and Cultural Critique.* Frankfurt: Campus Verlag, 2010.

Oren, Dan. *Joining the Club: A History of Jews and Yale.* New Haven, CT: Yale University Press, 1985.

Paige, D. D., ed. *The Letters of Ezra Pound 1907–1941.* New York: New Directions, 1971.

Parmar, Inderjeet. *Foundations of the American Century: The Ford, Carnegie, and Rockefeller Foundations in the Rise of American Power.* New York: Columbia University Press, 2012.

Pearson, Norman Holmes. *American Literary Fathers.* Edited by Shinji Takuwa. Kyoto, Japan: Apollon-Sha, 1965.

———. "The American Poet in Relation to Science." *American Quarterly* 1.2 (Summer 1949): 116–26.

———. *The American Writer and the Feeling for Community.* Tuscaloosa: University of Alabama Press, 1962.

———. "Among Recent Books." *Accent* 3.3 (Spring 1943): 185–86.

———. "Anderson and the New Puritanism." *Newberry Library Bulletin* 2.2 (December 1948): 52–63.

———. "Billy Budd: 'The King's Yarn.'" *American Quarterly* 3.2 (Summer 1951): 99–114.

———. "Both Longfellows." *University of Kansas City Review* 16.4 (Summer 1950): 245–53.

———, ed. *Decade: A Collection of Poems from the First Ten Years of the Wesleyan Poetry Program.* Middletown, CT: Wesleyan University Press, 1969.

———. "A Double Sense of Vision." *Yale Alumni Magazine* 39.3 (1975): 8–11.

———. "The Escape from Time: Poetry, Language, and Symbol: Stein, Pound, Eliot." In *Norman Holmes Pearson: Four Studies,* 59–69. Verona: Stamperia Valdonega, 1962.

———. "Foreword." In *Hermetic Definition,* by H.D., v–viii. New York: New Directions, 1972.

———. "Foreword." In *Regionalism and Beyond: Essays of Randall Stewart,* edited by George Core, xii–xix. Nashville, TN: Vanderbilt University Press, 1968.

———. "Hawthorne's Fiction and the Problems of Life." In *American Literary Fathers,* by Pearson, edited by Shinji Takuwa, 9–26. Kyoto, Japan: Apollon-Sha, 1965.

———. "Hawthorne's Usable Truth." In *"Hawthorne's Usable Truth" and Other Papers Presented at the Fiftieth Anniversary of New York Lambda Chapter, Phi Beta Kappa,* 7–21. Canton, NY: St. Lawrence University, 1950.

———. "Introduction." In *The Complete Novels and Selected Tales of Nathaniel Hawthorne,* vii–xv. New York: Modern Library, 1937.

———. "Introduction." In *The Double-Cross System in the War of 1939–1945*, by John Masterman, vii–xviii. New Haven, CT: Yale University Press, 1972.

———. "Introduction." In *Walden*, by Henry David Thoreau, v–xi. New York: Holt, Rinehart, and Winston, 1948.

———. "Ivy Oration." In *Gardner (Massachusetts) High School 1927 Yearbook*, 90–91.

———. "Lena Grove." *Shenandoah* 3.1 :3–7.

———. "Literary Forms and Types or a Defense of Polonius." In *English Institute Annual 1940*, edited by Rudolf Kirk, 61–72. New York: Columbia University Press, 1941.

———. "National Educational Defense Act." Review of Spillar, Thorp, et al., eds. *Literary History of the United States. Saturday Review*, November 27, 1948, 9–10, 33.

———. "The Nature and Possibilities of American Studies." In *Pacific Circle 2: Proceedings of the Third Biennial Conference of the Australia and New Zealand American Studies Association*, edited by Norman Harper: 1–9. St. Lucia: University of Queensland Press, 1972.

———. "The Nazi-Soviet Pact and the End of a Dream." In *America in Crisis: Fourteen Crucial Episodes in American History*, edited by Daniel Aaron, 327–48. New York: Alfred A. Knopf, 1952.

———. "The People Who Use the William Carlos Williams Collection at Yale." In *William Carlos Williams*, edited by Charles Angoff, 31–36. Rutherford, NJ: Farleigh Dickinson University Press, 1974.

———. "Problems in Literary Executorship." *Studies in Bibliography* 5 (1952/53): 3–20.

———. Review of *American Renaissance* by F. O. Matthiessen. *Decision*, November/December 1941, 107–11.

———. "Robert William Wright." In *Dictionary of American Biography*, edited by Allan Johnson and Dumas Malone, vol. 20:565. New York: Charles Scribner's Sons, 1936.

———. "Sinclair Lewis '07." *Yale Alumni Magazine*, March 1951, 10–11.

———. "Sophia Amelia Peabody Hawthorne." In *Notable American Women 1607–1950*, edited by Edward T. James, Janet Wilson James, and Paul Boyer: 162–63. Cambridge, MA: Harvard University Press, 1971.

———. "The Square Dollar Series." *Shenandoah* 7.1 (1955): 81–84.

———. "A Story by Hawthorne." *New England Quarterly* 6.1 (March 1933): 136–44.

———. "Surveying American Literature." *College English* 1.7 (April 1940): 583–88.

———. "Wallace Stevens and 'Old Higgs.'" *Trinity Review* (Trinity College, CT), May 1954, 35–36.

Perl, Jed. "Magnum Opus." *New Republic*, January 4, 2011, https://newrepublic.com/article/80844/the-picture-book-that-could-save-american-art.

Philby, Kim. *My Silent War: The Autobiography of a Spy.* New York: Random House, 2002.

Phillips Academy. *Pot-Pourri.* 1928.

Pierson, George Wilson. *A Yale Book of Numbers: Historical Statistics of the College and University, 1701–1976.* New Haven, CT: Yale University, 1983.

———. *Yale: The University College, 1921–1937.* New Haven, CT: Yale University Press, 1955.

Potter, David. "American Studies at Yale." *Yale Alumni Magazine,* January 1955, 11–14.

Pound, Ezra. *Guide to Kulchur.* New York: New Directions, 1968.

———. "A Retrospect." In *Literary Essays of Ezra Pound,* edited by T. S. Eliot, 3–14. New York: New Directions, 1954.

Price, Leah. *The Anthology and the Rise of the Novel: From Richardson to George Eliot.* New York: Cambridge University Press, 2000.

Raff, Daniel. "New York." In *The History of Oxford University Pres,* vol. 3, *1896–1970,* edited by Simon Eliot, 583–618. Oxford: Oxford University Press, 2013.

Rattray, David. "A Weekend with Ezra Pound." *Nation,* November 16, 1957, 343–49.

Richard, Mike. "Could It Be That Chair City Has Only One Chair Manufacturer Left?" *Gardner News,* July 29, 2021. https://www.thegardnernews.com/story/news/2021/07/29/then-and-now-s-k-pierce-standard-chair-manufacturers-gardner/8090340002/.

———. "During Its Glory Days, Goodnow-Pearson Couldn't Be Beat." *Gardner News,* July 24, 2008. https://www.thegardnernews.com/article/14/193663.

Richards, David Allan. *Skulls and Keys: The Hidden History of Yale's Secret Societies.* New York: Pegasus, 2017.

Richardson, Joan. *Wallace Stevens: A Biography; The Later Years, 1923–1955.* New York: Beech Tree Books, 1988.

Riesman, David, Nathan Glazer, and Reuel Denney. *The Lonely Crowd.* New Haven, CT: Yale University Press, 1950.

Robinson, Janice. *H.D.: The Life and Work of an American Poet.* Boston: Houghton Mifflin, 1982.

Rodgers, Daniel T. *As a City on a Hill: The Story of America's Most Famous Lay Sermon.* Princeton, NJ: Princeton University Press, 2018.

Rothfeld, Anne. "Nazi Looted Art, Part 2." *Prologue Magazine,* Summer 2002. https://www.archives.gov/publications/prologue/2002/summer/nazi-looted-art-2.html.

Salter, Michael. *US Intelligence, the Holocaust, and the Nuremberg Trials.* Vol. 2, *Seeking Accountability for Genocide and Cultural Plunder.* Leiden: Martinus Nijhoff, 2009.

Sands, Frederick. "At Last . . . I'll see some Eskimos," *Daily Mail* May 24, 1957.

———. "Mrs. Bryher, 60, Says: I'm Lucky to Have Come Back Alive." *Daily Mail*, n.d., 1957.

Santayana, George. *The Last Puritan: A Memoir in the Form of a Novel*. New York: Charles Scribner's Sons, 1936.

Sapir, Edward. "Culture, Genuine and Spurious." Edited and with an introduction by Alex Golub. Savage Minds Occasional Papers 5. 2013. https://core.ac.uk /download/pdf/18414428.pdf.

Sato, Hiroko. "NHP: The View of Japanese Scholars." *Pembroke Magazine* 8 (1976): 34–35.

Sayer, George. *Jack: A Life of C. S. Lewis*. Wheaton, IL: Crossway, 1994.

Schaffner, Perdita. "Glass in My Typewriter." *East Hampton Star*, May 15, 1975, 16.

———. "Keeper of the Flame." In *H.D.: Woman and Poet*, edited by Michael King, 27–33. Orono, ME: National Poetry Foundation, 1986.

———. "Running." *Iowa Review* 16.3 (Fall 1986): 7–13.

Schlesinger, Arthur M., Jr. *The Vital Center: The Politics of Freedom*. Boston: Houghton Mifflin, 1949.

Schrecker, Ellen. *Many Are the Crimes: McCarthyism in America*. Princeton, NJ: Princeton University Press, 1999.

Scott-Smith, Giles. "Building a Community around the Pax Americana." In *The US Government, Citizen Groups and the Cold War: The State-Private Network*, edited by Helen Laville and Hugh Wilford, 73–91. London: Routledge, 2006.

Seymour, Charles. "History of the College Plan." *Yale Alumni Weekly*, December 22, 1943.

Shelden, Michael. *Graham Greene: The Enemy Within*. New York: Random House, 1994.

Sherry, Vincent. *The Life of Graham Greene*. Vol. 2, *1939–1955*. New York: Viking, 1994.

Shumway, David. *Creating American Civilization: A Genealogy of American Literature as an Academic Discipline*. Minneapolis: University of Minnesota Press, 1994.

Skard, Sigmund. *American Studies in Europe: Their History and Present Organization*. 2 vols. Philadelphia: University of Pennsylvania Press, 1958.

Smith, Bradley F. *The Shadow Warriors: OSS and the Origins of the CIA*. Basic Books, 1983.

Smith, Richard Harris. *OSS: The Secret History of America's First Central Intelligence Agency*. Berkeley: University of California Press, 1972.

Smith, Sydney. Review of *Statistical Annals of the United States*, by Adam Seybert. *Edinburgh Review* 33 (1820): 69–80.

Soares, Joseph. *The Power of Privilege: Yale and America's Elite Colleges*. Stanford, CA: Stanford University Press, 2007.

Souhami, Diana. *No Modernism without Lesbians*. London: Head of Zeus, 2020.

Spiller, Robert E. "American Studies, Past, Present, and Future." In *Studies in*

American Culture: Dominant Ideas and Images, edited by Joseph J. Kwiat and Mary C. Turpie, 207–20. Minneapolis: University of Minnesota Press, 1960.

Spiller, Robert E., Willard Thorp, Thomas H. Johnson, Henry Seidel Canby, and Richard M. Ludwig, eds. *Literary History of the United States*. New York: Macmillan, 1948.

Stearns, Harold. "Preface." In *Civilization in the United States*, iii–viii. New York: Harcourt, Brace, 1922.

Stedman, Edmund Clarence. *Poets of America*. Boston: Riverside, 1885.

Stein, Gertrude. *The Autobiography of Alice B. Toklas*. New York: Harcourt, Brace, 1933.

Stevens, Holly, ed. *Letters of Wallace Stevens*. Berkeley: University of California Press, 1996.

Stevens, Wallace. *The Necessary Angel*. New York: Vintage, 1965.

———. "A Note on Poetry." In *Oxford Anthology of American Literature*, 1-vol. ed., edited by William Rose Benét and Norman Holmes Pearson, 1325. New York: Oxford University Press, 1938.

Synnott, Marcia Graham. *The Half-Opened Door: Discrimination and Admissions at Harvard, Yale, and Princeton, 1900–1970*. Westport, CT: Greenwood, 1979.

Thelin, John. *A History of American Higher Education*. Baltimore: Johns Hopkins University Press, 2004.

Tompkins, Jane. *Sensational Designs: The Cultural Work of American Fiction 1790–1860*. New York: Oxford University Press, 1986.

Trevelyan, Laura. *The Winchester: The Gun That Built an American Dynasty*. New Haven, CT: Yale University Press, 2016.

Turner, Catherine. *Marketing Modernism between the Two Wars*. Amherst: University of Massachusetts Press, 2003.

Turner, Frederick Jackson. "The Significance of the Frontier in American History." 1893. National Humanities Center. http://nationalhumanitiescenter.org/pds/gilded/empire/text1/turner.pdf.

Valenti, Patricia Dunlavy. "Sophia Peabody Hawthorne's *American Notebooks*." *Studies in the American Renaissance*, 1996, 115–85.

Valentine, John A. *The College Board and the School Curriculum*. New York: College Entrance Examination Board, 1987.

Vanderbilt, Kermit, *American Literature and the Academy*. Philadelphia: University of Pennsylvania Press, 1986.

Vidich, Arthur J. "Intelligence Agencies and the Universities: Further Implications of the Thesis Advanced by Sigmund Diamond in *Compromised Campus*." *International Journal of Politics, Culture, and Society* 6.3 (1993): 365–77.

Walker, Robert H., ed. *American Studies Abroad*. Westport, CT: Greenwood, 1975.

———. *American Studies in the United States: A Survey of College Programs*. Baton Rouge: Louisiana State University Press, 1957.

Wallerstein, Immanuel. "The Unintended Consequences of Cold War Area Studies." In *The Cold War and the University: Toward an Intellectual History of the Postwar Years*, edited by André Schiffrin, 195–232. New York: New Press, 1997.

Ward, Vicky. "The House That Guns Built." *Town and Country*, September 20, 2016. https://www.townandcountrymag.com/society/tradition/a7846/winchester-family/.

Wecter, Dixon. *The Saga of American Society*. New York: Charles Scribner's Sons, 1937.

Whyte, William. *The Organization Man*. New York: Simon and Schuster, 1956.

Williams, Stanley T. *The American Spirit in Letters*. New Haven, CT: Yale University Press, 1926.

———. *The Life of Washington Irving*. 2 vols. Oxford: Oxford University Press, 1935.

Williams, William Carlos. *The Autobiography of William Carlos Williams*. 1951. New York: New Directions, 1968.

Winks, Robin. *Cloak and Gown: Scholars in the Secret War, 1939–1961*. New York: Quill, 1987.

Winthrop, John. *Winthrop's Journal "History of New-England" 1630–1649*. Edited by James Kendall Hosmer. New York: Scribner's, 1908.

Wise, Gene. "'Paradigm Dramas' in American Studies: A Cultural and Institutional History of the Movement." *American Quarterly* 31.3 (1979): 293–337.

Wolfe, Tom. "In Tribute to Norman Holmes Pearson." Eulogy delivered November 11, 1975. *Pembroke Magazine* 8 (1976): 30.

Wolfe, Thomas. "A Western Journey." *Virginia Quarterly Review*, Summer 1939. https://www.vqronline.org/essay/western-journey.

Woloshyn, Tania Anne. "Nursing with Flare: The Operators of Light Therapy, c. 1890–1940." *Dermatological Nursing* 15.1 (March 2016): 47–52. https://www.ncbi.nlm.nih.gov/pmc/articles/PMC4936522/.

Wynne, Marjorie G. "Donald C. Gallup 1913–2000." *Yale Library Gazette* 76.1–2:16.

Zaretsky, Mark. "75 Years Later, New Haven Still Reshaping 'Urban Renewal.'" *New Haven Register*, September 29, 2018. https://www.nhregister.com/news/article/75-years-later-New-Haven-still-reshaping-the-13266864.php.

Zimmerman, Warren. ". . . To Him Who Waits . . ." *Yale Daily News*, November 24, 1954, 2, 6.

INDEX

Aaron, Daniel, 109, 301

Adams, Henry, 37

Adams, Léonie, 94, 239

Addiss, Jim, 313–14

Addiss, Justus, 313–14

Addiss, Susan (Sue), and Elizabeth (Lizzie) Tracy, 122, 125–27, 128–29, 134; post-war years of, 173, 175–76, 178–79, 251, 252–53, 312–14, 324–25; war years of, 150, 162

advertising industry, 278–80

aesthetic formalism, 93–94, 112–13, 119–20

Agassiz, Louis, 194, 196

Agee, Philip, 327

Agnew, Spiro, 319

Aiken, Conrad, 193, 239, 250, 305

Aldington, Perdita. *See* Schaffner, Perdita

Aldington, Richard, 223, 235, 240, 242, 247

Alger, Horatio, 26–27

All God's Chillun Got Wings (play), 63

Altsheler, Joseph, 25

American Century, 2, 8, 263, 272, 326

American Council of Learned Societies (ACLS), 265, 272, 282–83, 286, 290

American literature, initial neglect of, 49–53, 266

American studies, 6–7, 53–54, 70, 122, 125, 165–66, 170, 259, 262, 265–76, 285–87, 302–4, 308, 325, 326; in Australia and British Commonwealth, 282–86; in East Asia, 282; journals of, 265, 302, 317; the Sixties and, 316–18, 320; at

Yale, 174, 175, 251, 263, 265, 270–76, 286, 311, 318

American Studies Association (ASA), 3, 264, 265, 271, 282; Pearson's presidency of, 283, 286, 317; Radical Caucus within, 317, 318

American universities and national-security state, 1, 179, 262, 263–65, 273–74, 293

Anderson, Sherwood, 91, 178, 278, 288, 325

Angell, James, 40–41

Angleton, James Jesus, 115, 154–55, 157, 158, 169, 180, 295, 299

Ano, Fumio, 289

anthologies, history and purposes of, 79–81, 85–86

anti-Semitism, 57, 65, 67, 68, 73–74, 121, 130; Pound and, 190–91, 193, 194–95, 197–98, 204; at Yale, 42, 43

Arnold, Matthew, 50, 267, 268–69

Ashbery, John, 305

Auden, W. H., 5, 111, 118, 142, 188, 204, 220–21, 230; *Poets of the English Language* (with Pearson), 221–23, 307

Bak, Hans, 306

Ballantyne, R. M., 25, 251–52

Baltzell, E. Digby, 13, 17

Barbour, Ralph Henry, 25

Barnes, Djuna, 239

Barry, Elaine, 286

Barton, Melissa, 325

Bateson, Gregory, 273

Beach, Sylvia, 231

Pearson, Norman Holmes, travels of: Eastern Asia and Australia, 256, 282–90, 317, 319, 320, 322; Europe, 47, 56–69, 130, 141, 240, 241, 253–54; Mexican vacation, 171

Pearson, Susan Silliman Bennett: death of, 324; early years of, 122–29; postwar years of, 167, 171, 175–76, 178–79, 203, 224, 251, 290, 312–13, 315; war years of, 141–42, 151, 155, 162, 164

"People's Capitalism" campaign, 281

Phelps, William Lyon, 51, 104, 298

Philby, Harold Adrian Russell ("Kim"), 62, 156–57

Phillips Academy Andover, 4, 22–23, 29–31, 32–35, 39

Pierson, George, 38

Plato, 120

Poe, Edgar Allan, 52, 53, 78

Poetry (journal), 101, 105, 189, 233

Poets of the English Language (ed. Auden and Pearson), 221–23, 307

Pope, Alexander, 183

Porter, Cole, 39, 296

Porter, Katherine Anne, 193, 224, 325

Potter, David, 275

Pottle, Frederick, 298

Pound, Dorothy Shakespear, 192–93, 201, 204, 207

Pound, Ezra, 5–6, 53, 87, 100, 104, 175, 188, 189–207, 209, 221, 223, 246–47, 314, 321, 326, 327; Bollingen Prize controversy over, 190–93; the *Cantos*, 184, 187, 189, 190, 199–200, 201, 205–7, 209, 245, 246, 311; *Confucian Analects*, 193, 194; Eliot and, 101, 193, 204, 241; *Hilda's Book*, 201; imagism and, 185–86, 189–90; Pearson's assistance to, 193, 200; *Women of Trachis*, 200, 295. *See also under* H.D. (Hilda Doolittle)

Pound, Omar, 207

Powell, Lewis, 296

Pratt, Margaret, 287

Price, Leah, 80, 85–86

Prouty, Charles, 302

Puritanism, 5, 7–8, 11, 13–14, 17–18, 31, 35, 37, 53, 54, 90, 118, 122, 218, 279, 288, 289, 303, 321–22, 327; Bryer and, 252; H.D. and, 172, 228; modernism and, 187; negative connotations of, 7, 17, 277; Pearson's identification with, 7–8, 70, 107, 131, 165–66, 167, 278, 288, 294

Pynchon, Thomas, 320

Quiller-Couch, Arthur, 81

Rachewiltz, Mary de, 202–3, 207

racism, 24, 33–34, 195–96, 315–19

Ransom, John Crowe, 94, 223, 298, 300, 305

Reed, Ishmael, 320

Reed, John, 109

Ridge, Lola, 90, 224

Rinehart & Company, 177, 307

Rivera, Diego, 47

Robeson, Paul, 63, 88

Robinson, Edwin Arlington, 32, 84

Rockefeller Foundation, 271–72, 282

Roethke, Theodore, 306

Rogers, Ezekiel, 13–14

Roosevelt, Franklin Delano, 62–63, 68, 137, 204, 277

Ross, Harold, 277

Rosset, Barney, 236, 239, 240, 242

Rothschild, Victor, 161

Rudge, Olga, 201

Rukeyser, Muriel, 118, 134, 188, 203, 224–25, 230

Saint-Gaudens, Auguste, 267

Salinger, J. D., 278, 288–89

S.A.-Mann Brand (film), 65

Sandburg, Carl, 32, 53, 106

Sanders, Ed, 304–5, 355n26

Santayana, George, 7, 278

Sapir, Edward, 269

Sato, Hiroko, 290

Scarlet Letter, The (film), 29

Schaffner, John, 234

Schaffner, Perdita, 146, 154–55, 172, 229, 234, 235, 241, 256

Schaffner, Valentine, 234

Scharl, Josef, 117

Schellenberg, Walter, 150

Schlesinger, Arthur, Jr., 276, 278

Scholz, Jackson, 27

Schwartz, Delmore, 305

science fiction, 320, 322

Whitehead, Alfred North, 184

Whitman, Walt, 32, 50–51, 52, 53, 111, 113, 120, 267, 321

Whittemore, Reed, 115

Whyte, William, 294–95. *See also* Pearson, Norman Holmes: as Organization Man

Wilbur, Richard, 223, 296, 305

Wilde, Oscar, 60, 69

Wilder, Thornton, 87, 116, 218, 224, 239

Will, Hubert, 142

Williams, Floss, 211, 212, 214

Williams, Roger, 18, 277

Williams, Stanley T., 49, 51–54, 56, 64, 69–71, 75, 76, 94, 110–11, 114–15, 298, 302, 326; Oxford anthology project, 79, 81, 83, 85, 86

Williams, William Carlos, 5, 6, 26, 87, 88, 100, 188, 209–14; letters to and from, 101, 107, 110, 127–28, 165, 192, 210–11; *Paterson*, 187; Pound and, 193, 209–10; *Spring and All* bootleg, 245; *We Moderns* blurb on, by Pearson, 117. *See also under* H.D. (Hilda Doolittle)

Wimsatt, W. K., 298, 300, 301

Winchester, Oliver Fisher, and family, 122–23

Winks, Robin and Avril, 53, 291, 292, 353n78

Winthrop, John, 7–8, 14

Wise, Gene, 303, 304

Wolfe, Thomas, 87, 94, 95–96, 312

Wolfe, Tom, 199, 309, 311–12

Wolff, Kurt and Helen, 89, 118, 172, 233, 252

Woodson, Thomas, 308

Woolf, Virginia, 85, 182

Wordsworth, William, 117

World War II, 1, 4, 129–33, 137–66, 197, 262–63

Wright, Arthur Williams, 124

Wright, Robert William, 73

X-2 branch, 1, 2, 4, 8–9, 143–44, 147–52, 154, 158–63, 164–65, 174, 260; aftermath of, 168–69, 261

Yale Institute of International Studies, 271, 272

"Yale Report," 49

Yale Reports (radio program), 177, 204, 316

Yale University: Bryher on, 255; characteristics of, 37–42, 101, 115–16, 169–70, 173–74; founding of, 17, 37, 129; Harvard and Princeton compared to, 37–39, 264, 315; New Criticism at, 191–92, 199, 243, 298–301, 308, 326; postwar changes at, 264, 293–98; Pundits society at, 296, 297; the Sixties at, 294, 315–20; war years at, 129–30, 132–34; women at, 310, 315, 316; "Yale Man" ideal, 294, 310. *See also* Beinecke Rare Book and Manuscript Library; CIA (Central Intelligence Agency)

Yale University, Pearson at: student years, 4, 7, 35, 40–56, 60, 69–70, 109–10, 309; teaching assistantship, 71–73, 84; teaching career, 5, 8–9, 119, 127, 133–34, 163, 169–70, 173–77, 179, 181, 199–200, 243, 251, 259, 282, 286, 293–311, 315–20

Yeats, W. B., 63, 91, 120

youth culture, Pearson and, 288–89, 295, 320

Zabel, Morton Dauwen, 105, 110

Zaturenska, Marya. *See under* Gregory, Horace